Daniel Pindur

Value Creation in Successful LBOs

GABLER EDITION WISSENSCHAFT

Daniel Pindur

Value Creation in Successful LBOs

With a foreword by Prof. Dr. Frank Richter

Deutscher Universitäts-Verlag

Bibliografische Information Der Deutschen Nationalbibliothek
Die Deutsche Nationalbibliothek verzeichnet diese Publikation in der
Deutschen Nationalbibliografie; detaillierte bibliografische Daten sind im Internet über
<http://dnb.d-nb.de> abrufbar.

Dissertation Universität Ulm, 2006

1. Auflage September 2007

Lektorat: Frauke Schindler / Anita Wilke

Der Deutsche Universitäts-Verlag ist ein Unternehmen von Springer Science+Business Media.
www.duv.de

Umschlaggestaltung: Regine Zimmer, Dipl.-Designerin, Frankfurt/Main
Gedruckt auf säurefreiem und chlorfrei gebleichtem Papier
Printed in Germany

ISBN 978-3-8350-0852-6

Foreword

The empirical research contained in this book is unique. Daniel Pindur has put together a database of successful LBO transactions in the European market from 1993 to 2004. Next to insightful descriptive statistics of the representative sample, this database comprises purchase and disposal prices, interim cash flows and capital structure information. The novelty and granularity of this information enables the profound and first-time analysis of realized rates of returns on individual transaction level, and, even more important, the analysis of the various components and sources of such returns.

The covered successful LBO transactions generated significant returns to the buy-out firms. Failed and unrealized LBO investments, which have to be taken into consideration for a complete picture of LBO success rates as well, are not the topic of the present research. The question is rather what buy-out firms and their investors can learn from successful LBO transactions. Daniel Pindur provides answers to this question: an economic model of buy-out firms decomposes the economic success of realized investments and serves as the framework for identifying factors driving these components. Based thereupon the empirical work unveils the magnitude of these components and their relative contribution to the economic success of the covered transactions and reveals the relative importance of the various factors. Operational improvements seem to be of utmost importance, i.e. the increase in earnings over the holding period contributes by far most to value creation in these investments, with revenue growth being most important followed by profitability improvements. Cash-flow generation, mainly through discipline in capital expenditures and working capital management, comes next. Finally, the buy-out firms, which conducted the transactions covered in the database, were to some extent quite lucky, as they benefited substantially from multiple expansion during the holding period, i.e. from the fact that multiples paid at entry were significantly lower than multiples achieved at exit.

Furthermore, this book provides insightful and novel detail on various aspects and characteristics of successful LBO transactions, such as for example transaction cost, the impact of the divestiture mode and recapitalizations.

Findings presented in this book hence serve to much better understand the economics of buy-out investments and contribute some transparency and objectivity to a currently heated public debate regarding the economics of such investments. Further, buy-out firms will find benchmarks, which they can use in order to assess value creation potential of companies they are contemplating to invest in.

The same applies to industrial firms in the area of corporate strategy. Here, the "best-owner" question gets addressed, which includes an assessment of the relative capability and willingness to enhance profitability. The underlying question is, whether the ownership structure in the specific form of private equity makes a difference in terms of value creation and returns. The results included in this book suggest that this can be the case if done right.

Prof. Dr. Frank Richter

Acknowledgements

The idea for this thesis developed while I was working in the Investment Banking Division of Goldman Sachs and advising a buy-out firm on what was the largest German public-to-private LBO transaction at that time. The question how buy-out firms create value in LBO transactions had already attracted a lot of academic interest; however, related thorough, quantitative empirical research did not seem to exist. Without having received access from Goldman Sachs to a library of semi-public and confidential information booklets with raw financial data on numerous LBO transactions, the novel empirical research as presented in this book would clearly not have been possible. In this respect, special thanks go to Dr. Marcus Schenck and Karl Skjelbred for their support.

Most importantly, I would like to thank my doctoral thesis supervisor Professor Dr. Frank Richter who not only supported my ideas and intentions from the very beginning but who also served as invaluable sounding board for stimulating and challenging academic discussions throughout the development of this thesis. Also, I would like to acknowledge Professor Dr. Kai-Uwe Marten from the University of Ulm and Professor Dr. Dirk Schiereck from the European Business School, Oestrich-Winkel for serving as second and third referee for this thesis.

Particularly, I want to thank my friends for their support; mainly by making my academic leave a truly enjoyable and fun time.

I am deeply indebted to my parents who supported me in all respects throughout my education in a unique and outstanding manner. This book is dedicated to them.

Dr. Daniel Pindur

Contents

Detailed Contents

List of Charts

List of Tables

Symbols

AccPay	Accounts payable
AccRec	Accounts receivable
B	Firm-specific human capital costs of financial distress to management
C	Operating cash flow
CF	Cash flow
CI	Capital Invested
CMgmt	Change in (top) management during the holding period
CoGS	Cost of goods sold
D	Total debt; book value of total financial indebtedness
Dis	Discount in an equity offering
Div	Dividend
$E[\cdot]$	Expected value
	$E^P[\cdot]$ Expected value under the probability measure P
	$E^Q[\cdot]$ Expected value under the probability measure Q
E	Equity value
EBIT	Earnings before interest and taxes
EBITDA	Earnings before interest, taxes, deprecation and amortization
Employment	Number of employees
Employ-Mrg	Personnel Cost as % of Sales
ER	Excess return
ExpInd	Experience Index
F	Filtration
FCF	Free cash flow available for distribution to debt- and equityholders

I	Investment costs
Int	Net financial result
Int_{Cash}	Cash effective net financial result
Inv	End of period inventories
IRR	Internal Rate of Return
L	Leverage ratio defined as total debt (D) over $EBITDA_{LTM}$
$Labor\text{-}Prod$	Labor productivity; defined as revenues per employee
Liq	Liquidity
M	Market portfolio
N	Number of observations, sample size
ND	Net Debt; total financial liabilities less cash and cash equivalents
P	Purchase price
P/E	Price–Earnings ratio
PI	Profitability index
PME	Public market equivalent
Rev	Revenues
$ROIC$	Return on invested capital
$SG\&A$	Sales, general and administrative expenses
$Steady$	Investment (sample) without any acquisition and divestiture activity during the holding period
T	Point in time of the LBO exit transaction (exit)
Tax	Tax expenses
Tax_{Cash}	Cash effective tax expenses
TC	Transaction costs
TP	Total proceeds to equity investors in an LBO transaction

TS	Total sources
$U(\cdot)$	Utility
V	Entity value
W	Wealth
X	Amount
b	Non-pecuniary benefits
d	Down factor in a binomial model
g	Growth rate
	g^P Subjective growth rate under the probability measure P
	g^Q Subjective growth rate under the probability measure Q
i	Company index
j	Index
k	Alternative, comparable and available investment opportunity
l	Gearing ratio defined as total debt over entity value
ln	Natural logarithm
m	Transaction multiple $P/EBITDA_{LTM}$
n	Index
P	Probability of occurrence under the probability measure P
Q	Probability of occurrence under the probability measure Q
r	Return
	r_f Risk-free rate of return
	r_k Rate of return of a comparable, alternative investment opportunity
	r_M Rate of return of the market portfolio

t	Point in time of the LBO entry transaction (entry)
u	Up factor in a binomial model
~	Approximately
α	Remaining LBO equity investors' stake for a IPO exited investment
β	Beta
	β_A Asset beta
	β_E Equity beta
	β_L Levered beta; beta of a partially debt financed company
ε	Random variable; error term in a stochastic process
τ	Tax rate
σ	Standard deviation
σ^2	Variance
θ	Reinvestment rate
λ	Management's relative ownership stake

General Notation

- Throughout this thesis t indicates the entry point in time, T the exit point in time of the LBO investment.
- Negative values in tables are displayed in parentheses.
- Prefix Δ_ stands for the absolute difference of a variable at two different points in time; i.e. $Var_T - Var_t$; prefix *g_* indicates the growth rate of a variable, i.e. $var_{T-1} / var_{t-1} - 1$; prefix *c_* indicates the compounded annual growth rate of an investment, i.e. $(\text{var}_{T-1} / \text{var}_{t-1})^{\frac{12}{HP}} - 1$.
- Consistently the suffix (i) *cm* refers to a constant $P/EBITDA_{LTM}$ multiple at entry and at exit, (ii) *cRev* to constant revenues throughout the holding period, and (iii) *cMrg* to constant EBITDA-margin during the holding period.

Acronyms

APV	Adjusted present value
CAGR	Compounded annual growth rate
CAPM	Capital asset pricing model
CE	Continental Europe
CEO	Chief executive officer
CFO	Chief financial officer
CV	Control Variable
DCF	Discounted cash flow
DPI	Distributed total value to paid-in capital
DV	Dependent Variable
EI	Equity investor
EURIBOR	Euro Interbank Offered Rate
EVA	Economic value added
EVCA	European Venture Capital Association
GP	General partner
HP	Holding period
IAS	International accounting standards
I/B/E/S	Institutional brokers estimate system
IBO	Institutional Buyout
IPO	Initial Public Offering
IV	Independent Variable
JoF	Journal of finance
JoFE	Journal of financial economics

LBO	Leveraged buyout
LIBOR	London Interbank offered rate
LMBO	Leveraged management buyout
LP	Limited partner
LTM	Latest twelve months
Max	Maximum
MBO	Management buyout
Md	Median
Mgmt	Management
Min	Minimum
NAV	Net asset value
NPV	Net present value
NWC	Net Working Capital
PC	Primary component in an IPO
PE	Private equity
PPE	Plant, property and equipment
PV	Present value
RADR	Risk-adjusted discount rates
RNV	Risk-neutral valuation
SC	Secondary component in an IPO
SD	Senior debt
SIC	Standard industrial classification
SL	Security Line
Std	Standard deviation

SubD	Subordinated Debt
S&P	Standard & Poor's
TCF	Total cash flow
TM	Times money, i.e. distribution to paid-in capital
TVPI	Cumulative total value to paid-in capital
UK	United Kingdom
US	United States of America
US-GAAP	United States Generally Accepted Accounting Principles
Var	Variable
VC	Venture Capital
VE	Venture Economics
VIF	Variance inflation factor
WACC	Weighted average cost of capital
abs	Absolute
cont.	Continuous
e.g.	For example, for instance (Latin *exempli gratia*)
et al.	And others (Latin *et alii*)
f	And the following page
ff	And the following pages
i.e.	That is to say, in other words (Latin *id est*)
inj	Injection; in particular E_{inj} additional equity injection by equity investors
na	Not applicable
no.	Number
p.	Page

pp.	Pages
rel	Relative
vol.	Volume
vs.	Versus

I. Introduction

Ever since the extensive recovery in LBO activity, starting in the USA in the 80s, swashing to the UK in the early 90s and subsequently to Continental Europe, the LBO phenomenon has received significant attention in the academic literature.[1] Wealth effects to the variety of parties involved in LBO transactions seem to be at the forefront of interest as indicated by several different research streams.

However, due predominantly to the lack of available information on firms that have experienced and completed a LBO (henceforth realized LBO investments), empirical academic work on ex-post value creation and performance analysis is still in its infancy. Despite the current omnipresence and ever-increasing economic as well as political importance, the *PE* industry is still considered a relatively young industry. This in combination with the, in general, private nature of the industry results in a lack of the critical information required for value creation and performance analysis.

On fund/investor level recent advances with respect to value creation and performance analysis of *PE* as an asset class can be recorded.[2] But, however, value creation and performance analysis of individual LBO investments with a link to company- and transaction-specific information mainly remains a black box. Among others, value creation and performance analysis on investment level faces the challenge – both conceptually and empirically – of combining internal, investment-specific (i.e. rather microeconomic) aspects with external, market (i.e. rather macroeconomic) aspects. On the one hand established research streams on investment level lack the ultimate cash flow information from and to the LBO equity investors as the basis for any investment performance analysis. In light of this shortcoming previous empirical research frequently either applied (i) premia paid in public-to-private transactions[3] or (ii) selected pre- and post-buyout operational performance measures as

---

1 For reviews of LBO research see e.g. Fried, V. H./Hisrich, R. D. (1988), pp. 15-28, Barry, C. B. (1994), pp. 3-15, Wright, M./Robbie, K. (1998), pp. 521-570 and Berg, A./Gottschalg, O. (2003), pp. 42-47. For a review of the historical development of LBOs see e.g. Luippold, T. L. (1992), pp. 73ff and Schmid, H. (1994), pp. 47ff. Chapter II.A.1 provides a precise definition of LBOs for the purpose of this thesis.

2 Recent publications in the JoF (Kaplan, S. N./Schoar, A. (2005)) and JoFE (Cochrane, J. (2005)) highlight the relevance and actuality of LBO performance research. Basis for these advances are novel, in part proprietary databases capturing aggregated cash flow information on fund and investor level (see chapter I.A.2.3 for details).

3 In public-to-private (or synonymously going private) transactions, shareholders of a publicly held corporation are bought out by a management and/or a (group of) financial sponsor(s) who take a concentrated ownership position in a reconstituted privately held company and generally finance the transaction heavily with debt. See e.g. Lehn, K./Poulsen, A. (1989), p. 771. In the context of this thesis, these transactions will be considered as one type of LBO (see chapter II.A.3 for details).

imperfect proxies for value creation.[4] On the other hand, the novel research stream on the fund/investor level lacks investment-specific company and transaction information to analyze aspects of value creation on investment level. As a consequence the components and determinants of value creation on investment level remain puzzling.

Linking company- and transaction-specific information to LBO investment performance would apparently be of tremendous interest and seems like a missing piece in LBO research. Apparent questions arising in this context are numerous but shall be clustered for the current purpose into two categories.

- First, what are the components of value creation in LBO investments and what are the relative contributions of variations in (i) the firm's operating performance, (ii) its capital structure, and (iii) its relative valuation? Do operational performance improvements result rather from margin improvements or revenue growth? And are these improvements for instance at the expense of the firm's employees?
- Second, what are the factors triggering variations in these individual components and what are the corresponding theoretical foundations? Are for instance company- and transaction-specific aspects dominating the external, market related aspects? And what role do financial sponsors play?

Incidentally, such quantitative empirical evidence regarding realized LBO investments and determinants of value creation in particular adds to the objectiveness of a currently heated and widespread discussion regarding LBOs in general. The understanding of *PE* firms as *a plague of locusts* resembles much of the discussion on the controversy surrounding LBOs in the US where "[*t*]*hroughout the 1980s and well into the '90s, sceptics argued that LBOs simply provided a means for Wall Street financiers to earn paper profits by arbitraging differences between public and private markets.*"[5] In light of (i) the finite investment horizon, and (ii) the importance of the reputational asset can financial sponsors actually afford to chew companies up or is their involvement for the long-term good of the company? And would value be created in LBO investments without any favorable variation in relative transaction prices?

The novelty of this thesis therefore arises from conceptually and empirically decomposing and analyzing value creation in LBOs on investment level from a LBO equity investor perspective. Based on the LBO transaction model, the thesis applies for this purpose a two-tier framework of an internal and an external perspective. Such a framework (i) suitably and logically structures the conceptual discussion of value creation in LBO investments, and

---

4 See chapters I.A.2.1 and I.A.2.2 for further details regarding these empirical research streams.

5 See Allen, J. (1996), p.18.

(ii) provides guidance for the stepwise empirical performance analysis for a sample of 42 realized European LBO investments. Building upon a novel database with detailed company- and transaction-specific information, the empirical analysis addresses the aforementioned questions by (i) quantifying and decomposing LBO investment performance measures, and (ii) identifying determinants of value creation in LBO investments.

Following a brief discussion of the status of related theoretical and empirical research (chapter I.A), shortcomings and research gaps are concretized (chapter I.B) and the research design of this thesis for assessing value creation in LBO investments is outlined (chapter I.C).

A. On the Status of Research on Value Creation in LBOs

Research streams on value creation in LBOs are predominantly empirical in nature, though built upon various established theoretical approaches. Following a brief review of these theoretical approaches (chapter I.A.1) a threefold classification reviews relevant empirical work (chapter I.A.2). Efforts to assess value creation in LBOs have so far predominately focused on individual aspects only. The LBO entry transaction and the subsequent holding period of the investment have received substantial attention whereas the impact of the divestment of the investment, i.e. the exit phase, seems to have been researched to a much lesser extent, in particular quantitatively and on the individual investment level. *Holistic* approaches, comprising the for value creation to LBO equity investors essential entry, holding period and exit phases of the investment are rare – theoretically as well as empirically.

1. Theoretical Approaches to Analyzing Value Creation in LBOs

Other than in corporate acquisitions and mergers, synergy effects do not serve as the pre-eminent argument and source for explaining value creation in LBO investments.[6] Due to the presumably purely financial and non-strategic interest of private equity firms, a LBO as such should neither affect the market position of the bought-out company nor offer immediate room for cost-saving opportunities resulting from the combination or streamlining of operations or overhead functions.

In particular response to the neoclassic financial theory, various other theoretical approaches have emerged that serve to explain the LBO phenomena and analyze value creation in LBO investments. Some of these approaches offer starting points to validate the increasing popularity of LBOs in the US in the course of the 80s. Prior to a brief separate discussion Table 1 summarizes these theoretical approaches.

---

6 See e.g. Jensen, M. C./Ruback, R. S. (1983), pp. 5-50, Chatterjee, S. (1986), pp. 119-139 and Wöginger, H. (2004), pp. 235-262.

Table 1 Overview of Theoretical Approaches to Analyze Value Creation in LBOs[7]

Theoretical Approach	Main Thesis	Scientific Status	Practical Relevance	Important Papers
Neoclassic Financial Theory	Irrelevancy of financing decision for firm value Investment decision independent from consumption, savings and insurance decisions	Methodological basis for further theoretical approaches Assumptions completely rejected	non	Modigliani/Miller (1958) Hamada (1969) Fama (1970) Stiglitz (1974)
Property Rights Theory	Goods are assigned bundles of rights	Main methodological basis for further (institution economics) approaches	Design of Innovation-friendly organizations	Demsetz (1967) Cheung (1970) Alchian/Demsetz (1973)
Agency Theory	Agency conflicts and costs arising from independent utility maximization of the principal and the agent	Long-term thinking and altruistic behavior despite high relevance not considered	Design of delegation contracts	Ross (1973) Jensen/Meckling (1976) Grossman/Hart (1983)
Theory of Asymmetric Information Distribution	In markets with asymmetric information participants focus on average product characteristics	Various approaches not yet put together to a consistent theory	Information provision	Akerlof (1970) Leland/Pyle (1977) Campbell/Kracaw (1980) Rock (1986)
Transaction Cost Theory	Transaction costs make financing relationships more costly and reduce the probability of signing contracts	Low degree of specification for financial intermediaries	Clarification of the relevancy of Transaction Costs	Coase (1960) Benston/Smith (1976) Williamson (1985)

Source: Adopted from Schefczyk (2004), p. 128

1.1 Neoclassic Financial Theory

The groundbreaking work by Modigliani/Miller (1958) represents a first milestone of the neoclassic financial theory. Well-known *Proposition I* states that under numerous, restrictive assumptions, "*the market value of any firm is independent of its capital structure*"[8]. Based thereupon, *Proposition II* suggests that "*the expected yield of a share of stock is equal to the appropriate capitalization rate* [r_M] *for a pure equity stream in the class, plus a premium related to financial risk equal to the debt-to-equity ratio times the spread between* [r_M] *and* [r_f]."[9]

(1) $r_i = r_M + (r_M - r_f) D_i / E_i$

---

7 Further theoretical approaches not listed here include among others the *Knowledge-Based View*, the *Corporate Governance View*, the *Procedural Justice Theory* and *Investment Controlling*. For an introductory discussion in the context of LBOs see Meier, D. (2005), pp. 41-58.

8 See Modiglianin/Miller (1958), p. 268. The arbitrage-type argumentation of the neoclassic financial theory requires four restrictive assumptions: (i) perfect capital markets, (ii) free market access to anyone, (iii) identical information levels and homogeneous expectations, and (iv) predictable investment strategy according to accepted rules independent of financing decisions. See Fama (1978), pp. 273-274.

9 See Modigliani, F./Miller, M. H. (1958), p. 271.

With r_i= expected yield of share i, r_M= expected rate of return of the market portfolio, r_f= rate of interest for sure streams, D_i = the market value of debt for company i and E_i = the market value of company i's equity.

This financial leverage effect implies that the expected equity rate of return increases as the firm's debt–equity ratio increases but will in turn be exactly offset by an increasing riskiness and hence required equity rate of return, owing to the rising debt level.[10] According to MM's propositions I and II, investment and financing decisions can hence be completely separated.

Markowitz's (1952) seminal work regarding the portfolio selection theory represents a further milestone of the neoclassic financial theory.[11] Accordingly, portfolio diversification benefits imply that the risk-return profile can be improved by lowering the portfolio risk. Based on this, Sharpe (1964), Lintner (1965) and Mossin (1966) developed the Capital Asset Pricing Model (*CAPM*).[12] The existence of an efficient market portfolio builds upon the understanding that firm-specific, idiosyncratic risk can be entirely diversified and eliminated and hence should not be rewarded in perfect capital markets. Any traded security can be priced based on the specific amount of systematic risk it bears.

A third milestone represents the efficient market hypothesis with its three degrees of market efficiency as postulated by Fama (1970): accordingly, (i) current prices that reflect all relevant historical information characterize a weak form efficient market. (ii) When current prices incorporate all relevant publicly available information, the market is referred to as semi-strong efficient. (iii) A strong form efficient market requires current prices to additionally reflect all relevant private information.[13] In theory, competition among traders should imply in a capital market equilibrium that security prices incorporate all relevant information, are hence adequately priced and can be trusted. Any arbitrage opportunity is expected to be immediately exploited and hence ruled out.[14]

Although the M&M theorems and the efficient market hypothesis have been extremely helpful in structuring the logic of many valuation issues, they clearly do not reflect economic reality.[15] Also the neoclassic financial theory rules out financial intermediations such as LBO organizations since "*when markets are perfect and complete, the allocation of resources is Pareto efficient and there is no scope for intermediaries to improve welfare.*"[16] Deviating

---

10 See Brealey, R. A./Myers, S. C. (2003), pp. 227ff.

11 See Markowitz, H. (1952), pp. 77-91.

12 See Sharpe, W. F. (1964), pp. 425-442, Lintner, J. (1965), pp. 13-37 and Mossin, J. (1966), pp. 768-783.

13 See Fama, E. F. (1970), pp. 383-417.

14 For details regarding the arbitrage theory see e.g. Wilhelm, J. E. M. (1985), pp. 40-59.

15 See Jensen, M. C. (1993), p. 868.

16 See Allen, F./Santomero, A. M. (1997), p. 1462.

however, from the associated restrictive assumptions, there are a number of arguments contradicting the irrelevancy of financing decisions and serving to explain the existence of financial intermediation.[17] Empirical work questions the efficient information processing of capital markets and tends to support weak form informational efficiency and partially backs semi-strong form efficiency.[18] Further, Warner (1977) introduced the nowadays established argumentation that insolvency costs imply that the firm's financing decision is relevant to its market value.[19] In addition, firm value is also affected by the preference for taxation of interest payments rather than dividend payouts.[20] Accordingly, Jensen (1993) concludes that "*The 1980s control activities,* [...], *have demonstrated that the M&M theorems (while logically sound) are empirically incorrect. The evidence from LBOs, leveraged restructurings, takeovers, and venture capital firms has demonstrated dramatically that leverage, payout policy, and ownership structure (that is, who owns the firm's securities) do in fact affect organizational efficiency, cash flow, and, therefore, value.*"[21]

1.2 Institution Economics

Alternative theoretical approaches disengage from the restrictive assumptions of perfect capital markets with respect to information distribution and efficiency, costliness of transactions and insolvency, and are therefore generally applied to address value creation in LBOs on investment level. Given their relevance for this thesis the *Property Rights Theory*, *Agency Theory*, *Asymmetric Information Distribution* and the *Transaction Costs Approach* are briefly presented and subsumed under *Institution Economics.*[22]

Property Rights Theory

The Property Rights theoretical approach is "*characterized by a common emphasis on certain basic ideas concerning the interconnectedness of ownership rights, incentives, and economic behaviour*"[23]. Property Rights subsume any generally accepted (based on laws, tradition or conventions) right of disposition of goods in general and include (i) the right to use the good, (ii) the right of modification, (iii) the right to receive income from it, and (iv) the

---

17 See in particular Ross, S. A. (1973), Jensen, M. C./Meckling, W. (1976), Myers, S. C. (1977) and Myers/Majluf (1984) and the subsequent details on further theoretical approaches.

18 See e.g. Moeller, H. P. (1985), pp. 500-518 and Fama, E. F. (1991), pp. 1575-1614.

19 See Warner, J. B. (1977), pp. 337-347 and for anecdotal evidence e.g. Cutler, D. M./Summers, L. (1988), pp. 157-172.

20 See e.g. Deangelo, H./Masulis, R. W. (1980), pp. 3-29.

21 See e.g. Jensen, M. C. (1993), p. 868.

22 For a comparable discussion and classification see e.g. Picot, A., et al. (2001), pp. 46-61, Schefczyk, M. (2004), pp. 135-154 and Duffner, S. (2005), pp. 83. Alternatively, these theoretical approaches are frequently subsumed under *Theory of the Firm*.

23 See Furubotn, E. G./Pejovitch, S. (1972), p. 1137.

right to dispose of the good.[24] Property rights can either be held by a single individual or by a group of individuals;[25] in the latter case externalities arise. Externalities subsume any (positive or negative) effects resulting from the activity of an individual, "*which are neither compensated for on the market nor accumulated as costs for the individual in another manner*".[26] If information and negotiation were costless the optimal allocation of property rights would result in an efficient outcome where welfare losses from externalities are minimized. However, transaction costs arise through the preparation, exchange, policing and monitoring of property rights and related contracts.[27] As a consequence the efficient outcome results through optimizing the trade-off between the reductions of externalities on the one hand and increasing related transaction costs on the other.[28]

Any financing transaction can be considered a transition of property rights as investors receive rights and duties in exchange for their property.[29] With respect to LBOs, insights regarding control and monitoring aspects of the property rights theory are of relevance. In this respect, the property rights theory is generally considered the methodological basis for the *agency theory*, *asymmetric information distribution* and the *transaction costs approach*.[30]

Agency Theory

Agency theory deals with the specific situation and the corresponding problems where property rights are delegated from a principal to an agent.[31] More precisely agency theory is concerned with contractual problems that occur when "*one or more persons (principal(s)) engaged another person (the agent) to perform some service on their behalf which involves delegating some decision making authority to the agent*".[32] These two parties are characterized by different utility functions.[33] Since not all particularities resulting from this separation of

24 See e.g. Alchian, A. A./Demsetz, H. (1973), p. 17 and Furubotn, E. G./Pejovitch, S. (1974), p. 4.

25 See Demsetz, H. (1967), pp. 347.

26 See Picot, A., et al. (1997a), p. 116.

27 See e.g Demsetz, H. (1964), pp. 11f and Tietzel, M. (1981), p. 211.

28 See e.g. illustrative Picot, A., et al. (2001), pp. 47-49

29 See e.g. Schulz, E. (2000), p. 5.

30 See e.g. Schmidt, R. H. (1988), pp. 250f and Schefczyk, M. (2004), pp. 138f.

31 Major contributions forming agency theory as a part of institutions economics comprise Ross, S. A. (1973), Jensen, M. C./Meckling, W. (1976), Myers, S. C. (1977) and Grossman, S. J./Hart, O. (1983). Initial thoughts and considerations regarding unaligned interests between managers and shareholders of public corporations have already been presented by Berle, A. A./Means, G. C. (1932) and Marris, R. (1963).

32 Jensen, M. C./Meckling, W. (1976), p. 308. According to Fama, E. F./Jensen, M. C. (1983), pp. 301-325 this delegation is due to the specific knowledge and decision skills of the management and risk-sharing diversification efforts of the owners.

33 See e.g. Spremann, K. (1989), p. 6. Conflicts of interest arise among others by the different risk appetite of the two parties. Whereas the principal is generally considered risk neutral (i.e. indifferent between projects with the same expected value regardless of the variance), agents are assumed to be rather risk-averse (i.e.

ownership and control or decision and risk-bearing functions can be entirely fixed contractually residual control rights generally remain with the agent.[34] Managers will tend to use this discretionary power to maximize their individual utility rather than acting in the best interest of the principal since in their role as decision agents they do not bear a major share of the financial consequences of their decision. Therefore, in light of asymmetric information and resulting opportunistic behaviour on the part of the agent and corresponding disutilities on the part of the principal, agency theory deals with the contractual design of this relationship.[35]

For the current purpose two principal categories of agency conflicts shall be distinguished.[36]

- *Moral Hazard* (*Hidden Action*) subsumes any such action by the agent that increases his own utility at the expense of the principal's utility.[37] Problems of moral hazard arise after the closing of the contract in the form of the agent using the discretionary leeway resulting from either superior private information or insufficient monitoring of the agent's activities on the part of the principal. The recommended means of overcoming moral hazard are hence the reduction of information asymmetries and the alignment of interests/utility between the two parties

- *Holdup* (*Hidden Intention*) describes the opportunistic behaviour on the part of the agent to systematically benefit from the uncertainty of incomplete contracts. Following the closing of the contract and monetary commitments (i.e. investments) by the principal, the agent reveals his true intentions and – in light of the threat of sunk costs for the principal – might compel renegotiations.

The principal has various means of limiting and counteracting divergent agent behavior, such as reducing the agent's discretionary decision space, aligning the interest of management or implementing control mechanisms. However, a residual loss will remain as counteracting means cannot entirely eliminate non-congruent interests between the agent and the principal and costs of full enforcement of contracts exceed the benefits thereof. In this context, Jensen/Meckling (1976) introduced the basic notation of *agency costs* summarizing the costs of

---

preferring projects with less variance). See e.g. Eisenhardt, K. M. (1989), pp. 58f and Meier, D. (2005), p. 48.

34 See Shleifer, A./Vishny, R. (1997b) arguing that residual control rights remain with the agents as they have been chosen by the principal(s) for their specific knowledge and decision skills.

35 See e.g. Picot, A., et al. (2001), pp. 56ff.

36 For the following see Spremann, K. (1990), pp. 568-572. However, *adverse selection*, which is frequently seen as a third type of agency conflict, is for the understanding here (analogous to Schefczyk, M. (2004), pp. 139-152) considered separately under *Asymmetric Information Distribution*.

37 For details regarding *Moral Hazard* see chapter III.B.1.1 as well as Demougin, D./Jost, P.-J. (2001), pp. 46-67 in a general context and Schulz, E. (2000), pp. 56-63 in the context of PE investing.

divergent agent behavior, (i) the monitoring expenditures by the principal, (ii) the bonding expenditures by the agent, as well as (iii) the residual loss.[38]

As pointed out, agency theory is the generally applied lens to analyze operational performance effects of LBOs. To be detailed further in chapter III.B.1 the LBO business model and governance structure offers means to reduce any costs arising from the delegation of property rights which hence serves as a source of value in LBO investments.

Asymmetric Information Distribution

Considering information asymmetries between individuals/organizations providing capital and individuals/organizations seeking capital is apparently closely linked to the aforementioned agency theory. However, whereas in the context of LBOs, principal–agent theory primarily deals with the contractual relationship between investors and managers, the asymmetric information distribution also covers market transactions (such as an IPO or an auction process), which are not characterized by a hierarchical relationship. [39] This understanding merits a separate consideration here. According to Schefczyk (2004) reasons for these kinds of information asymmetries are threefold: (i) the preparation and provision of information is costly, (ii) the distribution of confidential information is sensitive, and (iii) the previously mentioned problem of *moral hazard* implies direct benefits of private information (and their expropriation).[40]

In markets that are characterized by asymmetric information, market participants are uncertain regarding the true quality of the offered product. *Hidden characteristics* prior to the signing of the contract potentially imply an *adverse selection* in the sense that good quality suppliers are incentivized to leave the market potentially causing a market breakdown in extreme cases.[41] Revealing private information represents a means of overcoming the problem of adverse selection. This is generally referred to as *signaling*.

Given the private nature of *PE* investing, the described information asymmetries are of particular relevance in the acquisition and the divestment phases. To be discussed further, information asymmetries between the seller and the acquirer can have a substantial impact on realized entry and exit prices in LBO investments.

---

38 See Jensen, M. C./Meckling, W. (1976), pp. 305ff.

39 See e.g. Schefczyk, M. (2004), pp. 149f.

40 See Schefczyk, M. (2004), p. 150.

41 See Akerlof, G. A. (1970), pp. 490-494.

Transaction Cost Theory

The transaction cost theory is closely related to the property rights theory. However, although the theory deals with the actual transfer of property rights, it is limited to the individual transaction only and therefore in a broad sense aims at explaining the existence of the firm as well as its organizational form.[42]

According to the transaction cost theory, criteria that will determine whether it is optimal to govern a transaction through a market setting or through the hierarchical, organizational setting of the firm are (i) the frequency of the transaction, (ii) the uncertainty of the transaction, and (iii) the asset specificity.[43] The objective function hereby is the minimization of transaction costs that arise from market imperfections[44], which reduces the cost of capital and hence increases the expected rate of return for investors. Based on these three criteria the probability that transaction cost is lowest in the firm setting is higher "*given high transaction frequency, the higher the internal uncertainty or asset specificity of a transaction*"[45].

Transaction costs are considered any such costs that arise through the interaction of transaction parties in the course of dealing with and exchanging property rights; depending on the transaction phase these include information costs, negotiation and execution costs as well as control costs.[46]

Financial intermediation such as *PE* investing implies at first, ceteris paribus, higher transaction costs through the involvement of an additional party.[47] However, given the repeated use of standardized financing instruments, financial intermediaries might enjoy comparative cost advantages, realize economies of scale and thus actually reduce transaction costs.[48]

2. Empirical Work to Assess Value Creation in LBOs

Efforts to empirically test the outlined theoretical approaches in the context of value creation analysis in LBOs on investment level and *PE* investing on an aggregated level are multifaceted. For the purpose of this thesis a threefold classification of (i) *Premia-Paid Studies*

---

42 See Williamson, O. E. (1985), pp. 35-41.

43 For details see e.g. Picot, A., et al. (2001), pp. 51ff and Meier, D. (2005), pp. 45ff based on Williamson, O. E. (1975).

44 See Williamson, O. E. (1985), p. 18.

45 See Meier, D. (2005), pp. 46-47 based on Mols, N. P. (2000), p. 238 Williamson, O. E. (1985), pp. 211ff and Picot, A., et al. (1997a), p. 109.

46 See Picot, A., et al. (1997b), p. 73.

47 See Hellwig, M. (1991), p. 42.

48 See Benston, G. J./Smith, C. W. (1976), pp. 215ff. Leland, H. E./Pyle, D. H. (1977), p. 383 notes that "*if there are economies of scale, one might expect organizations to exist which gather and sell information about particular classes of assets.*"

(ii) *Operational Performance Studies* (iii) *PE Performance Studies* serves to review relevant empirical work. Such classification (i) structures selected key contributions alongside three prominent approaches to proxy for value creation in LBO investments, (ii) provides an understanding of the status quo of relevant research, and (iii) creates bridges to shortcomings and research gaps in the subsequent chapter as the starting point for this thesis. Table 2 summarizes the three approaches. Details are subsequently discussed.

Table 2 Overview of Empirical Research Streams to Assess Value Creation in LBOs[49]

Approach	**Research Object**	**Perspective**	**Methodology**	**Important Papers**
Premia-Paid Studies	Going private transactions	Investment level Entry of the LBO investment Pre- as well as post-LBO equityholders	Acquisition premia as indication for expected value creation	Deangelo et al. (1984) Lehn/Poulsen (1989) Eddey et al. (1996) Andres et al. (2004)
Operational Performance Studies	Focus on going private transactions Rarely including divisional buyouts	Investament level Post-LBO stakeholders comprising equity- and debtholders, employees and the government	Variance analysis of pre- and post-LBO operational performance indicators Comparison of variations with industry levels	Baker/Wruck (1989) Smith (1990a) Opler (1992) Kaplan (1989a) Muscarella/Vetsuypens (1990)
PE Performance Studies	Going private as well as divisional, succession and secondary buyouts	Post-LBO equityholders on fund/investor level	Performance analysis of private equity as an asset class Comparison with the public market as alternative investment	Ljungqvist/Richardson (2003a) Evca (2004) Gottschalg et al. (2004) Kaplan/Schoar (2005)

Source: Own illustration

2.1 Premia-Paid Analysis in Public-to-Private Transactions

Substantial acquisition premia in US public-to-private transactions in the late 80s triggered a spate of research into the value creation of LBOs. This thesis refers to this first line of research as *Premia-Paid Studies.* Despite the presumably non-strategic nature of public-to-private LBO investments, empirical studies confirm acquisition premia that are statistically almost as highly significant as other control-changing devices such as tender offers, mergers and voluntary liquidations.[50] Pre-buyout public shareholders might consider this premium as the (fraction shared of total expected) value created through the LBO transaction. From a macroeconomic perspective the implicit line of reasoning in these studies is that the premium paid represents an indication of the total anticipated and expected value creation associated with the LBO.

---

49 For details regarding the research object and the perspective see chapters II.A and II.B respectively.

50 See Table 3 for details. For shareholder gains analyses resulting from tender offers, mergers and voluntary liquidations see among others Bradley, M., et al. (1988), Asquith, P. (1983) and Kim, E. H./Schatzberg, J. D. (1987) respectively.

Table 3 Selected Premia-Paid Studies in Public-to-Private Transactions[51]

Listed in chronological order; average cumulative abnormal return; numbers in brackets represent days prior (-) and after (+) the date of the first announcement [0]

Study	Approach	Analyzed Variables	Abnormal Return	Key Findings
Deangelo et al. (1984)	Gain-sharing analysis of the effect of 72 going-private proposals of US firms for the years 1973 to 1980 on public (minority) stockholder wealth — At announcement of proposal — For a sub-sample of withdrawn proposals	Offer outcome Extent of third-party participation Pre-offer managerial ownership Pre-announcement leakage of proposal	22.27% [-1 ; +1] 30.40% [-40 ; 0] Calculation of the cumulated average prediction error (CPE) to account for leakage	Statistically significant confirmation of the gain-sharing hypothesis: — Announcement premium comparable to merger cash tender premia — Decrease of stockholder wealth of 8.88% at withdrawal of the proposal — Presumably no exploitation of minority shareholders
Lehn/Poulsen (1989)[52]	Sample of 263 US going private transactions in the years 1980 to 1987 — Agency theoretical tests by contrasting firms that went private with a control sample (publicly traded corporation from the same industry and similar amount of equity) — Logit analysis with sub-periods prior and after to 1984 — Sub-samples with below and above median pre-buyout managerial ownership	Cash flow to equity value Total income taxes to equity value Historical sales growth as expected growth proxy Dummy variable for competing bids and/or takeover threat Pre-buyout managerial ownership	16.30% [-1 ; +1] 19.90% [-10 ; +10] 20.50% [-20 ; +20]	No confirmation of reduced agency costs for the total sample However, significant relationship for the sub-period from 1984 to 1987 between — premia paid to stockholders and undistributed cash flow — undistributed cash flow and a firm's decision to go private — low growth rates and a firm's decision to go private Going private transactions seem to be induced at least in part by the threat of hostile takeovers

[51] Further relevant studies not listed here include among others Amihud, Y. (1989), Cornett, M. M./Travlos, N. G. (1993), Frankfurter, G. M./Gunay, E. (1992), Marais, L., et al. (1989), Torabzadeh, K. M./Berlin, W. J. (1987), Warga, A./Welch, I. (1993), Carow, K. A./Roden, D. M. (1997) and Kieschnick, R. L. (1998). Hite, G. L./Vetsuypens, M. R. (1989) find significant abnormal return to parent company shareholders around the announcement of divisional buyout.

[52] *Note:* Kieschnick, R. L. (1998) revisited the analysis by Lehn, K./Poulsen, A. (1989) based on the same set of data and presents various different interpretations by accounting for the influence of the choice based sampling scheme, outliers in the data and potential mis-specified variables on the inferences. Accordingly, neither a firm's prior growth rate nor its prior level of free cash flow is a significant determinant for a decision to go private. Also the pre-buyout free cash flow level is not a significant determinant for the premium paid. Rather, the firm's size and potential tax saving opportunities seem to be determinants of the premium paid to take the firm private. In addition Kieschnick finds support for the overheated buyout market hypothesis presented by Kaplan, S. N./Stein, J. (1993). See Kieschnick, R. L. (1998), pp. 187-202.

Study	Approach	Analyzed Variables	Abnormal Return	Key Findings
Eddey et al. (1996)	Sample of 46 Australian going private transactions in the years 1988 to 1991 — Control sample (publicly traded corporation from the same industry and similar amount of equity) — OLS regression over one and four month intervals	Cash flow Dividend payout ratio Depreciation to total assets Growth proxy Managerial ownership Competing bids and/or takeover threat Ownership concentration Tax rate	27.72% [-2 ; 0] 30.78% [-30 ; 0] 27.15% [-120 ; 0]	Increasing premium with the level of ownership dispersion seems not to support inside information hypothesis Some evidence for LBOs being a response to an actual or perceived threat of a competing bid Statistically no direct support for reduced agency costs (presence of going privates despite a market being characterized by high growth rather than a lack of investment opportunities)
Andres et al. (2004)	Net sample of 99 European public-to-private transactions for the years 1996 to 2002 — Sub-sample analysis for UK vs. CE and for the UK sub-periods prior and after Dec-1999 — Multiple regression of abnormal returns on shareholder gain explaining variables — OLS regression over one and four month intervals	Free cash flow Free-float Managerial ownership Relative peer valuation (P/E) Share price development Illiquidity Legal protection (civil vs. common law) Labor productivity Taxes	13.83% [-1 ; 0] 27.01% [-30 ; +30]	Findings support and broaden US findings Statistically significant influence of (i) free float, (ii) historical share price performance and (iii) relative valuation to the firm's peer universe Private equity funds seem to "*scan the market for cross-sectionally and intertemporally undervalued target firms*" (p. 27)

Based on conducted due diligence, post-buyout equity investors theoretically set the premium such that on the one hand pre-buyout shareholders are encouraged to tender their shares and on the other hand cash flows arising from the potential investment in the form of dividend income during the holding period and the equity value at the time of the liquidation of the investment still justify the risk-return profile of the equity investors. Analyzing the relationship between premia paid and relevant firm characteristics tests for (i) cross-sectional differences of LBO vs. non-LBO companies as well as (ii) the assumptions of reduced agency costs resulting from the LBO governance structure and related organizational changes.

The conclusion of Torabzadeh/Berlin (1987) stresses the ex-ante view of the notation value creation in LBO investments in this first vogue of research. "*Stockholders of firms acquired through LBOs realize significant positive abnormal returns as a result of the buyout announcement. The findings support the notion of value creation in leveraged buyouts.*"[53] Similarly, Jensen (1989a) considers the premia-paid analysis as a viable approach to assess – what he refers to as – *total wealth effects* of LBOs. Accordingly, "*the equity returns* [*to post-*

53 See Torabzadeh, K. M./Berlin, W. J. (1987), p. 313.

buyout shareholders] are almost a pure risk premium and therefore independent of the amount invested. Calculating the returns on the entire capital base used to purchase the pre-buyout equity, or the fraction of the total wealth gains that go to pre-buyout shareholders, gives a better picture of the distribution of the total wealth created in the buyout."[54]

2.2 Operational Performance Studies

The second and to date most intense research stream to assess performance effects and proxy value creation in LBO investments are what this thesis refers to as *Operational Performance Studies*. Hereby value creation is generally inferred to by comparing pre- and post-buyout operational performance measures of the bought-out company. Deducing from improvements on value creation as a result of these measures it becomes evident to Palepu (1990), who reviews the findings of a number of studies on the economic consequences of buyouts and concludes that "[*R*]*esearch suggests that leveraged buyouts create value through significant operating performance improvements*".[55]

Apart from *Premia-Paid Studies* this research stream on value creation in LBOs takes a post-investment perspective by applying post-buyout financial information during the holding period. Comparable to *Premia-Paid Studies*, *Operational Performance Studies* predominately use reduced agency costs to explain favorable variations in operating performance measures post-LBO. The studies provide an understanding of whether, and to what extent, the *expected* value creation due to anticipated changes in corporate governance materializes in the form of improved financial performance. This, however, implies that financial performance improvements translate immediately into a higher, realizable firm value, thus leaving exit considerations aside. Similar to the methodology in *Premia-Paid Studies*, value creation in pure *Operational Performance Studies* is not an observed, analyzed or calculated variable but rather is assumed to be reflected by improved operating performance.

---

54 See Jensen, M. C. (1989a), p. 39. In this citation Jensen refers to results presented by Kaplan, S. N. (1989a) (see Table 4). For a brief discussion of the herein applied equity return measure see chapter I.B.3.

55 See Palepu, K. G. (1990), p. 247.

Table 4 Selected Operational Performance Studies[56]

Listed in chronological order

Study	Approach	Analyzed Variables	Key Findings
Selected Pure Operational Performance Studies			
Baker/Wruck (1989)	Detailed case study of the LBO of O.M. Scott & Sons Company including financial analysis and interviews Documentation of organizational changes that took place in response to the LBO Predominantly, qualitative analysis describing the LBO phenomenon based upon a variety of variables	Debt repayment schedule and debt covenants Management equity ownership, salaries and bonuses Purpose and composition of the board, operating partners NWC, employment, approaches to product markets	Confirmation of results of large-sample studies: heavy debt burden and management equity ownership lead to improved performance Identification of three factors that lead to organizational changes — Constraints of high leverage — Changes in incentives and compensation — Changes in the monitoring of top management "*Value was created by decentralizing decision making largely because managers were closely monitored and supported by an expert board of directors who were also equityholders*" (p. 189)
Smith (1990a)	Gross sample of 58 MBOs of public companies between 1977 and 1986 — Comparison of operating performance one year prior to two years after the LBO — Industry adjustment based on SIC codes — Sub-sample for MBOs with significant asset disposals (measured as >20% of net PPE)	Return on operating assets Return per employee Components of net working capital Discretionary items (R&D, advertising, maintenance & repair)	Significant increase of operating returns following the MBO before and after industry adjustment and consistent in both sub-samples Significant decrease of resources that are tied up in working capital items — Significant decrease in inventory holding period — Significant decrease in receivable collection period No support for significant cutbacks in discretionary items Significant decline of (relative) capital expenditures
Opler (1992)	Sample of 44 completed going private transactions in the years 1985 to 1989 — Comparison of operating performance one year prior to two years after the LBO — Industry adjustment based on three-digit SIC code	Operating profit margin CapEx Income Taxes R&D expenses Operating Profit per Employee	Absolute and relative (to industry peers) performance improvements: — Increase in the operating profits to sales ratio by 16.5% (11.6% industry-adjusted) — Increase in operating profit per employee by 31.8% (40.3% industry-adjusted) Sharp post-buyout decline in CapEx and income taxes and to a much lesser extent in R&D expenses Performance improvements "*cast[s] doubt on the contention that the collapse of the LBO market in 1989 and 1990 evidenced the unusual and transitory nature of the leveraged buyout transaction.*" (p. 33)

[56] Further relevant studies not listed here include among others Bull, I. (1989) , Long, W. F./Ravenscraft, D. J. (1993a), Long, W. F./Ravenscraft, D. J. (1993b), Ofek, E. (1994), Phan, P. H./Hill, C. W. L. (1995), Weir, C./Laing, D. (1998). For a review see e.g. Palepu, K. G. (1990), Schmid, H. (1994) and most recently Kitzmann, J. (2005). Questionnaire-based survey studies, in particular with a German focus, include Gräper, M. (1993), Jakoby, S. (2000).

Study	Approach	Analyzed Variables	Key Findings
Selected Reverse LBO Studies			
Kaplan (1989a)	Gross sample of 76 large Management buyouts of public companies between 1980 and 1986 — 48 companies with post-buyout financial information — 25 companies with exit valuation — Comparison of operating performance one year prior to two years after the LBO — Industry adjustment based on SIC codes	Operating Income CapEx Net Cash Flow Employment	Significant increases of operating income (before depreciation; margin increase by 19%) and net cash flow as well as significant decrease in CapEx (difference between operating income and CapEx increases by 96%) compared to both pre-buyout levels as well as inter-industry developments Median total market-adjusted return to pre- and post-buyout investors of 71.0% [-2 months, exit] Correlation analysis between total market-adjusted returns and operating changes give mixed support for the value of the operating changes Operating improvements and value increases presumably coming from improved incentives rather than layoffs or managerial exploitation of shareholders through inside information
Muscarella/ Vetsuypens (1990)	Gross sample of 72 US going privates (18) and divisional buyouts (54) that subsequently went public for the years 1976 to 1987 Governance structure, restructuring activities, performance, leverage and value analysis — Entire sample and sub-sample analysis for (i) divisional buyouts/going privates (ii) firms with acquisition and divestiture activities — Relative performance analysis compared to a control group of randomly drawn companies from COMPUSTAT	*Governance Structure:* Managerial Ownership, Compensation *Restructuring Activi -ties:* Redeployment of resources, operational efficiencies *Performance:* Sales, gross margin, operating margin, asset turnover, sales per employee, tax rates, CapEx, Employment *Leverage and value:* leverage, firm size, equity value	"*...data suggests that the buyout process created a new organizational structure, which appears to be more efficient than its public predecessor*" (p.1412) Post LBO changes in governance structure: — Substantial managerial ownership — Implementation of a variety of incentive schemes Numerous post-LBO restructuring initiatives to increase efficiency and performance — Significant improvement in accounting performance measures relative to the control group — Efficiency gains independent of the firm's acquisition and divestiture activity but more pronounced for divisional buyouts Median increase in firm size of 34%; very high returns on equity through extreme use of leverage
Selected Operational Performance Studies with or including European/German Focus			
Kitching (1989)	Sample of 110 US American and British MBOs (split roughly 60/40) completed prior to 1987 including going privates (~25%) and divisional buyouts (~75%) — Selection based on questionnaire responses and interviews from an initial identified sample of 320 transactions — Comparison of operating performance from entry to three years after the LBO	Revenues, cash flow, EBIT and net income Taxes NWC Managerial ownership Financing structure Employment Acquisitions and divestitures	"*...impressive efficiency gains*" (p. 77) Tax savings significantly larger for US LBOs Managers control on average 30% of the ownership, though only contributing 3% of the initial equity UK LBOs seem to be more conservatively financed than those in the US (7% vs. 37% junk bond financing) Employment remains stable Acquisition and divestiture activity more pronounced in the UK

For most studies, the perspective is limited to the entirety of post-buyout investors. First, the capital structure at entry is generally not considered. Consequently, a separate consideration of equity investors and debt investors is not feasible.[57] Second, the non-consideration of the LBO exit also prevents a more detailed analysis with respect to the type of investors. In this respect a sub-sample of *Operational Performance Studies* deserves special attention. IPO prospecti at the time of the exit of the investment generally serve as one source of post-LBO operational performance information; few studies though explicitly analyze so-called reverse LBOs in detail.[58] For LBO investments exited via IPO, the market price provides a valuation of the equity. Hence, from the perspective of the equity investor, value creation can be analyzed by comparing the equity values at exit and entry. This should then allow analyzing of how far operational performance improvements during the holding period translate into higher equity values at exit. However, as will be discussed further shortly, reverse LBO studies by Muscarella/Vetsuypens (1990) and partly by Kaplan (1989a), which apply IPO exit equity valuations for value creation analysis, face shortcomings, such as an inadequate equity valuation at entry and a lack of consideration of interim equity streams, that prevent or limit such analysis.[59]

Several studies put operating performance variations of the sample of LBOs into perspective by comparing their results to variations of (i) a randomly selected control group or (ii) a matching industry peer group.[60] The identification of an appropriate industry peer group is done either by assigning each LBO in the sample a peer company that matches the characteristics of the specific LBO as closely as possible, or by comparing the firms operating measures with industry-specific averages. In the latter case the use of the three or four digit SIC codes has been established as a standard. To evaluate relative operational performance improvements and to draw conclusions on the value creative effects of the LBO both approaches test for significant outperformance of the LBO compared to the assigned peer and the relevant industry respectively.

2.3 Private Equity Performance Studies

A relatively new though increasingly intense field of research regarding value creation in LBOs is the analysis of *PE* as an asset class. Rather than the analysis of an individual company on investment level this approach targets the analysis of aggregated cash flow information. On

---

57 See chapter II.B for details regarding these two investor types and an appropriate separation for the purpose of this thesis.

58 Going privates, which subsequently to a private holding period go public again, are referred to as *reverse LBOs*. See also chapter II.A.4.1.

59 See chapter I.B.3 for details.

60 See e.g. Kaplan, S. N. (1989a), Muscarella, C. J./Vetsuypens, M. R. (1990), Smith, A. J. (1990a), Opler, T. C. (1992) and most recently in a European context Kitzmann, J. (2005).

the one hand the aggregated consideration offers the opportunity to specify the risk and return profile of private equity and quantify the characteristics and their determinants. Such aggregated data account for the performance of not only successfully realized investments but also underperforming investments and write-offs. On the other hand, however, the aggregated cash flow perspective has failed so far to establish a link between company- and transaction-specific information and investment performance.

In the context of *PE Performance Studies* the perspective of value creation analysis can either be the private equity firm or so-called *General Partner* (GP), or the investors in the fund, i.e. the so-called *Limited Partners* (LP). Private equity firms are commonly structured as limited liability partnerships with limited partners committing funds for a finite lifetime.[61] GPs can draw on the cash whenever an appropriate investment opportunity arises and commit to (i) liquidize the investment in the course of the funds lifetime, and (ii) distribute the investment proceeds pro-rata net of the fund's compensation.[62] Performance analysis can either be on fund or investor level, where the latter reports the fund performance net of any fund expenses such as administrative expenses, taxes and fund compensation.[63] Fund compensation can be in a variety of forms. Generally the *PE* firm receives a fixed yearly management fee proportionate to the total committed fund size and on top participates in the overall performance either for each realized transaction or in the form of a percentage of the funds capital gain, the so-called *carried interest* or a combination of both. GP performance participation is generally tied to the achievement of some form of minimal fund performance (hurdle rate).[64]

Empirical studies in this research stream are generally based on confidential data provided by either *Venture Economics* (*VE*) or LPs, in particular so-called *fund-of-funds* that invest in a variety of individual *PE* funds simultaneously.[65]

---

61 See e.g. Wright, M./Robbie, K. (1998), pp. 532ff, Gompers, P. A./Lerner, J. (1999a), pp. 29ff and Bilo, S. (2002), p. 20.

62 For a recent study analyzing the contractual relation between GPs and LPs and factors affecting the contractual design see Schmidt, D./Wahrenburg, M. (2004).

63 For details regarding these performance measures see chapter II.C.3.

64 See e.g. Bader, H. (1996), pp. 155ff and Gompers, P. A./Lerner, J. (1999b), pp. 57-94. Gompers, P. A./Lerner, J. (1999a), pp. 3-44 find compensation across private equity partnerships to be relatively homogeneous with a standard compensation scheme of 1.5% to 2.5% annual management fee and 20% participation in profits, i.e. carried interest.

65 For details regarding the *fund-of-funds* concept see e.g. Von Daniels, H. (2004), pp. 19ff.

Table 5 Selected PE Performance Studies[66]

Listed in chronological order

Key Study	**Approach**	**Analyzed Variables**	**Key Findings**
Ljungqvist/Richardson (2003a)	Sample of 73 VC and LBO funds for the years 1981 to 1993 based on information provided by one LP — Detailed and precisely dated cash flow data by fund — Cash flow timing: draw-down and capital return schedules — Performance analysis with comparison to the S&P 500 (PI)[67] — Risk adjustment by assigning industry betas to portfolio companies — OLS regression analysis	Fund size First-time-fund Cash inflows into PE funds Portfolio betas Portfolio diversification — # of portfolio companies — Industry concentration (Herfindahl) — Fraction invested in dominant industry	Three years to invest 56.9% and six years to invest 90.5% of committed capital Average (unlevered) portfolio beta of 1.08 Risk-adjusted return (based upon calculated betas) on the order of 24% interpreted to represent illiquidity premium Excess returns (ERs) in the magnitude of five to eight percent compared to the aggregate public market (PM) ERs robust to assumptions about timing of investments in PM, measures of risk and measurement methodologies Cash inflow into private equity and the size of the fund found to be significant determinants of ERs
Evca (2004)	Sample of 881 venture and buyout funds — Performance measure based on pooled IRR[68] from fund inception to Dec-2003 — Performance trend analysis based on 1,3,5,10-year horizon IRRs[69] — Comparison to PM	Stage: VC vs. PE Fund Size Comparators (Morgan Stanley Euro Index, HSBC Small Company Index, JP Morgan Euro Bonds)	In the long run private equity returns outperform public markets Overall pooled IRR of 9.9% and 12.2% for buyout funds Large buyout funds (>€500m) perform relatively better than smaller funds Declining five-year rolling IRR due to difficult macroeconomic environment and limited exit opportunities

66 Further relevant studies not listed here include among others Kaplan, S. N./Stein, J. (1993), Gompers, P. A./Lerner, J. (1997), Moskowitz, T. J./Vissing-Jörgensen, A. (2002), Jones, C. M./Rhodes-Kropf, M. (2003), Schmidt, D. (2003) and Schmidt, D., et al. (2004), Kaserer, C./Diller, C. (2004) and Diller, C./Kaserer, C. (2005).

67 Profitability index (*PI*) compares an investment in PE relative to an alternative, comparable investment opportunity. See II.C.3.3 for details.

68 See Evca (2004) p. 10. The pooled IRR is "*[T]he IRR [net of fees and carried interest to the fund] is obtained by taking cash flows from inception together with the Residual Value for each fund and aggregating them into a pool as if they were a single fund.*"

69 See Evca (2004), p. 10. "*The Horizon IRR allows for an indication of performance trends in the industry. It uses the fund's net asset value at the beginning of the period [tracing back 1,3,5,10 years] as an initial cash outflow and the Residual Value at the end of the period as the terminal cash flow.*"

Key Study	Approach	Analyzed Variables	Key Findings
Gottschalg et al. (2004)	Dataset from VE with cash flow to investors and investment data for more than 500 mature US and European PE funds — Net performance (i.e. net of fees) analysis on fund level — Residual value of on-going investments proxied through historical conversion analysis Profitability index PI applied as performance measure	Distribution and takedown over time Book Value of the fund (mark-to-market) Real GDP growth rate BAA bond yields Credit spreads Market portfolio performance Option-based risk factors Aggregated P/E ratios	PE funds raised between 1980 and 1995 underperformed the public stock markets High cyclical exposure of PE funds — Strong correlation to valuation levels in the public markets as proxied by overall P/E ratios — Substantial left-tail risk, i.e. significantly higher losses during large market downturns but less sensitivity in favorable economic market environments Drivers of underperformance are small size, European focus and inexperienced fund
Kaplan/Schoar (2005)	Dataset from VE for VC and LBO funds in the period 1980 to 1997 with a net sample of 1090 funds Performance measures (IRR as reported, IRR as calculated and PME[70];all net of fees) for 746 funds (78% VC and 22% LBO funds) — Performance analysis with comparison to the S&P 500 — Analysis of characteristics of fund returns — Persistence Analysis	Fund Flows (timing) Fund Size Sequence (number of subsequent funds from the same general partner) Fund Survival Fund industry focus New funds entering the market	Large heterogeneity in returns across funds and time periods — Substantial persistence of funds; GPs who managed to outperform the industry with a fund are likely to do so again with subsequent funds and vice versa — Performance increases with fund size — Boom and bust type cycle: positive market-adjusted returns encourage entry that leads to negative market-adjusted returns, etc. i.e. poor performance of new entrants, in times of fund overcapacity, dilute overall industry performance Average PME for LBO funds of 0.93 and 1.21 for VC funds Potential underlying heterogeneity in the skill-set of GPs regarding quality of advice and access to proprietary deal-flow

Aforementioned *PE Performance Studies* analyze private equity on an aggregated level as asset class. Results are mixed and seem to be influenced to a great extent by the applied methodology and chosen benchmark. Remarkably though, several studies report a relative underperformance of PE as an asset class. Kaplan/Schoar (2005) find that *"[O]n average LBO fund returns net of fees are lower than those of the S&P 500"*.[71] However, the fund/investor perspective of *PE Performance Studies* substantially distorts value creation analysis of individual LBO investments. This is detailed further in the subsequent chapters.

70 Public market equivalent (*PME*) compares an investment in PE fund relative to an investment in the PM. See chapter II.C.3.3 for details.

71 See Kaplan, S. N./Schoar, A. (2005), p. 2.

B. Shortcomings and Research Gap

The brief overview of the status of research on value creation in LBOs in the previous chapter suggests the following three conclusions:

- First, mostly in response to the restrictive assumptions of the neoclassic financial theory, various analytical frameworks emerged, helping to theoretically explain and empirically analyze value creation in LBO investments. These theoretical frameworks throw light on the complex LBO value creation process from various perspectives and identify a variety of sources of value creation in LBO investments.

- Second, although the attempt to classify it in the previous chapter might suggest otherwise, empirical research on value creation in LBO investments is multifaceted. However, almost any empirical study induces *value creation in LBOs* through proxies. According to the classification presented, either (i) the acquisition premia paid to pre-buyout stockholders, (ii) the change in valuation-relevant operating accounting measures, or (iii) aggregated cash flow information were employed to deduce value creation.

- Therefore and third, there seems to be a clear lack of understanding and research for *value creation in LBO investments from a post-LBO equity investor perspective* in two respects: (i) the usage and discussion of a comprehensive framework capturing the entire LBO process holistically and despite this complexity still facilitating the consideration of the various sources of value creation in LBOs; (ii) an empirical analysis alongside such a framework based on the actual amount of value created in LBO investments from an equity investor perspective on investment level. Linking internal company- and transaction-specific information as well as external, market variables to LBO performance helps identify determinants of value creation in LBOs on investment level.

In this respect, it can be summarized that any shortcomings of previous empirical studies are based on the research object (chapter I.B.1), the perspective of the analysis (chapter I.B.2) or the notation of value creation (chapter I.B.3).

1. With Respect to the Research Object

With respect to the research object of various previous empirical studies on value creation in LBO transactions, a research gap seems to exist primarily regarding (i) the consideration and inclusion of all relevant steps in the LBO value creation process, but also concerning (ii) the geographical focus, and (iii) the types of analyzed LBO investments.

First, the exit mode of an LBO investment and in particular the relevance for value creation on investment level has received, if at all, very little attention in the academic literature so far, either from a theoretical or even an empirical perspective.[72] Consequently, empirical studies – in particular *Operating Performance Studies* – disregard the divestment process as a critical factor for value creation in LBOs and exclusively focus on internal, company-specific aspects. *PE Performance Studies* focus on realized investments and hence account for the divestment process. However, the impact on value creation can hereby not be excluded. Although some of these studies build upon cash flow information on direct investment level, they have a common shortcoming in that a linkage between company- and transaction-specific information (including the financial performance during the holding period and financing considerations) and this cash flow information on investment level cannot be established.

Second, empirical analysis on value creation in LBOs, as clustered in the preceding overview, has to date predominantly been conducted on US transactions. Early LBOs in the period of the mid to late 80s triggered a first vogue of academic research, followed by a notable decline in empirical publications thereafter, and a recently regained popularity in particular with respect to *PE Performance Studies*. Relevant work on European transactions is still relatively new and rare.[73]

Third, previous research seems to be biased towards the subset of public-to-private LBO transactions. For studies prevailing on value creation in LBOs through the analysis of premia paid this limitation is inherent. However, most operational performance studies also limit and hence bias the analysis to this sub-set of transactions given the non-availability of relevant data for previously privately held corporations.[74] Hence, the general notation of LBOs (and related terminologies) applied by several authors is based on a relatively narrow understanding, and more general post-buyout performance studies (comprising LBOs of various entry modes) would be desirable.[75] The analysis of the fund performance of *PE* as an asset class overcomes this shortcoming in that it includes LBOs of previously publicly as well as privately held corporations. However, these studies lack the individual investment as well as an equity investor perspective as discussed in the following chapter.

---

72 See e.g. Barry, C. B., et al. (1990), Brück, M. (1998), Prester, M. (2002), von Daniels, H. (2004) for exceptions. For a recent study detailing the impact of the exit mode in the context of venture capital see Cumming, D. J./Macintosh, J. G. (2003).

73 For a recent premia-paid study with European focus see e.g. Andres, C., et al. (2004); for a recent operational performance study see e.g. Kitzmann, J. (2005); aggregated fund studies generally include US as well as European funds; for a recent European study see e.g. Gottschalg, O., et al. (2004).

74 *Note:* In the case of public-to-private transactions, empirical analyses benefit from compulsory filed financial statements as a publicly held corporation. Further, the public listing provides an equity valuation in the form of market prices for the bought-out companies as a reference point.

75 See e.g. Kaplan, S. N. (1989a) and Smith, A. J. (1990b). Kitching, J. (1989), p. 74 correctly points out that "*[a]lthough public company buyouts attract the most media attention, they comprise a distinct minority of LBOs.*"

2. With Respect to the Perspective of the Analysis

The brief overview on the status of relevant empirical research indicates that value creation in LBOs has been analyzed from a variety of different perspectives. A research gap seems to exist though for studies taking a post-buyout equity investor perspective on investment level.

Chart 1 suggests that the ex-post analysis of LBOs can generally be accomplished on three levels: the *investment level* deals with individual direct investments and can be further specified by taking either the equity or the debt investor perspective. The *fund level* considers aggregated cash flow information on various investments undertaken by one and the same *PE* fund. Leaving investing management and potential co-equity investors aside, this perspective obviously considers only the (diluted) pro-rata *PE* fund ownership stake. The *investor level* takes the LP perspective by analyzing the return on the committed capital across various private equity funds, net of GP management fees and carried interest.

Chart 1 Perspectives for Analyzing Value Creation in LBOs

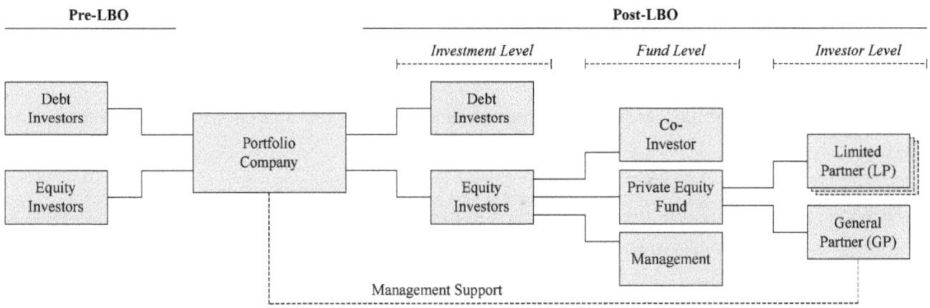

Source: Own Illustration

Premia-Paid Studies generally take an ex-ante, pre-buyout equity investor perspective. Apparently, such a perspective and the consideration of the entry does not include the holding period and the liquidation of the investment as integral parts of the LBO process and hence does not serve to analyze value creation in LBOs – especially as there is no mean value creation from a post-buyout equity investor perspective.

Operational Performance Studies commonly take the perspective of the entirety of post-LBO debt and equity investors. The financing structure of the LBO as a means for separating debt and equity investors and hence creating value is rarely – and even then frequently inappropriately – considered. Also, apart from a few exceptions, such studies neglect the specific limited time horizon of LBO investments by not considering the liquidation of the investment. Such a perspective cannot serve to analyze value creation in LBOs from a post-buyout equity investor perspective.

The third category, *PE Performance Studies* does capture the entire LBO process including the liquidation of the investment. However, such studies tend to take the perspective of the *PE* fund or its investors, in particular the LP perspective, by analyzing aggregated cash flow information of *PE* as an asset class. An inherent problem of these empirical studies is that frequently data applied are in aggregate rather than fund-by-fund form.[76] Further data are predominately self-reported and therefore likely biased.[77] Also *PE* funds as well as LPs often report *Fund* and *Investor IRRs* (as the generally applied performance measure) inconsistently. Whereas, some funds report annual and quarterly return series, which require the valuation of unrealized investments in the portfolio, others report returns of realized investments only. Despite the novelty of their insights these *PE Performance Studies* do not represent a means of assessing value creation in LBOs on an investment level from the post-buyout equity investor perspective.

For the purpose of analyzing value creation on investment level the post-buyout equity investor perspective is preferable. Compared to the fund investor perspective, the LBO investment equity investor perspective offers the advantage of not being diluted through fund fees and carried interest. *Fund IRRs* are weakened through carried interest not only of the fund but also of participating management. As already pointed out, a pre-buyout perspective can only analyze the fractional, anticipated amount of value creation shared with these investors at entry.

However, in light of this understanding, the post-buyout perspective might not necessarily reflect the total value creation of a LBO investment. Accordingly, such total value creation analysis ideally accounts for abnormal returns to pre-buyout shareholders earned at the time of entry. In public-to-private transactions pre-buyout shareholders are offered a premium on the undisturbed share price (see chapter I.A.2.1). With respect to other types of LBOs (see chapter II.A.3 for details) abnormal returns to pre-buyout shareholders are hardly quantifyable due to the non-availability of public market valuations. For the case of divisional buyouts, Hite and Vetsuypens (1989) analyzed the associated wealth effects to parent company shareholders. They find small but statistically significant wealth gains to pre-buyout shareholders suggesting that *"parent company stockholders share in the expected benefits of this change in ownership*

---

76 See Ljungqvist, A./Richardson, M. (2003a), Gottschalg, O., et al. (2004) and most recently Kaplan, S. N./Schoar, A. (2005) for exceptions.

77 Gompers, P. A./Lerner, J. (2000a), p. 250 argue that established PE organizations are usually more conservative in valuing investments during the holding period (and generally value at cost) compared to less established, inexperienced PE groups, which face tremendous pressure to raise follow-on-funds and thus might tend to overstate. For further details see also Gompers, P. A. (1996), pp. 133-156.

structure."[78] Accordingly, value creation analysis from the investor's point of view might underestimate the total value creation in LBO investments.

3. With Respect to the Notation of Value Creation

As a consequence of the various different perspectives, as well as vague and imprecise notational delimitations, the expression *value creation* has so far been used synonymously for various different phenomena in the context of LBOs. In most cases the notation has been used inappropriately regarding the common understanding of value creation in financial theory.[79] Value creation analysis in a strict sense requires the consideration of an alternative investment opportunity thereby accounting for the transaction-specific systematic risk.

Operational Performance Studies, with the – to my knowledge – only exception of Kaplan (1989a) and Muscarella/Vetsuypens (1990), have the common shortcoming that the link to value creation in LBOs is established by arguing that improved operational performance materializes and – ceteris paribus – leads to an increased entity and equity value when divesting the business. Baker/Wruck (1989), for instance, refer to value creation in the title as well as to the notation of value in the conclusion. However, the case study of the LBO of O.M. Scott & Sons Company fails to provide information on the equity valuation for the divestment of the business.

However, the studies by Kaplan (1989a) and Muscarella/Vetsuypens (1990) also reveal shortcomings regarding the performance analysis in LBOs from a post-buyout equity investor perspective, despite partially applying exit equity valuations: with respect to the equity return analyses, both studies seem to neglect any cash flows from or to the *PE* sponsors during the holding period and therefore face the shortcoming of not comprehensively capturing all interim equity streams.[80] Further, Muscarella/Vetsuypens (1990) define: "*Rates of return on equity are based on comparisons between the price per share paid at the LBO and the IPO offering price per share (adjusted for stock splits occurring under private ownership).*" and apply the notation of *shareholder wealth gains*.[81] Such calculation reflects the inherent problem regarding the comparability of the appropriate equity valuation at entry, i.e. the amount of equity contributed as a source of funds to finance the transaction and the comparable equity valuation at exit. Whereas the offering price per share at exit serves to determine the equity value of the portfolio company at exit, the price per share at entry is clearly a *use* of funds rather than an indication of the sponsor's equity contribution.

---

78 See Hite and Vetsuypens (1989), p. 953.

79 See chapter II.C for a detailed discussion of the notation value creation in LBOs.

80 See Kaplan, S. N. (1989a), pp. 235-240 and Muscarella, C. J./Vetsuypens, M. R. (1990), p.1410.

81 See Muscarella, C. J./Vetsuypens, M. R. (1990), p. 1410.

Kaplan (1989a), measures the nominal return to investors in post-buyout equity calculated as "*the market value of post-buyout common equity (and options) at the post-buyout valuation date divided by the total investment in post-buyout common equity (and options) at the going-private date.*"[82] Though this calculation more appropriately reflects the return on equity, common equity does not represent the cash in- and outflows to and from the LBO investment from the perspective of the LBO equity investor(s).[83] Alternatively, Kaplan (1989a) measures post-buyout return and market-adjusted return as the excess return to total capital consisting of the entirety of equity and debt financing. This return analysis does not require the differentiation between debt- and equity-financing instruments and hence small percentage estimation errors regarding the equity beta do not affect the calculation of expected returns to the same extent as when calculating equity returns.[84]

PE Performance Studies apply a variety of different IRRs – either reported by the *PE* funds or derived from reported, generally aggregated cash in- and outflows – as well as alternative performance measures as dependent variables. Again, given the aggregated rather than investment level perspective the link to a variety of company- and transaction- specific characteristics cannot be established. Only by linking such internal company- and transaction-specific aspects in combination with external capital market environment aspects to LBO performance and hence value creation facilitates an holistic analysis of determinants driving value creation in LBO investments.

To conclude, to the best of my knowledge no published study exists that comprehensively analyzes value creation in LBOs, both conceptually and empirically, from a post-buyout equity investor perspective on investment level, applying quantitative performance measures as the dependent and analyzed variables.[85]

C. Research Design to Assess Value Creation in LBOs

This thesis intends to overcome the aforementioned shortcomings with respect to value creation analysis in LBOs by discussing and empirically analyzing realized LBO investments on investment level from a post-buyout equity investor perspective. The research question this thesis addresses is: "*Which company and transaction-specific, as well as capital market related determinants and aspects drive to which extent performance and value creation in successful*

82 See Kaplan, S. N. (1989a), p. 238, Table 8, note c.

83 See chapter II.B for a detailed discussion of Total Proceeds and its components as the appropriate nominator to calculate returns for post-LBO equity investors.

84 See Kaplan, S. N. (1989a), p. 252.

85 For details regarding an appropriate value creation performance measure in the context of PE investing see chapter II.C.3 when specifying the objective function for this thesis.

LBO investments from the equity investor perspective?" With respect to the aforementioned classification of empirical research to value creation in LBOs, this thesis hence establishes the link between *Operational Performance Studies* and recently emerging literature on *PE Performance Studies* by considering the impact of company- and transaction-specific information as well as capital market related aspects on the performance of the investment. In doing so, this thesis is structured in three parts:

The *Introductory Part* comprises the introduction as well as chapter I dealing with preparatory considerations. Value creation in a strict sense from an equity investor perspective builds upon the time and risk adjusted analysis of *Total Proceeds* (*TP*) to the equity investor, relative to the corresponding capital invested. Hence any such ex-post analysis necessarily implies capturing all relevant cash flows associated with the investment: in the case of a LBO investment the equity contribution at entry, potential interim equity streams during the holding period and the residual equity value at exit. Equity investors in a LBO investment will be defined as any such investor having residual claims after all claims of third-party financial liability holders have been served. Consequently, chapter I comprises the clarification of the realized LBO investment as the research object (chapter II.A), the clarification of the post-buyout equity investor perspective (chapter II.B) and the definition of value creation in LBOs (chapter II.C).

The *Conceptual Part* comprises the theoretical analysis and the empirical study design. Chapter I starts with the discussion of the LBO transaction model. This model offers three distinctive advantages: first, by capturing and considering the entire LBO process, the model facilitates putting the equity value at exit and at entry into perspective, whereby equity values are calculated as the residual of the entity values less any (assumed, outstanding) third party net financial liabilities. Hence, given an entity and debt valuation at entry and at exit and accounting for interim equity streams, *Total Proceeds* to equity investors can be quantified. Second, *Total Proceeds* to equity investors can further be decomposed into five (non-mutually exclusive) components (i) *Earnings Variation*, (ii) *Multiple Variation*, (iii) a *Combined Earnings/Multiple Effect*, (iv) *Cumulated FCF Generation,* and (v) *Transaction Costs.* Third, a two-tier framework of an internal (*FCF effects*) as well as external (*variation in the transaction multiple*) perspective subsumes the above five components. This classification suitably structures both the subsequent discussion of various sources of value creation in LBO investments as well as the conducted empirical analysis that is based thereon. The internal *FCF effects* perspective considers next (i) the reduced agency costs hypotheses, (ii) the supporting impact of the financial sponsor referred to as *Management Support*, and also (iii) aspects of wealth transfer hypotheses. The discussion of sources of value creation with respect to the external perspective (*variation in the transaction multiple*) builds upon the risk-neutral valuation (*RNV*) framework. Subsequently, the impact of the capital market environment and potential information asymmetries in the divestment process are briefly discussed as two deviations from the stylized, RNV framework. Accordingly, chapter I starts with the consideration of the LBO transaction model (chapter III.A) and subsequently discusses in more detail aspects of value creation from an internal (chapter III.B) and an external perspective (chapter III.C).

Chapter IV starts with the specification of the research model. Given the outlined two-tier framework, the intention of the research model is first for a separate analysis of the internal and the external perspective and, based on this, the *holistic* analysis of value creation/performance measures for LBO investments. In a second step, hypotheses are derived regarding the impact of identified independent variables on the internal and external perspective and ultimately on the LBO performance (based upon previously detailed sources of value creation). Third, dependent variables are concretized.

The *Empirical Part* comprises the novel empirical analysis and the discussion of implications for value creation in LBOs. The empirical analysis in chapter V analyzes value creation in LBOs alongside the conceptual framework by applying a sample of 42 realized European LBO investments from the years 1993 to 2004 that have been exited via either an IPO or a secondary buyout. A newly created database comprising detailed deal-by-deal company- and transaction-specific information on investment level builds the basis. Based upon several hundred collected and derived pieces of information, this database enables the bottom-up, cash flow based performance analysis, linked to the impact of company- and transaction-specific information. First, descriptive statistics provide details regarding the characteristics of the analyzed sample. Second, novel insights result from the decomposition of *Total Proceeds* to equity investors according to the LBO transaction model and the subsequent analysis of sources of value creation in the context of the specified research model. Third, the detailed consideration of value creation/performance measures contributes quantitatively to the discussion of drivers of LBO performance and value creation in LBOs.

Chapter V concludes. Implications are discussed by (i) reviewing components of the LBO value creation process and their relative/absolute contribution to LBO performance and value creation, and (ii) summarizing the corresponding company-/transaction-specific and external/capital market environment related determinants.

Chart 2 Overview

Introductory Part	I. Introduction ▪ Status of Research ▪ Shortcomings and Research Gap ▪ Research Design	II. Preparatory Considerations ▪ Realized Investments ▪ Equity Investor Perspective ▪ Value Creation
Conceptual Part	III. Value Creation Analysis ▪ LBO Transaction Model ▪ Internal Perspective: FCF Effects ▪ External Perspective: Variation in the Transaction Multiple	IV. Study Outline ▪ Research Model ▪ Derivation of Hypotheses ▪ Operationalization of Variables
Empirical Part	V. Empirical Analysis ▪ Data Sample & Methodology ▪ Descriptive Statistics ▪ Total Proceeds & Components ▪ LBO Performance/Value Creation	VI. Implications ▪ Components of Value Creation ▪ Determinants of Value Creation ▪ Discussion & Outlook

II. Preparatory Considerations for Value Creation Analysis in LBOs on Investment Level

In response to the identified shortcomings the following chapters set the stage for the conceptual as well as empirical part by clarifying the research object (II.A), the perspective of the analysis (II.B) and the notation of value creation (II.C).

A. Research Object: Realized LBO Investments

This thesis takes the investment level perspective. Hence, the research object is the individual LBO investment and the corresponding direct cash flows from and to the various securityholders of the firm as illustrated in Chart 1, on page 23. Accordingly, the fund and investor level as defined in chapter I.B.2 are of minor relevance for the forthcoming conceptual and empirical analysis. Hence, to the extent possible, this thesis disregards the relationship between the LP and GP. Starting with a definition of LBOs for the purpose of this thesis (II.A.1) and relevant information on the LBO investment process (II.A.2), LBO entry (II.A.3) as well as exit modes (II.A.4) will be discussed briefly.

1. Defining Leveraged Buyouts

Despite the extensive amount of existing and further expanding academic literature and its omnipresence in corporate finance (in academia as well as in practice), no single, precise definition of the terminology LBO seems to exist.

Palepu's (1990) early definition of "*a transaction in which a group of private investors uses debt to purchase a corporation or a corporate division*"[86] shall serve as a starting point. For the purpose of this thesis, LBOs meet the following criteria: private investors consisting of a single (or a consortium of) private equity firm(s)[87], management of the target company and potentially third-party investors, acquire a controlling stake in a company or a subsidiary of a company.[88] Substantial debt financing against the target company's assets from "*banks and from buyers of subordinated public debt, which in the 1980s became known as junk bonds*"[89] constitutes probably the most well-known characteristic of LBOs. However, in this respect

---

86 See Palepu, K. G. (1990), p. 247. Further, in addition to a substantial increase in managerial ownership, significant changes in corporate governance, the lost access to public equity markets and a significant increase in the financial leverage are hereby argued to characterize LBOs.

87 See e.g. Berg, A. (2005), pp. 13-20 and Meier, D. (2005), pp. 23-27 for a detailed discussion of the terminology of private equity firm, its functions, dimensions for segmentation and structure. Henceforth, the terminologies private equity firm, buyout association and financial sponsor will be used synonymously.

88 The company that experiences a LBO is referred to as bought-out company, LBO firm/investment or – taking the perspective of the financial sponsor – as portfolio or target company.

89 See Shleifer, A./Vishny, R. (1997b), p. 766.

most definitions provide little clarity or precision regarding the notation of *'leveraged'*.[90] To use the words of Garfinkel (1989): "*The greatest ambiguity about what constitutes an LBO concerns the degree to which the purchase is financed with debt.*" Garfinkel (1989) mentions gearing ratios in the range of 80% to 90%; Easterwood et al. (1989) considers 85% as the appropriate threshold rate.[91] However, such high numbers need to be treated with great caution. The definition of *leveraged* implicitly requires a precise definition and delimitation of the various financing instruments available to fund the LBO. Chapter II.B discusses the various equity and debt financing instruments and illustrates how far an inappropriate delimitation of these two classes potentially results in overstating leverage and gearing ratios. For the purpose of this analysis, a transaction qualifies as *leveraged* when at least 50% of the total sources for the acquisition of the company are in the form of third-party financial liabilities. This 50% rate is in accordance with Sec (2001) stating that "[*i*]*f the transaction is 50 percent or more debt financed it is probably highly leveraged.*"[92]

A variety of types of LBOs exist with respect to the composition of the private investor group.[93] However, especially in practice, expressions such as LBO, institutional buyout (IBO), management buyout (MBO) or leveraged management buyout (LMBO) are often used – wrongly or not – interchangeably. A precise delimitation among these mentioned forms has been subject to extensive discussions in the academic literature but still remains contentious.[94] For instance according to Jakoby (2000) a restrictive characteristic of MBOs is that at least one manager remains with the LBO firm with the responsibility for the firm's day-to-day business.[95] Then Bergh (1998) considers a LBO as MBO when management owns an over-proportionate share of the company compared with industry standards.[96] Gräper (1993), argues that whereas management equity participation is a necessary condition for MBOs (but not for LBOs), significant third-party debt financing is a necessary condition for LBOs (but not for MBOs).[97] This thesis analyzes realized LBO investments: a finite, limited time perspective of the (equity) investors therefore represents, for the purpose of this thesis, a further constituting

---

90 See Garfinkel, M. R. (1989), p. 24 and Easterwood, J. C., et al. (1989), p. 30. For discussions of the terminology *leveraged* in the context of LBOs see also Then Bergh (1998) p. 8, Gräper, M. (1993), p. 4, Vest (1995), p. 14, Hoffmann, P./Ramke, R. (1992), p. 23, Berger (1993), p. 16, Schmid (1994) pp. 38-46.

91 See Garfinkel, M. R. (1989), p. 24.

92 See Sec (2001) and Mittendorfer, R. (2001), p. 141.

93 See e.g. Meier, D. (2005), p. 29 for a brief though comprehensive and Jakoby, S. (2000), pp. 11-49 for a detailed related discussion.

94 See e.g. Arbeitskreis finanzierung (1990), pp. 830-833, Hoffmann, P./Ramke, R. (1992) pp. 22-30 and Schmid, H. (1994), pp. 6-58.

95 See Jakoby, S. (2000), p. 19.

96 See Then Bergh, F. (1998), p. 11.

97 See Gräper, M. (1993), p. 8 (based on Ballwieser, W./Schmid, H. (1990)). For a discussion with a similar tenor see also Inderbitzin, M. (1993), p. 8ff.

characteristic of a LBO. This, in fact, necessarily requires the involvement of a (group of) financial investor(s), given their obligation according to the partnership agreement, to return committed funds to the LPs in the course of the fund's finite lifetime. This shall differentiate between a LBO and a pure MBO, which – assuming a majority managerial ownership stake – will presumably inevitably lack such a finite investment horizon. Therefore, while management itself does not hold the controlling stake in the business[98], its interests are generally aligned through ownership participation in the form of ordinary common stock, equity-like financing instruments and/or stock option schemes.[99]

With respect to the various financing stages of a firm, this thesis focuses on the later-stage financing of mature and established firms.[100] In this context, the notation of early stage and late stage financing can be applied to passably differentiate between Venture Capital (*VC*) and Private Equity (*PE*). These termini are still mostly used synonymously and ambivalently in both practice and academia.[101] This thesis focuses in the conceptual as well as the empirical analysis of comparably mature, established companies and hence on later-stage financing.

2. The LBO Investment Process

Given the nature of the LBO as an investment with a limited time horizon the LBO entry as such constitutes only one out of several sequential steps of the *PE* investment process.[102] Accordingly, the LBO process can be summarized to generally comprise six steps. (i) *Fund Raising* deals with the search and motivation of investors for the *PE* fund. Apart from high net worth individuals, potential LPs are primarily institutional investors such as pension funds and insurance companies.[103] In the (ii) *Deal Flow* phase the buyout firm screens potential investment opportunities of which those likely to generate the target rate of return are evaluated in the (iii) *Due Diligence and Valuation* phase.[104] The main purpose of this phase is

---

98 See e.g. Wallner, N. (1980), p. 20 stating that "[*t*]*he management never gets more than 50 percent of the equity unless the secured lenders are the only other participants in the deal*".

99 See e.g. Otto, H. J. (1990), 868-869, Berger, M. (1993), p. 217 and Thum, O. (2004), pp. 226f. According to Colman, R. D. (1981), pp. 532ff managerial incentivation in the course of LBOs does not necessarily imply cash equity investments by the management but necessarily involves significant contingent-compensation arrangements.

100 See e.g. Sahlman, W. A. (1990), p. 479 for an understanding of the various financing stages.

101 See e.g. Sahlman, W. A. (1990), pp. 473ff, Murray, G. C. (1999), pp. 351ff and Groh, A. P. (2004), pp. 16ff.

102 For a detailed discussion of the LBO process see e.g. Tyebjee, T. T./Bruno, A. V. (1984), pp. 1052-1054; Gorman, M. J./Sahlman, W. A. (1989), pp. 231-248; Bader, H. (1996), pp. 110-150; Wright, M./Robbie, K. (1998), pp. 535-553, Kraft, V. (2001a), pp. 128-147 and von Daniels, H. (2004), pp. 33-53.

103 For details, see e.g. Fried, V. H./Hisrich, R. D. (1992), pp. 29f, Schröder, C. (1992), pp. 122ff, Bader, H. (1996), pp. 110ff, Lerner, J. (2001), pp. 1-6 and Hagenmüller, M. (2004), pp. 1ff.

104 For details regarding the *Deal Flow* phase see e.g. Bygrave, W. D./Timmons, J. A. (1992), pp. 13f, Murray, G. C. (1995), pp. 1077-1106 and Wright, M./Robbie, K. (1998), p. 536. Meier, D. (2005), p. 20 notes that research in this field is still relatively limited despite the importance of deal flow generation in practice. For related details regarding the *Due Diligence and Valuation* (or Screening) phase see e.g. Korsukéwitz, K.

the elimination or at least diminution of information asymmetries between the current owner and the potential investor.[105] Types of due diligence include financial, tax, management, legal, environmental and insurance, technical, organizational and market due diligence.[106] The due diligence phase generally comprises a management presentation, management and expert discussions as well as site visits. Depending on the size of the transaction and the potential equity commitment, private equity firms generally engage various specialized external advisors to speed up and detail the due diligence process. The (iv) *Deal Structuring* phase comprises negotiations and investment details with the parties involved (primarily financing banks and equity investor consortia including co-investing funds and management) and ends with the investment, referred to henceforth as the *Entry* of the transaction. Apart from the financing structure, further critical aspects of this phase are the agreement regarding management incentive schemes, the fixation of control rights and related mechanisms for the private equity firm and the consideration of potential exit modes, i.e. divestment scenarios.[107] The (v) *Monitoring* phase constitutes the holding period of the investment starting with the entry of the transaction. In this phase the operational performance of the firm is intended to be improved through the reduction of agency conflicts and resulting agency costs or the active involvement of the financial investor in the target company's operations (what this thesis refers to as *Management Support*). Operational performance improvement and deleveraging are obviously the primary objectives at this stage. The final sixth phase, the (vi) *Exit*, also referred to as the divestment of the portfolio company, terminates the holding period from the equity investor perspective.[108] At times the return of capital to fund investors is considered as a seventh phase.

Evidently, not only does value creation on investment level occur during the holding period of the investment but it is also significantly affected from an equity investor perspective by the entry and exit phase. Hence, any such ex-post analysis inevitably requires the holistic consideration of the deal structuring and entry as well as monitoring phases, combined with the exit phase of the *PE* investment process.

(1976), pp. 39-155, Wright, M./Robbie, K. (1999), Brettel, M. (2002), pp. 305-325 and Cullinan, G., et al. (2004), pp.96-104.

105 See e.g. Thum, O. (2004), p. 220 and Richter, F. (2005), pp. 199ff.

106 See Marten, K.-U./Köhler, A. G. (1999), pp. 337-348 for a discussion of the various types of due diligence as well as their relative importance in M&A processes in the German context.

107 For a brief comparison of the different exit modes see chapter II.A.4. For further details regarding the investment phase see also Fried, V. H./Hisrich, R. D. (1988), p. 24, Trester, J. J. (1998), pp. 675-699, Kaplan, S. N./Stromberg, P. (2003), pp. 281-315, Brettel, M., et al. (2004), pp. 431-447.

108 For research regarding the divestment phase see footnote [72] as well as details in forthcoming chapter II.A.4.

Recapitalization

Restructuring or renegotiating the terms and conditions of the LBO investment's debt financing is referred to as *recapitalization* or *refinancing* and thus has to be differentiated from both the entry and the exit of a LBO. Reasons for a recapitalization can be numerous. The opportunity to lock in lower interest rates in a more favorable financing environment during the holding period potentially offsets transaction costs associated with the refinancing. A positive track record of the LBO investment presumably justifies higher leverage ratios. Also, in case of steady gearing ratios, such a track record triggers higher leverage, i.e. higher absolute amounts of debt, given an increase in the relevant cash flow measure for financing purposes, in practice generally EBITDA or EBITDA less capital expenditures for the trailing twelve months. Aspects indicating a positive track record are the ability to (i) handle and serve the heavy debt burden, (ii) improve the firm's operating performance, as well as (iii) meet or potentially outperform the business plan. Recapitalizations might allow the equity investors to recoup part of their investment in the form of an interim dividend payment, which – owing to restrictive debt covenants – wouldn't have been feasible without renegotiating the financing in place.

However, refinancing does generally not affect the ownership structure of the investment and hence is not considered as a mode of exit for the purpose of this thesis. Further, due to the unaffected ownership structure of the LBO, recapitalization does not imply the market valuation of the company's equity. Therefore recapitalization is not suitable for analyzing value creation in LBOs, which requires two equity market prices at different points in time based on the understanding of this thesis.

3. Modes of Entry for LBO Investments

As pointed out when defining LBOs, a variety of classifications exist with respect to types of LBOs. For the purpose of this thesis, such classification is made alongside the entry mode of the transaction, i.e. the principal seller of the bought-out company.[109] A first step differentiates mutual exclusively between (i) the involvement of public selling shareholders, i.e. the going private of a previously public company – referred to as *public-to-private* or *going private* (chapter II.A.3.1) and (ii) the existence of one or several private selling shareholders – also referred to as *private-to-private* (chapter II.A.3.2). Forthcoming analyses will hence not be

[109] For a general discussion of types of LBOs classified by seller see among others Wright, M., et al. (1987) pp. 14-30, Schwenkedel, S. (1991), pp. 13-17, Kropp, M. (1992), pp. 20-26 and Jakoby, S. (2000) pp. 35-49. Given the emphasis on the seller's motives, such classification frequently includes privatization and receivership LBOs/MBOs, which shall not be discussed separately here and can partially be subsumed under the presented structure.

limited to the well-known, probably most popular and in academic literature most frequently discussed entry mode of *going private*.

3.1 Public-to-Private Entry (Going Private)

Deangelo et al. (1984) define going private[110] as a means to "*restructure[s] corporate ownership by replacing the entire public stock ownership by an incumbent management group*", which frequently "*share[s] subsequent equity ownership with outside private investors who help finance the acquisition of publicly held stock.*"[111] Other than Deangelo et al. (1984), Richard/Weinheimer (2002) also consider the buyout of a division of a publicly listed corporation as *going private.*[112] In this respect this thesis follows Deangelo et al. (1984) and classifies any such LBO – being defined as in chapter II.A.1 – as *public-to-private* transaction when the entire bought-out corporation was previously publicly listed as an independent corporation.[113]

Hence, a constituting characteristic of *public-to-private* transactions is the fact that – other than in *private-to-private* transactions – the potential acquirer negotiates the potential buyout as such and the associated terms and conditions not with the owner of the corporation – the shareholders – but their delegates – the board of management.[114] Since management, however, belongs to the potential group of LBO equity investors through own equity contributions and/or equity incentive schemes, *public-to-private* transactions are characterized by an inherent conflict of interest. On the one hand, the fiduciary duty obliges management to act in the best interest of the shareholders, i.e. to maximize shareholder wealth. On the other hand, being a

---

110 *Going Private* is to be differentiated from *delisting*. While delisting refers to the withdrawal from one stock exchange, going private implies the delisting from all public notations and thus a restructuring of the ownership structure.

111 See Deangelo, H., et al. (1984), p. 367. A detailed discussion of the notation *going private* by Inderbitzin, M. (1993), pp. 4ff (and including delimitations to related terminologies) puts emphasis on the insider status of the acquirer – be it solely the incumbent management or management including associated, supportive private investors. For details regarding *Going Private* see also Borden, A. M. (1974), Deangelo, H./Deangelo, L. E. (1987), Lehn, K./Poulsen, A. (1989), Marais, L., et al. (1989), Kim, W. S./Lyn, E. O. (1991), Deangelo, H., et al. (1994) and most recently Achleitner, A.-K., et al. (2003). For empirical studies on going private see also Table 3 on page 12 and footnote [51].

112 Seemingly Muscarella, C. J./Vetsuypens, M. R. (1990), p. 1390 also consider buyouts of divisions of public corporations (what this thesis subsumes under *divisional buyout* according to chapter II.A.3.2) as *going privates*.

113 For a discussion of advantages and disadvantages of going private see Kulinski, J./Schiereck, D. (2003), pp. 181ff.

114 Special situations are so-called hostile or unfriendly takeovers, whereby the acquirer acts against management's will. However, financial sponsor led hostile takeovers are extremely rare in practice.

potential acquirer encourages management to exploit potential information asymmetries and act in their own best interest.[115]

Conflicts of interest most obviously arise in the negotiation phase but already the preparatory phase, prior to the buyout, is potentially characterized by divergences between management and shareholder interests. Public companies are hardly ever actively put up for sale, given the threat of adverse effects of a potentially failed sale process. Therefore, *public-to-private* transactions are generally in the form of exclusive one-on-one negotiations rather than structured auction processes and thus face the challenge of the highest levels of confidentiality and the threat of information leakage prior to the publication of the tender offer to public shareholders. In practice, this problem is addressed by – among other means – (i) the signing of a *confidentiality agreement* prior to any information exchange, and (ii) a *staged due diligence process*. Nonetheless, the potential acquirer requires in the course of the due diligence phase access to detailed insider information such as the company's strategy, competitive positioning and financial projections. Decisions regarding the extent of information exchange as well as whether to pursue or not at various stages remain the responsibility of the board of management.

Following the concretization of an imminent *going private* transaction, conflicts of interest are probably most severe during price negotiations. While on the one hand management ideally strives to maximize proceeds for shareholders in the form of the equity purchase price according to its fiduciary duty, simultaneously occurring negotiations regarding management equity contributions, incentive schemes and performance targets are often apparently counter effective. Transactions with these kinds of conflicts of interests are referred to as *non-arm's-length transactions*.[116]

3.2 Private-to-Private Entry

Given their non-public status, *private-to-private* transactions are generally characterized by a majority selling shareholder. *Private-to-private* transactions can further be separated alongside the selling shareholder being (i) a parent company, also referred to as divisional buyout or spin-off, (ii) a family, also known as succession buyout, and (iii) a financial sponsor, also referred to as secondary buyout. Being appropriate for the context of this thesis, such classification intends to be mutually exclusive though it does not claim to be collectively

115 For details regarding conflicts of interest and their management in public-to-private transactions see also Richter, F. (2005), pp. 227ff.

116 See e.g. Deangelo, H., et al. (1994), pp. 602-610. By contrast, transactions without any relationship between the target company and the acquirer are referred to as *'arm's-length acquisitions'* or synonymously *third party acquisitions*. See Inderbitzin, M. (1993), p. 13.

exhaustive. LBOs in the course of privatizations, for instance, involve the government as principal selling shareholder.

Divisional Buyout

According to Hite/Vetsuypens (1989) a divisional buyout is defined "*as the sale of a division, subsidiary, or other operating unit of a parent firm to members of the management of either the parent or the subunit being divested.* [..] *Equity ownership in the new firm is often shared with a buyout specialist who contributes equity capital and arranges debt financing*"[117]. Frequently, academics refer to one and the same phenomena as *spin-offs*.[118] From a seller's perspective, divisional buyouts are generally considered as non-core disposal businesses since a primary reason for the divestiture is argued to be the selling company's focus on its core competences.[119] In other words the motivation behind divisional buyouts is the belief that the value of the separated, standalone businesses exceeds the firm value prior to the spin-off.[120] In this context Hite/Vetsuypens (1989) argue that divisional buyouts "*1) represent an efficient reallocation of corporate resources to higher valued uses and 2) allow parent company stockholders to share in the expected benefits from this ownership change.*"[121]

Succession Buyout

A previously family-owned company might experience a LBO as one option to solve managerial and ownership succession problems. If no family-intern solution can be found (i) ownership can either remain with the initial family while the business is outsider-controlled, (ii) the family could transfer its shares into a foundation, or (iii) the business could be sold to a third party.[122] In the latter case, a LBO offers the opportunity for the company to remain broadly independent without being integrated into the organization of a specialized strategic buyer or a conglomerate. Potential further motives for a succession buyout might be the

---

117 See Hite, G. L./Vetsuypens, M. R. (1989), p. 954.

118 See e.g. Jakoby, S. (2000), pp. 35ff. For a detailed discussion of the terminology spin-off see e.g. Berger, M. (1993), pp. 10-13 and Hoffmann, P./Ramke, R. (1992) pp. 26-28. Ballwieser, W./Schmid, H. (1990) p. 300 argue that other than in the case of a buyout, a spin-off necessarily implies the foundation of a new company where the acquired assets are transferred to.

119 See e.g.Hite, G. L./Vetsuypens, M. R. (1989), pp. 953-970, Prahalad, C./Hamel, G. (1990), pp. 71-91 and Karsunky, R. (1992), p. 41. For a focus on core competences through (LBO) restructuring initiatives see also Achleitner, A.-K./Wahl, S. (2003).

120 *Note:* In analogy to the 1+1=3 philosophy in the case of synergies, Hershman, A. (1969) characterized the corresponding spin-off philosophy as 1-1=3. One and the same effect with significant attention in the academic literature is referred to as *conglomerate discount*. For the theoretical foundation see e.g. Aron, D. (1988), Stulz, R. M. (1990) and Rotemberg, J./Saloner, G. (1994), for recent empirical evidence supporting the conglomerate discount theory see e.g. Rajan, R., et al. (2000) and Burch, T. R./Nanda, V. (2003).

121 See Hite, G. L./Vetsuypens, M. R. (1989), p. 969.

122 See e.g. Huydts, H. J. M. A. (1992), p. 14, Spielmann, U. (1994), p.39 and Jakoby, S. (2000), p. 37. For detailed discussion of succession buyouts see in particular Huydts, H. J. M. A. (1992) and Bieler, S. (1996).

opportunity for the family (i) to retain a fraction of its shareholding by divesting only partially, (ii) to realize proceeds from the sale while continuing to be operationally involved in the business, as well as (iii) having access to equity capital for growth and acquisition initiatives under the umbrella of a (group of) financial investor(s).

Secondary Buyout

A transaction between two financial investors, i.e. the divestiture of the business from one financial investor to another is referred to as *secondary buyout.*[123] At first glance the rational and corresponding benefits of a secondary buyout seem questionable: why should a financial investor be in a better position to create value compared to its counterpart? First, it can be argued that *PE* funds increasingly develop some sort of strategic element such as in the form of detailed industry know-how, access to relevant management and industry specialists as well as synergy and spill-over effects from the fund's portfolio.[124] Second, timing aspects potentially favor a secondary buyout. Not only does the fund structure with a limited time horizon require the divestiture of the business at some point in time, but also a favorable financing environment with low financing rates and comparably high leverage ratios might benefit a secondary buyout transaction. Skeptics of secondary buyouts might claim that an asset, which has previously been owned by a financial sponsor has already realized '*low hanging fruits*' in the form of easy to implement and realize operational performance improvements. Accordingly, the potential for further improvements was expected to be limited. On the other hand however, successfully performing, previously financial sponsor owned companies, presumably demonstrated their ability (i) to cope with the heavy debt burden of an LBO, and (ii) to create value through deleveraging. Following this line of reasoning secondary buyouts might be assumed to be less risky as the uncertainty of the investment and hence the variance of returns should be reduced.

Secondary buyouts have to be differentiated from *secondaries*, the generally applied notation describing the additional offering of existing shares by current shareholders; in the context of LBOs the further sell-down of pre-IPO equity investors shares following the expiration of the lock-up period.

4. Modes of Exit for LBO Investments

As previously pointed out the finite time horizon is a key characteristic of *PE* investing and the corresponding exit a prerequisite for any ex-post LBO value creation assessment. Therefore,

---

123 *Note:* The notation *secondary buyout* is, particularly among practitioners, the generally applied expression for the described phenomenon. Alternatively, the expression *secondary purchase* (see Brück, M. (1998), p.41), though used synonymously here, emphasizes the entry mode, i.e. the acquirer perspective.

124 See chapter III.B.2 for related details.

and given some peculiarities in the forthcoming analyses, a brief discussion of the relevant exit modes is beneficial.

Academic literature frequently mentions five modes of exit: IPO, trade sale, secondary buyout, entire sale to the existing management and liquidation of the asset.[125] Quantifications regarding the relative importance of these five exit modes are generally based on data provided in EVCA yearbooks.[126] However, these statistics are of little relevance for the purpose and focus of this thesis and would be rather misleading in two respects: first, data comprise not only *later stage* buyout investments but also *seed*, *start-up* as well as *expansion* investments (which account for more than 80% in terms of number of exits). Second, the exit classification includes *refinancings* and *write-offs*.

Analogous to the discussion of the modes of entry, the following overview is structured alongside the status of the acquirer(s) into (i) *private-to-public* (chapter II.A.4.1) and (ii) *private-to-private* (chapter II.A.4.2) transactions.[127] Alternatively, the two *'traditional'* exit routes, the IPO and trade sale exit, could be viewed simplistically as *selling to the equity market*. Assuming that the acquiring company is publicly listed, a trade sale represents an indirect divestiture to the equity market as the marginal currency of the acquirer is its equity. Secondary buyouts on the other hand can be regarded as *selling to the credit market* since the marginal currency of financial investors is debt.

4.1 Private-to-Public Exit (Going Public)

In a *private-to-public* transaction the company and/or the equity investors dispose(s) of the firm's shares to the public market.[128] A potential reason for (the return to) public ownership might be that benefits of private ownership under the LBO governance structure have been fully appropriated and hence resources are deployed elsewhere more efficiently.[129] An IPO is characterized among others by a *primary and secondary share component*. Proceeds from selling existing shares (secondary component) flow to the owners of the shares, i.e. the equity investors of the investment. Proceeds from selling new shares (primary component) flow

---

125 See e.g. Kessel, B. (1991), pp. 60f, Bader, H. (1996), pp. 137ff, Then Bergh, F. (1998), p. 79 and Ivanova, A./Tzvetkova, R. (2001), pp. 165f. Given their irrelevance in the context of this thesis the latter two exit modes shall not be considered further.

126 See e.g. Brück, M. (1998), pp. 48-60 and von Daniels, H. (2004), pp. 44-54.

127 See e.g. Morris, P. (2005), pp. 3ff.

128 The analysis here shall be limited to the LBO equity investor perspective. For a discussion of the related (clearly perspective-depending) trade-off between public and private ownership in general see e.g. Gleisberg, R. (2003), Färber, H. (2005), Koehnemann, M. (2005). For a discussion of the IPO process see e.g. Ritter, J. (1999).

129 See Deangelo, H./Deangelo, L. E. (1987), p. 43. Further, empirical findings confirm that key benefits of the LBO governance structure such as high levels of managerial ownership and financial liabilities (see chapter III.B.1.2) remain following the IPO (see e.g. Holthausen, R. W./Larcker, D. F. (1996)).

directly to the issuing company and are generally used in parts or entirely to repay financial indebtedness. The issuance of new shares obviously dilutes the stake of the initial owners in the company. However, in the case that primary proceeds are used to repay outstanding quasi-equity financing instruments as defined in chapter II.B.2.2, LBO equityholders would benefit from the primary component.

Corporations that experienced a LBO in the form of a *going private* and subsequently go public again after the private holding period, i.e. a *public-to-private-to-public*, are also referred to as *reverse LBOs*.[130]

The listing of the LBO company's shares in a going public exit is accompanied by a variety of signaling effects:

- First, an exit via the public market as such receives substantial attention and is generally perceived positively, as the investment is considered a non-squeezed asset that is given public status. In this context a positive perception of financial sponsors might be considering these investors as intermediaries, facilitating the access of previously privately owned businesses to the capital market. Conversely however, if the company is to realize a substantially higher (relative) valuation in the exit than in the acquisition process, the approach and the business model of financial sponsors might be challenged and their reputation might suffer. In particular when the investment holding period is very short and the relative valuation differential between entry and exit accounts for the lion's share of *Total Proceeds* to equity investors, financial sponsors might be considered as arbitrageurs with no, or little, operating involvement in the company. To mention two prominent examples for what could be perceived as arbitrage between private and public markets as well as between regional markets: (i) equity investors in the *Charles Voegele* succession LBO in 1997 substantially benefited from the relative valuation differential between the private and public market and realized a multiple expansion of more than 100% (in terms of *P/EBITDA* multiple) in less than 20 months. Just recently equity investors in German chemical group *Celanese* arbitraged between the German and US public market and realized an approximate 2x EBITDA multiple expansion between the going private in Europe and the subsequent floatation in the US after a mere 12 months holding period. For the remainder of this thesis, investments that are characterized by high levels of multiple expansion in combination with a short holding period will be referred to as *quick-flips*.
- Second, the size of the secondary component signals the degree of ongoing commitment of the financial sponsor.[131] A substantial remaining stake in the company through a moderate

130 See e.g. Muscarella, C. J./Vetsuypens, M. R. (1990), p. 1390.

secondary component implies that the sponsor is not *cashing out* immediately and is thus generally perceived positively. Conversely however, an over proportionately high percentage of primary proceeds used to repay equity-like financing instruments is negatively regarded by the market, as it implies a cashing-out of the sponsor at the cost of the firm's growth opportunities as well as third-party financial liabilities level.

- Third, incumbent management normally remains in charge of the company in the course of the IPO, which too indicates their commitment to the firm. This, in combination with the continuing independency of the company (in particular when compared with the divestiture to a strategic acquirer) makes IPOs the generally preferred exit mode by management.

Potential negative signaling effects as well as market restrictions usually prohibit LBO equity investors from divesting the entirety of their existing shares. Thus, the IPO as such only represents a partial exit for the financial sponsor and the value of the entire investment has at first only partially been monetized. However, the IPO provides a liquid market for the shares of the portfolio company with the public market platform, offering the opportunity to liquidize the remaining, so far unrealized, though quoted, equity stake in the form of one or several further secondary placements. Given such partial exit the value of the remaining stake of the initial equity investors obviously remains exposed to market fluctuations. For the purpose of analyzing value creation in LBOs by applying two equity market valuations at two different points in time, the remainder of this thesis considers as default the IPO as the entire divestment for the pre-IPO equity investors and applies the IPO equity valuation as a basis for inferring on the equity value to these investors. To highlight the impact of the holding period, the empirical analysis in chapter V.E.2 provides insights regarding the sensitivity of equity investor returns.

A well-known pattern of equity issuances is the frequent incidence of underpricing, the so-called *IPO discount*, resulting fro m discrepancies between the offering price and the closing market price and thus abnormal initial returns to new equity investors.[132]

4.2 Private-to-Private Exit

Other than in the IPO exit, a *private-to-private* exit generally implies the immediate and entire divestiture of the company to a third party. In this sense a *private-to-private* sale is the cleaner exit in that LBO equity investors receive cash for their entire stake in the company.[133]

---

131 Details will be discussed in chapter III.C.2.2 when considering information asymmetries in the divestment phase as a potential source of value.

132 This aspect will be addressed further when considering potential information asymmetries in the divestment phase in chapter IV.B.2.3. For one of the first studies see Ibbotson, R. G./Jaffe, J. F. (1975). For a summary overview of related confirming studies and a brief discussion of potential reasons see also Ritter, J. (1999).

133 *Note:* The exception proves the role, though. In particular in secondary buyout private-to-private exits, the selling financial sponsor might remain interested with a minority co-ownership stake, potentially structured in the form of vendor loans (see chapter II.B.2.2 for details regarding this quasi-equity financing instrument).

With such a clear-cut exit the financial sponsor sacrifices future upside as well as downside potential, which it accommodates as pointed out in the case of the IPO exit.

While a *private-to-private* exit is – compared to an IPO – generally characterized by fewer information asymmetries it is potentially affected by peculiarities of an auction process. In the case of a structured divestment process, interested and invited parties receive a so-called *information memorandum*, comprising general company and industry information, detailed financial projections and further confidential data regarding the firm's future strategy. Additionally, a subsequent, detailed due diligence phase further aims to reduce latent information asymmetries between the seller and the acquirer. However, potential acquirers might face the so-called *winner's curse* effect, arising from the auction process, some details of which will be described in chapter III.C.2.2 when elucidating the impact of the divestment process.

Secondary Buyout

Similar to the mode of entry (see chapter II.A.3.2), the disposal of a portfolio company to a (group of) financial sponsor(s) represents a potential mode of exit for a LBO investment.[134] Particularly for smaller LBOs, contracts frequently include pre-emption rights for the existing management.[135] However, such divestiture of the portfolio company to the existing management will not be subsumed under secondary buyout here. In accordance with the previous definition of LBOs, a constituting characteristic shall be the involvement of a (group of) financial sponsor(s) with a controlling ownership stake. From the management point of view, a secondary buyout represents the opportunity to stay on with the company and preserve (at least partially) its independency, when the IPO is not an option.[136] Low financing rates, an abundance of *PE* money in the market[137] as well as obvious comparative disadvantages of alternative exit routs, are factors favoring secondary buyout exits.

Trade Sale

The divestiture of the LBO asset to a strategic investor is referred to as *trade sale*. The attractiveness of a trade sale is obviously determined by the strategic value of the company. A premium might be justified when the acquiring company is to realize and benefit from synergies and positive spill-over effects, market share gains or, primarily, market access. From

---

134 See also the relevant paragraph in chapter II.A.3.2 for few related details. Analogously to the entry mode, *secondary sale* (see e.g. Bader, H. (1996), p. 148) concretizes the notation of *secondary buyout* by emphasizing the exit, i.e. vendor perspective.

135 See e.g. Schmidtke, A. (1985), pp. 199f.

136 See von Daniels, H. (2004), p. 51.

137 See e.g. Kaplan, S. N./Stein, J. (1993), Gompers, P. A./Lerner, J. (2000b) and Kaplan, S. N./Schoar, A. (2005).

the acquirer's perspective value will be created as long as the NPV of all future synergies resulting from the acquisition exceed the premia paid on the stand-alone value of the business.[138] Luippold (1992) argues that operating and financial problems of the bought-out company increase the attractiveness for strategic investors. Given their detailed operating and strategic understanding, strategic investors are competent to implement required changes in the company's day-to-day operations.[139] Trade sales might, however, be opposed by management since the acquisition through a strategic investor generally implies the loss of independency and discretionary operational leeway.

B. Perspective: Equity Investors in LBOs

This thesis analyses value creation in LBOs on investment level from the equity investor point of view.[140] The equity investor perspective therefore comprises the private equity fund investor, investing management and potential third-party co-equity investors. To be borne in mind, any value creation and performance analysis will therefore be *before* the consideration of the equity ownership structure and corresponding changes therein during the holding period of the investment.

As pointed out in chapter I.C, value creation analysis based on cash in- and outflows to equity investors requires a consistent and comparable specification of the equity valuation of the company at entry vs. exit based on a clear-cut separation between equity and debt investors. An equity investor is considered any such investor in an LBO investment whose contingent claim remains as the residual when all claims of third-party debt investors have been served. This implies that any sort of funds provided and '*sponsored*' by either one of these equity investors will be considered as equity for the purpose of this thesis. In order to further specify this understanding, the remainder of this chapter first illustrates the concept of sources and uses in LBOs (chapter II.B.1). Thereafter the variety of forms of equity (chapter II.B.3) and debt (chapter II.B.3) financing instruments will be briefly presented.

1. The Concept of Sources and Uses in LBOs

Given the general non-strategic interest of financial sponsors, a newly founded acquisition vehicle, generally called *NewCo*, is set up for the purpose of acquiring the target company.

Based on the balance sheet concept with balancing amounts of assets and liabilities the financing of a LBO investment can be described through *sources of funds* (=liabilities) and *uses of funds* (=assets). *Sources of funds* are the sum of any form of equity, quasi-equity and

---

138 See e.g. Jansen, S. A., et al. (2001), p. 168.

139 See Luippold, T. L. (1992), p. 72.

140 See Chart 1, p. 23.

debt financing instruments applied for funding the acquisition representing the capitalization of *NewCo*. *Uses of funds* describe the application of the provided equity and debt financing sources. Funds available for the financing of the transaction are used to (i) pay the equity purchase price, (ii) settle any pre-buyout financial liabilities and (iii) assume the transaction costs of the acquisition. Existing pre-buyout financial liabilities in some instances might be rolled-over and hence represent not only a source but also a use of funds in which case total sources and uses can either be stated as gross or net values. Transaction costs associated with the LBO investment occur in the form of e.g. investment banking and other advisor fees, legal costs and financing fees.

Depending on the complexity of the individual transaction, a variety of forms of sources as well as uses of funds might exit; all of which however can be classified for the purpose of this thesis into either debt or equity financing instruments according to the '*sponsor*' of the funds. The *Total Sources* (*TS* or total consideration) of a LBO transaction equal the funding of *NewCo* and consequently the sum of all equity (*E*) and debt (*D*) financing instruments.[141]

(2) $TS_t = E_t + D_t$

Total Sources less excess cash in the business (*Liq*) will be referred to as the *net consideration*. The *enterprise* or *entity value* V_t of the business at entry results as the net consideration less *transaction costs* (*TS*) for the acquisition.

(3) $V_t = TS_t - Liq_t - TC_t$

For valuation purposes, market rather than book values of the financing instruments are of relevance. According to the concept of sources and uses, the market values shall equal the book values of the financing instruments at the time of entry. Hence the entity value calculation at entry can correctly be based on the total consideration. For the purpose of this thesis unfunded and underfunded pension obligations are neither considered as a source nor as a use in the LBO financing structures. Accordingly the derived entity values (*V*) are stated net of pension obligations.

Substituting TS_t in (3) with (2), the respective *equity value* E_t, i.e. the total equity contribution by the entirety of the equity investors, can be expressed as

(4) $E_t = V_t - D_t + Liq_t + TC_t$

$E_t = V_t - ND_t + TC_t$

141 Alternatively P_t could obviously be calculated based on the uses of funds.

Hereby *ND* stands for net financial liabilities (net debt). Although, any transaction costs (*TC*) are financed from the total sources of the acquisition, i.e. including any debt financing instruments, they are entirely assumed by the equity investors only. Any cash outflow associated with *TC* directly affects the equity value as the residual of the entity value of the investment less any third-party financial liabilities.

The presented concept of *sources* and *uses* of funds further highlights the importance and necessity of a clear-cut, consistent differentiation between debt and equity financing instruments for the analysis of value creation in LBO investments from an equity investor perspective.

The five criteria claim, reward, legal ordination, liability and maturity (=availability) are frequently applied to ideally differentiate pure equity and pure debt capital.[142] Accordingly, pure equity capital, other than pure debt capital, is characterized by a residual, quota share claim, success-dependent rewards, full ownership rights (information-, control- and voting rights) as well as unlimited liability and availability. Owing to the difficulties of a clear-cut separation alongside these criteria, *Mezzanine* in a broad sense is introduced as a third type of financing to subsume any form of hybrid financing instruments that cannot be clearly assigned to either category.[143] Discussions in the academic literature alongside these three *types of financing* are numerous, however not entirely appropriate for the purpose of this thesis as a clear-cut separation between funds provided by equityholders and funds provided by debtholders is required. In this context Chart 3 below classifies four categories of financing instruments, which will be briefly discussed hereafter.[144]

---

142 See e.g. Süchting, J. (1995), p. 28, Schmidt, R. H./Terberger, E. (1997) p. 20, Hinz, H./Dörscher, M. (2003), p. 3, Weinberger, N. (2005), chapter III.

143 See e.g. Suni, J. (2002), p. 8, Broda, B. M. (2003), p. 977, Hinz, H./Dörscher, M. (2003), p. 3, Müller, O. (2003), p.13, Rudolph, B. (2004), p.12 and Weinberger, N. (2005), chapter III. *Mezzanine in a strict sense* by contrast is in European LBOs the commonly applied notation for privately placed subordinated debt with a performance depending compensation component.

144 For a detailed and comprehensive discussion of the outlined classification as well as the corresponding financing instruments see Müller, O. (2003) and Weinberger, N. (2005).

Chart 3 Overview of Types of Financing[145] and the Corresponding Instruments

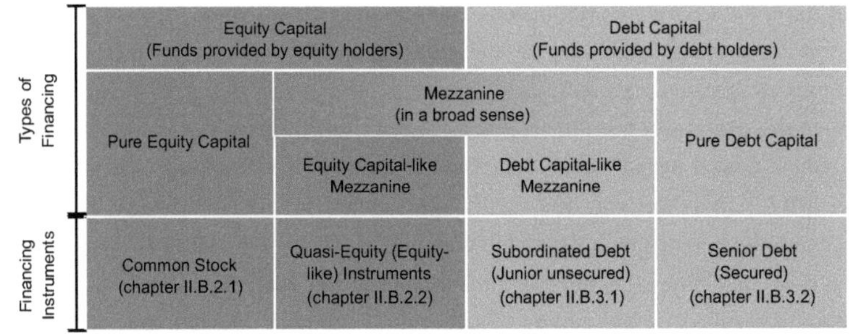

Source: Based on Weinberger (2005), chapter III

2. Equity Financing Instruments

The discussion of shortcomings and research gaps in chapter I.B highlighted a somewhat inappropriate classification of equity and debt financing instruments in some previous studies. Since value creation analysis from an equity investor perspective builds on putting *Total Proceeds* relative to the *Capital Invested* into perspective, any funds provided by the investors in the form of common stock (chapter II.B.2.1) as well as in the form of quasi-equity financing instruments (chapter II.B.2.2) will be considered as equity financing instruments. Consequently, the remainder of this thesis refers to *equity* as the entirety of all equity financing instruments and to *equity investor* as the respective provider/sponsor of these funds.

2.1 Common Stock

In accordance with the differentiating criteria between debt and equity mentioned above, common stock as equity in its purest form is a "*security representing ownership of a corporation*",[146] however, "*without priority for dividends or in bankruptcy*".[147] In this context and for the benefit of further discussions, equity may be seen as a contingent claim. Equityholders have a call option on the firm's assets, where the strike price is given by the debtholders' nominal claim (plus accrued interest). They will claim the residual of the firm's value and thus have unlimited upside potential.[148]

Financiers of equity in the form of common stock can be the *PE* fund investor, investing management and potential third-party co-equity investors. In particular in large-scale LBOs

145 *Note:* For the purpose of the LBO acquisition financing, the classification refers to external financing only; internal financing options from the firm's FCF generation are not considered here. For details regarding internal financing options see e.g. Drukarczyk, J. (1999), pp. 9ff.

146 See Brealey, R. A./Myers, S. C. (2003), p. 1041

147 See Ross, S. A., et al. (2000), p. 227.

148 See e.g. Stiglitz, J. E./Weiss, A. (1981), pp. 393ff and Ross, S. A., et al. (2002), pp. 10ff.

financial sponsors generally hold the majority of common stock to ensure their monitoring impact arising from the associated information-, control- and voting rights.[149] For a variety of reasons, such as for diversification purpose and reducing the portfolio exposure to a single investment, financial sponsors potentially co-venture with other sponsors or strategic investors. In order to align the interests between management and the financial sponsor majority owner, and thus to reduce related agency costs, management generally participates in the common stock of the LBO.[150] Management cash equity contribution is commonly high from the management perspective to ensure a creditable commitment, though presumably a relatively low percentage of total funds.[151] However, management can generally acquire equity at favorable terms (so-called *sweat equity*). Furthermore, complex management incentive schemes, with optional character linked to the achievement of various, a-priori specified targets, imply that management equity ownership frequently accrues over time.[152]

2.2 Quasi-Equity Financing Instruments

Types and forms of hybrid financing instruments, i.e. mezzanine in the broad sense are numerous. The respective instruments can neither be ascribed to pure equity nor pure debt based on the aforementioned five criteria. They are generally characterized by a risk-return profile between senior debt and common stock; i.e. the expected rate of return is superior while the rank is subordinated to senior debt and vice versa.[153] Most importantly a constituting characteristic of quasi-equity financing instruments is hence that they rank subordinated to any debt-financing in the case of insolvency.

Following Weinberger (2005) the subsequently listed hybrid financing instruments are considered quasi-equity financing instruments and therefore are included in the equity values when calculating *Total Proceeds* to equity investors.[154] In particular all hybrid financing instruments that are owned by the common stock equity investors, i.e. financial sponsors, management and third-party common stock investors are hereby included in capital invested at entry.

Vendor financing in the context of LBOs, where the seller of the company provides a loan to the acquirer and thus payment on part of the purchase price is deferred, are referred to as *vendor* or *seller notes*. Vendor loans are frequently applied for structuring earn-out models

---

149 See e.g. Hoffmann, P./Ramke, R. (1992), p. 95.

150 Managerial incentivation and alignment of interest as a mean to reduce agency costs are discussed in more detail in chapter III.B.1.2.

151 Kessel, B. (1998), p. 113 argues that management invests up to three times its annual salary in LBOs.

152 For details regarding management compensation and their incentivation in the context of LBOs see e.g. Becker, R. (2000), pp. 87-96.

153 See e.g Berger, M. (1993), pp. 185-204.

154 For a detailed discussion see Weinberger, N. (2005), chapter III.

with the amount to be paid being conditioned upon the future performance of the LBO. In this respect repayment of the loan is often linked to the achievement of predetermined performance measures such as absolute EBIT or EBITDA levels. Since vendor loans apparently align interests and reduce information asymmetries between the vendor and the acquirer they potentially help the seller to realize a higher purchase price.[155] Vendor loans will be considered as quasi-equity financing instruments, i.e. as equity, since (i) interest on vendor loans is generally low, (ii) their rank is subordinated to any other third-party financial liabilities and (iii) the seller thus faces a risk-return profile similar to that of common stock holders.[156]

Funds that are provided by the equity investors in the form of loans are referred to as *shareholder loans*. Like most vendor loans, shareholder loans are unsecured and also rank subordinate to any form of debt financing. Shareholder loans might be interest bearing, however, owing restrictive debt covenants, interest is generally accrued until maturity. Such a structure avoids the cash-interest outflow while nonetheless providing tax shield benefits.

A further quasi-equity financing instrument is *convertible bonds*. Convertible bonds are characterized by an embedded option that gives the holder of the instrument the right to convert the bond into a predetermined amount of shares of the underlying equity of the issuing company (or place in another company). *Warrants* also provide the owner with the option to purchase, at a predetermined price, a set number of the firm's shares until a fixed expiry date. However, other than in the case of a call option, warrants are settled by the company through the issuance of new shares.[157] A *bond with warrants* combines these two securities. As a differentiating criterion to a convertible bond the securities remain separately tradable.

Preferred stock, vendor loans and shareholder loans generally represent a significant part of total equity funds in LBO transactions. Quasi-equity financing instruments with optional character are frequently used in the context of management incentivation schemes.

As introductorily mentioned in the shortcomings, these aforementioned quasi-equity financing instruments (most importantly shareholder loans) are frequently erroneously considered and reported as financial liability and thus included in total indebtedness. Such mis-specification results in an understatement of total capital invested from an equity investor perspective at entry, and leverage ratios being (in part drastically) overstated.

---

155 See Richter, F./Timmreck, C. (2003), p. 247. Further, vendor loans might be beneficial for tax reasons and for accomplishing a faster execution of the transaction.

156 See e.g. Hoffmann, P./Ramke, R. (1992) p. 90, Kessel, B. (1998) p. 112, Müller, O. (2003), p. 231.

157 See Müller, O. (2003), p. 47.

3. Debt Financing Instruments

As pointed out in part one of this chapter, debt financing instruments – in the basic form – differ from equity financing instruments given their (generally) fixed claim, no success-dependent rewards, no ownership rights and in part limited liability[158] as well as availability. For the purpose of this thesis the two main instruments, *senior debt* (chapter II.B.3.1) and *subordinated debt* (chapter II.B.3.2) are distinguished.[159]

3.1 Senior Debt

Senior debt certifies a fixed claim and ranks first in case of insolvency.[160] In the case of LBO investments, the provision of senior debt financing is generally tied to so-called *conditions precedent.* These conditions precedent include among others (i) the right to participate in the *Due Diligence* process, (ii) *Representations & Warranties* with respect to firm-specific patents and licenses, (iii) in the most unspecified case, *material adverse change clauses* and most frequently, (iv) strict *covenants.*[161] Defaulting on the contractual, fixed claims or failing to meet either the agreed covenants or representation and warranties provides the lender with the right to accelerated debt repayment or even the cancellation of the financing contracts. Most frequently senior debt has a maturity of five to ten years with continuous, yearly interest payment and fixed repayment schedules.[162] Hereby the entire senior debt is structured in several term-loans that differ with respect to maturity and repayment schedules. Senior Debt is compensated through a spread (depending on the maturity and the default risk generally ranging between 2.25% and 3.25%) in excess of a floating base rate.[163]

3.2 Subordinated Debt

Other than senior debt, any debt that is not or insufficiently securitized is referred to as subordinated debt for which the legal ordination is hence subordinated to senior debt but still

---

158 *Note:* On the one hand the liability might be considered unlimited since despite a fixed claim the total loss of the committed capital is feasible. On the other hand however, debt generally ranks superordinated to equity in case of insolvency and on top might be secured through assets (see e.g. Volkart, R. (1999), pp. 1233f).

159 For further related details see e.g. Frommann, H. (1992), pp. 105ff and in particular Weinberger, N. (2005), chapter III.

160 See e.g. Frommann, H. (1992), p. 124 and Angbazo, L. A., et al. (1998), pp. 1252f. *Senior Secured Debt* refers to senior debt that is, other than *unsecured Senior Debt*, secured through operating assets.

161 See Weinberger, N. (2005), chapter III. Covenants can be separated into (*Negative* and *Affirmative*) *Maintenance* and *Financial Covenants*. Negative maintenance covenants include e.g. the constraint to dispose off or engage in the securitization of assets, constraints regarding the transfer of profits and constraints regarding borrowing additional, higher ranked debt. Affirmative maintenance covenants include e.g. control rights. Financial covenants include among others financing ratios such as a maximum leverage multiple or gearing ratio and interest coverage ratios as well.

162 See e.g. Müller, O. (2003), p. 227.

163 See Frommann, H. (1992), p. 125 and Suni, J. (2002), p. 6. The *Euribor* or *Libor* are the generally applied floating base rates. Interest rate adjustments are normally semi-annually.

senior to any equity financing instrument.[164] The higher associated risk and therefore expected rate of return of subordinated debt financing is either compensated through (i) higher fixed claims or (ii) the inclusion of success-dependent rewards, so-called *equity-kickers.*[165] Accordingly the differentiation between equity and debt financing instruments might at times be challenging, as pointed out repeatedly. However, for the purpose of a clear-cut separation between debt and equity financing, these funds are considered – in accordance with common practice – as debt financing instruments based on the understanding that the funds are not provided by LBO equity investors. The two most prominent types of subordinated debt financing in the context of *PE* investing are *High-Yield Bonds* and *Mezzanine in a strict sense.*

High-Yield Bonds

High-yield bonds are any such bonds whose long-term rating is considered sub-investment grade by at least one of the established rating agencies.[166] In the context of LBO financing the high default probability and hence risk premium arise from the high leverage and gearing ratio.[167] High-yield bonds in LBO financing can be structured in a variety of forms but most frequently have a maturity of seven to ten years, bear annual cash-interest payments and are fully repaid at maturity.[168] Standard compensation is in the form of a spread in the magnitude of around 4.5% to 7.0% on top of a floating base rate.[169] The popularity of high-yield bonds in Europe started in 1997 in the context of the Geberit buyout financing.[170]

Mezzanine in a Strict Sense

Despite frequently employed success-dependent remuneration components with equity character, mezzanine in a strict sense (henceforth *mezzanine*) is generally considered a hybrid financing instruments that belongs to the class of subordinated debt financing instruments.[171] Reasons therefore are, among others, the finite investment horizon of *mezzanine* financing of

---

164 See e.g. e.g. Mittendorfer, R. (2001), pp. 170ff and Frommann, H. (1992), p. 116.

165 See e.g. Frommann, H. (1992), p. 127 and Müller, O. (2003), p. 229

166 See e.g. Kessel, A. (1995), p. 90 and Müller-Trimbusch, J. (1999), p. 16. Established rating agencies (in the US referred to as nationally recognized statistical rating organizations) are Moody's Investors Service, Standard & Poor's as well as Fitch IBCA. The corresponding threshold levels for subinvestment grade for the first two agencies are BB+ and Ba1 respectively. Alternatively, high-yield bonds are frequently referred to as *junk bonds*.

167 See Volkart, R. (1999), p. 1234.

168 See e.g. e.g. Mittendorfer, R. (2001), pp. 173ff and Weinberger, N. (2005), chapter III. The various types of high-yield bonds include *zero-coupon bonds, payment-in-kinds bonds, deferred-interest bonds* or *step-up bonds*. For a detailed discussion of these various types see e.g. Tripp Howe, J. (1988), pp. 73ff.

169 See e.g. Müller, O. (2003), p. 213. However, given the tradability of high-yield bonds and the dependency of the compensation on the default probability, actual high-yield spreads are sensitive to not only systematic but also idiosyncratic risk (see Müller, O. (2003), p. 158).

170 Further details regarding the European high-yield market are provided by Weinberger, N. (2005), chapter III.

171 See e.g. Müller, O. (2003), pp. 22f and Weinberger, N. (2005), chapter III.

around five to ten years,[172] as well as the fact that *mezzanine* (although it ranks subordinated to senior debt) is secured with operating assets in case of insolvency.[173] Other than high-yield bonds, *mezzanine* financing is directly negotiated with the investors and hence individually structured.[174] As a consequence, compensation structures are very flexible, ranging from (i) a fixed cash component throughout the whole lifetime, over (ii) a spread rate on top of a floating base rate (comparable to high-yield bonds), to (iii) success-dependent components.[175] Success-dependent remuneration through warrants in combination with a reduced or accrued interest component apparently reduces the cash interest outflow during the holding period of the LBO but potentially dilutes the equity investors' stake at exit. Accordingly, expected returns on *mezzanine* financing exceed both senior debt and high-yield bonds given the subordinated securitization and the lower liquidity respectively.[176] In particular in complex financing structures, *mezzanine* is an increasingly applied subordinated debt financing instrument.[177]

C. Objective Function: Value Creation in LBOs

The following chapter defines *value creation* in the context of LBOs, thereby providing the operationalization of the principal objective function for the forthcoming analyses. Apparently, having specified the post-LBO equity investor perspective as the appropriate lens for analyzing value creation in LBOs, maximization of shareholder value is the only appropriate objective function.

According to the well-known net present value (*NPV*) concept a project is said to create value and hence the investment should be undertaken if the *PV* of the project exceeds the initial costs associated with the project.[178] In the context of an LBO, this implies that the LBO investment creates value, if the *PV* of all future cash flows to equity investors arising from the investment exceeds the initial equity contribution E_t.

Determining the PV of the future equity cash flows requires the specification of (i) total equity cash flows associated with an LBO investment, as well as (ii) the appropriate discount rate for these equity streams. The subsequent chapter II.C.1 details the sum of all equity cash flows associated with an LBO investment, referred to in this thesis as *Total Proceeds* (*TP*). The

172 See e.g. Suni, J. (2002), p. 8 and p. 11, Broda, B. M. (2003), p. 978 and Müller, O. (2003), p. 23.

173 See Müller, O. (2003), p. 23.

174 See e.g. Müller, O. (2003), p. 23 and Weinberger, N. (2005), chapter III.

175 See e.g. Mittendorfer, R. (2001), pp. 170ff and Weinberger, N. (2005), chapter III. Success-dependent remuneration can e.g. be in the form of a *back-end-loan-fee*, *accrued interest* or *warrants*.

176 See Rudolph, B. (2004), p. 12.

177 See Weinberger, N. (2005), chapter III for recent details regarding the development of the European Mezzanine market.

178 See e.g. Leroy, S. F. (1989), pp. 237ff.

following chapter II.C.2 discusses efforts to specify the appropriate discount rate for equity cash flows in an LBO investment. In light of apparent difficulties with the latter, chapter II.C.3 reviews various ex-post LBO investment value creation and performance measures.

1. Total Proceeds to Equityholders in LBOs

Total Proceeds (*TP*) represent the entirety of equity cash flows of a particular LBO investment. Hence from an equity investor perspective, *TP* is calculated as the sum of all cash inflows arising from the investment less the sum of all cash outflows associated with the LBO investment. Textbook literature generally applies the notation of *capital gains* to refer to the price appreciation of an investment; in the case of LBOs the difference in the equity value at entry and the equity value at exit. *Total Proceeds* to equity investors – as defined above for the purpose of this thesis – thus comprise *capital gains* plus any net interim equity streams.

Equity cash outflows primarily represent the initial equity contribution E_t, i.e. the portion of the funding at entry, '*sponsored*' by the entirety of equity investors (as defined in chapter II.B). Furthermore, any potential interim equity injections, i.e. any further funds for the portfolio company provided by these investors also account as equity cash outflows from the investor perspective. The sum of these two components is referred to as capital invested (*CI*) from hereonwards.

From the equity investor perspective, cash inflows represent at first the equity value E_T when the investment is exited. Furthermore, any interim equity streams to any form of equity financing instrument in any year n during the holding period, referred to as Div_n also qualify as equity cash inflows. According to this understanding, repayments of quasi-equity financing instruments, such as shareholder loans, are considered as interim dividend streams. Interim dividend payments to the equity investors generally call for the recapitalization of the firm's debt financing in place since restrictive debt covenants prevent the deployment of generated FCF other than for debt repayment purposes. Phrased differently, refinancings are generally a prerequisite facilitating interim dividend streams.

Thus, *TP* to equity investors equal the appreciation in the equity value plus the sum of any interim dividends less the sum of any interim equity injections.

$$(5) \quad TP = E_T - E_t + \sum_{n=t+1}^{T-1} Div_n - \sum_{n=t+1}^{T-1} E_{Inj,n}$$

The entirety of all dividend equity streams $\sum_{n=t+1}^{T-1} Div_n$ and all equity injections $\sum_{n=t+1}^{T-1} E_{Inj,n}$ in the course of the holding period is defined as $\sum_{n=t+1}^{T-1} E_n$ including the associated transaction costs $\sum_{n=t+1}^{T-1} TC_n$. Thus

$$(6) \quad TP = E_T - E_t + \sum_{n=t+1}^{T-1} E_n$$

2. Accounting for the Uncertainty of Total Proceeds or What's the Right Discount Rate

Positive *Total Proceeds* are necessary but not sufficient for value creation. As pointed out, value creation implies that the positive return (arising from positive *Total Proceeds*) of the investment exceeds the expected return of an alternative, comparable investment opportunity as the appropriate cost of capital for the investment.

CAPM and APT

The generally applied capital market models for quantifying expected returns for a set of uncertain, risky cash flows are the *CAPM* and the Arbitrage Pricing Theory[179] (*APT*). In the equilibrium of an arbitrage-free market these expected returns can be applied as the relevant cost of capital for the investment. According to the *CAPM*, the expected return for an investment $E[r_i]$ results as the risk-free interest rate (r_f) plus a premium, calculated as the excess market return times an indicator for the level of the investment's systematic risk, the well-known β factor.[180]

$$(7) \quad E[r_i] = r_f + \left(E[r_M] - r_f\right)\beta_A$$

Risk-adjusting cash flows to equity investors through the discount rate obviously requires the specification of the appropriate equity beta β_E. The question therefore arises how to transform the LBO portfolio companies asset beta β_A in light of the peculiarities regarding the LBO financing structure into β_E assuming that β_A were observable. First, accounting for proportionate debt financing, the firm's levered beta, β_L, results as the value-weighted average of the firm's equity beta and debt beta.[181]

---

179 See Ross, S. A. (1976).

180 As pointed out, investors will only be compensated for taking on systematic risk as company-specific, unsystematic risk can be completely eliminated through diversification. See chapter I.A.1.1.

181 See Ruback, R. S. (2002), p. 97.

$$(8) \quad \beta_L = \frac{E}{V_L}\beta_E + \frac{D}{V_L}\beta_D$$

Rearranging, the equity beta (β_E) results as

$$(9) \quad \beta_E = \left(\beta_L - \frac{D}{V_L}\beta_D\right) / \frac{E}{V_L}$$

To eliminate β_L an assumption regarding the debt financing policy has to be made. Assuming that in the course of the LBO transaction the company pursues a fixed debt policy with debt value D the value of the levered firm V_L results as the value of the unlevered firm V_U plus the value arising from the associated debt financing tax shield.[182]

$$(10) \quad V_L = V_U + V_{taxShield} = V_U + \tau D$$

Assuming that the riskiness of the interest tax shield equals the riskiness of the firm's financial liabilities, the firm's levered beta can be expressed as the value-weighted average of the unlevered beta β_A and the beta of the firm's financial liabilities β_D.

$$(11) \quad \beta_L = \frac{V_U}{V_L}\beta_A + \frac{\tau D}{V_L}\beta_D = \beta_A - \frac{\tau D}{V_L}(\beta_A - \beta_D)$$

Substituting β_L in equation (9) with the preceding expression and rearranging yields the firm's equity beta as ideally required for risk-adjustment in the discount rate of equity cash flows as a function of a firm's asset beta β_A, debt beta β_D, financing structure and tax rate τ.

$$(12) \quad \beta_E = \left(\beta_A - \frac{D}{V_L}(\beta_D + \tau(\beta_A - \beta_D))\right) / \frac{E}{V_L}$$

However, peculiarities regarding LBO investments question the applicability of the *CAPM* for assessing β_E and hence an appropriate risk-adjusted discount rate for LBO investments. Three primary reasons can be brought forward as to why the risk-and-return pattern of *PE* investments differ compared to those of traded stock even when considering comparable control factors such as growth expectations and profitability as well as the financial structure, β, industry and size:[183]

First, *Liquidity*. In addition to the uncertainty regarding the future operational performance of the bought-out company, the riskiness of LBO investments results to a large extent from the illiquidity of the investment due to the private nature of the transaction. The degree of liquidity of an investment is determined by the speed and certainty with which the investment can be

182 See Ruback, R. S. (2002), pp. 96f.

183 Based on Cochrane, J. (2005), p. 4.

sold/divested. Apart from potential interim equity streams, the capital is generally committed for the holding period of the investment. Therefore, owing to the absence of an institutionalized secondary market for trading individual *PE* investments, the realization of the divestment value is characterized by a high degree of uncertainty. Hence, the risk premium included in the appropriate discount rate needs not only to account for the systematic risk and the gearing ratio associated with the LBO investment but also to reflect this illiquidity of the investment in the form of an illiquidity premium. Research on asset prices indicates that liquidity is positively priced in capital markets. Reasons therefore are argued to be (i) an improved performance measurement, (ii) more informative stock prices, and (iii) the ability to easily redirect funds towards more efficient use.[184] Historically, empirical studies confirm illiquidity discounts in the magnitude of 20% to 74%.[185] Of particular interest for the context of this thesis are illiquidity studies that deal with transactions of shares in *PE* funds, i.e. among LPs. Thereby, the discount relative to the fund shares' (estimated) fair market value is approximated to range between 20-50%.[186] Gompers/Lerner (2000a) argue that given this illiquidity and the absence of follow-on revaluations of the investments, investors may substantially understate the effective volatility of the investment.[187] However, Gottschalg et al. (2004) point out that – in light of their finding of relatively low returns for *PE* as an asset class – the illiquidity discount might be overstated when considering LPs as large diversified institutional investors, putting only a relatively low fraction of their total investments into illiquid securities and hence presumably facing liquidity bottlenecks.[188]

Second, *Diversification*. As argued, investors in traded securities cannot demand any premium for taking on unsystematic risk. Other than systematic risk, unsystematic risk can be eliminated through a well-diversified portfolio. *PE* funds are generally insufficiently diversified.[189] While, in theory, the diversification aspect might as well be applied for a portfolio of *PE* investments, in practice, an individual LBO investment most likely represents a sizeable fraction of the *PE* fund. Whereas from a fund investor perspective this underdiversification might be of less relevance (assuming diversification of the entirety of

184 See e.g. Diamond, D. W./Dybvig, P. H. (1983), Amihud, Y./Mendelson, H. (1986) and Holmstrom, B./Tirole, J. (1993). Note, however, that there are argued to be also costs of liquidity such as a decreasing incentive for large shareholders to fulfill their monitoring duty (see e.g. Bhide, A. V. (1993)).

185 *Note:* Various types of illiquidity studies can be distinguished. Studies based on restricted stocks, which are temporarily banned from public trading (in general for two years), find average discounts in the range of 25% to 45%. Studies of private transactions preceding IPOs find average discounts of as much as 50%-74%. See Pratt, S. P. (1990) and Pratt, S. P., et al. (2000) for overviews, which provide an idea of the magnitude of the illiquidity discount. Both types of discount were found to be relatively stable over time.

186 See von Daniels, H. (2004), pp. 132f for an overview as well as the corresponding references referred to therein.

187 See e.g. Gompers, P. A./Lerner, J. (2000a), p 249.

188 See Gottschalg, O., et al. (2004), p. 26.

189 See e.g. Moskowitz, T. J./Vissing-Jörgensen, A. (2002), pp. 745ff.

investment activities i.e. on an aggregated level), it implies that unsystematic risk might very well need to be considered on fund level.

Third, *Monitoring and Governance.* Investors might require a premium for their efforts with respect to the reduction of agency costs and management support during the holding period of the investment. Such efforts presumably affect expected future cash flow claims arising from the investment. Additionally, however, a reasonable expected equity rate of return premium as a form of compensation could be considered.

Fund and Investor Level

On an aggregated, i.e. through various portfolio investments diversified, perspective the assessment of the riskiness of *PE* investing has only recently received considerable attention in the context of the emerging literature on aforementioned *PE Performance Studies*.[190]

Despite this recent popularity and steadily increasing data quality, time series measures of beta for *PE* as an asset class and the comparison to the public market (PM) seem inappropriate. The *PE* investment horizon and the corresponding fund lifetime of around ten years considerably limit the number of independent observations.[191] In light of this difficulty, Ljungqvist/Richardson (2003a) calculate hypothetical fund betas by *CI*-weighting the industry betas (according to Fama/French (1997)) assigned to the entirety of the fund's portfolio companies. Although such an approach leaves aside the potential benefits of substantial leverage in *PE* investing, the related analysis of cross-sectional differences between early stage and mature funds led the authors to conclude that "*systematic risk may not be one of the main determinants of the cross-section of private equity returns.*"[192] Similarly, Jones/Rhodes-Kropf (2003) conclude that in the context of *VC* and *PE* investing not only systematic but also idiosyncratic risk is priced, supporting the assessment by Ljungqvist/Richardson (2003a). Using quarterly return time series based on (subjective) Net Asset Values (*NAVs*) of a sample of 1,245 funds provided by *Thompson Venture Economics* Jones/Rhodes-Kropf approximate long-run betas in the magnitude of 0.65 for buyout funds.[193] Gottschalg et al. (2004), report diversification benefits of *PE* investing, i.e. hedging properties to the public market to be low. The corresponding average buyout fund beta is estimated at 1.7.[194] In light of (i) the reported

---

190 See chapter I.A.2.2.

191 See Ljungqvist, A./Richardson, M. (2003a), pp. 20f.

192 See Ljungqvist, A./Richardson, M. (2003a), p. 24.

193 See Jones, C. M./Rhodes-Kropf, M. (2003), pp. 0-40. The corresponding figure for VC funds is reported to be substantially higher at 1.80 expressing the higher related volatility. The shortcoming of subjective *Net Asset Values* compared with cash flow based financials is obvious (see also footnote [77] on page 24).

194 The calculation of this average fund beta is based on the methodology presented by Kaplan, S. N./Ruback, R. S. (1995) and mentioned in the context of risk assessment on investment level.

underperformance of *PE* as an asset class compared with the PM, and (ii) its disappointing hedging properties, the high levels of systematic risk investors bear by investing in *PE* seem not to be justified.[195] Schmidt (2003) analyzes diversification aspects of *PE* investments and finds the correlation with the public market to be low. Using bootstrap simulation, Schmidt (2003) concludes that portfolios comprising more than 15 portfolio investments eliminate 80% of non-systematic risk.[196] This by contrast would imply that idiosyncratic risk is priced fairly low in *PE* investing on fund/investor level.

Based upon the distribution of returns for fully realized funds Weidig/Mathonet (2004) report default probabilities, threshold rates and apply the standard deviation of realized returns as risk indicator.[197] For the sub-sample of buyout funds for the period 1983–1998 taken from *Venture Economics* the default probability (i.e. the probability of a total loss) is found to be 1%. The probability of a negative return amounts to 30%. An alternative – though given the focus of this thesis not further detailed – approach for risk assessment of *PE* investing is the analysis of publicly listed *PE* firms, where betas are observable. Apart from potential diversification benefits, several studies confirm a superior risk return profile for this asset class.[198]

Investment Level

There have been efforts to assess and ideally empirically quantify the riskiness of individual *PE* portfolio investments ever since, though this became particularly apparent in the context of what has previously been named *Operational Performance Studies.*[199] The ex-ante appraisal of an appropriate expected equity rate of return for an individual LBO investment based on standard capital market models is – as outlined – theoretically challenging. Preceding considerations on investor and fund level already imply that the riskiness of individual portfolio investments results to a large extent from the unsystematic operational risk, as systematic risk seems to be comparably low.[200]

Apart from the fact that unsystematic risk seems to be priced, the assessment of the appropriate riskiness of LBO portfolio companies faces two major challenges. First, and as

195 See Gottschalg, O., et al. (2004), pp. 1-53.

196 See Schmidt, D. (2003), pp. 0-54.

197 See Weidig, T./Mathonet, P. Y. (2004), pp. 1-33.

198 See e.g. Martin, J. D./Petty, W. J. (1983), Brophy, D. J./Guthner, M. W. (1988), pp. 187-206, pp. 401-410, Deibert (2004), pp. 24-25 and Zimmermann, H., et al. (2004), pp. 1-24. For a critical discussion see Bygrave, W. D., et al. (1989), pp. 95ff and Bygrave, W. D./Timmons, J. A. (1992), p. 152.

199 For a detailed, comprehensive overview and discussion of risk assessment and risk-adjusted performance measures in the context of PE investing see Groh, A. P. (2004), in particular pp. 179ff.

200 See also Bader, H. (1996), pp. 176-198. Ruhnka, J. C./Young, J. E. (1991) discusses qualitatively potential sources of risk in the context of VC and PE investing. For a brief discussion of types of operational risks see Schefczyk, M. (2004), p. 202.

pointed out previously, LBO investments are largely debt-funded and therefore exhibit high gearing ratios. Second, given the LBO business model with value creation through operational performance improvement and deleveraging, gearing ratios are expected to vary substantially between entry and exit. Not only is the entity value expected to increase but also the level of financial liabilities to decrease.

For a sample of 25 previously publicly traded LBOs, Kaplan (1989a) calculates market-adjusted returns applying the Scholes/Williams (1971) beta estimate for the firm's common stock estimated from 600 to 100 trading days prior to the buyout announcement. However, Kaplan (1989a) concludes that "[*b*]*ecause buyouts are initially financed with a small amount of equity, it is difficult to estimate the beta that should be applied to that equity. Most equity betas would initially exceed five.*"[201] In accordance with aforementioned findings, results by Kaplan/Stein (1990) suggest therefore that given the substantial financial leverage in LBOs the systematic risk of equity might be relatively low; much lower than expected.[202] Though their findings for twelve public recapitalizations for the years 1986–1988 should be interpreted for LBOs with great caution, the analysis documents a very modest average increase in beta of 30% compared to a hypothetical, predicted beta-increase of as much as 325%.[203] Based on this, Palepu (1990) deduces that the offsetting effect results from a reduced business risk of the bought-out company since higher operating cash flows resulting from organizational changes associated with the LBO cause asset betas to decrease.[204] Obviously, though, variations in operating margins do not necessarily represent the volatility of returns on invested capital from the perspective of the LBO equity investor, and hence do not serve as a measure for the risk of investor returns.

To conclude, standard capital market models seem somewhat unsuitable for determining expected equity rates of return for *PE* portfolio investments. Alternatives for considering the riskiness of *PE* investing from an ex-post perspective are pointed out in chapter II.C.3.3 when detailing alternative LBO performance measures.

3. Value Creation Performance Measures

Having specified *Total Proceeds* to equity investors and briefly highlighted the difficulties of assessing the appropriate discount rate, this chapter presents modes of ex-post performance analysis for *PE* investments in increasing order with regard to their theoretical foundation: (i) simple relative *TP* analysis – the so-called concept of *Times Money (TM)* – neither

---

201 See Kaplan, S. N. (1989a), p. 252.

202 See Kaplan, S. N./Stein, J. C. (1990), pp. 215-245

203 The hypothetical β is derived by unlevering and relevering the equity βs, assuming unaffected asset βs from the recapitalizations.

204 See Palepu, K. G. (1990), p. 256.

accounting for timing nor risk characteristics of the investment, (ii) the *Investment IRR* as timing-adjusted performance measure, and (iii) alternative performance measures against some form of benchmark intending to (partially) account for the riskiness of *PE* investing.

3.1 The Concept of Times Money

In analogy to the calculation of a securities *holding-period return (HPR)*[205] a first straightforward, simple, relative performance measure for LBO investments relates *Total Proceeds* to equity investors (*TP*) to the total amount of capital invested (*CI*).

$$(13)\quad TM = TP / CI$$

Specifically, applying the previously detailed components of *TP* and *CI*

$$(14)\quad TM = \left(E_T - E_t + \sum_{n=t}^{T} Div_n - \sum_{n=t}^{T} E_{Inj,n} \right) / \left(E_t + \sum_{n=t}^{T} E_{Inj,n} \right) - 1$$

Particularly in practice and on investment level this measure is referred to as the concept of *Times Money*.

TP and *TM* analysis is of high relevance for practitioners.[206] Due to fund dynamics and fund economics, the time value of money concept might be argued to be of less relevance.[207] As pointed out, *PE* funds are generally set up with a finite lifetime, during which the GP can draw from the commitment lines provided by LPs whenever a suitable investment opportunity arises. Realized proceeds are distributed immediately and are generally not reinvested. Assuming that LPs are rather *deep-pocket investors*[208], which commit funds for a period of ten years with an uncertain payback schedule and are thus presumably less sensitive to liquidity, the non-timing adjusted performance over the entire fund period might be of particular relevance. E.g. for the purpose of marketing historical performance when a new fund is launched, fund performance is most frequently communicated in these comparable, simple terms, on investor level the so-called *Ratio of Distributions to Paid-In Capital (DPI)*.[209]

However, the simple *Times Money* calculation apparently implies that such a measure neither accounts for the timing aspect of cash flows nor for the risk associated with their

---

205 See e.g. Bodie, Z., et al. (1999), pp. 132-133.

206 See e.g. Moreland, R./Reyes, J. E. (1992), pp. 44-48. Hielscher, U., et al. (2003) report that in their study 75% of the analyzed nationally and internationally investing financial sponsors apply among others *Times Money* as LBO performance measure.

207 See chapter I.A.2.3 for a very brief introduction to the fund concept.

208 Lerner, J./Schoar, A. (2004), p. 3 refer to *deep-pocket investors* as those investors who have a low likelihood of facing a liquidity shock.

209 Evca (2004), p.10 defines: "*The DPI measures the cumulative distributions returned to investors (Limited Partners) as a proportion of the cumulated paid-in capital. [...] This is also often called the "cash-on-cash return".*"

realization. For these reasons, comparability of investments based on this performance measure is limited and might be misleading.

3.2 IRR as Timing-Adjusted Performance Measure

The *Internal Rate of Return (IRR)* is the most commonly applied performance measure in the context of *PE* investing, in theory as well as in practice.[210] Taking the timing but not the riskiness of the cash flows into consideration, the IRR is the discount rate that implies the NPV of all future cash flows to be zero.[211] Generally

$$(15)\quad \sum_{n=t}^{T} CF_n (1+IRR)^{-n} = 0$$

Specifically, applying the previously discussed components of *TP*

$$(16)\quad -E_t + \sum_{n=t}^{T} \left(Div_n - E_{inj\,n}\right)\left(1+IRR\right)^{-n} + E_T(1+IRR)^{-T} = 0$$

In analogy to the perspectives of analyzing value creation in LBOs and in accordance with EVCA, three types of IRRs can be distinguished: (i) *Investor IRR*, (ii) *Fund IRR* and (iii) *Investment IRR.*[212]

The *Investor IRR* calculates the fund performance net of fund expenses by putting the cash in- and outflows to and from the LPs into perspective. As previously pointed out this is a frequently applied performance measure in aggregated *PE* performance studies (see chapter I.A.2.3). The *Fund IRR* is the gross IRR of realized and continuing investments and accordingly captures cash in- and outflows on fund level, gross of fund expenses and carried interest. The inclusion of continuing investments obviously raises the issue of appropriately valuing these investments.[213] Accordingly, a comparison of investor and *Fund IRRs* seems reasonable only for fully realized funds. *Investor* and *Fund IRRs* of funds that are not fully realized but are based on observable, realized cash flow data only (i.e. without the valuation of ongoing investments) are obviously characterized by the long-term nature of PE investing. Whereas cash outflows generally occur at the beginning of the funds' lifetime, proceeds from

---

210 For a discussion of the practical relevance and benefits of the IRR performance measure see e.g. Schober, A. (1996), Prester, M. (2002), Hielscher, U., et al. (2003). Most relevant empirical studies – especially private equity performance studies – apply the IRR performance measure at least as starting point for performance assessment in private equity (see chapter I.A.2.3). Ex-ante, the IRR is generally applied to assess the attractiveness of the investment and communicate target rate of returns to the LPs of the fund.

211 Brealey, R. A./Myers, S. C. (2003), p. 96.

212 For the various perspectives of analyzing LBO investments see chapter I.B.2 and chapter II.B. Evca (2003) refers to the three types as *Net Return to the Funder*, *Gross Return on All Investments* and *Gross Return on Realized Investments* respectively. For a discussion of the various types of IRR see also Bader, H. (1996) , pp. 310ff, Gull, J. (1999) pp. 46-48 and Schefczyk, M. (2004), pp. 198ff

213 See footnote [77] on page 24.

divesting investments are realized after the holding period towards the end of the funds' lifetime. The corresponding *hockey-stick-effect* is typical of such IRR calculations.[214] The *Investment IRR* is calculated as the gross return of a realized investment and thus represents the appropriate IRR performance measure for the purpose of this thesis. The calculation captures the entirety of cash flow streams on investment level, i.e. between the entirety of equity investors and the portfolio investment and is therefore before fund expenses and carried interest.

The *Investment IRR* disregards any ownership changes during the holding period as cash flows to all equity investors as defined in equation (16) (and hence including management) are applied. For this reason, comparing and potentially bridging the three types of IRR would be precarious and misleading. *Fund* and *Investor IRRs* only refer to a fraction of LBO equity investors as previously defined. As such, this is not distorting since a pro rata calculation values the respective cash in- and cash outflows as an equal percentage of total equity as in the case of a co-investing fund. However, leaving management as equity investor aside presumably understates value creation in LBOs. Complex and extensive management incentivation schemes in the form of option programs generally significantly dilute fund ownership over time until the liquidation of the investment, hence leading to depressed *Fund IRRs* when compared with the respective *Investment IRR*.

Given its arithmetic, the IRR performance measure has to be dealt with great caution.[215] Most importantly, the IRR arithmetic implicitly assumes that interim cash flows from the investment can be reinvested with the project's IRR. In other words, interim cash flows from the investment can presumably immediately be redeployed in investments with equally attractive prospects.

Although the associated drawbacks are particularly severe from an ex-ante perspective that uses the IRR as the decision rule for accepting or denying an investment opportunity, post-investment performance comparison must also be assessed in light of these pitfalls. Since *PE* funds are obviously interested in the absolute amount of wealth created and distributed to their LPs, an investment with a lower IRR might even be preferable given the IRR's inability to

---

214 See e.g. Bygrave, W. D., et al. (1989), pp. 98ff and Ljungqvist, A./Richardson, M. (2003a), p. 36.

215 *Note:* In this respect Brealey, R. A./Myers, S. C. (2003), pp. 98-105, list four pitfalls of the IRR performance measure: first for particular projects the NPV increases as the discount rate increases, obviously reducing the IRR investment decision rule to absurdity. Second, based on Descartes' rule of signs "*there can be as many different internal rates of return for a project as there are changes in the sign of the cash flows*" (see Brealey, R. A./Myers, S. C. (2003), p. 100). Third, given the fact that the IRR as relative performance measure does not account for the amount invested, basing the decision rule on the IRR potentially implies for mutually exclusive projects to decide for the project with the lower absolute NPV. Last, the IRR decision rule does not capture changes in the underlying risk-free interest rate and/or the risk premium as it implicitly assumes a flat opportunity cost of capital term structure. For further details regarding these pitfalls see also Ross, S. A., et al. (2000), pp. 261ff.

account for the amount of capital committed. Apart from mutually exclusive projects, this might be of particular relevance when (sizeable) investment opportunities rather than the required funds are scarce. The same line of reasoning challenges the IRR-based divestiture decision due to the re-investment premise of the IRR arithmetic. When investment opportunities are rare and associated with substantial transaction costs, a long-term investment with a lower IRR might still be preferable compared to a short-term investment with a higher IRR from an equity investor perspective. Even if the IRR were to decrease with the length of the holding period, an IRR in excess of the (assumed to be fix) fund's opportunity cost of capital is 'creating value'. This consideration in turn favors (partially) the simple *Times Money* performance measure.

Despite these aforementioned shortcomings, the standardization with respect to timing improves the direct comparability – both on investment and fund level. However, the calculation of the IRR as a one-dimensional (return) performance measure implies the non-consideration of the riskiness of the investment in the form of an appropriate opportunity cost of capital; as previously specified, the expected rate of return of an alternative, comparable investment opportunity. It could however be argued that this fact suits well the perspective of the equity investor on the investment level of this thesis: the *PE* fund acts as financial intermediary, investing from committed funds provided by LPs. Given restrictive partnership agreements that oblige GPs to invest almost exclusively in private companies, the *PE* market can be regarded as segmented from other asset classes.[216] Hence, from a financial sponsor perspective, an alternative investment opportunity can only be considered a LBO with similar risk and return characteristics that would have been made if the specific investment had not been entered into. However, this not only poses the quantification of the investment's expected equity rate of return and associated risk significant problems as previously discussed, but also the alternative investment approach is questionable from a scarcity of resources point of view. The current abundance of cash inflows in *PE* seems not to pose restrictions on the execution of an attractive investment opportunity, which satisfies the funds' expected equity rate of return. If at all, the scarcity of human resources required for the execution, as well as *PE* fund portfolio diversification effects, might validate this opportunity cost consideration. Hence given the equity investor perspective on investment level of this thesis the *Investment IRR* might already be considered as an appropriate lens to assess *value creation* in LBOs on investment level.

---

216 See Gompers, P. A./Lerner, J. (2000b), p. 286.

3.3 *Alternative Performance Measures*

In particular in the recent research stream of *PE* performance on fund/investor level (see chapter I.A.2.3) there is an ongoing debate regarding the measurement of returns and the assessment of performance of *PE* investing.[217] On the one hand the outlined shortcomings of the *Times Money* and IRR performance measure in the preceding chapter are apparent. On the other hand the difficulty of accounting for the uncertainty of TP and hence of *PE* investing became evident in chapter II.C.2.

In analogy to performance measurement and appraisal in the mutual funds industry, *Sharpe's*, *Treynor's* and *Jensen's measures* might be considered as risk-adjusted performance measures for *PE* investing.[218] However, being based on the CAPM, performance measurement of *PE* investing based on these three measures faces the challenge of appropriately quantifying the systematic risk of the *PE* investment (or the portfolio of investments from a fund/investor perspective). In a modified version, various *PE Performance Studies* apply a form of *Jensen's measure.* On investment level, the Excess IRR of a particular investment is calculated as the *Investment IRR* less the IRR of a benchmark investment.[219]

$$(17) \quad ER_i = IRR_i - IRR_k$$

The choice of the benchmark investment is obviously crucial. While the public market presumably does not represent the alternative investment opportunity for an individual LBO investment, considering the *PM* as benchmark provides the benefit of adjusting *PE* performances for market abnormalities.

As an alternative measure for relative *PE* performance assessment compared to a benchmark investment, various empirical *PE Performance Studies* apply the concept of the profitability index.[220] Hereby, the PV of all cash inflows (CF_i^{in}) is divided by the present value of all cash outflows (CF_i^{out}) for an individual investment opportunity.[221] The applied discount

---

217 For a detailed analysis regarding risk-adjusted performance measurement of PE investing see Groh, A. P. (2004). In the context of recent PE performance studies see in particular Kaserer, C./Diller, C. (2004), pp. 20ff, Gottschalg, O., et al. (2004), pp. 9-11, Kaplan, S. N./Schoar, A. (2005), pp. 1797ff and Ick, M. (2005), pp. 10ff.

218 See Sharpe, W. F. (1994), pp. 49ff, Treynor, J. L. (1965), pp. 63ff and Jensen, M. C. (1968), pp. 389ff respectively as well as Groh, A. P. (2004), pp. 78ff in the context of PE investing.

219 Similar to the calculation of the fund/investor IRR, the IRR of the benchmark portfolio is calculated for investing at the date of entry until the date of exit of the PE investment opportunity.

220 See e.g. Ljungqvist, A./Richardson, M. (2003a) and Gottschalg, O., et al. (2004). Kaplan, S. N./Schoar, A. (2005) and Kaserer, C./Diller, C. (2004) refer to a similar measure as the *Public Market Equivalent* (*PME*).

221 See Brealey, R. A./Myers, S. C. (2003), pp. 106f. Alternatively, the same methodology can obviously be applied on fund level with cash out- and inflows then representing cumulated cash flows of the entirety of portfolio investments.

rate ideally represents r_k, the return of an alternative, comparable and available investment opportunity.

$$(18) \quad PI = \frac{\sum_{n=t}^{T} CF_{ni}^{in} \prod_{j=t}^{n} (1+r_{kj})^{-1}}{\sum_{n=t}^{T} CF_{ni}^{out} \prod_{j=t}^{n} (1+r_{kj})^{-1}}$$

PE Performance Studies generally apply some form of public market index as benchmark investment.[222] By doing so the analysis implicitly presumes a beta of one for *PE* investing. Accordingly, *PIs* larger (smaller) than one imply an outperformance (underperformance) relative to the public market.

Comparing *PE* investing against the public market is particularly insightful on fund/investor level. However, the question regarding value creation on investment level is not specifically addressed unless the market rate of return r_M is assumed to represent the rate of return of the alternative investment opportunity r_k. Given the outlined failures and shortcomings of quantifying the alternative investment opportunity's rate of return the forthcoming empirical analysis applies illustrative benchmark values of r_k for the purpose of quantifying ERs and NPVs of the analyzed sample. *Excess Investment IRRs* are computed using the return of a public market index as benchmark. An illustrative NPV calculation uses (i) a representative *Fund IRR*,[223] (ii) the median *Investment IRR* of a control sample, as well as (iii) the median hypothetical IRR for the firm's operating performance (i.e. net of the impact of external market aspects)[224] as rates of return r_k for benchmark investments. Corresponding details and limitations are discussed in the respective chapter V.E.3 of the empirical analysis.

---

222 *Note:* The precise benchmark investment varies however across the different PE Performance Studies. Kaplan, S. N./Schoar, A. (2005) as well as Gottschalg, O., et al. (2004) apply some form of public stock market portfolio return as the appropriate rate for discounting *cash inflows*. Kaplan, S. N./Schoar, A. (2005) also use the public stock market portfolio returns for discounting *cash outflows*. Gottschalg, O., et al. (2004) argue that investors rely on short-term bonds as the alternative investment for the committed capital and accordingly apply the 30-day Treasury-bill yield for discounting *cash outflows*.

223 The average of the reported mean fund IRRs by two recent contributions is applied as a representative fund IRR. Alternatively it could be thought of to apply the ex-ante expected equity rate of return. Large established private equity funds frequently claim to work with the premises of an expected equity rate of return in the range of 20% to 30%. See e.g. Fenn, G. W., et al. (1997) , pp. 28-33.

224 Such a hypothetical Investment IRR is calculated by assuming – ceteris paribus – constant transaction multiples between the entry and the exit of the investment. See in particular the IRR sensitivity analysis in chapter V.E.2.2 for details.

III. Value Creation Analysis in the Context of the LBO Transaction Model

Preparatory considerations in the previous chapter emphasized that any value creation analysis in LBOs on investment level from an equity investor perspective (according to the understanding of this thesis) calls for the analysis of *Total Proceeds* in the sense expressed in equation (6) as a necessary starting point.

$$(19) \qquad TP = E_T - E_t + \sum_{n=t+1}^{T-1} E_n$$

with E representing the various equity streams at the time of the entry (t) and the exit (T) of the investment, as well as during the holding period in the form of interim dividends net of additional equity injections. Chapter III.A presents the LBO transaction model, and details in the context of this framework how *TP* to equity investors can be decomposed into five components, which can then be subsumed and classified alongside an internal and an external perspective. Chapter III.B then discusses theoretically sources of value creation with respect to the internal perspective, *FCF effects*. Chapter III.C focuses on sources of value creation with respect to the second, external perspective, *variation in the transaction multiple*.

A. The LBO Transaction Model

The LBO transaction model offers a straightforward, though comprehensive framework for analyzing variations in the market prices of LBO investments. The model provides the opportunity to (i) assess variations in the entity and equity value of the LBO company and the impact of financial leverage, as well as (ii) separate out the various components of *Total Proceeds* to equity investors, and (iii) distinguish an internal as well as an external perspective.

1. Financial Leverage and the Variation in the Entity and Equity Market Value

As defined in chapter II.A, LBOs are characterized, among others, by a significant amount of debt financing. The purchase price P_t, of the bought-out company is financed through a combination of debt and equity financing instruments as detailed in chapter II.B. Based on equation (4) and leaving aside transaction costs for the time being, the entity value of the target company equals

$$(20) \quad V_t = E_t + ND_t$$

Assuming further for the time being no interim equity streams from or to the equityholders implies that any FCF generated during the holding period of the investment is used to repay third-party financial liabilities. In this simplified case the variation in the equity value as the remainder results as the variation in the entity value less the variation in net financial liabilities from the initial investment in the liquidation of the investment.[225]

$$(21) \quad (E_T - E_t) = (V_T - V_t) - (ND_T - ND_t)$$

Defining the respective growth rates as $g^{V}_{T-t} = V_T / V_t - 1$, $g^{E}_{T-t} = E_T / E_t - 1$ and $g^{ND}_{T-t} = ND_T / ND_t - 1$ equation (21) reads as

$$(22) \quad E_t g^{E}_{T-t} = V_t g^{V}_{T-t} - ND_t g^{ND}_{T-t} = (E_t + ND_t) g^{V}_{T-t} - ND_t g^{ND}_{T-t}$$

The gearing ratio l_t be defined as $l_t = ND_t / V_t$. Hence

$$(23) \quad g^{E}_{T-t}(1 - l_t) = g^{V}_{T-t}(1 - l_t) + g^{V}_{T-t} l_t - g^{ND}_{T-t} l_t \text{ and}$$

$$(24) \quad g^{E}_{T-t} = g^{V}_{T-t} + \left(g^{V}_{T-t} - g^{ND}_{T-t}\right) \frac{l_t}{(1 - l_t)}$$

Interpreting (i) g^{E}_{T-t} as the expected rate of return of an unlevered company, (ii) g^{ND}_{T-t} as the expected rate of return of assumed financial liabilities and (iii) g^{V}_{T-t} as the expected rate of return of total assets, equation (24) nicely matches equation (1) of the Modigliani/Miller (1958) theorem for the no tax case.[226]

For the simplified case of no transaction costs and assuming no interim equity streams the concept of leverage in LBO transactions and related value creation is frequently visualized as illustrated in the following chart; with equation (21) becoming pictorial.

Chart 4 Simplified LBO Analysis[227]

Assuming no transaction costs and no interim equity streams

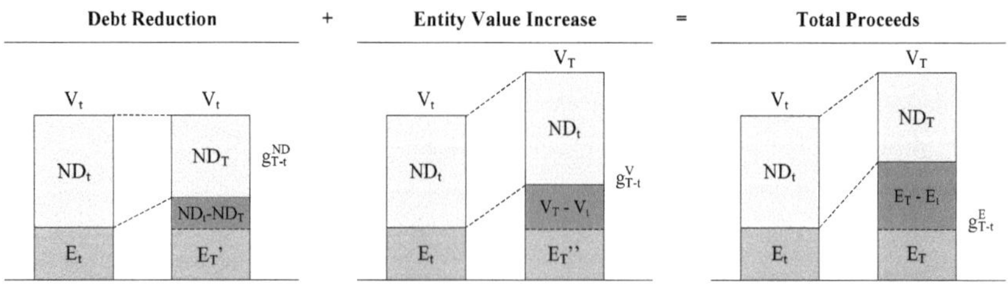

225 Based on Richter, F. (2005), pp. 175ff

226 See Richter, F. (2005), p. 175 and pp. 60ff.

227 Based on Mittendorfer, R. (2001), p. 151 and Weinberger, N. (2005), chapter III.

2. Components of Total Proceeds to Equity Investors

The following chapter details the LBO transaction model by (i) introducing transaction costs and interim equity streams in the form of dividends or capital injections based thereon, (ii) decomposing *Total Proceeds* to equity investors into its various components. It shows how components affecting *Total Proceeds* to equity investors can be clustered to result either from internal FCF generation or a – (primarily) externally induced – variation in the transaction multiple.

According to equation (4) the equity investment at the time of the entry is given as

$$(25)\quad E_t = V_t - D_t + Cash_t + TC_t$$

In LBO transactions, entity values are generally expressed as a multiple of any cash flow measure.[228] For the purpose of the following discussion C is used representatively for cash flow measure. In practice the most commonly applied measure is $EBITDA_{LTM}$. Other frequently considered cash flow measures for entity value multiples are, among others, $EBIT_{LTM}$ and $(EBITDA\text{-}CapEx)_{LTM}$. Replacing V_t by the product of the transaction multiple at entry m_t and the corresponding cash flow proxy C_t, and combining cash and total debt to net debt, equation (25) reads as

$$(26)\quad E_t = m_t C_t - ND_t + TC_t$$

Similar to equation (26) with respect to the valuation at entry, but taking into account that transaction costs at exit are borne by the acquirer, the equity value of the investments at the point in time of the exit E_T results as

$$(27)\quad E_T = m_T C_T - ND_T$$

Total Proceeds from an LBO investment are defined as the difference of cash inflows and cash outflows, including potential interim dividends and equity injection streams.

$$(28)\quad TP = E_T - E_t + \sum_{n=t+1}^{T-1} E_n$$

see equation (6), p. 53

228 For a discussion of entity and equity multiples and premises for use see also Herrmann, V. (2002), pp. 49-62 (as well as pp. 68-71 for a discussion of the relevance of multiples in corporate acquisitions), Richter, F./Herrmann, V. (2003), pp. 194ff and Kelleners, A. (2004), pp. 146-158.

Thus substituting the equity value at exit E_T and the equity value at entry E_t in equation (28) and defining $\sum_{n=t}^{T} TC_n$ as the total amount of transaction costs[229] yields for the LBO investment absolute *Total Proceeds* of:

$$(29)\quad TP = (m_T C_T + ND_T) - (m_t C_t + ND_t) + \sum_{n=t+1}^{T-1} E_n - \sum_{n=t}^{T} TC_n$$

Defining total debt repayment during the holding period as $\Delta D_{T-t} = ND_t - ND_T$ and the variation in the transaction multiple as $\Delta m_{T-t} = m_T - m_t$ equation (29) can be rewritten as

$$(30)\quad TP = m_t \Delta C_{T-t} + \Delta m_{T-t} C_t + \Delta m_{T-t} \Delta C_{T-t} + \Delta D_{T-t} + \sum_{n=t+1}^{T-1} E_n - \sum_{n=t}^{T} TC_n$$

EBITDA and the transaction multiple are multiplicative linked. This implies that the overall effect of variations in both the EBITDA level and the transaction multiple can not be entirely separated out. As soon as both variables change a fraction of the marginal increase is the result of both variables changing. The third term in equation (30) accounts for this combined effect.

Debt repayment and equity distributions can both be regarded as *uses* of cash, equity injections on the other hand as a *source* of cash. *FCF*, free cash flow available for distribution to debt and equityholders, can be defined as

$$(31)\quad FCF = EBITDA - Int_{Cash} - Tax_{Cash} - \Delta NWC - CapEx$$

Hence, the cumulated total amount of free cash flow available for distribution to debt- and equityholders generated during the holding period of the investment, $\sum_{n=t}^{T} FCF_n$, is *used* to either (i) reduce the amount of third party net financial liabilities by the amount ΔD_{T-t} or (ii) distribute interim dividend streams to the equityholders (net of equity injections and including payment of related transaction fees) in the amount $E_{T-t,int}$. Equation (30) then reads as

$$(32)\quad TP = m_t \Delta C_{T-t} + \Delta m_{T-t} C_t + \Delta m_{T-t} \Delta C_{T-t} + \sum_{n=t}^{T} FCF_n - \sum_{n=t}^{T} TC_n$$

Expressed in relative terms as percentage of *Total Proceeds*:

$$(33)\quad 1 = \frac{m_t \Delta C_{T-t}}{TP} + \frac{\Delta m_{T-t} C_T}{TP} + \frac{\Delta m_{T-t} \Delta C_{T-t}}{TP} + \frac{\sum_{n=t}^{T} FCF_n}{TP} - \frac{\sum_{n=t}^{T} TC_n}{TP}$$

[229] Comprising transaction costs at entry plus relevant transaction costs associated with equity in- and/or outflows during the holding period.

According to equation (33) five components of *Total Proceeds* to equity investors can be identified:

- *Earnings Variation* $\frac{m_t \Delta C_{T-t}}{TP}$: The (pure) change in the entity value of the company due to the change in the cash flow measure ΔC_{T-t} assuming no change in the transaction multiple at exit vs. entry

- *Multiple Variation* $\frac{\Delta m_{T-t} C_t}{TP}$: The (pure) change in the entity value of the company due to the change in the valuation level expressed by the variation of the transaction multiple with respect to the cash flow proxy C_t at entry

- *Combined Earnings/Multiple Effect* $\frac{\Delta m_{T-t} \Delta C_{T-t}}{TP}$: Resulting from the multiplicative, non-linear conjunction of C and the corresponding transaction multiple with respect to the entity value

- *Cumulated FCF Generation* $\frac{\sum_{n=t}^{T} FCF_n}{TP}$ (including any potential capital injections from the equity investor) during the holding period, which is either used to repay financial liabilities or to be distributed to the equity investors

- *Transaction Costs* $\frac{\sum_{n=t}^{T} TC_n}{TP}$ occurred during the holding period including transaction costs for the initial investment and if applicable for interim variations in the capital structure such as recapitalizations obviously negatively affecting *Total Proceeds*.

3. Perspectives of Value Creation in LBOs

Above decomposition of *Total Proceeds* is informative and in particular an empirical analysis alongside these five components will most likely reveal interesting results. In this respect, the forth component, *Cumulated FCF Generation* unambiguously indicates the relative value creation contribution through deleveraging (and potentially interim equity streams).

However, a separation between *Earnings Variation* and *Cumulated FCF Generation* is clearly not mutually exclusive when it comes to analyzing sources of value creation in LBOs. Factors driving *Earnings Variation* obviously impact *Cumulated FCF Generation*. *FCF* is defined as the sum of the operating and investing cash flow after cash taxes and cash interest expenses, i.e. the ultimate free cash flow available for debt repayment. Therefore by definition,

FCF comprehensively captures all factors that affect the level and that trigger a variation of the cash flow proxy *C*.

In order to account for this non-mutual exclusivity the components of *Total Proceeds* to equity investors will be clustered alongside two perspectives. First, the internal perspective subsumes all effects linked to the firm's ability to generate cash flow and thus will be referred to as *FCF effects*. Second, the external perspective relates to the variation of the transaction multiple from entry to exit $\Delta m_{T\text{-}t,i}$. Therefore:

$$(34) \quad \Delta E_{T-t} = f(FCF, \Delta m)$$

Potential interdependencies between the internal and the external perspective and thus regarding the mutual exclusivity of this separation will be addressed when considering the external perspective in detail.

Improved vs. Steady Operational Performance

The component *Earnings Variation* provides an indication for the impact of variations of EBITDA between the Entry and the Exit on the valuation of the investment. The component *Cumulated FCF Generation*, however, which is predominantly used to pay down debt, is affected in this respect not only by the *variation* in FCF but also by the corresponding *actual level* and the temporal pattern of variation during the holding period. According to equation (1) leverage boosts the realized equity rate of return as soon as the return on the unlevered firm exceeds the relevant cost of debt. Phrased differently, when the return on the unlevered firm exceeds the relevant cost of debt a LBO 'works' even without improving the firm's operations. Pure deleveraging through positive FCF generation, considering post-buyout capital structure implications of debt-servicing payments and associated tax effects but assuming *steady operational performance*, creates proceeds for the equity investors.[230] *Improved operational performance* during the holding period of the investment therefore double-impacts *Total Proceeds* to equity investors by not only (i) increasing firm value (assuming no variation in the transaction multiple) but also (ii) speeding up deleveraging of the company.

Improved operational performance can again be separated into two principal elements: Variations in levels of *FCF* (and thus of *C*) either result from (i) *revenue growth* or (ii) *FCF-Margin* improvements. According to the definition of *FCF* as the cash flow available for debt

---

230 *Note:* Focusing on this deleveraging aspect as a mean to generate proceeds for equity investors in LBO transactions even with steady operational performance led, among other things, to the understanding of an ideal LBO candidate as being characterized by high and stable FCF with unused borrowing capacities. See e.g. Smith, A. J. (1990b), pp. 19-25 and Schmid, H. (1994), pp. 90ff. Accordingly, the profile of attractive LBO candidates is that of "*mature, low-growth firms with strong, consistent, recession-resistant cash flows in "low-tech" industries.*" See Smith, A. J. (1990b), p. 19.

repayment (see equation (31)), *FCF-Margin* improvements also comprise reductions in relative *NWC* as well as capital expenditures.

In light of this understanding two brief remarks regarding previous empirical work on value creation in LBOs presented in chapter I.A.2, should be made: first, while most of the *Premia-Paid Studies* seem to fit well into the '*steady-operational-performance*' category by analyzing the relationship between firm characteristics and the likelihood of going private, the group of operational performance studies focuses rather on the impact of LBOs on variations in the firm's operations, i.e. on *improved operational performance* and in particular the FCF-Margin improvement element.[231] Second, once again it becomes evident that value creation analysis in LBOs on investment level is a complex construct with previous research – in particular empirically – focusing on selected single aspects only.

Chart 5 Overview on Value Creation Analysis in the Context of the LBO Transaction Model

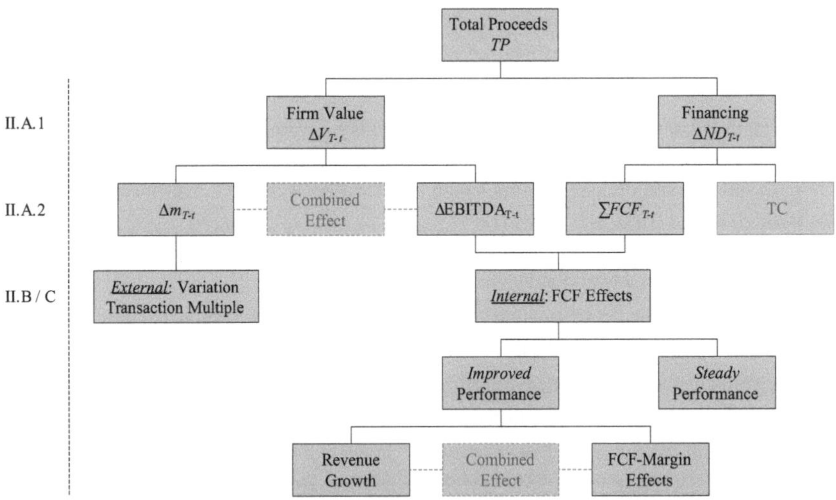

Source: Own illustration

Chart 5 summarizes the previously discussed decomposition of the LBO transaction model into its five identified components and the subsequent condensation into an internal as well as an external perspective as an appropriate two-tier framework for the remaining theoretical discussion and empirical analysis of this thesis.

---

[231] *Note:* The following chapters discuss, among other things, firm characteristics as indicators for the potential to improve the firm's operational performance during the holding period.

The following two chapters therefore adopt the two-tier framework of an internal (III.B) and an external (III.C) perspective for the purpose of analyzing sources of value creation in LBO transactions from an equity investor perspective.

B. Internal Perspective: FCF Effects

The previous chapter identified five non-mutually exclusive components of value creation in LBOs, which were then classified according to an internal perspective *FCF effects* and an external perspective *variation in the transaction multiple.* Internal, firm-specific effects of a LBO materialize in a variation of *FCF*, which then according to the presented transaction model affects at first and directly the components *Earnings Variation*, *Combined Earnings/Multiple Effect* and *Cumulated FCF Generation* over the course of the holding period of the investment.[232]

For the purpose of this thesis the brief discussion of sources of value creation with respect to the internal, *FCF effects* perspective shall be three-fold: first, based on relevant agency theoretical aspects the impact of reduced agency costs on *FCF effects* as a source of value creation is discussed in chapter III.B.1. Second, the impact of the (group of) financial sponsor(s) on operating performance improvements and the firm's strategy beyond the monitoring and control function are subsumed under *Management Support* and considered in chapter III.B.2. Third, for the purpose of completeness wealth transfer aspects in LBO investments are briefly discussed in chapter III.B.3.

1. Principal-Agent Theoretical Considerations

From the various theoretical approaches presented in chapter I.A.1, principal agent theory is most frequently applied to analyze internal, firm-specific value creation effects of LBOs. Applying principal-agent theoretical considerations for the internal perspective of the presented two-tier framework is well suited to the understanding of the principal agent theory as the theory of internal relationships of an institution.[233] In the mid to late 80s emerging literature on principal agent theory served well to justify the increasingly intense LBO activity. *Premia-Paid* and *Operational Performance Studies* mostly apply the argumentation of reduced agency costs to not only motivate the observed large acquisition premia in presumably non-strategic transactions but also explain the reported (abnormally) positive variations in accounting measures respectively.[234]

---

232 See chapter IV.B.2.1 for a discussion of potential interdependencies between the internal and the external perspective.

233 See Picot, A., et al. (2001), p. 57.

234 See chapters I.A.2.1 and I.A.2.2.

Before means of reducing agency costs in a LBO setting are presented in chapter III.B.1.2 a brief formal clarification of agency costs is beneficial.

1.1 A Clarification of Agency Costs

1.1.1 A Basic Model of Moral Hazard

The following basic model to elucidate agency costs resulting from the separation of ownership and control, based on Jensen/Meckling (1976), is highly suitable for the LBO context of this thesis.[235]

Consider an owner-manager controlled company that attracts the investment of outside equity investors. While such an outside investor is purely financially motivated, the utility of the owner-manager is determined through a combination of the maximization of firm value and the consumption of non-pecuniary benefits (henceforth *b*). Non-pecuniary benefits might comprise for instance perk consumption (such as physical appointments in the form of office space and office art) or the cultivation of personal relationships. On the one hand, being fractionally interested in the company the investor side of the owner-manager benefits from the maximization of firm value. On the other hand, the manager side of the owner-manager is inclined to consume non-pecuniary benefits, as the corresponding costs in the form of the reduction in firm value are borne only pro-rata.

The effects of such utility maximizing behavior on the part of the owner-manager are illustrated in Chart 6.

235 For the following analysis see Jensen, M. C./Meckling, W. (1976), in particular pp. 312-330.

Chart 6 Firm Value with Outside Equity Investment

The vertical axis depicts the entity value of the firm V; the horizontal axis depicts the amount of non-pecuniary benefits b consumed by the owner-manager; U_1, U_2 and U_3 represent the owner-manager's indifference curves between wealth (fractional firm ownership) and the consumption of non-pecuniary benefits; P_1 and P_2 represent the owner-manager substitution line

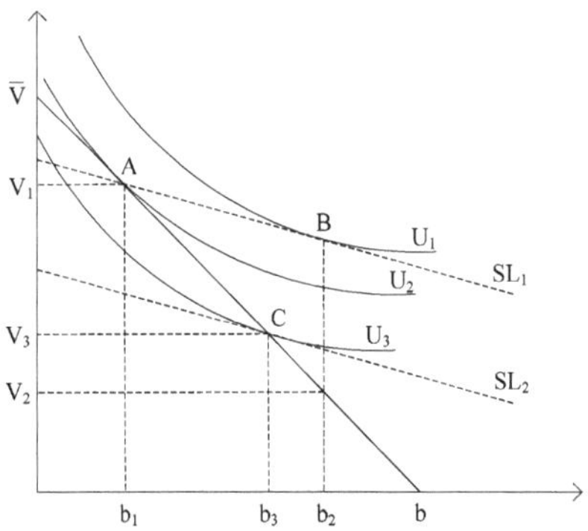

Source: Jensen/Meckling (1976), p. 316

The above outlined owner-manager budget constraint is displayed in Chart 6 alongside the line $\overline{V}b$. Assuming no consumption of non-pecuniary benefits, firm value equals $\overline{V}$; otherwise the value is linearly decreasing with *b*.[236] As the effects are exactly offsetting, the corresponding slope of the substitution line $\overline{V}b$, which depicts all feasible combinations of *V* and *b*, equals –1. The set of indifference curves U_1, U_2 and U_3 represents for different levels of owner-manager utility the feasible combinations of wealth and the consumption of perquisites that result in the owner-manager being equaled off. $\frac{\partial^2 U}{\partial^2 b} \geq 0$ and $\frac{\partial^2 U}{\partial^2 V} \geq 0$ determine the convex shape of the utility functions and indicate the positive though decreasing marginal utility for both wealth and non-pecuniary benefits. In the absence of any outside equity investors the maximization of owner-manager's utility results as the tangential intersection point *A* between the substitution line and the highest possible utility curve (U_2 in Chart 6). Accordingly, the corresponding Pareto efficient firm value V_1 results as the maximum firm value $\overline{V}$, less the amount of consumed non-pecuniary benefits b_1 according to the owner-manager's sole preferences.

This outcome changes when the owner-manager decides to sell the fraction $(1-\alpha)$ to an outside equity investor. Ceteris paribus (i.e. assuming at first identical levels of b_1) such outside investor will be willing to pay up to $(1-\alpha)V_1$ for this stake. However, following the

---

[236] *Note:* The presented analysis by Jensen, M. C./Meckling, W. (1976) assumes certain values for the firm as well as for the non-pecuniary benefits. This assumption can be relaxed however without loss of generality.

disposal of $(1-\alpha)$, $\overline{V}b$ no longer represents the adequate substitution line for the owner-manager. Costs arising from the consumption of non-pecuniary benefits are then partially borne by the outside investor; the owner-manager's substitution line is therefore illustrated by the line SL_1 with the slope equal to the negative of the retained ownership stake α.[237] In such a scenario though, point *A* no longer represents the utility maximizing combination of wealth and perquisites for the owner-manager as can easily be seen in Chart 6. The maximum now results as the tangency point *B* between the (modified) substitution line SL_1 and the highest possible indifference curve U_1. Following the involvement of the outside investor (starting from point *A*), the owner-manager would increase the consumption of non-pecuniary benefits to the level of b_2 as the corresponding wealth losses are partially borne by the outside investors; firm value then drops to V_2. In efficient capital markets outside equity investors will apparently anticipate such behavior by the owner-manager; i.e. the increased consumption of perquisites. Hence point *B* can clearly not represent an equilibrium situation. Given b_2, a rational outside equity investor would obviously at first be willing to pay no more than $(1-\alpha)V_2$ for his stake as his substitution line remains $\overline{V}b$. With a purchase price of $(1-\alpha)V_2$ manager-owner's level of utility apparently drops significantly and the outcome would no longer be utility maximizing from his point of view. Hence for a Pareto efficient equilibrium to establish the conjoint utility maximization has to be considered. Such equilibrium situation results where the tangential point of the manager-owner's substitution line and the corresponding indifference curve intersect the outside equity investor's substitution line $\overline{V}b$; point *C* in Chart 6. Pareto efficiency implies that the situation of no one party can be improved without harming the other party involved. The corresponding reduction in firm value is an indicator for the residual loss and is referred to by Jensen (1989b) as the *gross agency costs.*[238]

In the above framework the concept of monitoring and bonding activities can now be illustrated. Monitoring on behalf of the outside equity investors imposes restrictions on the consumption of perquisites by the owner-manager but triggers costs in the amount of *X*. Accordingly, firm value is now given by $V=\overline{V}-b(X,\alpha)-X$, implying that the substitution line (*SL*) from the perspective of the outside equity investors changes and is no longer given by $\overline{V}b$. Assuming positive though marginally decreasing benefits of monitoring (i.e. similar absolute reductions in the consumption of perquisites *b* by the manager-owner requires

237 *Note:* Taking into consideration that at point *A* the owner-manager has to be equaled off between remaining the 100% owner and selling partially to an outside investor implies that the substitution line P_1 necessarily crosses through point *A*.

238 See Jensen, M. C./Meckling, W. (1976), p. 319. Apparently the welfare loss to the manager-owner is less than V_1-V_3 times his fractional holding given the increase in the consumption of non-pecuniary benefits in the magnitude of b_3-b_1.

increasing monitoring efforts), the new substitution line for the outside equity investor SL^*_{EI} is convexly shaped as illustrated in Chart 7.

Chart 7 Firm Value and Control Mechanisms

The vertical axis depicts the entity value of the firm V; the horizontal axis depicts the amount of non-pecuniary benefits b consumed by the owner-manager

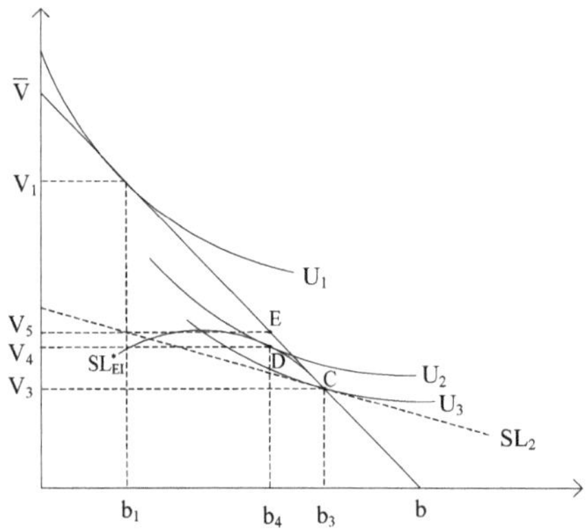

Source: Jensen/Meckling (1976), p. 324

The Pareto optimum results again through conjoint utility maximization; i.e. in the form of the tangency point *D* between the higher manager-owner's indifference curve U_4 and the outside equity investor's substitution line SL^*_{EI}. The induced reduction in *b* causes firm value to increase from V_3 to V_4. In the absence of any monitoring expenses of *X*, the corresponding firm value for the given level of b_4 would be V_5. As, however, point *E* does not represent an optimum from the manager-owner's perspective, a rational outside investor would have to expect the manager-owner to increase the consumption of *b*. Hence, *DE*, the vertical difference between $\overline{V}b$ and SL^*_{EI}, represents the amount of monitoring expenses *X*. Should activities on behalf of the manager-owner to signal self-imposed restrictions with respect to the consumption of non-pecuniary benefits (*bonding expenditures*) yield exactly the same trade-off for the manager-owner between wealth and perquisites, the substitution line for the outside investor and hence the above detailed results would be identical.

1.1.2 Basic Forms of Moral Hazard

Four different basic forms of moral hazard can be distinguished:[239] (i) insufficient managerial efforts, (ii) perk consumption, (iii) the risk incentive problem and (iv) the underinvestment problem.

The Effort Problem

Prior to the LBO transaction the problem of divergent managerial behavior through insufficient effort is particularly serious. Without appropriate incentivation managerial efforts to maximize shareholder wealth are obviously limited. Creative activities to explore new profitable ventures might be reduced and the motivation to rigorously pursue restructuring initiatives with the objective of increasing the operating profitability might be insufficient.[240] This problem prevails with outside equity investors and equity incentivized management. Given that benefits and returns have to be shared but efforts (such as in the form of less leisure) are entirely borne by management, marginal efforts are weighted against marginal benefits from value increase.[241] Formally, this trade-off can easily be shown.[242] Accordingly, equity-incentivized management's effort level decreases in the holding of outside equity investors.

Perk Consumption

The consumption of non-pecuniary benefits (such as luxurious company cars and office furniture) on behalf of the agent is referred to as perk consumption.[243] This classic example of agency costs in the context of a principal–agent relationship has been discussed in chapter III.B.1.1.1 and graphically illustrated in Chart 6. Perk consumption further comprises any investment that strengthens management's own position; also referred to as *management entrenchments*.[244] Since perk consumption requires excessive cash flows in the company, their existence and their reduction as a source of value in LBO transactions is frequently referred to as *Jensen's Free Cash Flow hypothesis*.[245] Accordingly, the "*problem is how to motivate managers to disgorge the cash rather than investing it below the cost of capital or wasting it*

---

239 See e.g. Kürsten, W. (1995), p. 230f and Schulz, E. (2000), p. 56 based on Jensen, M. C./Meckling, W. (1976) and Harris, M./Raviv, A. (1991).

240 See Jensen, M. C./Meckling, W. (1976), p. 313 and Baker, G. P., et al. (1988), p. 614.

241 See e.g. Schulz, E. (2000), pp. 57f.

242 See Kürsten, W. (1995), pp. 247f and Schulz, E. (2000), p. 57.

243 See Jensen, M. C./Meckling, W. (1976), p. 312.

244 See also Shleifer, A./Vishny, R. (1989), pp. 123-139. Personal motives of the manager potentially dominate investment decisions, which however, are not necessarily value destroying.

245 See Jensen, M. C. (1986), pp. 323-329. Note that Jensen defines free cash flow as operating cash flow less the amount of cash invested in positive NPV projects when discounted at the relevant cost of capital, and thus differs from the definition provided in chapter II.B in the form that only positive NPV projects are considered. Apart from the discussion here this thesis applies the previously introduced definition.

on organizational inefficiencies."[246] In case of managers' rewards being correlated more with the size than the market value of the company, management would be falsely encouraged to invest in potentially NPV negative projects purely for the sake of expansion and diversification regardless of market value implications.[247] Analytically, the obvious and graphical finding that the incentive for consuming non-pecuniary benefits is higher, the higher the outside equity investors' stake in the company, can be confirmed.[248]

The Risk Incentive Problem

Whereas the effort problem and perk consumption are considered agency costs in the context of outside equity financing, the risk incentive problem as well as the subsequently detailed underinvestment problem arise (predominantly) in the context of debt financing.

The risk incentive problem arises when management bases its financing and investment decisions on individual risk and reward preferences.[249] Accordingly, the risk incentive problem can have two forms. On the one hand, lacking appropriate incentive schemes prior to the LBO transaction, management is argued to be risk averse and therefore would tend to invest in less volatile projects.[250] On the other hand, following the LBO transaction and management's participation as equity investors, the leverage through outside equity as well as debt financing might incline management to undertake riskier projects.[251] The higher this leverage, the larger is the incentive for equity owners to undergo investment projects with higher variances as their appetite for risk increases. As illustrated in chapter II.B.2.1 residual equity claims have a call option character with the strike price equal to the nominal debt value and maturity equal to the duration of the debt. As the value of an option increases with variance, equityholders (and in particular management) might be inclined to invest in riskier, more volatile projects.[252] Rational debt investors apparently anticipate such opportunistic behavior on behalf of the equity owners and adjust their lending decision accordingly.[253]

---

246 See Jensen, M. C. (1986), p. 323. Agency costs are argued to be particularly high for companies with high levels of free cash flow in combination with few growth opportunities.

247 See e.g. Baker, G. P., et al. (1988), p. 609, Jensen, M. C./Murphy, K. (1990a), pp. 138ff and Liebeskind, J. P., et al. (1992), pp. 73ff.

248 See Kürsten, W. (1995), p. 244.

249 See e.g Jost, P. J. (1998), p. 289.

250 See e.g. Eisenhardt, K. M. (1989), p. 59.

251 See e.g. Stiglitz, J. E./Weiss, A. (1981), pp. 393ff. See also footnote [33].

252 This line of reasoning even implies that management equity investors might pursue investment opportunities with lower expected value but higher variances.

253 See Jensen, M. C./Meckling, W. (1976), pp. 334ff.

The Underinvestment Problem

A further serious incentive effect of financial liabilities on managerial decision making is based upon Myers (1977) and generally referred to as the *underinvestment* problem.[254] Consider a firm that applies a mix of debt and equity financing for the realization of an investment opportunity, whereby debt provisions are not earmarked, thus implying a discretionary power and flexibility for the owner-manager regarding the chosen level of investment, depending on the individual equity contribution. Since all proceeds from the investment flow to debtholders until a certain hurdle rate (based upon the fixed claim of debt financing) is reached, the incentive for equity investors to invest is reduced. Any additional investment would only benefit the debtholders in that the default probability is reduced at their benefit. As a consequence the actual level of investment can be lower for a partially debt-financed company compared with an unlevered firm.[255]

The preceding discussion of agency costs represents the classic understanding of basic forms of moral hazard and their mitigation. From an integrated perspective, this seems too simplistic, however.[256] In a broader sense agency costs comprise any such costs arising from asymmetric information.[257] The purpose of the subsequent chapter regarding means to reduce agency costs in the LBO governance structure is the identification of sources for value creation in LBO investments from an internal perspective. Given this purpose and the post-investment internal perspective, the presented understanding of agency costs seems fully appropriate. Further potential information asymmetries between management and outside equity investors at entry receive little support empirically. Lehn/Poulsen (1989) find that many public-to-private transactions are preceded by takeover rumors or competing bids and consider this finding to be inconsistent with the asymmetric information argument.[258] Deangelo (1986) presents evidence contradicting the hypothesis that management systematically understated earnings prior to the buyout.[259] Findings by Kaplan (1989a) even suggest that management tends to overstate earnings forecasts in proxy statements associated with buyout proposals.[260] Lee (1992) analyzes a sample of withdrawn buyout proposals and finds subsequent to the withdrawal no significant positive stock price performance.[261] The author interprets this

---

254 See Myers, S. C. (1977), pp. 147-175.

255 An analytical solution to the underinvestment problem can easily be shown and is among others provided by Kürsten, W. (1994), pp. 242ff and Schulz, E. (2000), pp. 62ff.

256 See Duffner, S. (2005), pp. 115ff

257 See. e.g. Hartmann-Wendels, T., et al. (1998), p. 99.

258 See Lehn, K./Poulsen, A. (1989), pp. 771ff.

259 See Deangelo, L. E. (1986), pp. 400ff.

260 See Kaplan, S. N. (1989a), pp. 247ff

261 See Lee, D. S. (1992), pp. 1061ff.

circumstance as an evidence against the argument that favorable inside information motivates a buyout proposal. The impact of potential information asymmetries between sellers and acquirers will however be further considered when detailing sources of value creation from an external perspective in chapter III.C.

Jensen/Meckling (1976) mention two further straightforward reasons, implying why (despite previously detailed agency costs of equity) ideally a corporation is not exclusively financed with financial liabilities: first, higher levels of debt increase the risk of bankruptcy and given this higher default probability costs of debt financing increase through the inclusion of a risk premium. This in fact in combination with the tax shield associated with debt financing led Modigliani/Miller (1963) to correct their famous irrelevance of financing theorem. Second, considering bondholders – like outside equity investors – as principals, the resulting principal–agent relationship is similarly characterized by monitoring and bonding expenses that ceteris paribus increase the costs of debt financing.[262]

1.2 Reducing Agency Costs in a LBO Governance Structure

As agency costs are not exogenous to the firm but can be influenced through changes in the ownership and governance structure LBOs are argued to reduce agency costs and thus create value.[263] In this light the LBO transaction model and corresponding governance structure as a means of reducing agency conflicts and resulting costs arising from the separation of ownership and control has been discussed extensively in the academic literature.[264] For the purpose here, the brief review to what extent LBO transactions offer the opportunity to change the governance structure, tackle the agency problem and thus reduce agency costs is three-fold; (i) the alignment of interest according to the *Incentive-Intensity Hypothesis*, (ii) the disciplining role of financial debt, and (iii) improved monitoring and controlling. A formal model on the reduction of agency costs by Garvey (1992) completes the analysis.

Managerial Ownership and the Incentive-Intensity Hypothesis

As illustrated, discrepancies between agent's and principal's individual utility maximization cause agency costs. According to the *Incentive-Intensity Hypothesis* any measure that intends to align the interests of the manager aims at reducing agency costs.[265] Equity participation from

262 See Jensen, M. C./Meckling, W. (1976), pp. 333ff

263 See Jensen, M. C. (1986), pp. 323ff. Note that for the purpose of this thesis to analyze value creation on investment level only first-level agency problems are considered. Given the structure of a buyout association as limited partnership, second-level agency issues obviously exist between the LP as principal and the GP as the agent. For a detailed discussion of related agency issues see e.g. Duffner, S. (2005).

264 See e.g. Schmid, H. (1994), pp. 194ff, Kessel, A. (1995), pp.25-78 and pp. 112-125, Hatzig, C. (1995), pp. 141ff and pp. 304ff and Then Bergh, F. (1998), pp. 91-211.

265 See e.g. Jensen, M. C. (1989b), pp. 61ff and Liebeskind, J. P., et al. (1992), pp. 73ff. Implicitly the *Incentive Intensity Hypothesis* thus assumes that prior to the LBO, managers might be falsely incentivized. Rather

own sources provides incentives in that it ties managerial decision making to own wealth effects and aligns interests with the owner more effectively than performance-based compensation.[266] Among others the LBO transaction model with a finite investment horizon, offers ownership incentivized managers the opportunity to fully cash-out or partially liquidize their investment in good time. In privately held, but non-LBO companies, this opportunity might be restricted owing the illiquidity of the equity. The action of committing own funds represents a more credible signal against any form of non-shareholder wealth maximizing behavior than any words.[267] Equity participation not only encourages management to undergo equity value increasing restructuring initiatives and pursue venture opportunities in core segments more rigorously but also refrains management from value destructive actions.[268] Regarding the consumption of perquisites, an incentivized management weighs the benefits of these perquisites against the corresponding reduction of its own equity stake in the firm as detailed in chapter III.B.1.1 and Chart 6.[269] Accordingly, this co-owner equity investor status is argued to lead into improved operating and investment decisions and hence translate into improved operating performance.[270] Note further that interest alignment through managerial ownership not only addresses the agency costs of equity but also those of debt. Following the argumentation of Jensen/Meckling (1976), management's incentive to invest in high variance projects decreases the higher the personal stake at risk.[271] Direct equity participation obviously represents only one means of aligning management's interest. Other measures might include sanctions, collateralized investments or quasi-equity financing instruments with optional character such as convertible debt.

Further, the *Incentive-Intensity Hypothesis* not only concerns equity participation of top management. Following the LBO, employee share ownership schemes and contracts (or at least performance-based compensation schemes) are generally introduced for a large number of employees, which then comprise interest-aligning, motivational evaluation and compensation patterns.[272]

---

than focusing on shareholders' wealth, managers might be more concerned with expanding and diversifying their business and focusing on personal rewards and status associated with the fact of an acquisition itself or the sheer size of the business.

266 See e.g. Deangelo, H./Deangelo, L. E. (1987), pp. 38ff, and Lichtenberg, F./Siegel, D. S. (1990), pp. 165ff.

267 See Leland, H. E./Pyle, D. H. (1977), p. 371

268 See e.g. Jensen, M. C./Meckling, W. (1976), pp. 305ff, Deangelo, H., et al. (1984), pp. 367ff, Hite, G. L./Vetsuypens, M. R. (1989), pp. 953ff and Smith, A. J. (1990a), 143ff.

269 See e.g. Duffner, S. (2005), pp. 146ff.

270 See e.g. Deangelo, H./Deangelo, L. E. (1987), pp. 38ff, and Easterwood, J. C., et al. (1989), pp. 30ff.

271 See Jensen, M. C./Meckling, W. (1976), pp. 334ff.

272 See e.g. Baker, G. P./Wruck, K. H. (1989), pp. 163ff and Muscarella, C. J./Vetsuypens, M. R. (1990), pp. 1389ff.

However, this line of reasoning is closely tied to the fact that effects of managerial ownership are not necessarily unanimously positive. The fact that management's equity participation generally represents a substantial part of its personnel wealth might have counter-productive effects. Assuming that managerial risk aversion increases with the amount of personnel wealth committed to the transaction the beneficial effects from (and thus optimal level of) up-front cash contribution seem to be capped. As pointed out, excessive risk aversion potentially harms the operating and investing decisions and thus the financial performance of the bought-out company.[273]

The brief illustration of basic forms of moral hazard implied that agency costs prevail with equity-incentivized management. Accordingly further non-monetary aspects need to be considered to align management's interest with the entirety of equity investors. For instance the pure participation in the LBO transaction and the entrepreneurial spirit accompanying the LBO might be stimulating and thus favor the alignment of interests and hence potentially entail operational performance improvements.[274]

Disciplining Role of Financial Debt

In order to reduce the amount of cash at its own discretion, management has to be forced to distribute the excess cash flow. Therefore, a principal means of reducing agency costs is swapping unspecified equity payment obligations for fixed debt-servicing payment obligations, by substituting equity with debt.[275] Given the firm's capital structure, distribution of excess cash flow is a combination of cash streams to the debt and equity investors according to the respective claims. In the case of a public corporation, equity cash streams can be either in the form of dividend payments or share repurchase programs, both of which are reversible by the management and thus signal little credibility regarding the distribution of excess cash flow. In the case of debt service obligations however, interest costs as well as debt repayment schedules are non- or little negotiable to management and represent a lasting cash outflow for the company. Since penalties for defaulting on debt service are more severe than penalties for reducing dividend payments "*the heavy debt burden forces managers to efficiently run the company to avoid default*"[276]. In this respect differences of debt and equity financing are

273 See e.g. Fama, E. F./Jensen, M. C. (1985), pp. 101ff, Morck, R., et al. (1988), pp. 293ff and Holthausen, R. W./Larcker, D. F. (1996), p. 295.

274 See e.g. Mittendorfer, R. (2001), p. 149. See forthcoming chapter III.B.2.1 for further details regarding the impact of the LBO organizational form.

275 See e.g. Vermaelen, T. (1981), pp. 139ff, Grossman, S. J./Hart, O. (1982), pp. 107ff and Jensen, M. C. (1986), pp. 323ff. as well #as Heinkel, R./Zechner, J. (1990) for a related formal theoretical model.

276 See Cotter, J. F./Peck, S. W. (2001), p. 102. Thompson, S., et al. (1992a) argues that management's motivation to safeguard its position arises not only from its equity stake at risk but also from its human capital locked into the corporation.

described by Stewart/Glassman (1988) as "[*e*]*quity is soft, debt hard. Equity is forgiving, debt insistent. Equity is a pillow, debt a sword.*"[277] As a consequence, the pre-commitment of corporate cash to service debt serves more compellingly as a disciplinary tool to force management to pay out excess cash flow to the firm's securityholders.[278]

The outlined benefits represent, however, only one side of the coin. Financial liabilities also trigger agency costs as previously discussed, implying that for the optimal debt level benefits have to be weighted against increasing costs.

In this context critics frequently argue that a focus on present profitability and the optimization of short-term operating cash flow to repay financial liabilities might come at the expense of long-term success and opportunities.[279] Commonly brought forward arguments are, among others, reduced maintenance capital expenditures as well as down-scaled expenditures for expansion and new projects which potentially weaken and threaten the firm's long-term competitive positioning and going concern. In particular for growth companies the heavy debt burden and associated debt service payment obligations could be restrictive. On the other hand however, it could be argued, that leverage is a function of expected revenue growth (rather than vice versa) as practitioners argue that firms with little growth prospects merit higher gearing ratios.

Improved Monitoring and Controlling

Improved monitoring and controlling through the presence of a majority equity investor constitutes a third mean to overcome or at least reduce principal agent conflicts between the management and equity investors in the course of a LBO transaction.[280] Prior to a LBO transaction, corporate governance systems are frequently characterized by control and monitoring deficiencies with respect to the objective function of shareholder value maximization. In practice a variety of internal as well as external corporate governance mechanisms are in place, which, however, only serve partially to counteract potential divergent agent behavior. External control mechanisms comprise the competition in product[281] and

---

277 See Stewart, B. G. I./Glassman, D. M. (1988), p. 82. According to a study by Gilson, S. C. (1989) managers of public corporations that come into financial distress are laid off in 52% of the cases and don't find employment with another publicly listed corporation for the consecutive three years.

278 See Lehn, K./Poulsen, A. (1989), p. 773. Phrased differently "*debt is a powerful agent for change.*" Jensen, M. C. (1989b), p. 67.

279 See e.g. Lei, D./Hitt, M. A. (1995), pp. 835ff.

280 See Jensen, M. C./Meckling, W. (1976), pp. 323ff, Shleifer, A./Vishny, R. (1986), pp. 461ff, Jensen, M. C. (1989a), pp. 35ff, Hellmann, T. F. (1994), pp. 1ff and Shleifer, A./Vishny, R. (1997b), pp. 737ff.

281 See e.g. Hart, O. (1983), 381f and Jensen, M. C./Murphy, K. (1990b), p. 252f. Accordingly competition in product markets can discipline management as firm's focusing less on shareholder value orientation are argued to have lower prospects.

labor[282] markets as well as the threat of hostile takeovers.[283] Internal control mechanisms include the supervisory board[284] as well as the controlling activities through individual shareholders.

However, external control mechanisms represent only insufficient means to trim down the above outlined forms of moral hazard between management and equity investors, and internal control mechanisms, in particular, have substantial shortcomings. First, members of the supervisory board potentially limit their control activities to a minimum in order to avoid financial distress of the company as effective control comes along with costs and efforts.[285] Second, in the case of dispersed ownership, small shareholders generally have only weak monitoring and controlling incentives given their little wealth at stake; the free rider problem prevents equity investors from scarifying resources and efforts to closely control and monitor the agent as soon as the costs associated with the controlling efforts exceed the fractional realizable increase in value.[286]

The LBO governance structure with a majority equity investor and a resulting emphasis on shareholder value maximization (partially) overcomes some of these shortcomings. The equity value objective function results hereby not only from the expected return on the committed funds but also from reputational considerations.[287] Accordingly, more effective monitoring and control of management due to the involvement of an *active investor* reduces divergent agent behavior such as insufficient efforts and the excessive consumption of perquisites. In this context Fama/Jensen (1983) argue that governance structures of LBOs effectively "*separate the ratification and monitoring of decisions from the initiation and implementation of the decisions.*"[288] According to Jensen (1989a) an active investor "*monitors management, sits on boards, is sometimes involved in dismissing management, is often intimately involved in the strategic direction of the company, and on occasion even manages.*"[289] Active board representations not only ease potential information asymmetries between management and investors but also offer investors the opportunity to continuously assess and control

282 See e.g. Fama, E. F. (1980), pp. 304ff and Shleifer, A./Vishny, R. (1997b), p. 738.

283 See e.g. Schafstein, D. (1988), pp. 185ff. Accordingly, the threat of a hostile takeover through raiders with private information can have a disciplining effect on managerial behavior.

284 See e.g. Fama, E. F./Jensen, M. C. (1983), pp. 322f.

285 See e.g. Coffee, J. C. J., et al. (1988), p. 86 and Baker, G. P., et al. (1988), p. 614.

286 See e.g. Furubotn, E. G./Pejovitch, S. (1972), p. 1149 and Shleifer, A./Vishny, R. (1986), pp. 463f.

287 See Jensen, M. C. (1989b), p. 65 and Shleifer, A./Vishny, R. (1997b), p. 754 and 764.

288 See Fama, E. F./Jensen, M. C. (1983), p. 301.

289 See Jensen, M. C. (1989a), p. 36.

management performance.[290] Following the LBO, supervisory boards are found to be smaller and more effective.[291]

For the special case of going private transactions, a further source of value creation is argued to be reduced spending in combination with the change from public to private ownership. Potential reductions include, but are not limited to, registration expenses, listing fees and other stockholder servicing costs such as costs for annual general meetings, which in their entirety Deangelo et al. (1984) refer to as "*real resource gains*".[292] Further, Andres et al. (2004) argue that costs (or losses of revenue) resulting from disclosure requirements potentially increase regulatory constraints or weaken the firm's competitive positions, and thus represent indirect costs from being publicly listed.[293] However, with respect to this particular source of value in LBO transactions, tests on the present value of associated savings from being privately held conducted by Travlos/Cornett (1993) for the US market could not explain shareholder gains in public-to-private transactions.[294]

A Formal Model on the Reduction of Agency Costs

Based on the seminal article by Myers (1977) that examines the underinvestment problem of debt for a given capital structure, several contributions vigorously analyze the signaling effects of financial debt.[295] In particular, in the broader context of the optimal capital structure discussion, the question regarding the optimal choice between debt and equity for the financing of an investment opportunity and asymmetric information regarding its quality is thereby addressed. By contrast, the following analysis aims at addressing the above outlined agency conflict based on Jensen (1986) in that the control mechanisms of financial liabilities counteract the managerial discretionary leeway through the pre-commitment of generated cash. Accordingly, suiting the context of this thesis of analyzing later stage LBO investment rather than start-up and seed venture capital investments, the perspective is rather on a mature firm with cash flows generated in excess of the amount needed for the financing of positive NPV projects. The question is hence how to motivate management to disgorge the cash rather than investing it in negative NPV projects. To put it another way, the effect of indebtedness on the mitigation of moral hazard rather than on adverse selection, should be addressed.

---

290 See e.g. Anders, G. (1992), pp. 79ff. and Palepu, K. G. (1990), p. 247.

291 See e.g. Cotter, J. F./Peck, S. W. (2001), p. 137.

292 See Deangelo, H., et al. (1984), p. 371.

293 See Andres, C., et al. (2004), p. 6.

294 See Travlos, N. G./Cornett, M. M. (1993), pp. 1-30.

295 See e.g. Myers, S. C./Majluf, N. S. (1984), pp. 187-221, Grammatikos, T., et al. (1988), pp. 227-335, Narayanan, M. (1988), pp. 39-51 and Heinkel, R./Zechner, J. (1990), pp. 3-24.

Garvey (1992) developed a model that illustrates how far management incentivation in the form of equity participation and third-party financial liabilities coincide in reducing agency costs in the outlined sense.[296] In accordance with the premise of a *mature* firm, and the presence of the described principal–agent conflict, the firm possesses an amount of internally generated (or through the issuance of debt in the amount *D* externally raised) cash in the amount of *X*. There are three possible means to deploy this cash. The firm might (i) invest the amount *I* into investment opportunities (such as expansion and acquisitions), (ii) keep a liquidity reserve *Liq* internally as cash on balance sheet (with apparently zero NPV), or (iii) distribute the remaining amount as dividends *Div*. Hence

(35) $X = I + Liq + Div$

An agency problem in the sense discussed in the previous chapter arises from tying managerial utility to *I*, i.e. *U(I)*. Accordingly, in the absence of any means to reduce potential divergent behaviour, shareholder value will not be maximized as negative NPV projects will be undertaken. The investment *I* yields an uncertain expected return $r_i + \varepsilon$ whereby ε is the random variable with mean zero indicating the uncertainty of the investment.[297] To establish the over-investment problem resulting from *U(I)* and in conflict with shareholder wealth maximization, rates of return on the investment are expected to be positive though marginally decreasing.

Apart from financial liabilities *D*, the model considers managerial shareholdings λ as well as the costs of financial distress (i.e. firm-specific human capital) to the management *B* as means to address the agency conflict.

The sequence of effects is in three stages. First, the level of managerial equity ownership λ and the level of *D* are set. In a next step management can choose the level of *I*, *Liq* and hence *Div*. Following the revelation of ε, investment proceeds are distributed to the equity- and debtholders in a third stage. Following the distribution of *Div* the firm will only be able to repay the assumed liabilities when the critical value $\hat{\varepsilon}$ equals at least $r_i + Liq + \hat{\varepsilon} = D$. Without the uncertainty of r_i, i.e. ε, incentivation through ownership would be sufficient to encourage management to decide ex-ante for an optimal *I'* such that $D = r_i^{'} + X - I$.[298] *Total Proceeds* to equity investors equal (i) the dividend *Div* plus – in case $r_i + \varepsilon > D - Liq$ – the excess return of

---

296 For the following based on Garvey, G. T. (1992), pp. 149-166.

297 *Note:* ε has a distribution and density function of F and *f* on the interval $[\varepsilon_l; \varepsilon_u]$. Ruling out diversification effects Garvey's model assumes for simplicity further that *f*(ε) is not a function of *I* and *Liq* and hence perfectly positively correlates with the market.

298 Further, to ensure that management's decision regarding *I* solely depends upon *U(I)*, let *Cash>I'* be assumed.

the investment over the amount required for repaying the part of financial liabilities D that is not covered by Liq. Hence

$$(36)\quad Div + \max[0, r_i + \varepsilon - (D - Liq)] = X - I - Liq + \max[0, r_i + \varepsilon + Liq - D]$$ [299]

When choosing Liq and I management apparently maximizes its total utility arising from (i) the fractional ownership in the firm, (ii) non-pecuniary benefits associated with the investment $U(I)$ and (iii) the personal costs of financial distress B weighted with the probability that the critical return $\hat{\varepsilon}$ is not realized and the firm hence defaults.

$$(37)\quad W = \lambda\left[\int_{\hat{\varepsilon}}^{\varepsilon^u} (r_i + \varepsilon + Liq - D) f(\varepsilon) d\varepsilon + X - I - Liq\right] - BF(\hat{\varepsilon}) + U(I)$$

Assuming that B, the personal cost of financial distress, is relatively low and hence management has on the one hand little incentive to keep liquidity reserves but on the other hand more incentives to either invest the capital or distribute it in the form of dividends, management's choice of liquidity reserves, Liq^* can be set to zero and equation (37) simplifies to

$$(38)\quad W = \lambda\left[\int_{\hat{\varepsilon}}^{\varepsilon^u} (r_i + \varepsilon - D) f(\varepsilon) d\varepsilon + X - I\right] - BF(\hat{\varepsilon}) + U(I)$$

Maximizing W through the setting of I^* implies $\partial W / \partial I = 0$

$$(39)\quad \lambda[r_i'(1 - F(\hat{\varepsilon})) - 1] + Br_i' f(\hat{\varepsilon}) + U'(I) = 0$$

Differentiating equation (39) with respect to λ confirms the well-known proposition that the level of I (and hence the level of pecuniary benefits in this model) decreases in managerial shareholding.

$$(40)\quad r_i'(1 - F(\hat{\varepsilon})) - 1 < 0$$

For equation (39) to hold, equation (40) needs to be negative, implying that a marginal increase in λ reduces the optimal level of I. Differentiating equation (40) with respect to D yields.

$$(41)\quad -R'(I) f(\hat{\varepsilon}) < 0$$

Given by definition positive values for r_i' and $f(\hat{\varepsilon})$ implies $-r_i' f(\hat{\varepsilon})$ to be negative. This indicates that the level of I decreases more rapidly, the higher the level of D.[300]

Hence apart from the fact that interest-bearing financial liabilities D reduce the amount of X through the corresponding fixed claims, D also coincides with managerial ownership in

---

299 Following similar considerations, proceeds to debtholders result as $min[D, r_i + \varepsilon + Liq]$.

300 See Garvey, G. T. (1992), p. 154.

reducing the deployment in potentially NPV negative projects that in the absence of these mechanisms are made only for management's own utility.

2. Management Support

The preceding chapter briefly elaborated on means aiming to reduce agency costs in an LBO governance structure. While active monitoring and control through the majority owner might be particularly pronounced and distinctive for an LBO setting, it might very well be argued that the means (i) managerial incentivation, and (ii) disciplinary role of debt could also be implemented in the absence of a LBO transaction. In light of this understanding the following chapter intends to first briefly highlight further peculiarities of an LBO as organizational form (chapter III.B.2.1) and based thereon touch upon further means to address value creation in LBOs from the financial sponsor's perspective (chapter III.B.2.2). Deviating from the previous assumption of a rather uninvolved and operationally as well as strategically detached outside equity investor, these efforts are subsumed under the expression *Management Support*. Related literature is predominately concerned with the earlier financing stage *VC* industry, emphasizing that hereby the operational and strategic involvement and guidance of the financial sponsor might be of higher relevance.[301] However, lacking formal, analytical theoretical models with respect to this operational and strategic impact, related studies are mostly descriptive in nature. According to Hellmann/Puri (2002), "*[a]n informal literature suggests that the role of venture capitalists extends beyond that of traditional financial intermediaries like banks, and that they play a broader role in the professionalization of the companies they finance*".[302]

2.1 The Impact of the PE Fund and the LBO Organizational Form

Fund Level with Direct Impact on the Investment Level

Given their role as buyout specialists[303], *PE* firms generally possess large networks from which they can source to add value to individual portfolio companies in a variety of means. Such networks potentially comprise (i) a pool of skilled (interim) managers capable of running a portfolio company, (ii) industry experts such as specialized business consultants or senior industry executives, as well as (iii) close relationships with professional service companies[304]. According to an analysis by Sapienza et al. (1996), *VC* companies consider their networking

301 See e.g. Sapienza, H. J., et al. (1996), pp. 439ff. Key contributions analyzing activities of the financial sponsor and the impact on value creation include Gorman, M. J./Sahlman, W. A. (1989), pp. 231-248, Macmillan, I. C., et al. (1989), pp. 27-47 and Sapienza, H. J., et al. (1996), pp. 439-469.

302 See Hellmann, T. F./Puri, M. (2002), p. 170.

303 See e.g. Baker, G. P./Montgomery, C. A. (1994), pp. 1-34

304 See e.g. Kraft, V. (2001b), pp. 256ff and Meier, D. (2005), p. 37.

roles as third most important, with the strategic involvement and the interpersonal role being ranked first and second.[305]

In this light, the question arises whether the level of experience of the *PE* firm positively affects *Management Support* and thus the performance of the bought-out company? Following the concept of learning through experience[306], more experienced *PE* firms have potentially better advisory capabilities, more expertise in executing deals and access to a larger and more valuable network. Baker/Montgomery (1994) argue that the execution of acquisitions represents the core competence of *PE* firms, a view favoring the learning-curve-effect based argumentation that experienced *PE* firms possess superior deal-making capabilities.[307] This alone does not necessarily imply a superior hands-on involvement of experienced *PE* firms. However, it might be argued that some financial sponsors provide better advice based on the experience of individual *PE* professionals. The experience of individual professionals is assumed to materialize in better performing investments.[308] In this context, Meier (2005), highlights the controversial effects of experience:[309] On the one hand, decision quality might increase due to an improved efficiency of the decision making process and the focus on key aspects of the decision.[310] On the other hand, however, experience might negatively affect decision making. Overconfidence and overestimation potentially result in detrimental effects on the level of experience.[311]

Investment Level

Apart from the governance structure that favors the reduction of agency costs, further inherent characteristics and peculiarities of the LBO organizational form indirectly stimulate value creation on investment level.

Due to the finite investment horizon of the LBO business model, LBO equity investors focus from day one on the future liquidation of the investment.[312] The clear shareholder value

---

305 See Sapienza, H. J., et al. (1996), pp. 439ff.

306 See Levitt, B./March, J. G. (1988), pp. 319ff.

307 See Baker, G. P./Montgomery, C. A. (1994), pp. 1-34. However, in the general acquisition context studies by Lubatkin, M. H. (1987) and Zollo, M./Gottschalg, O. (2004) fail to empirically support positive impact of execution experience on acquisition performance.

308 For a critical discussion of linking individual *PE* professional experience to *PE* fund experience see e.g. Meier, D. (2005), pp. 94f and p. 108.

309 See Meier, D. (2005), pp. 93ff.

310 See e.g. Chase, W. C./Simon, H. (1973), Choo, F./Trotman, K. T. (1991) and see Shepherd, D. A., et al. (2003), p. 383 for a recent overview of efficiency gains resulting from increasing experience.

311 See e.g. Oskamp, S. (1982) and Mahajan, J. (1992). See Shepherd, D. A., et al. (2003), pp. 383f for a recent overview of unfavorable effects resulting from more experience.

312 See e.g. Berglöf, E. (1994), pp. 247-267 for a control model between inside and outside equity investors based upon the incentive to exit.

maximization objective function unmistakably puts the emphasis on firm performance and the realization of agreed performance targets. This common goal and end in view, not only further aligns interests and efforts but also fosters the entrepreneurial spirit and the motivation of all parties involved.[313] Such good humor and positive atmosphere is by times referred to as *LBO fever*.[314]

Further, Phan/Hill (1995) argue that the LBO organizational form is characterized by (i) increased decentralization and (ii) reduced hierarchical complexity, both of which offer substantial room for efficiency gains and thus contribute indirectly to value creation in LBOs.[315] Increased decentralization not only comes along with beneficial motivational effects through the encouragement of personal responsibility but also should cause more effective decision making and might be seen as a strategy for tightening control within an organization.[316] Less hierarchical complexity resulting from streamlined operations and the emphasis on performance is expected to increase the organizational and bureaucratic efficiency.[317]

2.2 Means of Equity Investor's Operational and Strategic Involvement

Operational involvement

The formal clarification of agency costs in chapter III.B.1.1 assumes uninvolved and uninformed outside equity investors with pure financial interest. However, the preceding chapter on the LBO organizational form suggests that financial sponsors do have various means for intervening operationally beyond their role of active monitoring and control. A portfolio company might benefit from the aforementioned network aspect of *PE* firms directly in the form of (i) a new management, (ii) knowledge transfer, or indirectly through (iii) superior negotiation capabilities.

The management team is evidently crucial to the success of any LBO investment. Evans/Bishop (2001) argue that an unskilled management team causes a company's idiosyncratic risk to rise.[318] Accordingly, management not only affects the valuation through growth and profitability improvements of expected future cash flows but also through the

---

313 See e.g. Houlden, B. (1990), pp. 73-77. Samdani, S. G., et al. (2001), p. 100 point out that whereas in larger corporations extra effort is generally little rewarded (in particular as the value of stock option schemes, phantom shares or similar devices are subject to numerous forces outside the control of an individual), in an LBO setting extra efforts that are timely translate into cash at exit.

314 See e.g. Samdani, S. G., et al. (2001), p. 101.

315 See Phan, P. H./Hill, C. W. L. (1995), pp. 711ff. In this respect Easterwood, J. C., et al. (1989), 41 concretizes arguing that while operating decisions are decentralized, strategic decisions are centralized.

316 See Child, J. (1984).

317 See Phan, P. H./Hill, C. W. L. (1995), p. 713.

318 See Evans, F. C./Bishop, D. M. (2001), pp. 129-130.

uncertainty of their realization. Further, according to Manne (1965) and Jensen/Ruback (1983) and their theory on the market for corporate control in the context of mergers and takeovers, management competes for control over corporations.[319] Following the acquisition of a portfolio company, management is generally reviewed and the financial sponsor is potentially required to replace or complement the team in place.[320] Accordingly, a *PE* firm that commands a network of skilled (interim) managers (based on industry expertise, personal relationships and/or the experience of past investments), potentially enjoys a competitive advantage over competing *PE* firms in winning and successfully realizing an investment.[321] Also, in addition to frequent non-executive board representation(s) as a means of monitoring and controlling, *PE* firms sometimes send out their own professionals into portfolio companies assuming day-to-day operational responsibilities as part of the management team.[322] Following an LBO, the *PE* firm potentially also changes to the accountant of its choice for a variety of reasons.[323] Operational impact of the *PE* firm might further result in the form of knowledge transfers from other portfolio companies. Although, individual investments are generally operated completely independently, positive spill-over effects from exchanges of experience with respect to restructuring or growth initiatives are conceivable. Indirectly, benefits potentially accrue through superior negotiation capabilities of the *PE* company whether, for example, in the context of negotiating financing terms and conditions of follow-on funds or sale and purchase agreements when divesting or acquiring operations.

Strategic Involvement

Compared with the operational impact of LBOs and the corresponding analysis of variation in operational performance, strategic aspects of LBOs and in particular the impact of equity investors has received comparably little attention in the academic literature; both theoretically

319 See Manne, H. G. (1965), pp. 110ff and Jensen, M. C./Ruback, R. S. (1983), pp. 5ff.

320 See e.g. Shleifer, A./Vishny, R. (1986), p. 473, Sapienza, H. J. (1992), p. 13 and Hellmann, T. F. (1998), p. 58. In this context Lerner, J. (1994b) considers the change in top management as an indication of a need for more intense monitoring. See Lerner, J. (1994b) cited in Barry, C. B. (1994), p. 6.

321 Paisner, G. (2005), p. 2 cites Michael Smith, the chairman of CVC Capital Partners, "*Halfords, Debenhams, Kwik-Fit and the AA are examples of transactions where we used management teams from existing CVC portfolio companies to bring significant experience of the industry and the buy-out process. We have stuck to our investment model and have built an enormous body of experience from the deals we have completed. The more you do something, the better you get at it and the more you derisk transactions*".

322 See e.g. Lee, C. I., et al. (1992), pp. 58ff, Rosenstein, J., et al. (1993), pp. 99ff and Fried, V. H., et al. (1998), pp. 493ff.

323 Analyzing a sample of 234 firms that have changed auditors, Marten, K.-U. (1995) finds that firms with changes in majority ownership, such as an LBO, are significantly more likely to change auditors than firms without changes in majority ownership. See Marten, K.-U. (1995), pp. 718f.

as well as empirically.[324] There is, however, a growing understanding that strategic involvement on behalf of the financial sponsor substantially affects value creation in LBO investments, in particular in light of the finite investment horizon of the equity investors as (a variation in) the strategic direction is priced in the divestment phase.[325]

Predominately in early buyout research, *asset stripping* is considered a key motive for executing a LBO transaction.[326] The corresponding reasoning is that *PE* firms create value by breaking up conglomerates and removing the conglomerate discount by realizing higher values for the separated, individual businesses.[327] This over-simplistic view is altered towards an understanding of the LBO as a vehicle for corporate refocusing.[328] Selected disposals of non-core and/or underperforming operations to parties with higher valued use[329] help (i) to remove inter-company inefficiencies[330], and (ii) to reduce the overall complexity.[331]

Potentially complementary to selected disposals, *PE* firms might foster selected add-on acquisitions that strengthen the portfolio company's core competencies, increase its market share and aim at improving the operational performance through economies of scale.[332] In the extreme case *PE* firms acquire a selected portfolio company with the clear purpose of realizing a *roll-up* or *buy-and-build* strategy. In such case a nucleus (or plat-form) investment in a generally mature and sufficiently large, though fragmented industry is complemented through numerous add-on acquisitions with the objective of establishing a sizeable or even dominant market player.[333]

---

324 For a recent detailed analysis of strategic aspects of *PE* investing on fund level see Berg, A. (2005); Knoblauch, B. (2002) discusses the applicability of various value creation strategies (ranging from value chain deintegration to break-up) in the context of *PE* investing on investment level.

325 For a successful exit via trade sale or IPO, Seth, A./Easterwood, J. C. (1993) and Wiersema, M. F./Liebeskind, J. P. (1995) highlight among others the importance of strengthening core competencies with comparative advantages; the relevance of innovative efforts is emphasized by Markides, C. C. (1997) and Wright, M., et al. (2001); the necessity of a successful growth track record is stressed by Butler, P. A. (2001) and with respect to expected growth theoretically, fundamentally confirmed (see chapter III.C.1).

326 See e.g. Singh, H. (1993), pp. 147ff and Bhagat, S., et al. (1990), p. 44 arguing that "*the role of the raiders and MBO boutiques seems largely to take diversified firms, bust them up and sell the divisions to other firms in the same business*".

327 See e.g. Bhide, A. V. (1990), pp. 70-81 and Ramu, S. S. (1999) as well as Magowan, P. A. (1989), pp. 9ff for anecdotal evidence.

328 See e.g. Seth, A./Easterwood, J. C. (1993), pp. 251-273.

329 For disposals in the general context as a means of realizing a more focused diversification strategy see e.g. Hoskisson, R. E./Turk, T. A. (1990), pp. 459ff; in the special context of LBOs see for many Muscarella, C. J./Vetsuypens, M. R. (1990), pp. 1389ff and Anders, G. (1992) , pp. 79ff.

330 See e.g. Liebeskind, J. P., et al. (1992), pp. 73ff.

331 See e.g. Phan, P. H./Hill, C. W. L. (1995), pp. 704ff.

332 See e.g. Baker, G. P./Montgomery, C. A. (1994), pp. 1ff and Berg, A./Gottschalg, O. (2003), p. 24.

333 See e.g. Mills, K. G. (2000), p. 263, Samdani, S. G., et al. (2001), p. 105 and Knoblauch, B. (2002), pp. 84f. Allen, J. (1996) refers to such strategy as *leverage built-up*.

3. Wealth Transfer Hypotheses

This thesis applies the perspective of the post-buyout equity investor. For that reason, potential wealth transfers from other company stakeholders might also be considered as a source of value to these investors. [334] In the course of a LBO transaction wealth transfers potentially occur from (i) its bondholders, (ii) the firm's employees, and (iii) the government. Given the, for the most part, weak empirical support for the presented wealth transfer hypotheses (and even if than of minor magnitude) the forthcoming empirical analysis in chapter V tests for the wealth transfer hypotheses only indirectly. Since hence chapter IV does not derive testable hypotheses/operationalizations, the corresponding empirical evidence is discussed directly, subsequent to the brief discussion of the respective hypothesis.

3.1 Wealth Transfer from Bondholders

The principal theoretical argument for the detrimental effects of LBOs on bondholders of the target firm and the resulting wealth transfer to shareholders is argued to be the increased default risk caused by the incremental debt financing.[335] The default risk of a company that experiences a LBO is said to increase as most of the acquisition price is debt-financed and consequently the amount of equity that might serve to cover potential losses is limited. As a result of the increased default risk, the firm's rating will deteriorate and financing costs will increase. Whereas new debt investors are compensated according to the new risk-return profile, existing bondholders are expected to suffer as bond prices decrease given their nominal return but an increased risk profile. This loss in bondholder wealth might in turn be a source of value creation for shareholders.[336]

However, this view of an impaired value of debt due to additional financial liabilities arising from the LBO might be too simplistic for the following reasons:[337] first, some debt securities are convertible into common stock. Second, nonconvertible debt issues might be redeemed for cash, converted into other more favorable securities or renegotiated. Third, according to the reduced agency costs hypothesis, free cash flow available for distribution to debt- and equityholders is said to increase following a LBO. If this is so, fixed charge coverage ratios would increase ceteris paribus and higher absolute amounts of debt capacity could be justified, implying that the risk pattern might not change as dramatically as the increase in debt suggests and hence that financing costs would not necessarily rise.

---

334 Previous literature at times distinguishes from an outsider and macroeconomic perspective between wealth created and wealth transferred. See e.g. Muscarella, C. J./Vetsuypens, M. R. (1990). For detailed summary discussions regarding wealth transfers see e.g. Schmid, H. (1994), pp. 269ff and Kessel, A. (1995), pp. 99-112.

335 See e.g. Masulis, R. W. (1980), pp. 139ff.

336 For details regarding above line of reasoning see e.g. Lehn, K./Poulsen, A. (1990), pp. 199-217.

337 See Marais, L., et al. (1989), p. 156.

Further, bank loan financing is nowadays generally protected through restrictive change of control clauses. These change of ownership clauses require existing financial liabilities to be redeemed and entirely refinanced in combination with a LBO. Frequently, margin grids tie the bank loan interest margin to the company's leverage.[338] Even on the contrary, as bond terms in most cases include a put option for the holder, early calls of outstanding bonds at the point in time of the LBO entry transaction usually trigger an early redemption premium.[339] In such cases existing financial liabilities might in the extreme case be considered as *uses* of value rather than *sources* of value in LBO investments. In the case of Grohe's Secondary buyout by the Texas Pacific Group in July 2004 the financial sponsor had to bear €37m of early redemption costs in combination with the bond outstanding from the financing of Grohe's initial buyout in 1999/2000. This *use* of value represented approximately 2.5% of the acquisition price in 2004.

Empirical Evidence

Overall empirical evidence is mixed, mostly limited to public-to-private transactions and generally suffers from relatively small sample sizes.[340] If at all a primary source of value creation, the empirical findings suggest that the magnitudes of these types of wealth transfers are insufficient to explain much of the shareholder gains in analyzed samples of public-to-private transactions.

Cook et al. (1992) conducted an empirical analysis of bondholder wealth effects of MBOs based on a sample of 29 US American MBOs during the years 1981–1989. The authors found significant bondholder wealth losses of about 3% associated with the announcement of the buyouts.[341] This finding is supported by Asquith/Wizman (1990). Based on a sample of 214 nonconvertible bonds issued by 65 US American buyout targets between 1980 and 1988 the authors conclude that (i) bondholders suffer on average statistically significant losses, (ii) bondholder gains and losses are correlated with the respective covenant protection level,

338 *Note:* In practice, financing conditions are generally fixed and based on current and forecasted (i) leverage ratios such as Total Debt/EBITDA or Total Debt/(EBITDA-CapEx) and (ii) interest coverage ratios such as the total interest cover (EBITDA/Total Interest Expense) or total fixed charge cover (EBITDA less CapEx less cash taxes less changes in NWC divided by cash interest expenses and mandatory debt repayments).

339 Studies by Cook, D. O., et al. (1992) and Asquith, P./Wizman, T. A. (1990) confirm for bonds a positive correlation between the degree of protection and returns. The presence of these clauses might promote managerial entrenchment as agency costs of equity increase. See e.g. Kahan, M./Klausner, M. (1993), pp. 931-982.

340 For an overview of research on bondholder wealth effects of takeovers, in general, and leveraged buyouts, in particular see Cook, D. O., et al. (1992).

341 See Cook, D. O., et al. (1992), pp. 102-113.

and (iii) the type of covenant protection strongly affects the disposition of bonds, e.g. whether they remain outstanding, are called or tendered.[342]

Conversely, results by Marais et al. (1989) are non-confirmative for this wealth transfer hypothesis. According to their sample of 290 US American going-private proposals from 1974 to 1985, over two-third of senior securities (mainly private, non-convertible debt) remained outstanding following the buyout without any stated revisions in the explicit terms of the contract. Further, based on the finding of negative though non-significant abnormal returns of non-convertible debt, LBOs are argued not to redistribute wealth.[343]

An empirical study by Kaplan/Stein (1990) of twelve public leveraged recapitalizations confirms the increase of riskiness for the post-recapitalization debt.[344] The only modest increase in equity betas implies higher debt riskiness and/or reduced asset betas. Depending on the assumption of an unchanged or reduced asset beta the average implied beta for post-recapitalization debt is found to be 0.65 and 0.40 respectively.

The well-known buyout of RJR Nabisco in 1988 provides supportive, anecdotal evidence. Following the first announcement of the transaction, one outstanding bond declined by as much as 16.5% whereas RJR Nabisco's share price jumped by more than 61%.[345]

3.2 Wealth Transfer from Employees

Wealth transfers from employees in the course of a LBO might occur in the form of reduced wages and salaries, extended working hours, fewer fringe benefits, termination of/or cuts in the firms' pension plan or in the worst case employee layoffs.[346] It is frequently argued that not only do the majority of employees not participate in the post-buyout value creation process but also that the buyout process offers restructuring opportunities that are at the expense of the employees.

Empirical Evidence

Empirically, the wealth-transfer-from-employees hypothesis could not so far be clearly confirmed. In their respective studies neither Palepu (1990) nor Kaplan (1989a) find significant support for the hypothesis, regarding both a decrease in the workforce as well as total compensation levels.[347] With respect to the effect of a LBO transaction on the relative

---

342 See Asquith, P./Wizman, T. A. (1990), pp. 195-213.

343 See Marais, L., et al. (1989), pp. 167-187.

344 See Kaplan, S. N./Stein, J. C. (1990), pp. 215-245 as well as chapter II.C.2.

345 See Wallace, A. (1988).

346 See e.g. Shleifer, A./Summers, L. (1988), pp. 33ff and Kropp, M. (1992), p. 114. For details regarding the negative effect of a LBO on employee pension schemes see Ippolito, R. A./James, W. M. (1992), p. 165.

347 See Palepu, K. G. (1990), pp. 247-262 and Kaplan, S. N. (1989a), pp. 217-254.

composition of the workforce, Lichtenberg/Siegel (1990) analyzed total factor productivity for manufacturing plants involved in going privates or divisional buyouts. The authors conclude from a change in relative wages between production and non-production workforce that LBOs are "*organizational innovations that are relatively production-labor using and non-production-labor saving*".[348] This is in-line with the argumentation that LBOs are streamlining corporate overheads, hierarchy and back-offices.

3.3 *Wealth Transfer from the Government*

Significant corporate tax savings are presumably the most popular and hence most intensively discussed wealth transfer hypothesis.[349] Sources for potential tax savings in LBOs (i.e. "*truffles from the tax man*"[350]) are threefold.

First and most obvious, interest expenses are tax deductible yielding a valuable tax shield. Given the heavy debt financing of LBOs, interest expenses tend to increase, thereby reducing the taxable income and thus corporate taxes. Further benefits arise from accrued interest payment structures of various quasi-equity financing instruments. Whereas the related accounting interest expenses are tax deductible, the corresponding cash effect is accrued until maturity.

Second, asset step-ups are a potential source for tax savings. Opportunities arise when the firm's assets are revalued according to their current market value in the course of the LBO acquisition structure.[351] Higher book values imply an increased depreciation base and accordingly higher depreciation charges for the remaining lifetime of the assets. The associated positive tax shield from depreciation charges with no cash outflow represents a source of value.

Third, the US American literature, in particular, considers Employee Stock Ownership Plans (ESOPs) to be a potential source for tax savings in the course of a LBO transaction.[352] Under an ESOP the borrower can deduct not only interest but also principal payments from taxable income. However, Kaplan (1989b) argues that in practice tax benefits from ESOP are low as "*principal repayments to the ESOP loan over time may effectively replace employer contributions to the employee plan.*"[353]

---

348 See Lichtenberg, F./Siegel, D. S. (1990), p. 180.

349 For a general discussion of the tax-savings hypothesis in LBOs see, among others, Lowenstein, L. (1985), pp. 730-784, Kaplan, S. N. (1989b), pp. 611-632, Schipper, K./Smith, A. (1991), pp. 295-341, Newbould, G. D., et al. (1992), pp. 50-57 and Frankfurter, G. M./Gunay, E. (1992), pp. 82-95.

350 See Lowenstein, L. (1985), p. 759.

351 A potential positive difference between the purchase price and the book value of the assets can be either allocated through revaluation of the assets or booked as goodwill.

352 See e.g. Lehn, K./Poulsen, A. (1989), p. 772 and Kaplan, S. N. (1989b), p. 612 and pp. 622-623.

353 See Kaplan, S. N. (1989b), p. 622.

Apparently, the above discussed sources of tax savings depend to a large extent on the applied tax regulations. These not only differ significantly across countries but also over time, which dramatically limits a general discussion of tax savings opportunities. Some academics have argued that tax reforms have already removed much of the tax savings opportunities of previous buyouts.[354] Also, LBOs not only affect tax payments on the level of the bought-out company in the form of incremental interest and depreciation deductions but also pre-buyout shareholders and LBO debtholders. Miller, Merton H. (1977) argues that new interest deductions and interest income to lenders should have an offsetting effect resulting in no tax advantage overall.[355] Jensen et al. (1989) refer to this offsetting effect by pointing out that LBOs provide sources of tax revenues to the state's Treasury through "*(i) taxes on capital gains realized by the pre-buyout shareholders, (ii) taxes on operating cash flow increases from buyouts, (iii) taxes on interest income received by buyout lenders, and (iv) taxes on capital gains from post-buyout asset sales.*"[356]

Empirical Evidence

Kaplan (1989b) conducted one of the first and most extensive studies of the impact of tax savings opportunities on premia paid in going-private transactions. His analysis comprises 76 US MBOs between 1980 and 1986.[357] Overall Kaplan provides evidence for a strongly significant relation between tax savings and premia paid. This finding in fact supports the argumentation that potential future tax savings/value creation opportunities need to be shared with pre-buyout public shareholders. Savings from increased interest deductions are based on calculations applying the post-LBO gearing ratio. In various scenarios Kaplan analyses the impact of (i) varying the effective tax rate from a maximum of 46% (representing the maximum corporate tax rate at that time) to a lower bound of 15%, (ii) including and excluding the benefits of asset step-ups, and (iii) differentiating between constant debt level, i.e. no debt repayment, and continuous debt repayment over the course of eight years. Accordingly, total potential tax savings are estimated to range from a minimum of 21.0% to a maximum of 142.6% of the acquisition premia paid. Further evidence is provided by Schipper/Smith (1991). Analyzing a sample of 83 US LBOs in the years 1982 to 1986 incremental tax deductions seem

354 See e.g. Newbould, G. D., et al. (1992), pp. 50-57 and Baker, G. P./Smith, G. D. (1998).

355 See Miller, M. H. (1977), pp. 261-278.

356 See Palepu, K. G. (1990), p. 254.

357 See Kaplan, S. N. (1989b), pp. 611-632. Of the aforementioned three potential explanations for tax savings Kaplan focuses on increased interest and depreciation deductions. In addition to the expected low tax benefits from borrowing under an ESOP plan, only five out of a possible 76 LBO companies made use of ESOPs in Kaplan's sample.

to result mostly from additional deductions and, to a much lesser extent, from additional depreciation deductions resulting from asset step-ups.[358]

With respect to the macroeconomic tax effect of LBOs, including pre-buyout shareholders, lenders and the government, Jensen et al. (1989) estimate the PV of future federal tax revenues following a LBO to substantially increase by as much as 61% above the corresponding level in the absence of a LBO.[359]

C. External Perspective: Variation in the Transaction Multiple

The decomposition of the LBO transaction model in chapter III.A identified in addition to *FCF effects* the *variation in the transaction multiple* as the second complementary perspective for value creation analysis in a LBO investment. A detailed discussion of valuation and transaction multiples is supported by their high practical relevance. In particular in the field of private equity, LBO transactions and the related financing process, multiples are an established and widely used valuation technique and *common language* for price, leverage and financing discussions.

The following chapters further detail value creation in LBO investments in the context of this external perspective. Chapter III.C.1 sets the stage for this analysis by theoretically discussing *valuation* multiples in the risk-neutral valuation (*RNV*) framework. The objective is to identify in a first step factors that fundamentally drive variations in the valuation multiple. However, given its ex-post perspective on value creation in LBO investments this thesis is concerned with the variation in the *transaction* multiple, based on empirically observable entity, net debt and hence equity prices at entry and at exit of the investment. Realized prices and thus the respective transaction multiple might deviate significantly from the theoretically correct value and corresponding valuation multiple of the assets for a variety of reasons. Disengaging from the conceptual RNV framework, chapter III.C.2 therefore briefly elucidates two supplementary approaches intending to explain discrepancies between valuation and transaction multiples. In this light, chapter III.C.2.1 details the impact of the capital market environment on transaction multiples. Potential information asymmetries in the divestment phase are considered as an influencing factor for variations in the transaction multiple in chapter III.C.2.2.

---

358 See Schipper, K./Smith, A. (1991), pp. 295-341. Apparently a mere ⅓ of analyzed companies stepped-up the asset base following the LBO.

359 See Jensen, M. C., et al. (1989), pp. 61-74. Summers, L. H. (1989), however disputes such estimates by questioning the likely overestimated LBO debtholder tax payments.

1. Conceptual Valuation Framework

A theoretical consideration of valuation multiples in the context of the LBO transaction model requires the specification of a conceptual valuation framework comprising an underlying valuation theorem as well as an underlying stochastic model for future cash flows.

Two fundamental approaches for the valuation of the expected realizations of future cash flow streams differ in the methodology of how to consider investors' risk aversion. On the one hand, the concept of risk-adjusted discount rates (*RADR*) accounts for riskiness by discounting unconditional cash flow expectations with a risk premium on top of the risk-free discount rate.[360] As briefly pointed out in chapter II.C.2 the CAPM as the generally applied capital market model serves for the quantification of the corresponding investment-specific risk premium. Thereby factors affecting the systematic riskiness regarding the realization of expected future cash flow streams of the investment are subsumed in the well-known beta factor.[361] On the other hand, the concept of risk-neutral valuation (*RNV*) transforms unconditional cash flow expectations into certainty equivalents, which can then be discounted at the risk-free rate of return.[362] In other words in the RNV theorem the adjustment for uncertainty occurs in the future cash flow streams by applying certainty equivalents instead of risky cash flows.[363]

The RADR approach has well-known theoretical and empirical shortcomings.[364] One of the key specifications of the CAPM, the expected market risk premium, is not observable and as a consequence computations are generally based on historical estimates. Whereas this shortcoming of an explicit assumption on the risk premium can be overcome with the RNV theorem, the application of the RNV approach demands the specification of the risk-neutral probability that is required to transform unconditional cash flow expectations into certainty equivalents. For the purpose here, to identify factors impacting variations in the transaction multiple through variations in the theoretically correct valuation multiple of the LBO transaction, the RNV theorem shall be applied.

---

360 For details regarding the RADR approach see standard corporate finance textbook literature such as Ross, S. A., et al. (2002) and Brealey, R. A./Myers, S. C. (2003).

361 See chapter II.C and in particular equation (7).

362 For the theoretical foundation of this approach see Duffie, D. (1988) and Pliska, S. R. (1997). For further details see also Richter, F. (2001), Richter, F. (2002b) and Richter, F. (2004a). For a recent detailed work on the concept of RNV – in particular in the context of valuation with multiples – see Kelleners, A. (2004). For a discussion of certainty equivalents see Laux, H. (1998), pp. 211ff.

363 See Richter, F. (2004b) for a detailed comparison of the two theories.

364 See e.g. Ballwieser, W. (1993), p. 165 and Richter, F. (2002a), p. 61.

1.1 The Risk-Neutral Valuation Theorem

The risk-neutral valuation theorem is well-known from option pricing theory. Accordingly the value V_{ti} of a given asset i is the sum of all future cash flows under the risk neutral probability measure Q discounted at the risk-free rate r_f.[365]

$$(42) \quad V_{ti} = \sum_{n=t}^{T} \frac{E^Q[C_{ni}|F_n]}{(1+r_f)^n}$$

The filtration F_n thereby represents the set of available information at time n, on which basis the probability measure Q creates certainty equivalents $E^Q[C_{ni}|F_n]$.[366] Discounted at the respective risk-free rate r_f these certainty equivalents lead to a value V_{ni} in consistence with the assumption of arbitrage-free markets. In other words the probability distribution Q ("*certainty equivalent probability*"[367]) leads to certainty equivalents, which perfectly replicate the expected cash flow streams of a portfolio of risk-free assets.[368]

The probability measure Q is hence to be differentiated from the probability measure P. Whereas Q yields conditional certainty equivalents, P creates subjective, unconditional investor expectations of future cash flow streams as applied in the *RADR* approach. Assuming positive correlation of the company's cash flow with the cash flows from the market portfolio, risk-averse investors will obviously expect less under Q than under P:[369]

$$(43) \quad E^Q[C_{ni}|F_0] < E_P[C_{ni}]$$

1.2 The Binomial Cash Flow Model

Two principal different schools of thoughts exist for trends, patterns and dependencies of financial time series with respect to the predictability of a stochastic process based on historically realized and observable data. On the one hand it is argued that some predictability of future realizations comes from intertemporal dependencies of a stochastic variable in a financial time series.[370] According to this linearity, historical realizations were to obtain valuable information for the estimation of future realizations. On the other hand, the *Random-*

365 See e.g. Richter, F. (2001), pp. 175ff.

366 A filtration specifies the development and distribution of information in the course of a stochastic process. See e.g. Duffie, D. (1988), pp. 130ff.

367 See Richter, F. (2002b), p. 138.

368 See e.g. Ross, S. A. (1987), p. 374 and Richter, F. (2004a), pp. 368ff.

369 See Richter, F. (2002a), p. 62.

370 See e.g. Edwards, R. D./Magee, J. (1976), p. 8.

Walk Hypothesis argues that future realizations are independent from historical patterns.[371] Only the current level, not historical realizations, are of relevance for the upcoming realization. In particular this implies that the probability for the transformation of a stochastic variable from one realization in period n to the other realization in period $n+1$ is independent from the state of the variable.[372] Authors in favor of the *Random-Walk Hypothesis* argue that in efficient markets any kind of predictability of future realizations of a stochastic variable would immediately be eliminated through a relevant trading strategy in order to comply with the argument of an arbitrage-free market.[373]

Since the following analysis is based on the argument of arbitrage-free capital markets, the *Random-Walk Hypothesis* will be applied. A frequently used process to model properties of financial time series in the context of the *Random-Walk Hypothesis* and in the absence of the true stochastic model of future cash flows is the binomial model.[374]

Being based on the *Bernoulli* experiment, there are only two potential outcomes in a one-period binomial process with the respective probabilities of p and $1-p$.[375] Accordingly, the cash flow for the period $n+1$ either moves up or down by the factors $u_{n+1,i}$ or $d_{n+1,i}$ respectively.[376]

(44) $$C_{n+1,i} \in \{C_{ni}u_{n+1,i}; C_{ni}d_{n+1,i}\}$$

The up and down factors u_{ni} and d_{ni} have a reciprocal relationship with $0 < d_{ni} < u_{ni}$. Given the subjective probability measure $P = \{p, (1-p)\}$ and the set of available information at time n, expressed by the filtration F_n, investors will form their view regarding the unconditional expected cash flow for the subsequent period as:[377]

(45) $$E^P[C_{n+1,i} | F_n] = pC_{n,i}u_{n,i} + (1-p)C_{n,i}d_{n,i}$$

---

371 Osborne, M. (1959) first theoretically described and founded the random-walk hypothesis by transferring the concept of the Brownian motion into financial theory. For the application the random-walk hypothesis in the context of option pricing see Hull, J. C. (2003). See e.g. Kelleners, A. (2004), pp. 22-42 for a comparison of the two methods and some related empirical evidence.

372 See Wunsch, G./Schreiber, H. (1984), pp. 107-113 and Hull, J. C. (2003), p. 216.

373 See e.g. Fama, E. F. (1970), pp. 386f.

374 *Note:* The binomial model frequently serves as the stochastic process in option pricing theory. The theoretical foundation for a binomial option pricing formula was developed by Cox, J. C., et al. (1979). According to Richter, F. (2002b), p. 137 the use of the binomial model in the context of valuation with multiples is suitable as it can easily be generalized and given its ease of applicability.

375 A series of consecutive, independent realizations with constant probabilities according to the Bernoulli experiment is referred to as a Bernoulli sequence.

376 See Richter, F. (2002b), p. 137.

377 See Richter, F. (2001), pp. 178-179.

Therefore, according to the binomial model set-up, the expected cash flow either increases by $C_{ni}(u_{ni}-1)$ with the probability p or decreases by $C_{ni}(d_{ni}-1)$ with the probability $(1-p)$. The relevant growth rate reads as:

$$(46)\quad E^P\left[(1+g^P_{n+1,i}\middle|F_n\right]=\frac{E^P\left[C_{n+1,i}\middle|F_n\right]}{E^P\left[C_{ni}\right]}=pu_{ni}+(1-p)d_{ni}$$

Applying these variables, time-specific expected growth rates for any future cash flow can be expressed through a combination of the cash flow C_{ni} and the relevant expected, subjective growth rates.[378]

$$(47)\quad E^P\left[C_{ni}\middle|F_n\right]=C_{ni}\prod\nolimits_{j=1}^{t}(1+g^q_{ji})\ \text{with: } (1+g^q_{ni})=pu_{ni}+(1-p)d_{ni}$$

As mentioned previously, the RNV approach is based on security equivalents instead of unconditional, expected cash flow as in the RADR approach. Applying the respective risk-neutral probability measure with the assumed binomial cash flow model $Q=\{q,(1-q)\}$, equation (47) reads as:

$$(48)\quad E^Q\left[C_{ni}\middle|F_n\right]=C_{ni}\prod\nolimits_{j=1}^{t}(1+g^q_{ni})\ \text{with: } (1+g^q_{ni})=qu_{ni}+(1-q)d_{ni}$$

whereby g^q represents the risk-adjusted growth rate under the probability measure Q. The up and down factors u_{ni} and d_{ni} are identical for both probability measures since the RNV valuation theorem argues for a modification of the expected growth rates through adjustments in the *certainty equivalent probability*.

Subjective growth expectations can now be applied to solve for the up and down factors $u_{t,i}$ and d_{ni} numerically. For the special case of a recombining binomial model the relationship between u_{ni} and d_{ni} simplifies to[379]

$$(49)\quad d_{ni}=\frac{1}{u_{ni}}$$

Substituting d_{ni} in equation (48) yields for u_{ni}

$$(50)\quad u_{ni}=\frac{1+g^p_{ni}}{2p}+\sqrt{\left(\frac{1+g^p_{ni}}{2p}\right)^2-\frac{1-p}{p}}\ \text{whereby: } \sigma_{ni}=\sqrt{\left(\frac{1+g^p_{ni}}{2p}\right)^2-\frac{1-p}{p}}$$

---

378 See Richter, F. (2002b), pp. 140-142.

379 See Richter, F. (2002a), p. 63. The assumption of a recombining binomial model is no limitation but a simplification. A general formula for a non-recombining can be found in Richter, F. (2002a), pp. 71-72.

For the special case of $p = 0.5$ equation (50) reduces to

$$(51) \quad u_{ni} = 1 + g_{ni}^{p} + \sqrt{\left(1 + g_{ni}^{p}\right)^{2} - 1} \text{ whereby: } \sigma_{ni} = \sqrt{\left(1 + g_{ni}^{p}\right)^{2} - 1}$$

Replacing now d_{ni} and u_{ni} in equation (48) with the expression derived above yields

$$(52) \qquad (1 + g_{ni}^{q}) = q(1 + g_{ni}^{p} + \sigma_{ni}) + (1 - q)(1 + g_{ni}^{p} + \sigma_{ni})^{-1}$$

Extending the second term of the equation with $(1 + g_{ni}^{p} - \sigma_{ni})$ and rearranging yields

$$(53) \qquad (1 + g_{ni}^{q}) = q(1 + g_{ni}^{p} + \sigma_{ni}) + (1 - q)(1 + g_{ni}^{p} - \sigma_{ni}) \text{ with: } \sigma_{ni} = \sqrt{\left(1 + g_{ni}^{p}\right)^{2} - 1}$$

As a result, the risk-neutral probability q remains the only unspecified variable that is required for a transformation of subjective growth expectations into security equivalents for the case of a recombining binomial model with $p = 0.5$.

1.3 Valuation with Multiples

The previous two chapters provided a specification of the underlying valuation theorem as well as the underlying cash flow process. The value of a company can hence be expressed through the combination of the RNV approach with the binomial cash flow model. With C representing the cash flow of an all-equity financed firm the equity value E_{ti} results as:[380]

$$(54) \quad E_{ti} = C_{ti} \sum_{n=t}^{T} \prod_{j=t}^{n} \frac{1 + g_{ji}^{q}}{1 + r_f} \text{ with: } (1 + g_{ni}^{q}) = q u_{ni} + (1 - q) d_{ni}$$

As the RNV framework is applied, the risk-neutral, time-specific, conditional growth rate of the cash flow C g_{ni}^{q} is discounted at the risk-free interest rate r_f.

Similar, applying the entity approach to firm valuation with TCF representing the cash flow to equity as well as debtholders, the entity value V_{ti} results as:

$$(55) \quad V_{ti} = TCF_{ti} \sum_{n=t}^{T} \prod_{j=t}^{n} \frac{1 + g_{ji}^{q}}{1 + wacc_{ji}^{q}} \text{ with: } (1 + g_{ni}^{q}) = q u_{ni} + (1 - q) d_{ni}$$

$wacc_{ji}^{q}$ represents the conditional weighted average cost of capital under the probability measure Q.[381]

---

380 See e.g. Richter, F. (2004b), p. 24.

381 The presented model represents a simplification with respect to the consideration of personal income taxes in the valuation equation. See Richter, F. (2004b) for a detailed discussion of personal income taxes in this context.

(56) $wacc_{ji}^{q} = r_f(1-\tau)l_{j-1,i} + r_E^q(1-l_{j-1,i})$

Under the risk-neutral probability measure Q, the equity rate of return r_E^q equals the risk-free interest rate r_f. Accordingly equation (56) can be rearranged to

(57) $wacc_{ji}^{q} = r_f(1-\tau l_{j-1,i})$

Equation (55) represents the relevant valuation formula for variable, i.e. period-specific growth rates and gearing ratio. For the simplified case of constant growth rates and assuming constant gearing ratio equation (56) reduces to the well-known *Gordon-Growth* formula.[382]

(58) $V_{ti} = TCF_{ti}\dfrac{1+g_i^q}{wacc_i^q - g_i^q}$

with: $g_i^q = \left(qu_i + (1-q)/u_i\right) - 1$ according to (46), (49)

with: $u_i = \dfrac{1+g_i^p}{2p} + \sqrt{\left(\dfrac{1+g_i^p}{2p}\right)^2 - \dfrac{1-p}{p}}$ according to (50)

and: $wacc_i^q = r_f(1-\tau l_i)$ according to (57)

Derivation of the V/EBITDA Multiple

As mentioned before the *V/EBITDA* multiple is of particular importance for practitioners in the field of LBOs. Relative acquisition prices, leverage, financing ratios and financial covenant ratios are generally expressed in the form of this EBITDA entity multiple. In order to derive *V/EBITDA* in the context of the RNV framework TCF needs to be decomposed in a first step. As defined in chapter II.B:

(59) $TCF = EBITDA - CapEx - \Delta NWC - Tax$

θ be defined as the reinvestment rate, being the fraction of the firm's after-tax EBITDA that is reinvested (including depreciation and amortization) into the firm.[383] Applying the stylized corporate tax rate τ, equation (59) can be rewritten as:

(60) $TCF = EBITDA(1-\theta)(1-\tau)$

In combination with equation (58) and equation (57) the relevant *V/EBITDA* multiple results as

382 See Gordon, M. J. (1962), pp. 43-54 for the principals of the Gordon-Growth formula.

383 See e.g. Herrmann, V. (2002), pp. 53f and Richter, F./Herrmann, V. (2003), pp. 194ff.

$$(61)\quad \frac{V_{ti}}{EBITDA_{ti}} = (1-\theta)(1-\tau)\frac{1+g_i^q}{r_f(1-\tau l_i)-g_i^q}$$

with: $g_i^q = \left(qu_i + (1-q)/u_i\right) - 1$ according to (46), (49)

with: $u_i = \frac{1+g_i^p}{2p} + \sqrt{\left(\frac{1+g_i^p}{2p}\right)^2 - \frac{1-p}{p}}$ according to (50)

The reinvestment rate θ deserves some more attention. Assuming that growth results from the reinvestment of the firm's cash flows and assuming further that the return on these new investments equals the current return on the firm's assets, i.e. ROIC, than θ can be expressed as

$$(62)\quad \theta = \frac{g_i^q}{ROIC_i}$$

With this equation (61) reads as

$$(63)\quad \frac{V_{ti}}{EBITDA_{ti}} = (1-\tau)\left(1-\frac{g_i^q}{ROIC_i}\right)\frac{1+g_i^q}{r_f(1-\tau l_i)-g_i^q}$$

Hence, in the framework of the RNV theorem and following the above assumptions the theoretically derived *V/EBITDA* valuation multiple is a function of (i) the risk-free interest-rate r_f, (ii) the growth rate g_i, (iii) the firm's current profitability expressed as $ROIC_i$, (iv) the corporate tax rate τ and, given the tax shield from debt financing (v) the gearing ratio l_i.

Interdependency between the Internal and the External Perspective

Equation (63) highlights an additional layer of complexity in the presented two-tier framework of an internal and an external perspective. As previously pointed out this separation might be considered commonly exhaustive but, owing to interdependencies between the two perspectives, not mutually exclusive. The previous chapter derived the theoretically correct valuation multiple. Assuming that the transaction multiple is to a large extent fundamentally driven, variations in the transaction multiple in LBO transactions might result from internal *FCF effects*. Although in equation (63), g_i^q represents the firm's expected long-term EBITDA growth rate, it could be argued that operational performance improvements as well as revenue expansions during the holding period lift the company on a new growth track and hence merit a higher valuation/transaction multiple. Similarly, higher levels of *ROIC* in the denominator increase the expression in brackets and hence should foster a positive variation in the valuation/transaction multiple. In other words, companies that manage to increase the performance relative to the capital employed would deserve a multiple expansion.

Despite these interdependencies, the presented two-tier framework serves well the purpose of a structured discussion and analysis of value creation in LBOs in the context of this thesis. Individual effects and sources of value creation can be contemplated separately at first and in a second step be considered jointly with respect to the impact on the performance of the LBO transaction.

2. From the Valuation to the Transaction Multiple

The previous chapter theoretically derived the *V/EBITDA* valuation multiple and its impacting factors in the context of the RNV framework. Transaction multiples in LBO transactions (at entry as well as at exit) express purchase prices as a multiple of any cash flow measure; most commonly $EBITDA_{LTM}$. For this purpose the notation *transaction multiple* has hence been applied to clearly differentiate from theoretically founded valuation multiples as discussed in the preceding chapter.

For the following discussion of transaction multiples it is beneficial to introduce a further – rather practical – understanding regarding their constitution and components, which shall contribute towards explaining their variations. Chapter II.B intended for a clear-cut differentiation of sources of financing between equity and debt financing instruments. Like purchase prices financing ratios of total debt and its components are frequently expressed as multiples of $EBITDA_{LTM}$. Accordingly, the total purchase price multiple (i.e. transaction multiple) can be stated as a combination of the total debt EBITDA multiple (referred to as leverage L) and the relative total debt contribution (the gearing ratio l).[384]

$$(64)\quad m_t = \frac{P_t}{EBITDA_{LTM}} \frac{D_t}{D_t} = \frac{L_t}{l_t}$$

Various levels of transaction multiples resulting from the combination of leverage L_t and the corresponding financing structure $(1\text{-}l_t)$ are illustrated in Chart 8.

384 See also Richter, F. (2005), pp. 179f.

Chart 8 Sources of Funds and the Transaction Multiple

EBITDA transaction multiple m_t as a combination of leverage L_t (expressed through Total Debt as a multiple of EBITDA) and the relative equity contribution $1\text{-}l_t$

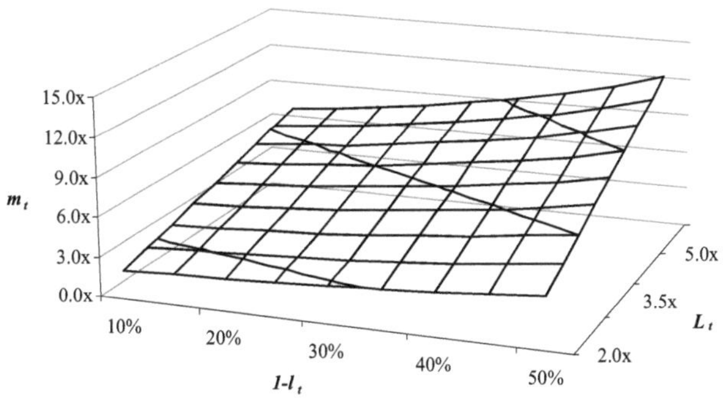

Source: Own illustration

As briefly pointed out, the applicability of the conceptual valuation framework and hence the practical relevance of theoretically derived valuation multiples is subject to various restrictive assumptions. Be it in the context of the RADR or the RNV framework, changes in the equity market valuation of a publicly or privately held firm should be determined by changes either regarding expectations of its future expected cash flows or its cost of capital. In their article on *the limits of arbitrage* Shleifer/Vishny (1997a) build among others upon circumstances that restrict the arbitrage-free argumentation and therefore potentially serve to justify deviations between valuation and transactions multiples. Accordingly, the remainder of this chapter intends to briefly detail the impact of the capital market environment (chapter III.C.2.1) and potential information asymmetries (chapter III.C.2.2) to identify further factors affecting (variations in) transaction multiples in LBO transactions.

2.1 *Market Timing, Supply and Demand and the Impact of the Capital Market Environment*

This chapter considers – based on introductory *market timing* reflections – basic *supply and demand* considerations for the equity and debt capital market.

Market Timing

In light of the finite investment horizon of financial sponsors, the vital question arises whether these intermediaries possess a *timing* ability to benefit from changes in the state of capital markets in the sense of buying at a relatively low price and selling at a relatively high price.

In particular, with respect to the performance of mutual funds market timing ability has received extensive attention in the academic literature. [385] Empirical results are mixed.[386] Assessing market timing abilities in the context of the private equity asset class differs from the mutual funds asset class in two respects.[387] First, as pointed out in chapter II.C.2 when considering the risk component, *PE* investments are characterized by a high degree of illiquidity. In the absence of a secondary market for these investments, daily or monthly prices as required for standard timing models are not observable. Apart from potential interim equity streams, cash flows between the *PE* firm and the portfolio company are limited for the investment and divestment cases when reconcilable equity valuations are available. Second, investment decisions are taken much less frequently in the field of private equity than in the mutual funds industry. Whereas the cash/equity securities composition varies for the mutual funds asset class on a daily basis, Ljungqvist/Richardson (2003a) find the average number of portfolio investments for the analyzed sample of 54 *PE* funds to be 16.1 during the fund's lifetime.[388] Accordingly, Schmidt et al. (2004) hypothesize that the cautious decision regarding the entry and – presumably of more relevance – the precise exit point in time constitute market timing ability rather than the frequent buy/sell and corresponding cash/equity securities portfolio composition decision. Given this non-applicability of standard market timing measures, Schmidt/Nowak et al. analyze the correlation between the relative market valuation and the monthly investment and divestment activity level.[389] The underlying line of reasoning implies that executing investments (divestments) in times of relatively low (high) market valuations signals market timing capabilities. Using a sample of 70 realized *VC* and buyout funds with deal-by-deal cash flow data, investment timing abilities of private equity fund managers can be confirmed. Surprisingly though, divestment timing ability can not be found to be statistically significant, even when considering the 1998–2000 bubble period.[390]

---

385 First theoretical measures for fund managers security selection capabilities were developed by e.g. Jensen, M. C. (1968), Black, F., et al. (1972) and Jensen, M. C. (1972). Models testing for the timing ability of fund managers with respect to the allocation of funds between cash and equity securities were developed by Merton, R. C. (1981) and Henriksson, R. D./Merton, R. C. (1981).

386 Based on empirical findings confirming non-constant risk-structures of mutual funds over time (thereby invalidating assumptions of Jensen's and Black et al. models), several studies including Kon, S./Jen, F. C. (1979) and Fabozzi, F./Francis, J. C. (1979) conclude that market timing affects fund managers' investment decisions. However, results by Treynor, J. L./Mazuy, K. (1966) and Henriksson, R. D. (1984) are little supportive for the market timing hypothesis.

387 See Schmidt, D., et al. (2004), pp. 10ff.

388 See Ljungqvist, A./Richardson, M. (2003a), p. 39. For the total sample of 73 funds (comprising 19 VC funds) it takes on average six years for 90% of the committed capital to be invested. For a sub-sample of 157 funds raised prior to 1995 and with more than 50% of the capital invested, Gottschalg, O., et al. (2004) report a mean (median) number of 16.5 (12.0) direct investments.

389 See Schmidt, D., et al. (2004), pp. 12ff. The relative market valuation relates an equity market index to the 36-months-moving-averages of the index. The investment (divestment) activity level relates negative (positive) cash flows for the period to total negative (positive) cash flows for the funds lifetime.

390 See Schmidt, D., et al. (2004), pp. 1- 33.

Also on fund level, Kaplan/Schoar (2005) confirm the above line of reasoning by analyzing the timing aspects of fundraising: funds raised in boom times are likely to underperform.[391]

However, some arguments can be brought forward against this market timing hypothesis; most importantly that fund economics might significantly affect the investment and divestment decision. First, a *PE* investment can be considered as a shortened put option. Given the finitely committed capital, the divestment option needs to be exercised when the end of the fund lifetime approaches. Furthermore, the pressure to deploy non-invested committed capital is likely to increase towards the end of the investment period of the fund and the undrawn fraction of the committed funds; a phenomenon known as *window dressing*. Also the timing of follow-on fundraising might affect the funds' activity level. As a consequence *PE* firms might be required to divest well-performing investments opportunely and potentially delay the divestment of underperforming assets regardless of the state of the capital market environment.[392]

When briefly discussing potential exit modes in chapter II.A.4 it has been mentioned that an alternative view for clustering exit modes could be (i) selling to the equity capital market, compared with (ii) selling to the credit (i.e. debt) capital market. This understanding shall serve here to structure the remaining discussion of the impact of the state of the capital markets.

2.1.1 Equity Capital Markets

The State of the Private Equity Capital Market

The effect of increasing cash inflows into the market for LBOs has been discussed steadily in the academic literature.[393] In particular following the seminal article by Gompers/Lerner (2000b) the phenomenon of *money chasing deals* has received attention in most recent *PE Performance Studies.*[394] The quintessence of the underlying line of reasoning is that increasing capital inflows into the *PE* industry causes transaction prices to increase, i.e. "*too much money [is] chasing too few deals*".[395] Gompers/Lerner argue applying the market for direct portfolio investments: as long as perfect substitutes exist for a given security, demand curves for the asset should be infinitely price elastic.[396] Accordingly, purchase prices of private firms should

---

391 See Kaplan, S. N./Schoar, A. (2005), pp. 1791-1823.

392 Kaplan, S. N./Schoar, A. (2005) find that better performing funds are more likely to raise follow-on and larger funds.

393 See Kaplan, S. N./Stein, J. (1993), pp. 313ff, Allen, J. (1996), pp. 18ff, Kieschnick, R. L. (1998), pp. 187ff, Gompers, P. A./Lerner, J. (2000b), pp. 281 and Inderst, R./Müller, H. M. (2004), pp. 319ff.

394 See Table 5 on page 19.

395 See Gompers, P. A./Lerner, J. (2000b), p. 282.

396 See also Shleifer, A. (1986), p. 579. Shleifer notes that most common capital market theorems such as the CAPM and the APT predict (almost) infinitely price elastic demand curves. Accordingly the "*stock price is an unbiased predictor of underlying value, maintained through the working or arbitrage.*"

be unaffected by increasing capital inflows, as long as these inflows are unrelated to expected future cash flows and the corresponding cost of capital, i.e. as long as they are exogenous. However, accounting for the peculiarities of *PE* investing and considering the *PE* market as being segmented from other asset classes, demand can no longer be considered as being infinitely elastic and even exogenous increases in fund inflows trigger rising prices. Furthermore, should case fund inflows be endogenous, e.g. a more promising outlook for private companies triggers higher levels of committed funds to the asset class, prices and fund inflows would increase simultaneously. Based on Gompers/Lerner (1999c), Inderst/Müller (2004) consider fund inflows to be endogenous in the long run.[397]

For the purpose here, the stylized effects of an increased supply in *PE* shall be illustrated through the combined consideration of the market for *PE* funds and the market for *PE* investments as shown in Chart 9.

Chart 9 The effect of increased supply in private equity funds on the price of private equity investments

S and D indicate supply and demand curves respectively; E denotes cumulated committed equity funds to the private equity industry; V denotes the corresponding cumulated entity valuation for the entirety of direct investments; E[r_E] and P^V denote the respective equilibrium prices

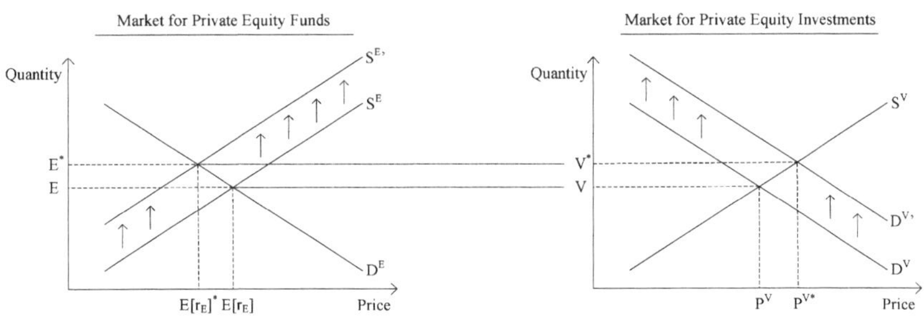

Source: Own illustration

The market for *PE* funds is characterized by the amount of total funds *E* and the corresponding equilibrium price for the asset: the expected equity rate of return $E_t[r_t]$. Owing to variations in factors affecting the supply of private equity funds other than changing $E_t[r_t]$ triggers shifts in the supply curve S^E. Such factors increasing the supply and hence shifting the curve up (S^E ->S^{E}') might for instance contribute to a better understanding of *PE* as an asset class, and an increased appreciation of the diversification benefits of *PE*. Accordingly, investors are willing to commit a higher aggregated amount E^* for the corresponding

397 See Inderst, R./Müller, H. M. (2004), p. 331. According to Gompers, P. A./Lerner, J. (1999c), p. 25 "*The skills needed for successful venture capital investing are difficult and time-consuming to acquire. During periods when the supply or demand for venture capital has shifted, adjustments in the number of venture capitalists and venture capital organizations appear to take place very slowly.*"

price $\mathrm{E}_t[r_t]^*$; with $\mathrm{E}_t[r_t]^* < \mathrm{E}_t[r_t]$ assuming a downward sloping, not an infinitely elastic demand curve for *PE* funds. Considering *PE* as a segmented asset and assuming further constant debt supply, the increased equity supply E^* translates into higher demand V^* for *PE* investments. In the respective market the demand curve D^V shifts up (D^{V}'). Following the shortage at P^V, the market mechanism causes prices to bid up to finally clear the market at P^{V}'. The more elastic S^V, the more of the increased demand translates into investment volume (and hence demand D^E in the *PE* capital market) and absorbs potential price increases for *PE* investments.

Fund inflows thus presumably not only affect transaction prices at entry but also at exit. In the divestment phase the state of the *PE* capital market potentially affects the attractiveness of a secondary buyout exit.

The State of the Public Equity Capital Market

As in the case of private equity, the state of the public equity capital market might impact transaction prices of private equity investments at entry as well as at exit. Considering a going private transaction or a LBO in general as selling to the credit market, a relatively unattractive equity capital market as the alternative medium to the credit market seems beneficial from the financial investor perspective. At entry, the financial sponsor interested in the LBO investment competes directly not only with the alternative of an IPO (in case of a divisional, succession or secondary buyout) but also with the alternative of a trade sale; both alternatives benefit from an attractive public equity capital market environment. In other words if demand/appetite for assets on the part of the public equity capital market is low, prices fall and entry levels for financial sponsors are becoming relatively more attractive. Conversely, in the divestment phase demand for the asset boosts the price and obviously divestment proceeds for the LBO equity investors. Hence a favorable equity capital market environment, which stimulates not only an IPO but also a trade sale to a strategic investor, is desirable. In a favorable public equity capital market environment, investors might be more enthusiastic about financing add-on acquisitions (i.e. trade sales from the LBO perspective) through capital increases.

Whereas the private equity capital market argumentation was based on supply-side considerations, the public equity capital market argumentation builds upon basic demand-side considerations. Though rather straightforward, the basics are illustrated in Chart 10, for the purpose of completeness.

Chart 10 The effect of an increasing demand for IPOs

S and D indicate supply and demand curves respectively; E denotes cumulated public equity for IPOs; P^E denotes the respective equilibrium price

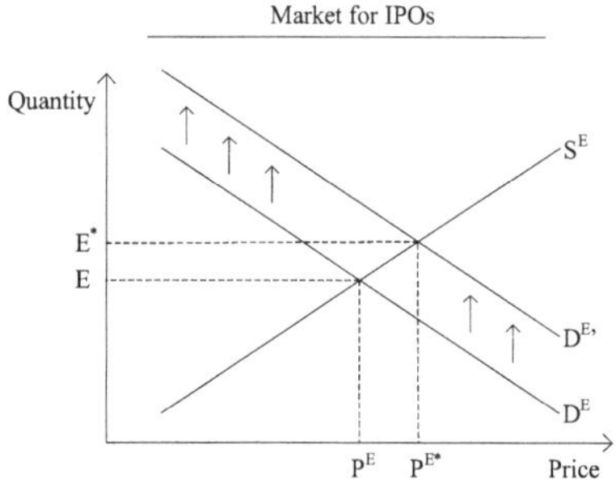

Source: Own illustration

Following an exogenous shock, the demand curve for new public equity investments shifts up (D^E -> D^{E}'). In response to the shortage at the prevailing equilibrium price P^E, the market mechanism (in combination with an anything but infinitely price elastic supply curve S^E) implies that the price for the asset increases to P^{V*}. Such an exogenous demand shock might result for instance from irrational expectations or variations in diversification considerations and resulting investors' willingness to invest a higher fraction of their wealth in equity securities. An attractive public equity capital market is hence characterized by a large appetite for IPOs and is frequently referred to as *Hot Issues Market*.[398]

With a similar line of reasoning, equilibrium prices for new issuances might decrease following a negative shock causing the demand curve to shift down. In such a scenario, with relatively low prices in the alternative market, financial sponsors potentially benefit in the form of attractive entry prices.

2.1.2 Debt Capital Markets

Maximum Debt Capacity Approach to Valuation

Introductory equation (64) expressed the simple relation between the leverage of an investment (expressed in terms of a multiple of $EBITDA_{LTM}$) and the relative purchase price (expressed as $V/EBITDA_{LTM}$ multiple). Based thereupon and assuming for the time being that financial sponsors draw on as many third-party financial liabilities as possible for the funding of the transaction, the relative purchase price m_t is then determined by the maximum leveragability L_t^{max} for the asset and a minimum acceptable/required equity contribution l_t^*.

398 See e.g. Ibbotson, R. G./Jaffe, J. F. (1975) and Ritter, J. (1984).

$$(65)\quad m_t = \frac{L_t^{\max}}{1-(1-l_t^*)}$$

Ideally LBO financing structures apply the maximum amount of debt. As described, gearing not only boosts the realized equity rate of return (as soon as the return on the invested capital exceeds the costs of debt financing) but also provides disciplinary control and tax benefits as pointed out in chapter III.B.1.2 and chapter III.B.3.3. Based upon L^{max}, the *PE* firm then commits the minimum required amount of equity that on the one hand suffices to outbid potential competing financial and/or strategic buyers and exceeds the attractiveness of alternative exit modes but on the other hand still satisfies their expected return in terms of *Times Money* and/or *Investment IRR*. According to equation (16) the realization of the expected return apparently depends upon the timing and magnitude of equity cash out- and inflows associated with the investment. The inherent circularity is obvious: the exit cash in-flow results as the selling price P_T less the remaining amount of third-party financial liabilities ND_T.[399] ND_T is determined by the cumulated amount of *FCF* generated during the holding period, which itself is a function of the initial amount of debt ND_t and the corresponding terms and conditions of the financing.[400]

Since the purchase price according to this line of reasoning results from the financing structure based on the maximum leverage, the approach might also be referred to as *maximum debt capacity approach to valuation*. This understanding of the determination of the (relative) purchase price is for instance highlighted by Mills (2000) stating that after "*the creation of the 'junk bond' market, the unsecured portion of the capital structure became cheaper and larger. This allowed investors to bid up multiple, because they could pay more for a deal (all other factors being equal) and still net the same returns.*"[401]

Analogous to considerations regarding the state of the *PE* capital market, the following Chart 11 applies supply-side argumentation to address stylized effects of the impact of debt capital market attractiveness.[402]

399 See equation (27) on page 69.

400 For an analogous line of reasoning see also Spremann, K. (1991) p. 281 and Mittendorfer, R. (2001), pp. 154-155 in the context of determining the maximum equity purchase price at entry under the premise of a target equity rate of return.

401 See Mills, K. G. (2000), p. 262. Interestingly in this context, Kaplan, S. N./Stein, J. C. (1990), p. 243 argues that (assuming 90% (permanent) gearing and 12% cost of debt) "*Each 1% mispricing of the interest rate on the debt would allow a buyer to bid up to 7.5% more than the true value of the firm*".

402 For the following increasing benefits of leverage are assumed.

Chart 11 The Effect of Increased Supply in Debt Capital on the Price of Private Equity Investments

S and D indicate supply and demand curves respectively; D denotes cumulated debt capital funds for the private equity industry; V denotes the corresponding cumulated entity valuation for the entirety of direct investments; P^D and P^V stand for the respective equilibrium prices

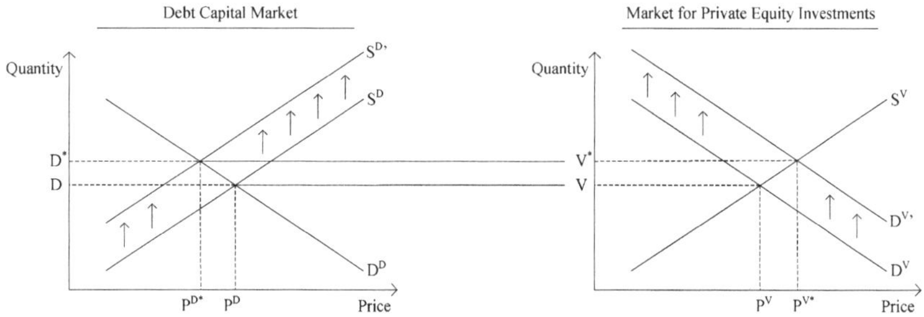

Source: Own illustration

Let the starting point again be an exogenously induced supply-side shock (S^D -> S^D') causing prices for debt capital financing to decrease, P^D -> P^{D*}, and (given the assumption of a standard, i.e. downward-slopping, demand curve) the market equilibrium amount of debt capital to increase, D -> D^*. Assuming for simplicity constant absolute equity contributions the increasing demand for debt capital implies evidently – ceteris paribus – higher purchase prices P^{V*} in the market for *PE* investments.

2.2 *Information Asymmetries and Competition in the Divestment Process*

The exit mode and the corresponding process can have a substantial impact on the realized price of the asset and hence on the relative performance of the investment from the equity investor perspective.

- In case of an IPO exited LBO investment, the divestment process might be characterized by substantial information asymmetries between the seller (i.e. the LBO equity investors) as insider and the acquirer (i.e. institutional and public investors) as outsider. Furthermore, information asymmetries potentially arise between the different groups of acquirers. Large institutional investors might benefit from relatively detailed and private information regarding the firm's operational performance, the competitive positioning and its strategy prior to an IPO through so-called *Road-shows*. Public minority investors, however, solely rely on the information provided in the Offering Prospectus.

- In a secondary buyout (or a trade sale) by contrast, the divestment process is most frequently arranged in the form of an auction process and generally comprises detailed due diligence as outlined in chapter II.A.2. Hereby the potential acquirers are granted access to confidential information and latest financials as well as to senior management. This education with respect to the firm's current and projected financial performance aims at reducing information asymmetries and thus putting the interested parties in a position to submit informed bids. However, inefficiencies might result through an auction process set-up.

Given these peculiarities of the divestment process with respect to the exit mode, potential implications on the (relative) valuation of an investment shall briefly be addressed separately. Information asymmetries with a focus on the seller/acquirer relationship are considered in the subsequent chapter; the impact of the competition in auction processes thereafter.

2.2.1 Information Asymmetries between the Seller and the Acquirer in Private-to-Public Transactions

A fundamental problem with issuing equity is potential opportunism by insiders with superior knowledge. The circumstance of insider information has been addressed from a variety of perspectives. Information asymmetry might occur (i) between the issuer and its advisors (the underwriter and/or auditor), (ii) between informed and uninformed investors, or (iii) between the issuer (including associated advisor) and new investors/the market. A market failure of the type described by Akerlof (1970) as the *market for 'lemons'* might result, when insiders fail to credibly communicate their intentions.[403] Accordingly, related means/efforts to overcome information asymmetries are manifold and are generally subsumed under the *signaling hypothesis*. Two in practice most commonly observed and in theory most frequently discussed signals in the divestment process, (i) the under-pricing phenomenon, and (ii) the retained ownership shall briefly be addressed.[404]

Underpricing in an IPO

Baron (1982) models information asymmetries between the issuer and the underwriter. Underwriters are assumed to be more knowledgeable regarding the demand and true market price for the new issuance than the issuing firm itself. Hereby under-pricing is seen as an indicator for uncertainty. The more uncertain the equity issuer with respect to the true market price, the greater the need for underwriter advice. Reducing the probability of under-subscription and increasing the reputational benefits for the underwriter, they are compensated

403 See Akerlof, G. A. (1970), pp. 488ff.

404 Other variables to convey information about firm quality might for instance be the compensation structure of management, the quality of the board of directors/supervisory board and the publication of private operating results.

for their superior insights through underpricing.[405] Empirical findings by Muscarella/ Vetsuypens (1989) are however unsupportive.[406]

Rock's (1986) model is concerned with information asymmetries between informed and uninformed investors. In a market with over- and underpriced IPOs, informed investors bid only for the latter ones, leaving uninformed investors with a higher proportion of the over-priced IPOs. Accordingly, new issues are required to be sufficiently under-priced in order to compensate uninformed investors for the uncertainty/risk they bear and motivate them to participate in the IPO market.[407] Again, under-pricing of the new issuance is found to be an efficient outcome.

In the context of IPO exited LBO- and *VC* investments, financial sponsors are frequently attested a certification role. Based on the *Certification Hypothesis* presented in Booth/Smith (1986) several papers analyze and compare the properties of financial sponsor backed IPOs.[408] It is generally confirmed that the reputational signaling of the involvement of financial sponsors leads to lower issue under-pricing and thus maximizes net proceeds to the issuer.[409] In the context of the framework of this thesis, financial sponsor certification in an IPO could hence be seen (analogously to the considerations in chapter III.B.2) as some form of *Management Support* on behalf of the financial sponsor in the divestment process.

Signaling with Retained Ownership

Leland/Pyle (1977) (henceforth LP) were the first to develop a model accounting for the fraction of ownership retained by the issuer in an IPO setting in the context of the information asymmetries and signaling hypothesis.[410] The line of reasoning starts with an under-diversified owner of a private firm. Generally such an owner would prefer to shift idiosyncratic risk to well-diversified investors through an IPO of his firm. By retaining a substantial amount of the private firm's equity (and hence its firm-specific risk), the owner can credibly send a signal to the market regarding the quality of the firm. The model yields a separating equilibrium (an equilibrium which efficiently separates lower quality and higher quality issuing firms), in which investors correctly infer firm value from the retention signal provided by the owner of

405 See Baron, D. P. (1982), pp. 955-976.

406 See Muscarella, C. J./Vetsuypens, M. R. (1989), pp. 125-135. The authors find self-underwritten IPOs, i.e. investment bankers marketing their own securities, to be significantly more under-priced than IPOs of firms with different issuers and underwriters.

407 See Rock, K. (1986), pp. 187-212 and most recently e.g. Richter, F. (2005), pp. 190-194.

408 See Booth, J. R./Smith, R. L. (1986), pp. 261-281. the certification argument is based upon the reputational signaling hypothesis developed by Klein, B./Leffler, K. (1981).

409 See. e.g. Barry, C. B., et al. (1990), pp. 447ff, Megginson, W. L./Weiss, K. A. (1991), pp. 879ff and Saadouni, B. S., et al. (1996), pp. 47ff.

410 See Leland, H. E./Pyle, D. H. (1977), pp. 371-387.

the firm. Higher fractional retained holdings signal larger cash flows. Empirical support of the model is provided amongst others by Downes/Heinkel (1982) and Clarkson et al. (1991).[411]

Combined Signaling

The LP model applies only one signal, the retained ownership fraction. This implies that cash flows of the project/firm are known and observable as only one parameter can be unknown. Various models extended the univariate LP signaling model.[412] For the purpose of this thesis relevant parts of the model provided by Grinblatt/Hwang (1989) (henceforth GH) shall briefly be reviewed.[413] This GH model builds upon the LP framework though applies the issue's offering price next to the fractional holding of the owner as a second signal.

Consider a three-date world. At date 0 the investment requires a capital outlay I by the owner (henceforth the issuer). The investment returns a cash flow of $\mu+\tilde{C}_2$ at date 2 and an independent random cash flow $\tilde{C}_1$ at date 1, whereby $\tilde{C}_1$ and $\tilde{C}_2$ have zero means and variances of σ^2. As in the LP framework the owner markets (for under-diversification reasons) the investment to the investing public. In case the owner's private information regarding μ exceeds that of the investing public, the issuer can employ (i) α, the fraction of the new issue retained, as well as (ii) P, the issue offering price, as the two signals to credibly communicate his information. If no signaling of the true μ occurs at date 0, public investors will learn the true project mean in the course of period 1 with probability p. This is a fundamental difference compared with the LP model. Other than in the model presented here, in the LP model the expected value of the project is revealed to outsiders with certainty at date 1 and the variance is already known at date 0.

The presented GH model further assumes that the owner intends to sell the remaining fractional holding ($1-\alpha$) at date 1. The objective function is to maximize the date 1 expected utility according to the assumed linear expected utility in the form

$$(66)\quad E\left(U\left(\tilde{W}_1\right)\right)=E\left(\tilde{W}_1\right)-\frac{b}{2}\sigma^2\left(\tilde{W}_1\right)$$

---

[411] See Downes, D. H./Heinkel, R. (1982), pp. 1-10 and Clarkson, P. M., et al. (1991), pp. 115-131.

[412] See e.g. Allen, F./Faulhaber, G. (1989), Grinblatt, M./Hwang, C. Y. (1989), Welch, I. (1989), Datar, S. M., et al. (1991), and Courteau, L. (1995).

[413] For the following see Grinblatt, M./Hwang, C. Y. (1989), pp. 383-420.

Similar to the LP model, the owner chooses according to his budget any combination of (i) a risk-free asset[414], (ii) the market portfolio, and (iii) equity shares in his investment; with all assets being priced based on information available to outside investors.

First, the special case of known variance and hence signaling by the fractional holding only is considered. According to the outlined set-up, the end of date 1 wealth $\tilde{W}_1$ results as follows: at date 0 the initial wealth position W_0 is used to invest the amount M into the market portfolio and the amount I into the private firm. From the issuance of all shares other than his retained fraction with the discount Dis, the issuer receives $(1-\alpha)(\mu(\alpha)-Dis)$. Uninformed, though signaled, outside investors expect date 2 cash flows to be $\mu(\alpha)$ and hence value their corresponding stake at $(1-\alpha)\mu(\alpha)$. From the perspective of the issuer the investment returns between date 0 and date 1 $\alpha(\tilde{\hat{\mu}}+\tilde{C}_1)$ and the investment in the market portfolio returns $M(1+\tilde{r}_M)$. Accordingly, the end of period 1 wealth results as

(67) $\tilde{W}_1=\alpha(\tilde{\hat{\mu}}+\tilde{C}_1)+M(1+\tilde{r}_M)+[W_0+(1-\alpha)(\mu(\alpha)-Dis)-M-I]$

Unless the outside investors learn with probability p during period 1 the true μ of the project the value of expected date 2 cash flows is evaluated with the signaling schedule $\mu(\alpha)$ (i.e. at date 1 $\tilde{\hat{\mu}}=\mu$ with probability p and $\tilde{\hat{\mu}}=\mu(\alpha)$ with probability $1\text{-}p$).

Hence, the expected value and the corresponding variance result as

(68) $E(\tilde{\hat{\mu}})=p\mu+(1-p)\mu(\alpha)$

and

(69) $\operatorname{var}(\tilde{\hat{\mu}})=p(1-p)(\mu-\mu(\alpha))^2$

respectively. In combination with equations (68) and (75) the expected end of period 1 wealth $E(\tilde{W}_1)$ and the corresponding variance can be expressed as

(70) $E(\tilde{W}_1)=\alpha[p\mu+(1-p)\mu(\alpha)]+M\bar{r}_M+[W_0+(1-\alpha)(\mu(\alpha)-Dis)-I]$

and

(71) $E(\tilde{W}_1)=\alpha^2\sigma^2+\delta^2\sigma_M^2+\alpha^2p(1-p)(\mu-\mu(\alpha))^2$

The end of period 1 expected utility then results as

---

414 Without loss of generality the model assumes the risk-free rate to be zero.

(72) $$E\left(U(\tilde{W}_1)\right)=\alpha\left[p\mu+(1-p)\mu(\alpha)\right]+M\tilde{r}_M+\left[W_0+(1-\alpha)(\mu(\alpha)-Dis)-I\right]$$
$$-\frac{b}{2}\left[\alpha^2\sigma^2+M^2\sigma_M^2+\alpha^2 p(1-p)(\mu-\mu(\alpha))^2\right]$$

The partial differentiations of equation (72) with respect to α and δ are first order conditions for the maximizations of expected utility.

Accordingly, differentiating equation (72) with respect to M $\left(\frac{\partial E\left(U(\tilde{W}_1)\right)}{\partial M}=0\right)$ implies

(73) $$\delta=\frac{\tilde{r}_M}{b\sigma_M^2}$$

Differentiating equation (72) with respect to α $\left(\frac{\partial E\left(U(\tilde{W}_1)\right)}{\partial \alpha}=0\right)$ implies

(74) $$p\mu+(1-p\alpha)\mu_\alpha(\alpha)-p\mu(\alpha)-\alpha b\sigma^2-\frac{b}{2}p(1-p)$$
$$\left[2\alpha(\mu(\alpha)-\mu)^2+2\alpha^2(\mu(\alpha)-\mu)\mu_\alpha(\alpha)\right]=0$$

Assuming a self-fulfilling belief $\mu(\alpha)=\mu$, equation (74) reduces to[415]

(75) $$\mu_\alpha(\alpha)=\frac{\alpha}{1-\alpha p}b\sigma^2$$

The unique solution to this differential equation equals

(76) $$\mu(\alpha)=-\frac{1}{p^2}b\sigma^2\left(\ln(1-\alpha p)+\alpha p\right)+c$$

with c being the constant of the integration.

Thus, in this one-signal world, with signaling through retained ownership only, the unique Pareto-dominant signaling schedule can then be shown to result as $\mu(\alpha)=-\frac{1}{p^2}b\sigma^2\left(\ln(1-\alpha p)+\alpha p\right)+I$.[416] The benefit of not only signaling with the retained fractional ownership is revealed in equation (76). The equation indicates that a higher variance issuer has higher expected value. In case of unknown variance, high variance issuers might be willing to bear the costs of a further signal. Here the GH model argues that "*in a separating equilibrium, the*

415 See Grinblatt, M./Hwang, C. Y. (1989), p. 399.

416 See Grinblatt, M./Hwang, C. Y. (1989), pp. 399f.

portion of the signaling schedule for the Lowest Variance Issuer $\left[\sigma_L^2\right]$ *must be a separating signaling schedule for the case where the variance is known.*"[417]

To illustrate the effect of signaling with underpricing only, the following two-stage game between a *High Mean Issuer* and a *Low Mean Issuer* shall briefly be considered. A Low Mean Issuer that decides not to underprice receives $(1-\alpha)\mu^L$ at date 0 and regardless of whether outside investors learn the true μ the issuer will get $\alpha(\mu^L + \widetilde{C}_{1,L})$ at date 1. In case a Low Mean Issuer falsely signals (through underpricing) to be of high quality the corresponding payoffs are $(1-\alpha)(\mu^D - Dis)$ at date 0 and depending on the state at date 1, i.e. if the true μ is revealed, either $\alpha(\mu^L + \widetilde{C}_{1,L})$ with probability p or $\alpha(\mu^H + \widetilde{C}_{1,L})$ with probability *1-p*. Hence, the initial cost of falsely signaling $(1-\alpha)(Dis - \mu^D + \mu^L)$, face potential benefits of $p0 + (1-p)\alpha(\mu^H - \mu^L)$. This cost–benefit trade-off implies that for

$$(77) \quad \mu^H = \mu^L + \frac{1-\alpha}{1-\alpha p} Dis$$

the Low Mean Issuer is deterred from mimicking the High Mean Issuer and therefore in his own best interest decides not to underprice.

Considering finally the case or the conjoint signaling by the fractional holding and the underpricing builds upon the similar equation (67) for date 1 wealth; except for replacing $\mu(\alpha)$ with $\mu(\alpha, Dis)$.

$$(78) \quad \widetilde{W}_1 = \alpha\left(\tilde{\bar{\mu}} + \widetilde{C}_1\right) + M\left(1 + \widetilde{r}_M\right) + \left[W_0 + (1-\alpha)(\mu(\alpha, Dis) - Dis) - M - I\right]$$

Similarly the expected utility results as

$$(79) \quad E\left(U(\widetilde{W}_1)\right) = \alpha\left[p\mu + (1-p)\mu(\alpha, Dis)\right] + M\widetilde{r}_M + \left[W_0 + (1-\alpha)(\mu(\alpha, Dis) - Dis) - I\right]$$
$$-\frac{b}{2}\left[\alpha^2\sigma^2 + M^2\sigma_M^2 + \alpha^2 p(1-p)(\mu - \mu(\alpha, Dis))^2\right]$$

Following substitutions with equation (73) and (77) into (79) and deriving the first order condition, the following signaling schedules for $\mu(\alpha, Dis)$ and $\sigma^2(\alpha, Dis)$ result (see Appendix A for details):

$$(80) \quad \mu(\alpha, Dis) = \mu^L(\alpha) + \frac{1-\alpha}{1-\alpha p} Dis$$

---

417 See Grinblatt, M./Hwang, C. Y. (1989), p. 404.

(81) $\sigma^2(\alpha, Dis) = \sigma_L^2 + \frac{(1-\alpha)p}{(1-\alpha p)\alpha b} Dis$

Equation (81) reveals a positive relation between the fractional retained holding and the degree of underpricing.

To conclude, if the variance is unknown, issuers might want to signal the quality of their firm through a combination of their fractional holding and underpricing. The presented model argues for a positive relation between these two signals. The intuition hereby is that high quality issuers bear the IPO discount to differentiate themselves from lower quality issuers and rely upon the fact that they can recoup the cost of signaling in subsequent issuances.

2.2.2 Winner's Curse in Auctioned Private-to-Private Transactions

As pointed out, private-to-private transactions mitigate information asymmetries between the seller and the potential acquirer through the exchange of confidential information in a due diligence process. However, in order to establish a market, supply and demand mechanism in private-to-private transactions, companies are generally sold in an auction process.

A phenomenon referred to as *winner's curse* stalks the pages of the literature on (common value) auctions.[418] Common value auctions are characterized by the fact that the auctioned item has the same value for all bidders.[419] Kagel et al. (1989) argue the winner's curse to result "*from bidder's failure to account for the adverse selection problem inherent in winning auctions for items of uncertain value.*"[420] In other words, the winner's curse as a form of judgmental failure may result in common value auctions where "*bidders usually win the item when they have the highest, or one of the highest, estimates of value.*"[421] Accordingly, winning an auction is not based upon an unbiased estimate of value but rather results from the biased, estimated value conditional upon having the highest private information signal. Assuming risk neutrality or risk aversion of the bidders, this implies on average negative profits for inexperienced bidders.[422] The impact of the winner's curse on acquirer's profitability has first been empirically observed in the offshore oil business. Capen et al. (1971) notes that in auctions for offshore tracts "*the winner tends to be the player who most over-estimated the true tract value.*"[423]

---

418 For early contributions to the phenomenon of the winner's curse see. e.g. Miller, E. M. (1977), pp. 1151-1168, Cassing, J./Douglas, R. W. (1980), pp. 110-121 and Cox, J. C./Isaac, M. R. (1984), pp. 579-592.

419 See Kagel, J. H./Levin, D. (1986), p. 895.

420 See Kagel, J. H., et al. (1989), p. 241.

421 See Kagel, J. H./Levin, D. (1999), p. 900.

422 See Kagel, J. H./Levin, D. (1999), pp. 899ff.

423 See Capen, E. C., et al. (1971), p. 643.

Several side aspects of the winner's curse phenomenon in the context of auctions have received detailed attention in the academic literature. Kagel/Richard (2001) focus on differences between inexperienced and super-experienced bidders in common value auctions. Among others, their experimental study reveals that super-experienced bidders have learned to overcome the winner's curse as they bid below the expected value conditional on winning the item and hence earn on average positive profits.[424] In their seminal paper Kagel/Levin (1986) derive that the revelation of public information about the value of the company increases revenues of the seller absent the winner's curse but interestingly decreases revenues of the seller in the presence of the winner's curse.[425] Further, the authors report that a larger number of bidders results in more aggressive bidding. Mares/Harstad (2003) and Kagel/Levin (1999) analyze the private disclosure of information to only selected bidders in common value auctions. Hereby, the authors conclude that – in particular when super-experienced bidders are present – sellers can increase their revenues by selectively revealing private information compared with a systematic information structure.[426]

The implications for the divestment phase and hence the variation in the transaction multiple of LBO investments are obvious. Selling an investment through an auction process creates a competitive environment and ensures that the seller maximizes disposal proceeds by selling to the strategic or financial investor with the highest estimate of value.

[424] See Kagel, J. H./Richard, J.-F. (2001), pp. 408-419.

[425] See Kagel, J. H./Levin, D. (1986), pp. 894-920.

[426] See Mares, V./Harstad, R. M. (2003), pp. 264 and Kagel, J. H./Levin, D. (1999), pp. 1219ff.

IV. Research Model, Derivation of Hypotheses and Operationalization of Variables

A. Research Model

Purpose of this thesis is the analysis of value creation in LBOs on investment level from a post-LBO equity investor perspective. *Total Proceeds* to these equity investors are the prerequisite for any such value creation analysis; next to a time, and appropriate risk adjustment as discussed in chapter II.C.

For the purpose of a structured discussion, the five non-mutually exclusive components resulting from the decomposition of *Total Proceeds* were subsumed according to the framework of an internal perspective *FCF effects* and an external perspective *variation in the transaction multiple* (chapter III.A). Theoretical sources of value creation for both perspectives were subsequently discussed in chapter III.B and III.C respectively.

In this light, the research model to empirically assess value creation in LBOs on investment level has the following conceptual design:

Chart 12 Conceptual Research Model

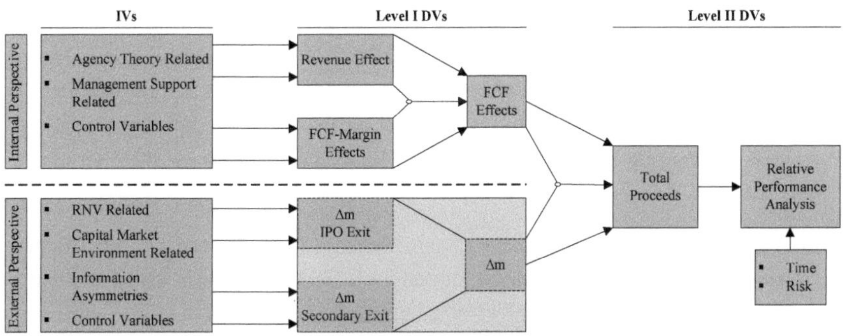

Source: Own illustration

- Based on the two-tier discussion regarding sources of value creation in LBO investments, hypotheses for the impact of independent variables (IVs) on (i) *FCF effects*, and (ii) the *variation in the transaction multiple* and therefore implicitly on value creation and the performance of the investment are derived in a first step. The derivation of each individual hypothesis is based on previous discussions with respect to the internal perspective in chapter III.B and the external perspective in chapter III.C. Separate hypotheses for control variables complement the analysis.

- Operationalization of dependent variables (*DVs*) with respect to the internal as well as the external perspective will be referred to as *Level I DVs*; the relative performance measures and their constituents as *Level II DVs.*

- Other than with respect to the external perspective, the operationalization of the internal perspective is not straightforward as *FCF effects* as such does not represent a single, quantifiable and observable dependent variable.
  - *Revenue effect* and *FCF-Margin effects* as the two principal components of *FCF effects* are considered separately (see also chapter III.A.3); *FCF-Margin effects* are operationalized through the variation analysis of the various accounting components of FCF during the holding period. Accordingly, a variety of individual measures represent *FCF-effects.*
  - Based on previous considerations in chapter III.C, the analysis of the *variation in the transaction multiple* separates IPO and secondary buyout exited LBOs.

- The analysis is based on the central underlying assumption that prior to the LBO, bought-out companies are characterized by organizational inefficiencies that improve in the course of the LBO holding period. Based thereupon, expectations for a positive or negative variation of internal perspective *Level I DPs* are formulated using simple accounting algebra.

- The analysis of value creation performance measures and their components (*Level II DPs*) represents the primary objective of this thesis. Based upon previous analyses, *Times Money*, the *Investment IRR* and *Alternative Performance Measures* can be (i) descriptively quantified and (partially) decomposed, as well as (ii) (partially) inferringly analyzed. Accordingly, not only the overall impact of the identified independent variables but also the relative impact of the components is considered.

- Finally, the relationship of the various LBO performance measures is considered. This puts the various findings of the individual measures into perspective and provides illustrative insights regarding the interconnectivity of these measures.

B. Derivation of Hypotheses and Operationalization of Independent Variables

Based on previous considerations in chapter III.B and III.C and the resulting outlined conceptual research model, the following chapter derives hypotheses and operationalizes IVs for the empirical analysis. This faces three major challenges:

- First, the holistic approach to assess value creation in LBOs combines various aspects of the complex value creation process. As repeatedly pointed out the presented framework of an internal as well as external perspective builds upon numerous individual sources of value.

While each aspect merited – in part extensive – research on its own, this thesis strives for the integrated view of these various sources.

- Second, the following empirical analysis is based on a proprietary, newly created database with information taken from public, semi-public and confidential primary sources of date (see chapter V.A for details). The outlined research model requires objective and quantifiable variables. Other than with a questionnaire-based survey technique, qualitative, non-observable variables shall not be operationalized through a (subjective) rating scale.
- Third, the empirical analysis comprises 42 realized LBO investments. Apparently, this poses restrictions not only on the methodology of the analysis (see chapter V.B for details) but also on the number of hypotheses, and thus IVs, to be analyzed.

In due consideration of these challenges the following chapters derive hypotheses alongside the outlined conceptual two-tier framework with an internal (chapter IV.B.1) and external (chapter IV.B.2) perspective. Control Variables (CVs) for both perspectives are discussed separately (chapter IV.B.3).

1. Internal Perspective: FCF Effects

Analogous to chapter III.B *agency cost reduction* related aspects (chapter IV.B.1.1) and *Management Support* related aspects (chapter IV.B.1.2) shall be distinguished.

1.1 Agency Cost Reduction Related

The first set of hypotheses and related, operationalized independent variables addresses the extent of agency problems prior to the LBO and thereupon means to overcome, or at least reduce, corresponding agency costs as discussed in chapter III.B.1.2. Given the identification of the three major means to reduce agency costs, an empirical analysis should aim to control for (i) monitoring and control, (ii) managerial ownership and the incentive intensity hypothesis, as well as (iii) the disciplinary role of financial debt.

1.1.1 Size and Profitability

First, firm size and profitability are applied as proxies for pre-LBO agency problems in the form of monitoring and control. Assuming that organizational inefficiencies tend to be higher in large corporations the potential to reduce agency costs and thus to improve operating margins should be higher for relatively large firms. In their seminal article Jensen/Meckling (1976) hypothesize that the larger the firm becomes the larger are the total agency costs because it is likely that the monitoring function is inherently more difficult and expensive in a larger corporation.[427] On the other hand growth rate basics imply that compared with smaller

---

[427] See Jensen, M. C./Meckling, W. (1976), p. 348.

firms, larger firms might grow less fast. Accordingly, academic literature predominately hypothesises a positive effect of firm size on operational performance improvements of the portfolio company. Conversely, the revenues effect is expected to be negatively related to size. Empirical results are confirmative.[428]

H_Int_1a: *The larger the firm at entry, the higher are potential FCF-Margin effects but the lower is the revenue effect. The combined effect on FCF effects and hence the LBO investment performance is unpredicted.*

The effect of the firm's profitability on *FCF effects* is similarly controversial. With respect to *revenue growth*, profitable firms should experience higher growth rates due to the internally generated cash, which can be used for growth investments and acquisitions. Regarding *FCF-Margin effects* two opposing effects coincide: on the one hand, agency theory argues that the level of divergent managerial behavior is higher for firms with high levels of undistributed cash flow since the corporation's profitability offers room for perk consumption and thus misuse. On the other hand, the pressure to improve operating margins should be higher for relatively unprofitable companies. In particular when the profitability level is low and the threat of not being able to serve the fixed debt financing claims is omnipresent, the incentive to improve operating margins should be higher. In other words, we expect that relative improvements to operating performance are larger for LBOs of underperforming firms than for LBOs of average or normal performers. Furthermore, it seems questionable whether any accounting measure could meaningfully serve to test the first line of reasoning. Accounting measures are generally stated net of the consumption of any fringe benefits (which presumably become apparent in SG&A costs), implying that their level inappropriately reflects the potential to improve the firm's performance. Long/Ravenscraft (1993b) empirically confirm the latter view. In the analyzed sample comprising a gross number of 209 LBOs, the pre-LBO profitability measure is the statistically most powerful variable in explaining performance improvements subsequent to a LBO.[429] For these reasons the respective hypothesis postulates:

H_Int_1b: *The lower the profitability of the firm at entry, the lower the revenue growth, but the higher FCF-Margin effects during the holding period. The combined effect on FCF effects and hence the LBO investment performance is unpredicted.*

---

428 See e.g. Long, W. F./Ravenscraft, D. J. (1993b), pp. 16f and p. 22 as well as Schefczyk, M. (2004), pp. 217ff; both applying revenues for operationalizing *size*.

429 See Long, W. F./Ravenscraft, D. J. (1993b), pp. 21f; pre-LBO operating income margins were applied as profitability measure.

For the purpose of the following empirical analysis, size and profitability will be operationalized through the firm's revenues and EBITDA-margin for the latest available LTM period prior to the LBO: Rev_{t-1}[430] and $EBITDA\text{-}Mrg_{t-1}$[431].

1.1.2 Managerial Incentivation

Chapter III.B.1.2 discussed the alignment of interests between shareholders and managers in the context of the incentive-intensity hypothesis as a means to reduce divergent managerial behavior and thus reduce agency costs in LBO investments. Equity holdings transform managers into co-owners and thus decrease the degree of separation between ownership and control and increase the extent of common interest between investors and its management. As argued, efforts are expected to increase, perk consumption to decrease and the underinvestment as well as the risk incentive problem to be mitigated. An underlying assumption for this line of reasoning is that pre-LBO managerial alignment of interest has been suboptimal, due either to insufficient equity holdings or inappropriate incentive schemes.

Direct empirical support is provided by Phan/Hill (1995) confirming a statistically significant relationship between management stockholdings and variations in operational performance (measured as the difference in labor productivity) three and five years following the LBO. Based upon a sample of 214 US American LBOs in the years 1986 and 1989, these results imply that "*management stockholdings may have the most enduring impact upon firm efficiency.*"[432] Similarly though not in the direct context of LBOs, studies by Wruck (1989) and Morck et al. (1988) confirm the direct association between (variations in) equity ownership and (variations in) accounting performance.[433]

Related empirical findings are similarly supportive and consistent, though differ substantially with respect to the operationalization of the dependent variable. In premia-paid

---

430 With respect to *size* forthcoming regression analyses were also run using $Assets_{t-1}$ and TS_t as well as a z-standardized variable comprising Rev_{t-1}, $Assets_{t-1}$, TS_t as the respective IV (for a brief discussion of difficulties regarding assets as variable and/or denominator for ratio analysis see chapter V.B). Given the high correlation between the variables, results were broadly comparable. Factor analysis identified Rev_{t-1} as the appropriate size indicator. Further, despite a higher level of skewness Rev_{t-1} rather than ln_Rev_{t-1} was applied. First, the *Kolmogorov-Smirnov* test can not reject the validity of the assumption of normally distributed revenues (Rev_{t-1}) as size indicator in the sample. Second, the correlation between size and profitability is lower for Rev_{t-1} than for ln_Rev_{t-1} as the size indicator, thus reducing multicollinearity of the analysis (see Table 66 in the Appendix).

431 *EBITDA-Mrg* has been chosen pre capital expenditures to account for the theoretical argument that resources are potentially allocated to negative NPV projects pre-LBO. The ex-ante differentiation between positive and negative NPV projects is not feasible from an outsider perspective.

432 See Phan, P. H./Hill, C. W. L. (1995), p. 733.

433 See Wruck, K. H. (1989), pp. 3ff and Morck, R., et al. (1988), pp. 293ff. Both studies, however, describe a nonmonotonic relation between managerial ownership and (non-LBO) firm performance, which – given that the average percentage equity holding in the analyzed sample of LBOs here is much larger – shall not be considered in this analysis.

studies, Grammatikos/Swary and Travlos/Millon found higher cumulated abnormal returns for pure management-led buyouts.[434] Assuming that the premia paid serves as an indicator for the expected value creation, stock markets seem to anticipate buyout transactions with no financial sponsor involvement, i.e. the purest form of managerial incentivation, to be more successful.[435] Jakoby (2000) reports a tendency for investments with a higher post-MBO managerial ownership stake to be more successful.[436] An inverse relation between management equity participation and defaults on debt payments is found by Kaplan/Stein (1993).[437] Further evidence in the form of the incentive-intensity hypothesis is provided by Wright et al. (1994) and Thompson et al. (1992b) who report a statistically significant negative relation between managerial incentivation and the failure of an MBO[438] and confirm the theoretically predicted relation between managerial equity ownership and the return on invested capital[439]. Finally, in a case study comparing Kroger's recapitalization and Safeway's LBO, Denis (1994) argues the differences in managerial incentivation to be causally for significant differences in post-LBO performance.[440] Conversely however, analyzing a sample of 398 firms and after controlling for observed firm characteristics as well as firm fixed effects, Himmelberg et al. (1999) find managerial ownership not to affect firm performance.[441]

Based upon the aforementioned reasoning and mostly supportive empirical results, *FCF-Margin effects* are thus expected to be higher, the higher management is incentivized, although positive effects of managerial ownership are expected to show a marginally decreasing utility.

H_Int_2: *The degree of management incentivation has a positive impact on FCF-Margin effects and thus the performance of the LBO investment.*

The empirical analysis will employ management's relative diluted ownership stake at exit λ as indicator for management incentivation. The level of managerial ownership participation can either be assessed relative to the total equity contribution or in absolute terms. Both measures are imperfect: on the one hand it could be argued that the optimal relative participation is lower for larger firms as the work effort and the riskiness of the investment, which investing management weighs against the expected benefits, increase under-proportionately with the size

434 Cited in Amihud, Y. (1989), p. 7.

435 See Schmid, H. (1994), p. 285.

436 See Jakoby, S. (2000), p. 276. Note, however, that the study is based (other than this study) on MBOs with an average managerial ownership stake in excess of 70%. Further, the dependent variable indicating the success of the MBO is operationalized as binary 0/1 variable based on the calculation of a *success index* (pp. 129-136).

437 See Kaplan, S. N./Stein, J. (1993), pp. 354f.

438 See Wright, M., et al. (1994), pp. 21-40.

439 See Thompson, S., et al. (1992b), pp. 413-430.

440 See Denis, D. J. (1994), pp. 193ff.

441 See Himmelberg, C. P., et al. (1999), pp. 353-384.

of the firm.[442] On the other hand it seems reasonable to assume that the group of incentivized top-management and hierarchical levels increases with firm size, thereby challenging the absolute and favouring the relative consideration. Empirical results in this study indicate the relative consideration to be the better proxy. As pointed out previously, management incentivation schemes are highly complex, generally tailored to the specific transaction and comprising optional components. For that reason the ultimate, relative diluted ownership stake at exit is applied to account for potential ownership appreciation over the course of the investment period. In doing so, the variable captures the upside potential for management and associated motivational effects from potential ownership appreciation.

1.1.3 Disciplining Debt

Chapter III.B.1.2 stressed the disciplinary role of third-party financial liabilities. Debt service payments, the combination of interest payments and debt repayments resulting from the heavy debt burden of the LBO, decrease managements' discretionary leeway for deploying the firm's cash flow. Baker/Montgomery (1994) consider this pre-committed capital as an outsourced controlling system that institutionalizes monitoring of management.[443] The pressure to improve the operational performance of the business and reduce cash outflows (e.g. in the form of capital expenditures or inefficiently managed NWC) should therefore be higher, the higher the level of debt financing of the business, though with a marginal decreasing utility of additional debt. However, the extent of debt financing is expected to negatively affect revenue growth. Not only the pre-commitment to service debt, but also the reduced flexibility potentially dissuades growth initiatives.[444]

With respect to the overall performance of an LBO investment, debt financing increases ex-ante the riskiness of the investment; which expressed in the form of higher β increases the expected equity rate of return as discussed in chapter II.C.2. In an ex-post consideration of realized, and thus by definition to some extent *successful*, investments debt financing (i.e. to be precise the gearing ratio) boosts the realized equity rate of return, i.e. the performance of the investment expressed as *Times Money* or *Investment IRR* as soon as the return on the firm's assets exceeds post-tax costs of debt (see equation (1)).

For a sample of going private transactions, Frankfurter/Gunay (1992) find a statistically significant relationship between the benefits of debt financing (expected tax savings and pre-commitment of generated cash for debt servicing) and the cumulated abnormal return earned

---

442 See e.g. Forst, M. (1993), p. 85.

443 See Baker, G. P./Montgomery, C. A. (1994), pp. 1-34.

444 See e.g. Gifford Jr., D. (2001), p. 18.

by pre-buyout stockholders.[445] Lehn/Poulsen (1989) report a significant relation between undistributed FCF and the decision to go private, also backing the presented argumentation of unused borrowing capacity and a disciplinary role of financial debt.[446] Related evidence is provided by Maloney et al. (1993) in that indebtedness improves managerial decision making in the context of acquisitions.[447] Similar to managerial ownership (though as reported presumably less important), Phan/Hill (1995) identify the level of debt to significantly affect the performance of the analyzed LBO investments. In order to test the hypothesis that high levels of debt oblige management to disgorge generated cash flows, Long/Ravenscraft (1993b) compare the operating performance of a set of LBOs to non-leveraged going private transactions.[448] The coefficient of the corresponding dummy is significantly negative as predicted. In addition to these empirical studies, further anecdotal evidence supporting the basic argumentation that managerial incentivation favors the performance/success of LBO transactions is provided by Baker/Wruck (1989), pp. 163ff and Anders (1992), pp. 80f. Therefore:

H_Int_3: *The higher the debt financing at entry, the lower the revenue growth effect, but the higher FCF-Margin effects and thus the better the LBO investment performance.*

The gearing ratio l_t – defined as total debt as percentage of total capitalization (see chapter II.B.1) – at entry will be considered for partially proxying beneficial disciplinary effects of debt financing.

1.2 Management Support Related

Means of operational impact of the (group of) financial sponsor(s) on *FCF effects* have previously been subsumed under *Management Support* and discussed in chapter III.B.2. When it comes to empirically testing for *Management Support* two questions arise: First, what factors representatively indicate the level of *Management Support* provided by the (group of) financial sponsor(s)? Second, owing to the difficulty of quantitatively assessing such factors, how can qualitative indicators be operationalized for testing the impact on the performance of an investment?

Empirical studies testing for *Management Support* generally apply a questionnaire-based survey methodology, since indications of the extent of *Management Support* are of a rather qualitative nature. In their seminal study Macmillan et al. (1989) identified 20 ordinal variables

445 See Frankfurter, G. M./Gunay, E. (1992), pp. 82-95.

446 See Lehn, K./Poulsen, A. (1989), pp. 771ff.

447 See Maloney, M. T., et al. (1993), pp. 189-217.

448 See Long, W. F./Ravenscraft, D. J. (1993b), p. 17 and p. 23.

for questionnaire-based survey technique in order to measure involvement of the *PE* firms. Based on factor analysis the four identified factors were (i) development of operations, (ii) management selection, (iii) personnel management, and (iv) financial.[449] Due to the quantitative nature of the forthcoming empirical analysis, with objective, observable variables, the three subsequently detailed indications, (i) change in management, (ii) divestiture and acquisition activity, and (iii) the *PE* sponsor experience will be applied for indicating *Management Support* effects. Obviously, this set-up constrains the ability to test for rather qualitative aspects such as organizational changes or motivations and tasks of people involved, which could either be surveyed or captured in individual case studies.[450] However, in light of the outlined research design, the necessity of a quantitative analysis and related benefits are evident.

1.2.1 Change in Management

Following the argumentation presented in chapter III.B.2.2 and assuming that *PE* firms ideally command a network of senior executives capable to run – at least intermediately – a portfolio company, it can be argued that changes in the top management subsequent to a LBO entry transaction install a more efficient management team. While this line of reasoning implies positive impacts on the LBO performance, a contradictory argumentation based on the resource based view of a corporation might consider management turnover as a loss of experience and expertise, which ought to coincide with negative performance effects.[451]

Related empirical support is provided by Denis/Serrano (1996). Following unsuccessful control contests, (i) management turnover is reported to be concentrated in underperforming companies with outside equity investors acquiring an ownership stake, and (ii) management turnover in combination with outside blockholding is found to coincide with successful post-contest asset restructuring.[452]

Assuming that *PE* firms actively and intentionally bring about changes in management in the course of the LBO transaction, this thesis follows a priori the first argumentation and thus postulates the following working hypothesis:

---

449 See Macmillan, I. C., et al. (1989), pp. 27ff. For a recent empirical study applying a slightly modified questionnaire structure see Meier, D. (2005). Further related questionnaire-based survey studies, though with a focus on venture capital and early financing stages or rather smaller MBO companies, include among others Sapienza, H. J. (1992), Barney, J. B., et al. (1996), Jakoby, S. (2000), Brinkrolf, A. (2002) and Schefczyk, M. (2004).

450 For case studies on LBO investment level see e.g. Baker, G. P./Wruck, K. H. (1989), pp. 163-190, Baker, G. P. (1992), pp. 1081-1119 and Denis, D. J. (1994), pp. 193-224.

451 See e.g. Barney, J. B./Wright, P. M. (1988). In this respect Cannella, A. A., Jr./Hambrick, D. C. (1993) empirically confirm negative performance effects of managerial turnover in takeovers.

452 See Denis, D. J./Serrano, J. M. (1996), pp. 239-266.

H_Int_4: *Changes in a firm's top management positively affect revenue growth as well as FCF-Margin effects and thus the performance of the LBO investment.*

The binary variable *CMgmt* dummies changes in the firm's top-management and takes the value of one if the Chairman, the CEO or the CFO were replaced during the holding period of the investment.

1.2.2 Divestiture and Acquisition Activity

In theory as well as in practice a frequently brought-forward argument claims that LBO companies dispose of non-core business activities during the holding period.[453] The respective argumentation as a source of value creation is twofold: first the disposal of non-core or underperforming assets is argued to be a means of streamlining or restructuring the business and transferring ownership to a party with a higher valued use.[454] Second – and probably an even more prominent line of reasoning – cash disposal proceeds help repay financial liabilities and reduce the firm's heavy debt burden associated with the LBO.[455] Muscarella/Vetsuypens (1990) argue that according to Jensen (1986) "*the bonding effects of high leverage may help correct ill-conceived past diversification strategies*".[456] Therefore disposal activity should coincide with positive *FCF-Margin effects*. It has been argued in chapter III.B.2.2 that selected, majority-owner approved acquisitions during the holding period strengthen the company's core business, offer opportunities for synergies and economies of scale and therefore also foster positive *FCF-Margin effects.* Gompers (2002) argues that *PE* firms add value when it comes to acquisitions and divestitures on investment level given their expertise in executing transactions.[457]

Empirical findings are mixed. Hite et al. (1987) find positive stock market reactions in response to asset sales in the context of general corporate divestiture activity.[458] However, Long/Ravenscraft (1993b) fail to empirically confirm significant results regarding the performance impact of a dummy variable accounting for LBOs that divested more than 30% of

---

453 See among others Deangelo, H., et al. (1984), pp. 367ff, Kaplan, S. N./Stein, J. (1993), p. 333, Inderbitzin, M. (1993), p. 8, Mills, K. G. (2000), p. 262.

454 See e.g. Easterwood, J. C. (1998), pp. 133ff.

455 *Note:* Frequently, debt financing term sheets include covenants imposing the firm to use any proceeds from asset disposals exclusively to repay outstanding indebtedness. In some cases, financing terms are even negotiated with so-called disposal bridges, which are based on or imply the immediate disposal of some of the firm's asset to lower total leverage shortly after the transaction. In the case of add-on acquisitions, additional borrowings are sometimes used in combination with cash generated endogenously, which obviously also immediately impacts leverage.

456 See Muscarella, C. J./Vetsuypens, M. R. (1990), p. 1397.

457 See Gompers, P. A. (2002), p. 6.

458 See Hite, G. L., et al. (1987), pp. 229-252.

total assets in the three years following the LBO.[459] Easterwood (1998) analyzes a sample of 41 LBO investments in the 1980s regarding 134 divestments undertaken by these firms during their holding period. Using bond returns for publicly traded debt as proxy to measure wealth effects of the divestment announcement, the author finds that, on average, divestments are not associated with significant wealth effects.[460]

As a working hypothesis, this thesis predicts ex-ante positive effects of acquisition and divestiture activity.

H_Int_5: *Significant disposals and/or acquisitions during the holding period positively affect FCF-Margin effects and hence the performance of the LBO investment.*

Let *Disp* be defined as a binary 0/1 variable taking the value of one if the bought-out company underwent at least one significant disposal in any year *t* during the holding period. Analogously, let *Acq* be defined as a binary 0/1 variable taking the value of one if the bought-out company acquired significantly in any year *t* during the holding period. A divestiture or an acquisition is considered significant if the transaction value exceeds 5% of the firm's total assets in the relevant year. The variable *steady* is a binary 0/1 variable that takes the value of one if the portfolio company neither disposed of nor acquired significant assets during the holding period.

1.2.3 Private Equity Firm Experience

Chapter III.B.2 argued that *PE* firms add value to portfolio companies not only through monitoring and controlling but also through advising and hands-on involvement in the business. Various means such as an efficient network of industry specialists, specific industry knowledge and relevant operational experience of private equity professionals were mentioned.

On investment level, some empirical findings regarding the impact of experience are unsupportive. Meier (2005) tested for the impact of experience of individual *PE* professionals on *value added to buyouts* and could not confirm a significant relationship.[461] Similarly, De Clerq/Sapienza (2002) found no significance for *PE* firm experience analyzing a sample of 263 portfolio companies. GP experience is thereby operationalized through the partner's average *PE* experience.[462]

---

459 See Long, W. F./Ravenscraft, D. J. (1993b), p. 22.

460 See Easterwood, J. C. (1998), pp. 129-159.

461 See Meier, D. (2005), pp. 159f.

462 See De Clerq, D./Sapienza, H. J. (2002).

On fund level, results are mixed; though in part experience could be found to significantly affect fund performance. Burgel/Murray (2000) distinguish analyzed funds on the basis of whether the fund is a first-time or follow-up fund, and found weak significant support for the experience hypothesis.[463] Conversely, Ljungqvist/Richardson (2003a) fail to confirm a statistical significance for their simplistic proxy (dummy variable for first-time fund) for experience.[464] Kaplan/Schoar (2005) report a strong heterogeneity of *PE* fund returns with respect to the fund experience, whereby experience is operationalized based on the sequence number of a fund.[465] This persistence phenomenon in *PE* funds' returns is also confirmed by Gottschalg et al. (2004).[466] Related evidence that experience improves performance is provided by steadily decreasing percentage write-offs in consecutive funds of *CVC Capital Partners*. Whereas 18.2% of the first fund's investments needed to be written off, the corresponding figure declined to 7.4% in the second fund and amounts for the almost fully realized third fund are still zero percent.[467]

In light of these findings, it could be presumed that experience effects result on fund level rather than on investment level. Potentially, more experienced funds take better decisions regarding the investment as such and therefore presumably bear less complete write-offs than inexperienced funds. Therefore, this thesis hypothesises that experience alone does not positively influence *FCF effects* of the bought-out company.

H_Int_6: *The level of experience of the financial sponsor is not expected to affect FCF-effects and thus the performance of the investment.*

Preceding discussions indicate that operationalizing experience is challenging and troublesome. This particularly holds true given the quantitative, database-based nature of the empirical analysis. Following Rosenstein et al. (1993), experience is operationalized by distinguishing between established and other private equity firms.[468] For the purpose of this thesis, a *PE* firm will be considered as established when it belongs to the top-20 group of *PE* firms when ranked according to the amount of capital invested. In this case the binary variable *ExpInd* will take the value of one.

---

463 See Burgel, O./Murray, G. C. (2000).

464 See Ljungqvist, A./Richardson, M. (2003a), pp. 25f.

465 See Kaplan, S. N./Schoar, A. (2005), pp. 1791-1823. Hereby superior management and advisory from the fund to the LBO investment are mentioned as a potential explanation for superior returns for established and experienced funds. However, persistence is found to be more pronounced for venture capital funds.

466 See Gottschalg, O., et al. (2004), pp. 1-53.

467 See Paisner, G. (2005), p. 2.

468 See Rosenstein, J., et al. (1993), pp. 99-113.

2. External Perspective: Variation in the Transaction Multiple

2.1 Conceptual Valuation Framework Related

Chapter III.C.1.3 derived the formula for the EBITDA valuation multiple in the context of the risk-neutral valuation framework.

$$\frac{V_{ti}}{EBITDA_{ti}} = (1-\tau)\left(1-\frac{g_i^q}{ROIC_i}\right)\frac{1+g_i^q}{r_f(1-\tau l_i)-g_i^q} \quad (82)$$

The corresponding identification of constituting factors of this *V/EBITDA* multiple are hence not only subject to the restrictive assumptions of the presented valuation framework but are also based upon various simplifying assumptions. First, given the simplification of perpetuity growth, the risk-adjusted growth rate is implicitly assumed to remain constant. Similarly, the firm's gearing ratio and its pay-out ratio are assumed to be constant over time. Also the assumption of an infinite life-time for the corporation implicitly assumes the absence of any risk of insolvency. Apparently these restrictions are hardly ever fulfilled in reality. Nonetheless the theoretical discussion serves the purpose of this analysis well by illustrating the theoretical link between valuation multiples and influencing control factors.[469] The stylized setting of the model helps identify factors that ideally fundamentally drive variations in the *valuation* multiple. Therefore, assuming that the *transaction* multiple is determined to a large extent by the fundamental value of the company, these factors were to impact variations in the transaction multiple.

From the various identified factors, variations in the risk-adjusted growth rate and the risk-free interest rate will be considered as influencing factors for variations in the transaction multiple. Owing to the relatively short holding period of the investments and given the heterogeneity of the different tax regimes across the considered European countries, the corporate tax rate τ as well as q are assumed not to differ between the entry and exit date.[470] Further, the depreciation charge as percentage of EBITDA is assumed to be constant. Finally, owing to restrictions with respect to the operationalization of future growth expectations, ROIC as an indicator of the firm's current profitability level will to some extent be subsumed under this growth variable.

---

469 For a similar line of reasoning in the context of the selection of comparable companies based on identified control factors see e.g. Herrmann, V. (2002), p. 62 and Richter, F./Herrmann, V. (2003), pp. 194ff.

470 Note however, that any variations of the corporate tax rate not only impacts the theoretically correct valuation multiple directly but also indirectly through variations in q.

2.1.1 Risk-free Interest Rate

According to equation (63) variations in the risk-free interest rate r_f have reciprocal effects on the EBITDA valuation multiple. Increases in the risk-free interest rate, cause the theoretical valuation multiple to decrease and vice versa. This is quite intuitive when considering the risk-free interest rate as the expected rate of return for a comparable (and available) investment opportunity. Given an increase in this opportunity costs should lead to a decrease in the relative attractiveness (i.e. the price and valuation multiple) of the alternative investment opportunity.

Relevant empirical work regarding the impact of r_f can be cited for both the context of valuation multiples as well as the context of private equity performance. With respect to *PE* fund performance, Gottschalg et al. (2004) report a relative underperformance for funds that entered investments in times when interest rates were high.[471]

Given the purpose of this thesis is to analyze realized LBO investments and in particular the relative variations in the transaction multiple between the entry and the exit, the relative differential of the risk-free interest rate for the entry/exit points in time are considered. Based on previous considerations, multiple expansion is expected to be higher, the higher the decrease in the risk-free interest rate during the holding period. The expected corresponding effect on the performance of the LBO transaction is straightforward and supplemented by an amplifying effect on *Cumulated FCF Generation*, i.e. debt repayment.

In light of the two-tier framework of the analysis as well as the diverse operationalization of internal FCF effects before interest and taxes (see chapter IV.C.1), the risk-free interest rate is not considered an independent variable for the internal perspective. It shall be noted however, that the cumulated amount of FCF available for debt repayment is apparently higher, the lower the risk-free interest rate and hence the debt financing costs for the portfolio company. For *Level II DVs* this effect coincides with the discussed effect of variations in the risk-free rate on the transaction multiple.

H_Ext_1: *The lower the risk-free interest-rate differential between exit and entry, the higher the variation of the transaction multiple and thus the better the LBO investment performance.*

The difference between the interest rate of the 10-year UK government bond at exit and at entry will be applied as independent variable and referred to as $\Delta\_r_{f,T-t}$.[472]

---

471 See Gottschalg, O., et al. (2004), pp. 18f.

472 The ten year UK government bond rate will be applied as the risk-free interest rate.

2.1.2 Growth Expectations

Apart from r_f, the expected, long-term, risk-neutral growth rate g^q is the second considered key determinant of the valuation multiple in the setting of the discussed, stylized valuation framework as indicated by equation (63). The theoretically predicted impact of expected growth rates of various equity and entity cash flow measures on the corresponding equity and entity multiples is largely empirically confirmed.[473] Accordingly, analogous to the risk-free interest rate, any variation in the transaction multiple between the entry and the exit of a LBO investment should be positively driven by a variation in the expected growth rate.

H_Ext_2: *The higher the differential of the expected, long-term, risk-neutral growth rate between exit and entry, the higher the variation of the transaction multiple and thus the better the LBO investment performance.*

Operationalizing the expected, certainty equivalent growth rate is troublesome. First, given the private status of the considered companies, consensus market estimates for key performance measures such as I/B/E/S estimates are generally not available and hence are not an option. Second, *Tobin's Q*, calculated as assets market value over the corresponding book value and frequently applied in *Operational Performance Studies*, is barely applicable due to, among others, distortions in asset book values resulting from asset step-ups during the holding period of the investment.[474] Third, management projections are forward looking but face the shortcoming that apart from the fact that they are very infrequently available for the analyzed sample, they are subjective estimates on behalf of the management and hence likely biased. Forecasts by financing banks on the other hand are comparably objective but are also not consistently available for the considered investments at entry and at exit. A related considered option is the comparison of these projections at entry with actual realizations during the holding period. If a company manages to outperform its business plan it could be argued that it lifts the firm onto a different growth pattern. However, data availability also rules out this opportunity although the financial projections at entry only would be sufficient.[475] Accordingly, projections by management and/or financing banks are not an option either. Further variations in q obviously affect the variation in the expected, risk-neutral growth rate.

---

473 See e.g. Zarowin, P. (1990), pp. 439-454, Lakonishok, J., et al. (1994), pp. 1541-1578 and Richter, F./Herrmann, V. (2003), pp. 194-219.

474 Further, in the case of LBOs acquisition prices would need to serve as indicators of market value. Accordingly, methodologically flawed, a ratio applying the investment's acquisition price would be applied to test for variations in the relative acquisition price.

475 *Note:* This approach is restricted in that the comparison of projections with actual realizations is misleading for investments that are characterized by substantial acquisition and divestiture activity during the holding period. Solely for informational purposes, projections of financing banks with actual realizations at exit are compared for *Rev*, *EBITDA* and *EBITDA-Mrg* for a reduced sample in chapter V.D.2.1.1.

In light of these difficulties, this thesis applies the relative difference between the EBITDA CAGR for the 2-year period prior to the buyout and the EBITDA CAGR during the holding period as indicator for the difference in expected growth rates. The consideration of the change in EBITDA CAGR during the holding period compared with pre-buyout levels is required as the consideration of one historical growth rate (i.e. the EBITDA CAGR from entry to exit) would be misleading. Accordingly a company with higher EBITDA growth rates during the holding period does not necessarily merit higher multiple expansion as potentially these higher growth rates were priced at entry in the form of higher growth expectations. However, this reasoning is again not as unambiguous as it might seem: this thesis considers the relative variation in the transaction multiple as the dependent variable. Assuming that low growth expectations come along with low absolute multiples than – ceteris paribus – variations in the multiple might indeed be argued to be higher, the higher the EBITDA growth rate during the holding period. The consideration of the relative difference implies that the expected multiple expansion will be higher the more the company succeeds in growing EBITDA faster during the holding period than prior to the buyout. This approach, however, apparently faces the shortcoming of the underlying assumptions that current levels of profitability and hence EBITDA growth form the basis for the expectations regarding future growth rates.[476]

2.2 Capital Market Environment Related

Deviating from the stylized world of the RNV theorem, it has been argued that the state of the capital market environment affects variations in the transaction multiple. In accordance with previous discussions in chapter III.C.2 and given the considered exit modes of IPO and secondary buyout exited LBOs, the attractiveness of the (i) equity, and (ii) debt capital market have been distinguished.

2.2.1 Equity Capital Market Attractiveness

When considering the impact of the state of the equity capital markets in chapter III.C.2.1.1 a distinction was made between the private equity and public equity market. On the one hand the supply of private equity fund inflows was argued to boost prices in the market for *PE* investments. On the other hand the accessibility of the public equity market and demand/appetite for IPOs and reverse LBOs impacts the entry as well as the exit multiple of a transaction. LBO investments will be *cheaper* at entry in terms of entry transaction multiple when equity market valuations are low – having a direct impact in the case of going privates and indirectly affecting alternatives for the seller in case of divisional, succession and secondary buyouts. At exit the public equity market *appetite* obviously determines the feasibility and the economics of the IPO exit mode.

---

476 Similarly historical growth rates to proxy future realizations were applied by Lehn, K./Poulsen, A. (1989), pp. 771ff.

Empirical research is supportive. Gompers/Lerner (2000b) analyze the direct impact of fund inflows on valuation. Applying a sample of more than 4,000 direct *VC* investments, (absolute, adjusted) valuation levels are found to increase by 7%–21% following a doubling of fund inflows.[477] Further, numerous aggregated fund studies empirically confirm the theoretically predicted impact of capital inflows on fund performance.[478]

With respect to the public equity market, research seems to confirm the ability of *VC* and *PE* funds to time the market for IPO exits.[479] Lerner (1994a) compares the occurrence of IPOs with the occurrence of private financings and an appropriate industry equity index. Applying a non-parametric mean comparison test, IPOs are confirmed to occur (highly statistically significant) in times of relatively high equity valuations.[480] Implicitly, Ritter (1991) and Loughhran/Ritter (1993) also confirm IPO timing abilities by showing that poor performance of IPOs relative to the market can be partially attributed to their concentration around equity market peaks.[481]

For the purpose of this thesis the states of the two sub-markets – *PE* and *PM* – will be subsumed under *equity capital market attractiveness*. Methodologically, this is justified in two respects. First, it seems reasonable to assume and is empirically supported that the attractiveness of the two sub-markets coincide. Gompers (1998) argues that "*high returns in the venture industry resulting from the active initial public offering market has spurred greater fundraising.*"[482] Bivariate correlations between standard proxy variables for the respective state of the sub-market are very highly significant with positive coefficients in excess of 90%.[483]. Second, a conjoint consideration adheres to the frequently aforementioned sole separation between equity and debt capital financing. Regardless of *PE* and *PM*, an increased allocation of fund resources to the respective markets leads to increased prices in the market for *PE* investments. Hypothesis *H_Ext_3_IPO* hence postulates:

H_Ext_3_IPO: *The variation in the transaction multiple and thus the performance of the IPO exited LBO investment will be higher, the higher the differential of the relative equity market attractiveness between exit and entry.*

---

477 See Gompers, P. A./Lerner, J. (2000b), pp. 281-325. Findings are reported to be robust with respect to controlling for various firm characteristics, public market valuations of comparable firms and expected returns.

478 See e.g. Ljungqvist, A./Richardson, M. (2003a), Gottschalg, O., et al. (2004) and Kaplan, S. N./Schoar, A. (2005). See also Table 5 on page 19.

479 See e.g. Barry, C. B., et al. (1990), pp. 445-471 and Lerner, J. (1994a), 293-316.

480 The finding remains significant even when detrending the index by a GDP deflator and inflation.

481 See Ritter, J. (1991) and Loughhran, T./Ritter, J. (1993) cited in Lerner, J. (1994a), p. 294.

482 See Gompers, P. A. (1998), p. 1090.

483 Diller, C./Kaserer, C. (2005), p. 28 report a correlation coefficient of 0.95 for the number of (Germen) IPOs and capital inflows into buyout funds.

Various proxy parameters could be thought of to operationalize the attractiveness of the equity market environment. Das et al. (2002) and Diller/Kaserer (2005) applied the number of IPOs as an indicator for the level of '*hotness*' of the equity capital market.[484] Gottschalg et al. (2004) considered the market portfolio return during the investment and the average earning-to-price ratio (for all stocks listed on the NYSE/AMEX/NASDAQ) at exit.

This thesis employs the monthly number of (UK and continental European) IPOs as the appropriate indicator. The corresponding dependent variable is the variation in the transaction multiple. Therefore, the independent variable *Δ_#_IPOs* is calculated as the difference between the number of IPOs in the month of exit and the number of IPOs in the month of entry. As a higher number of IPOs points to a relatively more attractive equity market environment, the variation in the transaction multiple is predicted to be higher, the higher *Δ_#_IPOs*. Alternative, considered possibilities were the relevant difference for (i) UK, European and combined equity volumes issued and (ii) the DJStoxx index. Very high correlations between the differences of the number of IPOs with the volume of equity issuances (0.788) and with the DJStoxx Index (0.641) confirm the validity of these three measures and the redundancy of considering the variables separately. Factor analysis identified the differential of the number of IPOs as the appropriate indicator for equity capital market attractiveness. Apart from this, the variation in the DJStoxx index has not been considered further as it correlates highly (0.780) with the variable *Time* detailed in chapter IV.B.3.

2.2.2 Debt Capital Market Attractiveness

Chapter III.C.2.1.2 briefly touched upon the positive impact of a favorable debt capital market environment on (relative) transaction prices in the market for *PE* investments. Based on financing supply considerations it has been argued that decreasing *prices* for debt as well as higher leverage ratios in a *hot* financing market benefit the maximum amount of debt used in the LBO financing structure. Ceteris paribus, relative transaction prices expressed in the form of *P/EBITDA* multiples are expected to be higher. *Prices* for debt (such as the *yield-to-maturity* for a bond) are generally expressed through a base rate plus a credit spread indicating the riskiness of the particular debt security. The previously mentioned operationalization of the risk-free interest rate, the 10-year government bond rate, is frequently applied as the appropriate base rate.

---

484 To test for the expected *Times Money* multiple in their sample of investment level financing rounds, Das, S. R., et al. (2002) apply a dummy variable indicating hot IPO markets for the years 1986, 1991-1997 and 1999-2000. In their fund level study, Diller, C./Kaserer, C. (2005) employ the number of German IPOs as indicator.

On fund level, Gottschalg et al. (2004) empirically confirm the predicted impact of credit spreads. Funds with direct investments entered into in times when credit spreads were high are found to underperform.[485]

H_Ext_3_Sec: *The variation in the transaction multiple and thus the performance of the secondary buyout-exited LBO investment will be higher, the higher the differential of the relative financing market attractiveness between exit and entry.*

The aforementioned decomposition of the *price* for debt provides a straightforward operationalization for debt capital market attractiveness. The risk-free interest rate r_f is already applied as an operationalized independent variable in the context of the RNV approach. For the purpose of this thesis the attractiveness of the credit market is hence operationalized through the credit spread for European BB[486] rated companies.[487] A lower spread indicates a *hotter* and thus for the purpose of LBO financing a more attractive credit market. Accordingly, the variable *Δ_spread* is defined as the average spread for the month of exit less the average spread for the month of entry for each considered transaction. The variation in the transaction multiple is predicted to be higher the lower *Δ_spread*.

2.3 Information Asymmetries Related

2.3.1 IPO Exit Characteristics

Signaling aspects in combination with information asymmetries in the IPO divestment process have been elucidated in chapter III.C.2.2.1. It has been illustrated that a trade-off might exist between on the one hand realizing a maximum share price at the time of the IPO and on the other hand differentiating itself from lower quality issuers and thus facilitating a further seasoned offering of the remaining stake through an IPO discount. Underpricing would obviously depress the observed transaction multiple at exit. Ibbotson/Fjaffe (1975) first conjectures that IPOs are underpricing to "*'leave a good taste' in investors' mouths' so that future underwritings from the same issuer could be sold at attractive prices*"[488]. Equation (81) established a positive relation between the fractional ownership α and the degree of underpricing *Dis*.

---

485 See Gottschalg, O., et al. (2004), pp. 18f.

486 According to Standard and Poor's bond ratings, bonds of companies, which don't make the cut to investment grade status, are ranked BB and are referred to as junk bonds. See also chapter II.B.3.2.

487 Alternatively, the LBO bond volume could also be thought of as indicator for the credit market attractiveness. However, the credit spread has been applied as it is considered the purer indicator.

488 See Ibbotson, R. G./Jaffe, J. F. (1975), p. 1030.

$$(83) \quad \sigma^2(\alpha, Dis) = \sigma_L^2 + \frac{(1-\alpha)p}{(1-\alpha p)\alpha b} Dis$$

Consequently, if pre-IPO equity investors do not underprice and intend to realize maximum proceeds in the IPO, their motivation to maximally reduce the retained ownership stake is strong. High levels of retained ownership would obviously imply exposing a higher stake to the post-IPO threat of being exposed as a lower quality issuer and increasing the dependency on follow-on secondary offerings. In the absence of IPO discounts, issuers potentially forgo a favorable future secondary offering with more enthusiastic investors. This line of reasoning that IPO underpricing relates positively to future seasoned offerings is applied – apart from the presented GH model – in signaling models by Welch (1989) and Allen/Faulhaber (1989). In this respect Gale/Stiglitz (1989) however argue that (i) the infrequency with which insiders such as management and financial sponsors sell securities, and (ii) potential lock-up arrangements, imply that there are unlikely to be any penalties for falsely signaling in an IPO in the foreseeable future.[489] On the contrary, the benefits of cheating are immediate and presumably large.[490] Following the first line of reasoning high multiple expansion would – ceteris paribus – signal relatively unattractive prospects for the company as the insider owner employs the IPO to minimize its retained ownership stake.

Empirically, various studies analyze IPO discounts, some in particular the impact of retained ownership by the issuer. Analyzing a sample of 39 IPO exited MBOs Saadouni et al. (1996) report a statistically significant negative relation between IPO discounts and the insider's retained ownership.[491] Similarly Hogan et al. (2001) predict and empirically confirm underpricing to be higher, the higher the level of insider ownership, whereby insider ownership represents the percentage of post-IPO relative to the percentage of pre-IPO insider ownership.[492] In other words, the reduction of insider ownership will come along with little underpricing.

H_Ext_4a_IPO: *The variation in the transaction multiple and thus the performance of the IPO exited LBO investment will be higher, the higher the exploration of information asymmetries in the divestment process.*

The preceding argumentation implied that the pre-IPO equity investors' intention to minimize their post-IPO exposure, i.e. to cash out as much as possible in the IPO, might signal the exploration of information asymmetries between the seller and the acquirer. When it comes to

489 See Gale, I./Stiglitz, J. E. (1989), pp. 469ff.

490 See also Megginson, W. L./Weiss, K. A. (1991), p. 881.

491 See Saadouni, B. S., et al. (1996), pp. 47-60.

492 See Hogan, K. M., et al. (2001), pp. 1-18.

operationalizing this exploration, the post-IPO free float seems at first glance to be the intuitive indicator. Let free float be defined as the percentage ownership of the company, which following the IPO is not held by pre-IPO equityholders. However, a high post-IPO free float does not necessarily result from a high secondary component but might simply be triggered by a high primary component. Hence, a measure accounting for the relative contribution of the primary and the secondary component seems preferable. Further, as mentioned in chapter II.A.4.1, proceeds from the primary component might be used to repay or redeem quasi-equity financing instruments, most importantly shareholder loans and preference shares. Similarly to secondary proceeds, the repayment of quasi-equity financing instruments through primary proceeds implies cashing out on behalf of the LBO equity investors. For these reasons, this thesis considers α as the remaining stake of the total equity value from the pre-IPO equity investor perspective at the time of the IPO that has not been realized. Accordingly α is defined as the issuer's remaining amount of equity and quasi-equity financing instruments divided by the pre-IPO equity valuation, i.e. E_T. Hence, the relation between α and the variation in the transaction multiple is predicted to be negative.

2.3.2 Relative Entry Valuation

Previous hypotheses and the corresponding operationalizations base the argumentation on the variation of the respective independent variable between entry and exit (see e.g. $\Delta\_r_{f,T-t}$ for hypothesis *H_Ext_1* and *Δ_#_IPOs* for hypothesis *H_Ext_4_IPO*). Relative variations rather than absolute levels of the independent variables are predicted to cause relative variations in the transaction multiples. In this light, operationalizing relative variations in information asymmetries is troublesome: ideally the analysis should account for the differences regarding the exploration of information asymmetries in the investment & divestment phase. Hence, the aforementioned hypothesis regarding information asymmetries faces the shortcoming in that only the exit is considered and hence the relative variation compared with the entry is neglected. To partly overcome this deficiency, a further variable shall be introduced that intends to account for the relative valuation level at entry.

Weinberger (2005) reports high, statistically significant, negative correlations between the relative valuation (expressed as entity value over $EBITDA_{LTM}$ or $EBITDA_{LTM}$-$CapEx$) and the relative total debt contribution. Based on this finding and in accordance with equation (64), it could be argued that a relatively high gearing, i.e. a low relative equity contribution implies a relatively low transaction multiple at entry. It is important to note that the purpose of the analysis is the relative comparison of transaction multiples at entry and at exit of a particular investment and not across various different investments. With this in mind the above argumentation might become perspicuous when assuming that a particular LBO investment can be assigned a *natural* gearing ratio. In the case that (due for instance to capital market environment particularities or information asymmetries) the entry transaction is characterized by a comparably high gearing, the acquisition might be considered a *lucky buy* and a multiple expansion at exit becomes more likely.

Further, Kaplan/Schoar (2005) argue that proprietary access to transactions, i.e. the so-called proprietary deal-flow, could be one potential explanation for the observed heterogeneity of funds with respect to performance and the consistent outperformance of few, presumably higher quality, established and better skilled funds.[493] Proprietary deal-flow implies the absence of any competition and hence presumably lower relative valuations as argued in chapter III.C.2.2.2. Consistent with the findings reported by Weinberger (2005), lower relative purchase prices come along with higher relative debt levels as *PE* firms need to contribute relatively less equity compared with auction processes. The presented line of reasoning is supported in practice. Frequently purchase price increases in auction come exclusively from equity or at least highly under-proportionately from debt, implying an increasing gearing ratio.

Based upon these considerations the following working hypothesis is formulated:

H_ext_4b: *The higher the gearing at entry the higher will be the multiple expansion at exit and thus the performance of the LBO investment.*

In line with previous notation and definition the gearing at entry l_t will be defined as the fraction of net third party financial liabilities ND_t of total sources TS_t.

3. Control Variables

Three further aspects merit a closer consideration. As pointed out, the analysis of realized LBO investments is not limited to *going private* transactions but rather subsumes LBOs of different entry modes as described in chapter II.A.3. Hence, a separate consideration of the entry mode might be insightful. The forthcoming empirical analysis, however, considers European investments for the time period 1993 to 2004. Thus considerations with respect to the region and the time also seem valuable.

Regional Consideration

A general tenor of the discussion in chapter III.B has been that the LBO corporate governance structure facilitates operating a company in the best interests of its shareholders, the LBO equity investors. Critically, however, it has been remarked that the means to achieve this shareholder value orientation could also be implemented for non-LBO companies, thus achieving similar or at least comparable results with respect to shareholder value orientation. Corporate governance mechanisms that in principal similarly address the previously discussed

---

493 See Kaplan, S. N./Schoar, A. (2005), pp. 1-45.

means to reduce agency costs inherent in the separation of ownership and control are numerous and presumably vary considerably across countries.

The line of reasoning regarding the impact of regional differences on the performance of LBO investments can be twofold. On the one hand, it might be argued that a shareholder value-oriented country, with a developed *PE* market offers a general framework to implement performance enhancing initiatives and thus should be characterized by better performing investments. On the other hand, however, an investment might perform better in countries with relatively little shareholder value orientation. While this, at first, sounds counterintuitive, it seems reasonable to assume that the *potential* to improve the bought-out firm's operational performance beyond its current level ought to be higher in countries (i.e. corporate governance systems), where relatively little emphasis has been put on shareholder value orientation prior to the LBO. In other words, in countries where basics for shareholder value increasing governance structures are already in place, statutory and enforceable by shareholders, the positive *FCF effects* of the LBO should be lower since the respective improvement potential through a LBO governance structure are limited.

This controversial argumentation also applies to the external perspective, the variation in the transaction multiple. On the one hand, the higher developed the capital markets, i.e. the more attractive potential exit modes via the equity capital or debt capital market, the higher presumably the variation in the transaction multiple. On the other hand, the more shareholder value oriented the country and the higher developed its capital markets are in terms of depth and liquidity, the lower the related information asymmetries and the higher the transparency, and thus the lower the variation in the transaction multiple.

The UK is generally considered the most developed *PE* market in Europe.[494] Jeng/Wells (2000) find the reason for that to be three institutional factors: private pension funds, labor market rigidities and IPO exit modes, highlighting the importance of country-specific peculiarities of the corporate governance system. Witt (2003) discusses in detail country-specific differences in Europe with respect to the prevailing corporate governance systems, structured alongside nine characterizing criteria.[495] Witt hereby argues that distinguishing peculiarities for the market-oriented, British corporate governance system are among others (i) a so-called one-tier-system, (ii) a low degree of statutory regulations, (iii) the importance of

---

494 See e.g. Jeng, L. A./Wells, P. C. (2000), Leopold, G., et al. (2003), pp. 241ff.

495 See Witt, P. (2003), pp. 78-106. The nine characterizing criteria are the objective function and the management of the corporation, control through exercise of voting rights, control through the capital and labor markets, control through publicity, control through liability and control through compensation.

institutional investors, (iv) a liquid and developed capital market, and (v) the high relevance of (hostile) takeover attempts.[496]

Interestingly in this respect, Manigart et al. (2002) find that UK *VC* firms have substantially higher required returns compared to Belgium, France and the Netherlands.[497] In their recent premia-paid study of going privates in the European market Andres et al. (2004) report higher premia for UK companies, though cannot confirm this to be statistically significant.[498]

As a working hypothesis, this thesis follows the first line of reasoning and hence postulates ex-ante a positive impact of market-oriented corporate governance systems and thus for UK investments.

H_CV_1: *Both FCF-Margin effects as well as the variation in the transaction multiple and thus the performance of the LBO should be higher for more shareholder value oriented countries.*

In order to empirically test for a regional effect in the sample, the binary variable *Region* takes the value of one for UK investments and zero for Continental European (CE) investments.

EntryMode

It has previously been argued that the *change* in the governance structure associated with an LBO sets the stage for improvements in the firm's operations through reduced agency costs. The level of such operational performance improvement potential obviously depends on the degree of change i.e. on the degree of disparity between the pre- and post-buyout governance structure to the extent they facilitate shareholder control. In this respect Hite/Vetsuypens (1989) argue that divisional buyouts are less likely to suffer from the absence of *arm's length bargaining* between the acquirer and the seller compared to going private transactions.[499] However, it could be argued that in the pre-buyout governance structure of divisional buyouts as well as in going private transactions the management of the company has been delegated from the shareholders to a group of managers. Resulting principal–agent problems and benefits of reducing related agency costs should apply for both types. Conversely, improvement effects through reduced agency costs should be lower for LBOs with a comparable pre-LBO governance structure that already allowed the exercising of shareholder control. Given this argumentation, it seems beneficial to apply the classification of Wright/Robbie (1997) who

---

496 See Witt, P. (2003), p. 98.

497 See Manigart, S., et al. (2002), pp. 291-312.

498 See Andres, C., et al. (2004), pp. 1-39.

499 See Hite, G. L./Vetsuypens, M. R. (1989), pp. 953ff.

differentiate between previously management-controlled and previously owner-controlled LBOs.[500]

So far operational performance studies have predominantly focused on *going private* transactions and hence research including other modes of entry is comparably rare. Hite/Vetsuypens (1989) analyzed abnormal returns to public parent companies around the announcement of divisional buyouts. The finding of statistically significant abnormal returns to the parent company might suggest that the buyout is expected to create value and the seller shares associated expected benefits.[501] In their reverse LBO study, comprising 18 going private and 54 divisional buyouts, Muscarella/Vetsuypens (1990) report more pronounced efficiency gains for divisional buyouts.[502] Further, Desbrières/Schatt (2002) find that while the operational performance of the analyzed sample of French MBOs falls following the completion of the transaction, this reported downturn is less pronounced for divisional buyouts than for succession buyouts.[503] While not directly confirmative, these findings support the above line of reasoning in that the alternative argumentation seems invalidated.

Further, Wruck (1989) reports that changes in firm value around the announcement of private sales of equity are strongly correlated with the resulting degree of ownership concentration.[504] Based thereupon, it could be hypothesized that in the case of LBOs the (anticipated) value creation is higher, the higher the disparity between pre- and post-LBO ownership concentration. In other words, if the LBO company is already owner-controlled and characterized by a high degree of ownership concentration, post-LBO improvement potentials should be lower. In the absence of further empirical evidence, the thesis follows this line of reasoning and predicts that *FCF-effects* ought to be higher for previously management-controlled companies.

With respect to the external perspective the thesis hypothesizes in line with the above argumentation for *FCF-effects*, that entry transaction multiples are inflated in that they comprise a premium to be paid to pre-LBO equity shareholders for the anticipated operational improvements. Meaning, for the case of previously management-controlled companies (where anticipated operational improvements are presumably higher) the expected value creation needs to be shared with pre-LBO owners. Accordingly, variations in the transaction multiple from entry to exit are predicted to be lower for previously management controlled

---

500 See Wright, M./Robbie, K. (1997), pp. 227-249.

501 See Hite, G. L./Vetsuypens, M. R. (1989), pp. 953-970.

502 See Wruck, K. H. (1989), pp. 3-28

503 See Desbrières, P./Schatt, A. (2002), pp. 695-729.

504 See Muscarella, C. J./Vetsuypens, M. R. (1990), pp. 1389-1413.

companies.[505] Ainina/Mohan (1991) argues that IPO exits of previously publicly owned corporations as well as of divisional buyouts are presumably characterized by less uncertainty regarding their quality and performance. Following this line of reasoning, previously owner-controlled companies should demand higher IPO discounts (to tolerate the higher degree of uncertainty) and should hence come along with lower levels of multiple variation. For the context of this thesis this argumentation is considered less relevant. For companies of the size analyzed in the empirical part, IPO prospecti generally comprise detailed, audited financial information for at least the last three years prior to the IPO, which is assumed to rule out potential informational disadvantages for previously less transparent, i.e. owner-controlled companies. Hence, the corresponding working hypothesis postulates:

H_CV_2: *While FCF-Margin effects are predicted to be lower, variations in the transaction multiple are predicted to be higher for pre-LBO owner-controlled compared with pre-LBO management-controlled companies.*

For the purpose of this thesis, and following the classification of LBOs in chapter II.A.3, divisional buyouts and going privates are considered previously management-controlled LBOs whereas succession and secondary buyouts are considered previously owner-controlled LBOs. The binary variable *EntryMode* will take the value of one for previously management-controlled (*Mgmt-cont.*) and zero for previously owner-controlled (*Ow-cont.*) LBOs.

Time Considerations

With respect to time effects two lines of reasoning, though not mutually exclusive, seem to coincide:

First, a similar argumentation compared to regional considerations can be brought forward. Decreasing benefits of a change towards the LBO governance structure should trigger a decreasing LBO performance over time. A variety of macro- and micro-economic factors such as the established free-market economy, globalization, the liberalization of capital markets, the public debate on corporate governance and corresponding legislation have led to an increased shareholder value orientation and improved efficiency through tighter cost control over time.[506] In like manner, these factors improved the depth and liquidity of capital markets and thus reduced related market imperfections. In other words benefits resulting from the LBO-specific corporate governance system as well as from variations in the transaction multiple should be decreasing over time.

---

505 See Ainina, M. F./Mohan, N. K. (1991), pp. 393ff.

506 See e.g. Wright, M./Robbie, K. (1996), pp. 691ff.

Second, *PE* markets are getting more developed and mature.[507] This too, is expected to increase market efficiency, through e.g. higher transparency and standardized acquisition and divestiture processes. As hinted repeatedly, excessive cash inflows in the *PE* market are expected to drive up purchase prices based on simple supply and demand considerations and foster the phenomenon of *money chasing deals*.[508]

According to Mills (2000), LBO performance decreases historically over time, with the argumentation, however, based on the varying relative importance of components of *Total Proceeds*.[509] Andres et al. (2004) report substantially lower acquisition premia for the sub-sample of UK going private transactions post-1999. Assuming the premia to be a valid indicator for expected benefits, this finding potentially hints at decreasing LBO performance over time. Empirical support for the fact that intense competition in the *PE* market negatively affects LBO performance could be confirmed by Long/Ravenscraft (1993b) on investment level and by Ljungqvist/Richardson (2003a) on fund/investor level, among others.[510] Assuming such competition to increase over time supports the following hypothesis.

H_CV_3: *FCF-Margin effects, the variation in the transaction multiple and thus the LBO investment performance are expected to be lower for recent transactions.*

To empirically test for general timing effects the binary 0/1 variable *Time* dichotomizes the analyzed sample according to the median date of entry and takes the value of zero for early transactions and one for recent transactions.

507 See e.g. Gompers, P. A. (1994), Jeng, L. A./Wells, P. C. (2000), pp. 249ff, Leopold, G., et al. (2003), pp. 205ff.

508 See chapter III.C.2.1.2 and in particular Gompers, P. A./Lerner, J. (2000b), pp. 281-325.

509 See Mills, K. G. (2000), pp. 261-273. According to his classification in three eras, in the period until mid 1990 emphasis was put on any returns resulting from leverage and associated benefits, while the period of the early to late 1990s was characterized by variations in the transaction multiple. The third era since the late 1990s is argued to focus on operational improvement.

510 See Long, W. F./Ravenscraft, D. J. (1993b), pp. 0-36 and Ljungqvist, A./Richardson, M. (2003a), pp. 1-41.

Table 6 Summary Hypotheses

		Hypothesis	Variable
Internal Perspective			
H_Int_1a	Size	The larger the firm at entry, the higher are potential FCF-Margin effects but the lower is the revenue effect. The combined effect on FCF effects and hence the LBO investment performance is unpredicted.	Rev_{t-1}
H_Int_1b	Profitability	The lower the profitability of the firm at entry, the lower the revenue growth, but the higher FCF-Margin effects during the holding period. The combined effect on FCF effects and hence the LBO investment performance is unpredicted.	$EBITDA\text{-}Mrg_{t-1}$
H_Int_2	Mgmt. Incentivation	The degree of management incentivation has a positive impact on FCF-Margin effects and thus the performance of the LBO investment.	λ
H_Int_3	Disciplining Debt	The higher the debt financing at entry, the lower the revenue growth effect, but the higher FCF-Margin effects and thus the better the LBO investment performance.	l_t
H_Int_4	Change in Mgmt	Changes in a firm's top management positively affect revenue growth as well as FCF-Margin effects and thus the performance of the LBO investment.	*CMgmt*
H_Int_5	Disp/Acq Activity	Significant disposals and/or acquisitions during the holding period positively affect FCF-Margin effects and hence the overall performance.	*Steady*
H_Int_6	PE Firm Experience	The level of experience of the financial sponsor is not expected to affect FCF-effects and thus the performance of the investment.	*ExpInd*
External Perspective			
H_Ext_1	Risk-free interest rate	The lower the risk-free interest-rate differential between exit and entry, the higher the variation of the transaction multiple and thus the better the LBO investment performance.	Δ_r_f
H_Ext_2	Long-term growth	The higher the differential of the expected, long-term, risk-neutral growth rate between exit and entry, the higher the variation of the transaction multiple and thus the better the LBO investment performance.	Δ_g_{EBITDA}
H_Ext_3_IPO	Equity Market Attractiveness	The variation in the transaction multiple and thus the performance of the IPO exited LBO investment will be higher, the higher the differential of the relative equity market attractiveness between exit and entry.	*Δ_#_IPOs*
H_Ext_3_Sec	Financing Market Attractiveness	The variation in the transaction multiple and thus the performance of the secondary exited LBO investment will be higher, the higher the differential of the relative financing market attractiveness between exit and entry.	*Δ_spread*
H_Ext_4a_IPO	Information Asymmetries	The variation in the transaction multiple and thus the performance of the IPO exited LBO investment will be higher, the higher the information asymmetries in the divestment process.	α
H_Ext_4b	Relative Entry Price	The higher the gearing at entry the higher will be the multiple expansion at exit and thus the performance of the LBO investment.	l_t
Control Variables			
H_CV_1	Region	Both FCF-Margin effects as well as the variation in the transaction multiple and thus the performance of the LBO should be lower for more shareholder value oriented countries.	*Region*
H_CV_2	Entry Mode	While FCF-Margin effects are predicted to be lower, variations in the transaction multiple are predicted to be higher for pre-LBO owner-controlled compared with pre-LBO management-controlled companies.	*EntryMode*
H_CV_3	Time	FCF-Margin effects, the variation in the transaction multiple and thus the LBO investment performance are expected to be lower for recent transactions.	*Time*

C. Operationalization of Dependent Variables

Existing empirical research on *Value Creation* in LBOs operationalizes the objective function in a variety of forms, ranging from purely qualitative indicators through the construction of some form of hypothetical performance indications to purely quantitative indicators.[511] Introductory considerations regarding the notation of value creation emphasized the necessity of quantifying LBO performance measures as defined in chapter II.C as the objective function and hence dependent variable for LBO research on investment level. No empirical study on investment level seems to exit that links company- and transaction-specific information to a quantified LBO performance measure on investment level.

According to the outlined research model, the empirical analysis comprises *Level I* and *Level II DVs*. The analysis of relative LBO performance measures (*Level II DVs*) represents the ultimate objective of this thesis. The LBO transaction model, its decomposition and the resulting two-tier framework with an internal and an external perspective, serve to improve the tangibility of the complex LBO value creation process. Having previously derived hypotheses regarding the impact of identified independent variables on *Revenue Growth*, *FCF-Margin effects*, *Multiple Variation* and ultimately value creation/LBO performance measures, the forthcoming chapter details the various applied *Level I DVs*.

1. Internal Perspective: FCF Effects

Chapter III.A.2 decomposed the LBO transaction model into its five principal components. For the then-following discussion the internal *FCF effects* perspective subsumed all effects resulting from variations in the firm's *FCF*. Any such variations either result from *Revenue Growth* or *FCF-Margin effects*. For the purpose of increasing the accuracy of the analysis and in order to account for potential offsetting effects on an aggregated level, *FCF-Margin effects* shall in the following further be broken down alongside the various FCF accounting components.

Analyzing the various accounting components of *FCF* provides the following advantages:

- First, pure descriptive statistics on absolute and relative variations of individual *FCF* components provide insight into how the bought-out firm's operations are affected from entry to exit of the investment. Among others this helps clarifying myths surrounding LBO investments and potentially disproves some stereotypical, cut and dried prejudices.
- Second, considering variations in the *FCF* components as *DVs* facilitates testing for the discussed sources of value creation in LBOs alongside the previously derived hypotheses. In

[511] For an overview of the various operationalizations of dependent variables in PE research see e.g. Schefczyk, M. (2004), pp. 182ff as well as pp. 195ff for a critical discussion.

doing so annualized variations in the form of CAGRs are generally applied for testing the derived hypotheses in order to improve comparability across various investments and account for investment-specific holding periods.[512] Considering the various components of *FCF* instead of variations in *FCF* obviously increases the level of detail. Such granularity potentially confirms the significant impact of sources of value in LBOs, which otherwise in the case of aggregated considerations only would have been unrecognized due to offsetting effects.

- Third, once having quantified the contribution of the *Cumulated FCF Generation* component to *Total Proceeds* the analysis of variations in the *FCF* components will allow separating out the *improved* compared to the *steady operational performance* element.
- Fourth, relative contributions of variations in individual *FCF* components to overall LBO performance can be quantified.

FCF available for debt repayment as defined in chapter II.B.1 comprises the operating and the investing element.

1.1 Operating Cash Flow

EBITDA, Revenue Growth and EBITDA-Margin

FCF effects have been separated into *Revenue Growth* and *FCF-Margin effects*. Chapter IV.B accounted for this separation when hypotheses were derived. The absolute EBITDA level is the starting point for the *FCF* calculation as defined in II.B.1 and obviously results as the product of revenues and the corresponding margin. In order to test the aforementioned hypotheses, revenue growth and variations in the EBITDA-Margin during the holding period will therefore be applied as a first set of *DVs*. Applying variations in the absolute EBITDA level as a further dependent variable will test for the aggregated effect.

In light of the discussed sources of value creation in LBOs and based on the previously derived hypotheses all three variables are expected to be positive, significantly different from zero.

CoGS-Margin and SG&A-Margin

The analysis of variations in the operating cost structure can further be broken up into CoGS and SG&A costs. Potential causes for reductions in the CoGS-Margin (e.g. a new sourcing agreement, improved purchasing power and better negotiation tactics) do not necessarily require the involvement of a financial sponsor. However, given their clear focus on efficiency and value creation, financial sponsors presumably simply pursue cost cutting initiatives more

---

512 See chapter V.B for a discussion of the applied methodology and chapter VI.C for a discussion of related shortcomings and benefits of potential adjustments.

rigorously. Strong incentives and motivation to avoid unnecessary overhead spending as well as eventually private information about potential overhead cost saving opportunities should lead to a less bureaucratic structure and hence to a reduction of SG&A expenses following the LBO.[513] As cost positions, both CoGS and SG&A expenses have an inverse relationship with EBITDA.

Hypotheses in the previous chapter suggest that variations from entry to exit in the CoGS- as well as the SG&A-Margin are negative, significantly different from zero.

Employment Details and R&D-Margin

The separate examination of personnel costs as a component of operating costs in combination with the aforementioned components of EBITDA is no longer mutually exclusive as personnel expenses are generally included in both CoGS and SG&A. However, for the sake of precision and the specific argument of wealth transfer from employees being a source of value creation, personnel costs and employment details in general are worth considering separately.

Chapter III.B.3.2 briefly explained the well-established argument that LBOs do create value through efficiency improvements in the form of increased labor productivity. Therefore, in addition to a variation in the personnel costs margin, labor productivity should be considered as a second variable. Labor productivity, measured as revenues per employee is expected to increase during the holding period of the investment, whereas – ceteris paribus – personnel costs relative to revenues should decrease.

The two aforementioned variables are obviously directly or indirectly dependent on the employment level. Absolute employment effects have been at the centre of interest in the recent public controversy regarding LBO investments in Germany with advocates questioning heretical claims that LBOs were to 'destroy' jobs.[514] However, simple accounting algebra implies that employment levels do not necessarily need to decrease for wealth transfers from employees in a strict sense to occur. Personnel costs as percentage of sales decrease (and thus contribute to efficiency improvements and increased EBITDA-Margins and therefore increased EBITDA levels) as long as increases in labor productivity outweigh increases in personnel costs per employee. An analysis of all related variables – in particular variations in employment levels – will contribute objectivity to such discussions.

In addition, even a decrease in personnel costs per employee would not necessarily imply a wealth transfer from employees. Negative variations in such a ratio might result from changes

---

513 See e.g. Easterwood, J. C., et al. (1989), Butler, P. A. (2001) and Samdani, S. G., et al. (2001).

514 See e.g. Westerwelle, G. (2005), Keese, C. (2005).

in the relative constitution of a firm's workforce.[515] Further, it could be argued that following a LBO, employees on various levels would participate in the success of the LBO through equity option schemes and thus only tolerate moderately increasing cash compensations during the holding period of the investment.

Similar to employment considerations, it would be interesting to consider research and development (R&D) costs separately. Based on research indicating that firms with high debt burdens scarify R&D spending for debt servicing payments, the significant increase in debt levels in the course of LBOs is expected to cause corresponding cuts.[516] Proponents of this view argue that in an LBO "*one of the things that get squeezed is R&D, because that's an investment in the future. Whatever costs are postponable are likely to go by the boards.*"[517] Again though, a counter argument could be that postponed R&D expenses lower future prospects of the firm and thus would decrease the price to be realized when exiting the investment. In this context KKR (1989) argue that even contrary pre-LBO managers with unaligned interests are little incentivized to spend on R&D, lacking their long-term perspective. Empirical results regarding the impact of LBOs on R&D spending are mixed.[518] Whereas Smith (1990b) and Long/Ravenscraft (1993c) find decreasing R&D spending following the LBO, KKR (1989), Bull (1989) and Lichtenberg/Siegel (1990) report increases in R&D activity. Bruton/Scifres (1992), conclude that "*it appears the buyout left firm's posture towards R&D largely unchanged.*"[519]

Therefore, and given the controversy, argumentation variations in relative R&D spending are not expected to be significantly different from zero.

Cash Net Financial Result

The cash net financial result as the next component of *FCF* brings circularity into play. The firm's capital structure affects the financial result and – assuming that *FCF* is used to repay financial liabilities – vice versa. Variations in the cash net financial result are driven by the firm's financing at entry, the circularity with leverage, and clearly further influencing factors such as the individual financing terms and conditions. For these reasons, the cash net financial result will not be considered as a dependent variable for testing the above hypotheses regarding the impact of a set of independent variables on the bought-out firm's performance. Nonetheless,

---

515 See e.g. Lichtenberg, F./Siegel, D. S. (1990) who find a relative shift towards blue-collar workers.

516 See e.g. Baysinger, B./Hoskinsson, R. E. (1989), pp. 310-332, Graebner, U. A. (1991), p. 84.

517 Walter Adams, Michigan State University, cited in Skryzcki, C. (1988).

518 For a review of relevant studies see e.g. Zahra, S. A./Fescina, M. (1991) and Bruton, G. D./Scifres, E. (1992).

519 See Bruton, G. D./Scifres, E. (1992), p. 18.

the role of cash interest for the analysis of *Cumulated FCF Generation* and thus *Total Proceeds* will be of particular interest.

Variations in cash interest expense from entry to exit are expected to be negative, significantly different from zero.

Furthermore, the relation between cash interest and accounting interest expenses might be worth considering. By accruing interest, the firm benefits from the tax shield of the P&L interest charge but postpones the related cash outflow as interest expenses are capitalized. Regarding debt financing instruments, the effect might be negligible. Restrictive debt covenants imply that any excess cash needs to be fully applied for repayment. In a stylized world with only one debt financing instrument the effect to the debtholder should therefore be identical, assuming that sufficient cash would be generated to meet the debt servicing costs. However, with respect to equity financing instruments, shareholders fully benefit from the tax advantage of accrued interest. For that reason it will be revealing to analyze how far LBO companies apply such structures.

The corresponding ratio, cash interest expense relative to the total accounting interest expenses for the first full year following the LBO, is expected to be smaller than one.

Cash Taxes

As discussed in chapter III.B.3.3, the *tax-savings hypothesis* postulates the well-known tax shield effect of interest expenses, implying that cash taxes ought to decrease significantly following the LBO. In this respect cash taxes as a percentage of EBIT prior to the LBO compared to the corresponding average figure during the holding period, are applied to approximate and descriptively analyze variations in cash tax expenses as a consequence of the LBO. However, for similar reasons like the cash net financial result, cash taxes will not be considered as a separate *DV*.

In light of the familiar argumentation, variations in cash taxes are thus expected to be positive, significantly different from zero.

Change in Net Working Capital

Let *NWC* in the narrow sense and for the purpose of this thesis be defined as inventories (including advances) *Inv*, plus accounts receivable (including prepayments) *AccRec*, less accounts payable (including advances from customers) *AccPay*.

Predominantly due to the reduced agency cost hypotheses *NWC* as a percentage of sales ought to decrease during the holding period. The previously outlined mechanisms of incentivation and control push managers towards stricter cash control and fewer *NWC* inefficiencies. Obviously, however, reduced *NWC* as a percentage of sales does not necessarily imply cash inflow for the period resulting from decreasing *NWC* in absolute terms. Increased revenues might trigger *NWC* related cash outflows despite decreasing relative levels.

Consequently, variations in *NWC-rel, Inv-rel* and *AccRec-rel* are expected to be negative, variations in *AccPay-rel* to be positive, significantly different from zero.

1.2 Net Investing Cash Flow

Capital expenditures (*CapEx*) include investments of the LBO company for maintenance and expansion. Cash outflows for acquisitions and proceeds from divestitures are not included and are treated separately. Since capital expenditures represent immediate cash outflow for the company the, at first, obvious objective for equity investors with a finite investment time horizon is to reduce related spendings to the minimum, acceptable level. Agency theory argues in this respect that aligned interests and control minimize management inducements wasting cash resources on negative NPV projects.

However, there is clearly a flip-side to the coin and a downside to short-term cash maximization through squeezed *CapEx* levels. First, in the long-run postponed maintenance spending might result in obsolescence and underinvestment, potentially yielding efficiency disadvantages and a weakened competitive position. This in turn will negatively impact firm value.[520] Second, the high absolute debt burden and cash restrictions from debt servicing payments eventually prevent companies investing in promising long-term, positive NPV projects, which the company would otherwise, i.e. with a not fully exploited borrowing capacity, have undertaken. Such passiveness might again result in competitive disadvantages resulting from delayed strategic repositioning, thereby also causing value destruction. Often neglected but of high relevance, both aspects potentially lower the exit valuation of the investment; a fact apparently not in the best interests of the equity investors even – or in particular – in light of their limited investment horizon.

To conclude, owing to the focus on cash generation and potential excessive non-value adding spending pre-LBO, variations in relative capital expenditures from entry to exit are expected to be on average negative, significantly different from zero.

2. External Perspective: Variation in the Transaction Multiple

The operationalization of the external perspective dependent variable is, in particular compared with the internal perspective, straightforward. Following considerations in chapter

---

520 Holthausen, R. W./Larcker, D. F. (1996), pp. 293ff provide evidence that *CapEx* levels of IPO exited LBO companies are prior to the IPO below the level of the median firm in the same industry and subsequent to the LBO return to the median level.

III.C.1, *EBITDA* and *V/EBITDA* will be applied as the cash flow for valuation purposes and the corresponding ratio of entity value relative to *EBITDA*, i.e. the *EBITDA* multiple. From hereon *V/EBITDA* is referred to as m.

Theoretical discussions and the subsequent derivation of hypotheses imply the separate consideration of IPO exited and secondary exited LBO investments.

3. LBO Performance Measures

The discussion of LBO performance in chapter II.C.3 started with *Times Money* (*TM*). Owing the well-known deficiency of not accounting for the different holding periods of the investments, *TM* is descriptively but not inferringly analyzed in the empirical part. Any regression analysis with *TM* would apparently be misleading and meaningless as the identified independent variables will account for the investment specific holding period. Following introductory considerations, the time-adjusted *Investment IRR* is applied as the key *Level II DV* given its practical relevance and – despite some mentioned shortcomings – its theoretical foundation. The empirical analysis provides further *Investment IRR* sensitivity analyses in the sense of hypothetically calculating for each individual investment in the analyzed sample *Investment IRRs* assuming constant key value drivers such as the transaction multiple, revenues and EBITDA-margin from entry to exit of the investment. By keeping these value drivers constant, the analysis strips out the respective net *Investment IRR* contributions. Applying these hypothetically derived, artificial *Investment IRRs* as further dependent variables ideally confirms the then preceding results with respect to independent variables driving variations in the internal and the external perspective dependent variables. As detailed in chapter II.C.3.3, alternative LBO performance measures comprise (i) excess returns (*ER*) and (ii) NPVs with three illustrative rates of return for alternative investment opportunities as outlined.

Chart 13 summarizes the concretization of the previously outlined conceptual research model following the preceding formulation of the hypotheses regarding the impact of identified independent variables on the operationalized dependent variables.

Chart 13 Detailed Research Model

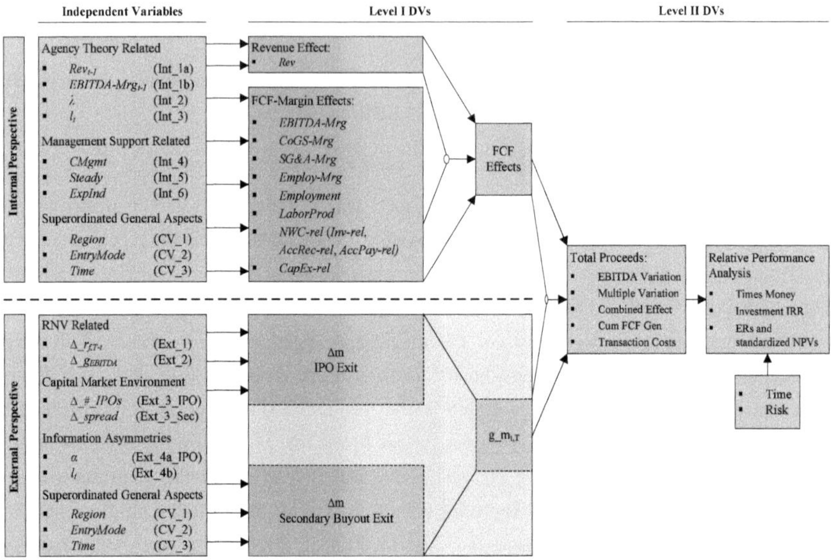

Source: Own illustration

V. Empirical Analysis

This thesis intends to analyze value creation in LBOs from an equity investor point of view on investment level. According to the outlined research model and based upon a deal-by-deal, bottom-up calculation of *Total Proceeds* (*TP*), the empirical analysis provides novel insights in several respects. First, the decomposition of TP to equity investors on investment level into its various components as outlined in chapter III.A.2. Second, the separate analysis of factors driving the variation in identified dependent variables alongside the applied two-tier framework of an internal and external perspective. Third, the holistic, i.e. conjoint, consideration of relevant identified company- and transaction-specific as well as macroeconomic factors regarding the impact on value creation on investment level.

Accordingly, the empirical analysis starts with the description of the data sample (chapter V.A) and the applied methodology (chapter V.B). Following descriptive statistics of the independent variables (chapter V.C), TP to equity investors is decomposed and successively analyzed with respect to the internal and external perspective (chapter V.D). The descriptive and inferring performance analysis including sensitivity analyses recombines these two perspectives (chapter V.E).

A. Data Sample

Several recently published contributions analyze cash flow data between LPs and GPs;[521] some of which with cash flow information on direct investment level.[522] Despite the novelty of this approach and the resulting insights, these studies face the common shortcoming in that the impact of corresponding detailed company- and transaction-specific information on the various return analyses cannot be assessed. The applied data sources generally record cash flow information only in an aggregated form on fund/investor level. In other words, the linkage between investment characteristics and the performance of the investment cannot be established. No such study seems to exist.[523] This might be due predominantly to the following two main reasons:

- Analyzing realized investments highlights two of the inherent problems with quantitative analysis in the field of LBO investments:

---

521 See Chapter I.A.2.3 and the corresponding Table 5 with footnote [66].

522 See e.g. Ljungqvist, A./Richardson, M. (2003a), Gottschalg, O., et al. (2004) and Kaplan, S. N./Schoar, A. (2005).

523 Please refer to chapter I.A.2. To some extend Kaplan, S. N. (1989a) and Muscarella, C. J./Vetsuypens, M. R. (1990) applied the variation in valuations at exit and at entry as a means to analyze value creation in LBOs; facing however the limitations and shortcomings previously described.

— First, despite its steadily increasing importance and omnipresence as illustrated by both an increase in the number of deals and a rising average size per deal[524] the LBO industry is still considered a relatively young industry. Analyzing *realized* investments stresses the problem of a representative number of adequate investments as it apparently implies the LBO entry transaction dating back for the holding period of the investment.

— Second, given the private nature of the business, the analysis of realized LBO investments is complicated by the fact that it builds upon detailed financial information regarding the respective investment not only at entry and at exit but also during the holding period. As outlined, the analysis requires at least capturing all interim equity streams to and from the investor and ideally benefits from detailed interim cash flow information for debt pay-down analysis.

- The equity investor perspective of the analysis requires a detailed and – most importantly – consistent separation of debt and equity financing instruments.[525] Any variations in the relevant financing instruments might be due to or trigger interim equity cash flow streams to and/or from the equityholder that need to be captured in order to adequately calculate TP as the prerequisite for value creation analysis.

These aspects have significant implications on the sample of realized investments for the empirical analysis as detailed in the following chapter.

1. Investment Selection Criteria

The empirical analysis comprises a total number of 42 realized LBO investments. This is the result of a gross number of relevant selected investments meeting pre-defined criteria less a number of transactions that needed to be excluded for the lack of detailed, comprehensive and consistent financial information.

Identification of Potential Investments

The empirical analysis covers (i) European realized LBO investments with (ii) an entry entity valuation of minimum €150m, (iii) the entry not dating back further than 1993, (iv) that have been exited via (v) an IPO or via a Secondary Buyout until Dec-2004. More precisely, in

---

524 According to Thomson Financial (2005) the annual number of European LBO transactions increased with a CAGR of 3.2% from 752 in 1995 to 966 in 2003. In the same period of time the deal volume soared from €20.1bn in 1995 to €74.9bn in 2003 implying an increase in the average size per transaction to €26.7m to €77.5m over the eight year period.

525 See chapter II.B for a brief discussion of financing instruments in LBO transactions and in particular chapter II.B.1 with respect to the importance of a clear separation between debt and equity financing for the purpose of this thesis.

light of the introductory identified shortcomings and for the purpose of the outlined research model, the relevant considered investments satisfy the following criteria:

- Given the shortcoming of previous research with respect to the research object (see chapter I.B.1) this thesis focuses exclusively on European investments. *European* meaning that the business under review is headquartered in a European country. *Realized LBO Investment* refers to the definition provided in chapter II.A.
- According to equation (20), entity value refers to the sum of all debt and equity financing instruments less cash and cash equivalents and less transaction costs associated with the initial LBO transaction. Investments under review are characterized by an entry entity value of larger than €150m applying the relevant spot exchange rate to the € at the date of closing. The consideration of larger investments only improves the availability and consistency of the detailed required financial information prior to the buyout as well as during the holding period and at exit. With respect to the various financing stages the €150m threshold emphasizes the focus on later-stage financing investments only. As pointed out the thesis intends to refrain from considering early stage seed, start-up and expansion financing investments, which are presumably more affected by qualitative factors such as, among others, the entrepreneur, the particular product and related lifecycle and patent aspects.
- The analysis covers any such defined realized investments with the entry occurring after January 1993 and the (partial) exit taking place before December of 2004.
- From the number of exit modes classified in chapter II.A.4 only the exit via an IPO and the exit via a secondary buyout are considered. Trade sales to strategic investors are per definition not included in this analysis due to lack of appropriate and consistent financial information. Trade sales generally do not trigger the publication of certain public or semi-public/confidential documentations that are taken as a crucial primary source of information for the identified and selected investments. As pointed out, pure recapitalizations of the company's financing in place are not considered as they provide – if at all – subjective equity valuations from the current owner.[526]

The identification and quantification of an appropriate target population based upon these criteria is troublesome. Numerous, in part professional, organizations provide secondary data for the European buyout market.[527] However, the precise formulation of the mentioned

---

526 However, recapitalizations during the holding period of the investment obviously need to be taken into account as they might trigger cash flow streams to the equity investors and hence affect TP.

527 Such organizations comprise among others (i) the *European Private Equity & Venture Capital Organization (EVCA)* which represents the European buyout associations, (ii) university departments such as the *Insead Buyout Research Program* or the *Center for Management Buyout Research* (*CMBOR*) at the Nottingham university, (iii) professional capital market data providers such as the *Standard & Poor's (S&P)* rating

investment selection criteria seems to pose restrictions to most of these secondary data providers, questioning the unequivocal identification of a correct target population. Most data providers seem to struggle either with the precise entity valuation of the business, the exit record or at least the precise clarification of the exit mode. [528] Applying several of the aforementioned secondary data providers simultaneously, an initial gross sample of 73 investments that precisely meet the outlined selection criteria is identified.[529]

Sources of Information and Resulting Limitations

Empirically testing the outlined research model requires a detailed, comprehensive and consistent set of financial information data. *Level I DVs* call for comprehensive and consistent income statement and cash flow statement financial items from prior to the entry until the exit of the investment. The considered *Level II DVs*, i.e. the LBO performance and value creation measures, are based upon a consistent specification of the entity, net debt and hence equity value of the business at entry as well as at exit of the investment. Further various identified company- and transaction-specific information that serve as independent variables are needed.[530]

This need for a considerable amount of detailed and in particular consistent financial information for the identified 73 investments, in combination with the respective constraints of secondary data providers obviously calls for a newly created, proprietary database. The following sources of primary data have been applied for setting up such database.

- Publicly filed information is available in the form of (i) *IPO prospecti* for those investments exited via an IPO, (ii) *20-F* and *Bond Prospectuses* for those investments being partly financed by a bond issuance, (iii) *Offer Documents* for those investments where the entry was in the form of a taking private of a formerly publicly traded company, and (iv) *Annual Reports* for those companies that – even if not obliged – continued to publish audited financials.
- In addition to this publicly available information, *Goldman Sachs International* granted access to a library of specific, semi-public and confidential documents. These documents include *Information Memoranda* and *Bank Books*. Information Memoranda are prepared in the process of setting up a company for sale and are made available to interested potential

agency, *Initiative Europe*, *Bloomberg* and *Thomson Financial* as well as (iv) journals and commercial databases such as the *European Venture Capital Journal* and *mergermarket* and *CEPRES*.

528 For details see chapter V.A.3 when discussing the representativity of the analyzed sample.

529 This identification is primarily based on the *Initiative Europe* database as of Oct-2004, *Bloomberg*, *Thomson Financial* and searches in the appropriate press.

530 For further details regarding financial data see chapter V.B.1.

buyers of the business. Such documents generally include detailed historical financials and projections by its current owner regarding the expected future financial performance. So-called Bank Books are prepared for the syndication of senior loans and mezzanine tranches in the context of LBO financing and are made available to banks and further financial institutions being interested in acquiring part of such financial liability. Given the nature of LBO transactions as being financed through a significant portion by financial liabilities, these transactions generally trigger loan syndication and consequently the preparation of Bank Books. In addition to historical and projected financial information these documents also contain information regarding the financing sources and uses of the particular transaction and therefore facilitate the valuation of the business.

- Pressruns for the individual bought-out companies for the time period from 12 months prior to the entry to (ideally) 18 months following the exit of the investment complement the aforementioned primary sources and frequently served to clarify the precise staging of the events.

The amount of detailed financial information required for the outlined analysis poses restrictions on the number of analyzed investments and reduces the sample size from 73 considered investments initially to a final sample of 42 investments. Key criteria for the consideration of an investment in the final sample are (i) the undoubted calculation of *Total Proceeds*[531] to equity investors, as well as (ii) the consistent availability of revenue and EBITDA figures for the two years prior to the buyout and throughout the holding period.[532] Apparently numerous other data (such as the entirety of the identified independent variables) are irredeemable for the outlined research model. However, the creation of the database indicated the aforementioned two criteria to be the most critical. Furthermore, with respect to the various identified internal perspective FCF effects dependent variables, selected missing information is occasionally tolerated as this only reduces the respective sample size and does not require discarding the entire investment. Apart from difficulties with respect to the specification of TP and consistent revenues and EBITDA information, reasons to condemn an initially considered investment include (i) a not reconcilable transaction structure at the time of the entry, (ii) significant business-transforming acquisitions or divestitures during the holding period that make a like-for-like comparison either impossible due to insufficient detailed financial information, or meaningless in light of the change in business scope, (iii) inconsistent

---

531 The undoubted calculation of TP requires detailed capital structure information at entry and at exit as well as the capturing of interim equity streams from and to the LBO equity investors.

532 *Note:* Revenues and EBITDA information represent the key operating financial information as their variation reveals a company's growth and profitability pattern. Further a consistent EBITDA number is the prerequisite for the analysis in the variation of the transaction multiple between entry and exit as outlined in chapter III.C.1.3.

financial information due to changes in the accounting standards in the holding period compared with pre-LBO financials, or even (iv) negative EBITDA figures.

Chart 14 summarizes country, entry and exit date information for the final sample comprising 28 IPO exited and 14 secondary buyout exited LBO investments.

Chart 14 Final Sample of Realized European LBO Investments

Country, Entry and Exit year information for the Total sample of 42 realized LBO investments; note that IPOs are considered for the time being as entire exits; accordingly, the first trading day represents the exit date

IPO exited Investments				**Secondary Buyout exited Investments**			
Company	**Country**	**Entry**	**Exit**	**Company**	**Country**	**Entry**	**Exit**
Alfa Laval	Sweden	2000	2002	Actaris	France	2001	2003
Charles Voegele	Switzerland	1997	1999	ATU	Germany	2002	2004
Comp. Gen. dc Sante	France	1997	2001	Baxi	UK	2000	2004
Dignity	UK	2002	2004	Clondalkin	Ireland	1999	2004
Eircom	Ireland	2001	2004	Frans Bonhomme	France	2000	2003
EuroDollar	UK	1993	1994	Friedrich Grohe	Germany	1999	2004
Findexa	Norway	2001	2004	Gala Group - 1	Uk	1997	2000
Geberit	Switzerland	1997	1999	Gala Group - 2	Uk	2001	2003
Halfords	UK	2002	2004	Guala	Italy	1998	2000
HMV	UK	1998	2002	IMO	UK	2002	2004
Interpump	Italy	1996	1996	Materis	France	2001	2003
Intertek	UK	1996	2002	Nycomed	Norway	1999	2002
Intrum Justitia	Sweden	1998	2002	Picard	France	2001	2004
Jessorps	UK	2002	2004	William Hill - 1	UK	1997	1999
Leica Geosystems	Switzerland	1998	2000				
McBride	UK	1993	1995				
MDIS	UK	1993	1994				
Mettler Toledo	Switzerland	1996	1997				
Neopost	France	1997	1999				
New Look	UK	1995	1998				
Perlos	Finland	1997	1999				
PHS	UK	1999	2001				
Tarkett	Germany	1994	1995				
Thorn	UK	1993	1994				
William Hill - 2	UK	1999	2002				
Willis Corroon	UK	1998	2001				
Wincor	Germany	1999	2004				
Yell	UK	2001	2003				

2. Potential Sample Bias

Based on the Investment Selection Criteria

Due to the specified investment selection criteria the initial sample of considered investments is already characterized by a sample-selection bias.[533] First, the analysis of realized LBO investments represents by definition an analysis of successful LBO investments. Analyzing realized investments not only excludes per se write-offs, but it could also be argued

533 See e.g. Maddala, G. S. (1991), pp. 797ff for details regarding sample selection biases.

that financial sponsors tend to hold on to an underperforming investment and the exit is accordingly postponed. Conversely, if the market is *hot*, i.e. the market offers the opportunity for a successful (partial) flotation of the business, financial sponsors will tend to realize the investment. For instance from a fund perspective it might be wiser to hold on to an underperforming investment, as negative or below expectations returns that dilute the overall fund performance do not need to be accounted for until their realization.

Accordingly, when compared with the entirety of LBO investments the initial sample is already characterized by atypically successful investments – what is referred to as *survivor bias*. Kitching (1989) refers to this phenomenon as LBO plums ripen before lemons, meaning that detailed information is available for outperforming investments.[534] In a recent study analyzing over seven thousand financing rounds, Cochrane (2005) corrects this survivor bias by modeling the probabilities of exits applying a maximum likelihood estimation method.[535] However, Kaplan (1989a) argues against such survivor bias of above-average performing LBOs. Accordingly *"the most successful buyouts may not need to raise additional funds in the public capital market and may remain private* [*whereas*] *less successful buyouts may need to return to the public capital markets or obtain funds from corporate buyer."*[536] Similarly, Muscarella/Vetsuypens (1990), pp. 1389ff argue that corporations go public again as, ex-post, the benefits of private ownership presumably turned out to be smaller than expected.[537] With respect to the initial sample of identified investments, a potential selection bias might further result from the analysis of IPO and secondary buyout exit modes only (i.e. the exclusion of trade sale exits). However, this thesis considers the entirety of investments meeting the previously specified selection criteria as the target population and any interpretation of the forthcoming results has hence to be seen in this context and might not be extended to non-considered investments such as Trade-Sale exited LBOs.

Based on the Exclusion of Investments

Discarding certain deals due to the non-availability of crucial financial information might trigger a further selection bias on the level of the final sample of analyzed investments. On the one hand it could be argued that more detailed financial information is available for successfully performing buyouts and therefore the lack of detailed information can be considered as an indication of underperformance. On the other hand, however, the secretiveness and non-availability of entry financials could well be considered as a sign of satisfying or above-expectation performance. *Private* equity investors prefer to maintain

---

534 See Kitching, J. (1989), pp. 74 ff.

535 See Cochrane, J. (2005), pp. 3-52.

536 See Kaplan, S. N. (1989a), pp. 220ff.

537 Muscarella, C. J./Vetsuypens, M. R. (1990), pp. 1389ff.

silence regarding the monetary success of their investment. Furthermore, the higher the complexity of the transaction structure, the lower obviously the associated transparency, the higher the associated uncertainty and the higher the potential upside for a successful LBO investment. In this respect the latter two arguments contradict the assumption of a selection bias towards a more successful LBO transaction by excluding specific transactions due to the lack of available financial information or the associated complexity.

Based on the Sources of Information

In addition to the sample bias resulting from the transaction criteria, a further bias might result from the respective sources of information. Kaplan (1989a) distinguishes in his set of post-buyout financial information of 76 LBOs between mandatorily and voluntarily filed financial statements.[538] Accordingly, those companies that were obliged to file financial statements due to outstanding publicly held debt issued in connection with the acquisition (or immediately thereafter) are argued to present financials that are unconditional on (and consequently represent unbiased measures of) post-buyout performance. Contrary thereto, the sample of LBOs that file financial statements for the purpose of the divestiture or recapitalization of the business are expected to present financials that are conditional on (and consequently represent biased measures of) post-buyout performance. However, in this respect Kaplan (1989a) concludes that "*if a selection biased is present, it is small.*"[539] Due to the variety of sources of financial information and the explicit focus on consistency of financial data across the entire holding period no bias test on conditional and unconditional financial information is conducted.[540]

3. Tests for Representativeness

Tests for representativeness generally aim to compare certain characteristics of the selected sample to those of the identified target population. It has been noted however that the identification of the precise target population in light of the specified criteria is troublesome and questionable. By definition given the specification of the selection criteria the initial as well as the final sample are characterized by a survivor bias. However, potential selection biases with respect to the final sample of 42 investments compared with the initially identified 73 investments seem less worrying. Selection biases based on the exclusion of certain investments as well as based on the sources of information do not appear to be systematic. To

---

538 See Kaplan, S. N. (1989a), pp. 217ff.

539 See Kaplan, S. N. (1989a), pp. 231-234.

540 Desbrières, P./Schatt, A. (2002), points to a comparable selection bias in the form of subjectively influenced post-LBO accounting data. Related evidence contradicting this view is presented by Deangelo, L. E. (1986), pp. 400-420. Analyzing the accounting decisions of managers for a sample of 64 firms that announced their intention to go private in the years 1973-1982 no evidence could be found for potentially artificially depressed reported financials prior to the buyout.

provide further clarification some tests for representativeness are conducted, which compare the final sample of 42 investments against two control samples. Both samples match the selection criteria as closely as possible though apparently do (and can) not represent a target population.

- *Initiative Europe* Control Sample.[541] Searching the *Initiative Europe* database for investments in accordance with the specified criteria faces two major challenges. First, for numerous investments, transaction prices are not disclosed. Second, while the database appears to capture entry information very comprehensively, it seems to lack comprehensiveness with respect to exit records and related details. For the purpose of identifying a control sample all such investments post 1993 are selected that (i) either record transaction prices larger than €150m or in the case of *not disclosed* are classified as *buyouts*[542] and (ii) are recorded as *exited*. Accordingly, control sample *CS_1a* comprises 209 such defined realized investments. Selecting IPO and secondary buyout exited investments only reduced the sample to 99 investments and will be named *CS_1b*.
- *CEPRES* control sample.[543] CEPRES records among others cash flow information on investment level. Accordingly, the comparison to the analyzed sample with respect to the *Investment IRR* is feasible.[544] Regarding the selection criteria problems arise however, with respect to the precise entity valuation at entry and the delimitation of the exit mode.[545] An initial selection including write-offs and only partially exited investments comprises 438 investments. Excluding these write-offs and focusing on investments with flotation or complete exits only, reduces this initial selection to the control sample *CS_2* comprising 128 LBO investments.

541 See Initiative Europe (2004).

542 Selecting investments with transaction prices only would inappropriately and disproportionately reduce the control sample. The classification as *buyout* differentiates an investment from other categories such as *early stage* and *expansion* and therefore seems to fit the focus of this thesis on later stage financing.

543 See Cepres (2005). Special thanks go to Dr. Daniel Schmidt of CEPRES for providing – anonymously with respect to the investments – data required for the conducted control tests.

544 In order to exclude write-offs and partial exits, *Investment IRRs* below 5% are excluded. Similarly, in order to account for the impact of extreme outliers at the upper end, *Investment IRRs* are capped at 400%.

545 The control sample circumvents the difficulty with respect to (i) the entity valuation by selecting large scale LBOs only (which obviously rules out a control test with respect to the size) and (ii) the exit mode by excluding all definite trade sales.

Table 7 Tests of Representativity

Control samples CS_1a, CS_1b and CS_2 as previously specified; non-parametric Chi-square tests are applied for binary scaled variables (Region and ExitMode), non-parametric Mann-Whitney tests for continuously scaled variables (P_t and Investment IRR)

			Control Samples		
Tested Variable	**Scale**		**CS_1a**	**CS_1b**	**CS_2**
		N	209	99	128
Region	binary	*Chi-square*	.515	1.606	.041
		Sig. (two-tailed)	.535	.209	.757
P_t	cont.	*Z-Statistics*	(1.361)	(1.040)	na
		Sig. (two-tailed)	.174	.298	na
Investment IRR	cont.	*Z-Statistics*	na	na	(.238)
		Sig. (two-tailed)	na	na	.812
ExitMode	binary	Chi-square	na	2.100	na
		Sig. (two-tailed)	na	.121	na

Given the outlined investment selection criteria and data availability of the control samples, the considered variables for tests of representativity are *Region*, the purchase price (= observed entity value) at entry P_t, the *Investment IRR* and the *ExitMode.* The forthcoming descriptive analysis provides details regarding these variables for the analyzed sample.

The only variable consistently available for the three control samples is *Region*. In accordance with the operationalization of *Region*, UK and Continental European (CE) investments are distinguished. Despite the small sample size of only 42 realized investments, non-paramentric *Chi-square* tests results indicate that, compared with the three control samples, the analyzed sample is representative with respect to *Region* (see Table 7). Entity values at entry (P_t) are available for the Initiative Europe control samples *CS_1a* and *CS_1b* only. Using non-parametric *Mann-Whitney* tests, the analyzed sample can also be considered representative with respect to entity values at entry. Interestingly, results for the reduced control sample *CS_1b* for IPO and secondary buyout exits indicate even representativeness. Particularly noteworthy is the test of representativity regarding the *Investment IRRs*. A non-parametric Mann-Whitney test comparing the analyzed sample with the *CEPRES* control sample *CS_2* yields 81.2%. This result for a control test with a sample that derives *Investment IRRs* based on fund cash flow information not only confirms the representativity of the analyzed sample but also provides confidence with respect to the applied, highly sensitive bottom-up calculation of *Investment IRRs* based on company and transaction information. The (by comparison) lowest level of significance (12.1%) is found with respect to the *ExitMode.* Accordingly, secondary buyout exited transactions seem to be (though not significant statistically) overrepresented in the analyzed sample.

B. Methodology

1. Financial Data

Total Proceeds

As defined in chapter II.C, the bottom-up calculation of value creation requires first the specification of *Total Proceeds*, i.e. the entirety of cash flows between the portfolio company and the equity investors, as the appropriate nominator. According to equation (28), *TP* from an equity investor perspective equal the variation in the equity value of the firm plus any net interim equity streams.

(84) $$TP = E_T - E_t + \sum_{n=t+1}^{T-1} E_n$$ see equation (28), p. 69

As pointed out before, owing to the absence of a secondary market for trading direct *PE* investments and hence the absence of market prices, any value creation analysis therefore requires (i) the observation of at least two market prices for the equity value of the business as generally provided at the point in time of the entry and exit of the business, as well as (ii) the capturing of the entirety of interim equity streams.

Company- and Transaction-Specific Information

The discussed dependent variables, in particular operationalized *FCF effects* variables, require further attention. There are two principle types of variables: absolute and relative ones. Apart from EBITDA levels and revenue levels (as one of EBITDA's two components) the remaining operationalized variables are of a relative nature. Relative variables improve comparability across various investments, in particular in light of the heterogeneity of the sample with respect to various analyzed variables. Unless stated otherwise for particular cash flow components, the standard denominator for variables expressed in relative terms is revenues of the same period.[546] Throughout the empirical analysis relative variables will generally be denoted with the suffix *–Mrg* or *–rel.*

FCF effects are operationalized through the analysis of variations in FCF-constituting variables from the entry to the exit of the investment. The point in time of the entry is as mentioned before denoted by *t*; the point in time of the exit, *T*. Throughout the empirical analysis trailing entry financial information will be referred to as the LTM period with the

546 *Note:* Alternatively the firm's assets in the same period could be applied as denominator. This thesis refrains from doing so owing distortions from step-up accounting in the course of LBOs as discussed in chapter III.B.3.3. Since data for comparable pre-LBO asset values are hardly available, pre-buyout asset values would have to be adjusted by the difference between the purchase price and the asset book value. This however, especially when using the variable as denominator, offers substantial room for significant inaccuracies and distortions and thus seems inferior to using sales as the appropriate denominator.

latest comprehensively available company financials prior to the LBO and is denoted by $t{-}1$. Trailing exit financial information refers to the LTM period with the latest comprehensively available company financials prior to the divestment of the asset and is denoted consistently by $T{-}1$.

Applying LTM numbers based on quarterly available financial information improves the accuracy of any related analysis; in particular in light of relatively short holding periods of only two to three years. The improved accuracy not only applies to the holding period until the exit but also to the reference numbers prior to the LBO. Direct investments are obviously characterized by different holding periods (*HP*), denoted by $t{-}T$, which requires appropriate adjustment for the purpose of comparability. For the purpose of discussing *FCF effects*, variations of a particular variable regardless of absolute or negative nature are displayed in three different modes:

- *Absolute* variations, denoted by the prefix Δ, simply calculate the difference between the variable at two different points in time: $var_{T-1} - var_{t-1}$.
- *Relative* variations, generally referred to as *growth* and denoted by the prefix g, put the value of the variable at exit relative to the value at entry into perspective: $var_{T-1} / var_{t-1} - 1$.
- Calculating the compounded annual growth rate (CAGR) with monthly accuracy, annualizes the relative variation by accounting for the different lengths of the investment: $\left(\text{var}_{T-1}/\,\text{var}_{t-1}\right)^{\frac{12}{HP}} - 1$; corresponding variables are denoted by the prefix c.[547]

If applicable, descriptive statistics of the variations in FCF components will comprise these three types of variations. Since for relative variables all types are expressed in percentages, interpretations have to be made, and conclusions have to be drawn cautiously. Important to note further that the strict calculation of variation in the sense Var_{T-1} minus/divided by Var_{t-1} implies that signs have to be considered carefully. To give an example: a positive sign for any of the above variation measures implies favorable EBITDA-Margin improvements though unfavorable CoGS-Margin variations.

Consistency

Consistency of the analyzed financial information is obviously of utmost importance for the outlined research model. This concerns consistency (i) in the variations analysis as well as (ii) in the cross-sectional comparison. Comparing any financial information at two different

547 *Note:* Parallels to the discussion of value creation and related performance measure in LBOs in chapter II.C are obvious. Whereas absolute variations equal *Total Proceeds*, *Times Money* puts these proceeds relative to capital invested into perspective and *IRR* accounts for time aspects.

points in time (i.e. at entry and at exit or during the holding period) requires precisely the same definition and consistent understanding of exceptional one-off items or other adjustments. In particular the analysis of *Total Proceeds* as the basis for the relative LBO investment performance analysis builds upon a consistent definition of equity and debt financing instruments at entry and at exit as well as related cash flows. The same applies for the comparisons across various investments.

A complication arises from the non-industry adjusted comparison of various accounting measures. This deficiency is partially circumvented by considering growth rates and CAGRs during the holding period only and hence abstracting from absolute margin considerations of the dependent variables. Identical relative variations in any relative accounting ratio might be argued to be equally valuable as the impact on *EBITDA Variation* as a component of value creation is determined by the relative variation thereof. Further, the purpose of this thesis is the analysis of determinants driving value creation in a particular LBO investment relative to the entire sample of successfully realized LBO investments. An industry comparison of operational performance improvements through the analysis of a matching control sample is thus not necessarily required.[548] With respect to the external perspective, variation in the transaction multiple, such industry comparison seems even less relevant.[549]

Treatment of Divestitures and Acquisitions During the Holding Period

Interim divestitures and acquisitions represent a severe problem for detailed value creation analysis in LBOs and in particular for the analysis of variations in FCF components. With respect to the decomposition of the LBO transaction model divestitures and acquisitions will be considered as occurred. With respect to the decomposition of *Total Proceeds* to equity investors, disposals and acquisitions predominantly affect *EBITDA Variation* and *Cumulated FCF Generation.* While in the case of acquisitions the *EBITDA Variation* component is presumably inflated and the FCF Generation component is understated, effects are evidently opposite for disposals. *Cumulated FCF Generation* itself is doubly affected with inverse effects in the form of cash in- (out)- flows in the investing element and the missing (additional) operating contribution in the operating element for disposals (acquisitions). With respect to *Multiple Variation* the inclusion of transactions with significant disposals and acquisitions during the holding period implicitly assumes that the expected, long-term, risk-neutral growth

548 For Operational Performance Studies comprising industry peer-group comparisons see e.g. Kaplan, S. N. (1989a), Muscarella, C. J./Vetsuypens, M. R. (1990), Smith, A. J. (1990a), Opler, T. C. (1992) and most recently in a European context Kitzmann, J. (2005).

549 Richter, F./Herrmann, V. (2003), p. 217 conclude from their findings that "*industry classification (at least when using SIC codes as proxy) does not contain superior information to that already controlled for using the theoretically derived factors*", which question the consideration of an industry classification as control variable at least for the external perspective.

rate remains unaffected. Applying relative variables and year-end figures as the appropriate denominator partially controls for divestiture and acquisition activity. The purpose of this thesis is the ex-post analysis of value creation in LBOs on investment level and in this light the analysis of variations in FCF components, which exculpates applying financials as reported.

For the purpose of accuracy, however, the upcoming analyses will be conducted and results will be displayed separately for a reduced sample of transactions without any acquisition and divestiture activity during the holding period. Throughout the empirical analysis this sub-sample is referred to as the *steady sample.*

2. Statistical methods

Statistical methods for the purpose of this thesis can be separated into descriptive and inferring statistics.

Descriptive Statistics

Given its novelty in several respects, the empirical analysis comprises substantial descriptive statistics. Quantitative research regarding *PE* in general and in particular with respect to the outlined research model is still very rare. Therefore, not only all operationalized independent and derived dependent variables, but also further calculated variables, are described throughout the entire empirical analysis with the following template form.

	Average	Median	% Positive Variations	Std. Dev.	Minimum	Maximum	N
Var	$\overline{X}$	X_{Md}	$X_{>0}/X$	X_{Std}	X_{Min}	X_{Max}	N

Apart from standard descriptive statistics, the percentage of positive (negative) variations of the considered variable is shown when appropriate.

In order to control for the formulated expectations regarding the variations of the various Level I Dependent Variables, *Z-statistic* testing for differences from zero is applied. Internal and external independent variables, dependent variables as well as further calculated, insightful variables in the course of the empirical analysis are analyzed for the sub-samples of the three identified binary control variables, *Region*, *EntryMode* and *Time*. Corresponding details (Average and Median) are shown in Appendix C in the following form:

		Total Sample	By Region		By EntryMode		By Time	
			UK	CE	Mgmt-Controlled	Owner-Controlled	Pre Sep-1998	Post Sep-1998
Var	Average	$\overline{X}$	$\overline{X}_{UK}$	$\overline{X}_{CE}$	$\overline{X}_{MC}$	$\overline{X}_{OC}$	$\overline{X}_{Pre}$	$\overline{X}_{Post}$
	Median	X_{Md}	$X_{Md, UK}$	$X_{Md, CE}$	$X_{Md, MC}$	$X_{Md, OC}$	$X_{Md, Pre}$	$X_{Md, Post}$

Statistically significant findings based on non-parametric mean comparison tests are referred to in the main part. *Mann-Whitney* tests are applied for continuously or ordinally scaled variables that severely violate distributional assumptions of parametric tests. *Chi-square* tests are used for binary-scaled variables.

Inferring Statistics

The discussed small sample size with a maximum of 42 observations, constrains the applicability of second generation multivariate analyses such as structural equation models. Given its robustness and ease of application, OLS regression analysis is employed to test the previously postulated hypothesis regarding the effect of the identified independent variable.[550] In a first step the separately derived independent variables for the internal as well as the external perspective are tested on *Level I DVs*. The corresponding, predicted signs of the coefficients of the identified independent variables based upon (i) the formulated hypotheses and (ii) expectations regarding the variation of the dependent variables are displayed in Table 51 in the Appendix. In a second step variables for which in the first step, a significant impact could be confirmed for at least three operationalized *FCF effects* are regressed on *Level II DVs*, i.e. the LBO investment performance and value creation measures. Standard procedure is the comprehensive multiple OLS regression analysis comprising all identified independent variables. In case constraints regarding the data availability of one of the identified dependent variables limit the number of observations to less than 30, stepwise regression analysis is used. In a few cases, owing to restrictions with respect to the sample size, correlation results only are reported.

Various tests are conducted to control for the premises of the OLS regression analysis.[551]

- *Multicollinearity* of independent variables is tested for in two respects. First, Table 66 in Appendix F displays the corresponding correlation matrix. None of the *Pearson correlation coefficients* exceeds 0.43. Among others, the premise of only weak correlated independent variables affect in part the operationalization of certain variables as discussed in chapter IV.B. Second, *VIF* (Variance Inflation Factors) are considered in any conducted regression analysis for each included independent variable. The maximum observed value is 2.376 (see Table 67 in the Appendix). There is no formal cut-off point for multicollinearity though a rule of thumb generally considers VIF values lower than five as not critical.[552]

- *Normal distribution* of dependent variables is controlled for with the *Kolmogorov-Smirnov* test. Even based on a 10% significance level the assumption of normal distribution does not

---

550 For a discussion of the robustness of the OLS regression model see e.g. Cohen, J., et al. (2003).

551 See any standard statistic textbook such as Backhaus, K., et al. (2003) or Bortz, J. (2005).

552 See e.g. Myers, R. H. (1986).

have to be rejected for any of the considered dependent variables (see Table 67 in the Appendix).

- *Autocorrelation* of residuals is controlled for with the *Durbin-Watson* test. Due to the small sample size the *grey area* between the lower and the upper limit for negative as well as positive autocorrelation is particularly wide. For the total of 18 tested dependent variables no significance is found for either positive or negative autocorrelation. However, internal perspective (i) revenues CAGR ($c\_Rev_{t-1,T-1}$) and therefore also EBITDA CAGR ($c\_EBITDA_{t-1,T-1}$) lies within the grey area for positive autocorrelation, and (ii) (capital expenditures CAGR) $c\_CapEx\text{-}rel_{t-1,T-1}$ lies within the grey area for negative autocorrelation (see Table 67 in the Appendix).

C. Independent Variables Descriptive Statistics

This chapter presents descriptive statistics for the identified independent variables structured alongside the previously discussed structure of Control Variables (chapter V.C.1), Purely Internal Perspective Aspects (chapter V.C.2) and Purely External Perspective Aspects (chapter V.C.3).

1. Control Variables

Regional Considerations

The thesis analyzes European investments only. Out of the total sample of 42 transactions, exactly 50% of the companies were registered in the UK, six in France, four in Germany, five in the Nordic Region (including Denmark, Finland, Norway and Sweden) and the remaining seven companies were based in another European country. The relatively high fraction of UK companies is notable. One potential explanation is the fact that the tremendous increase in US LBO transactions in the 80s first swashed to the UK and from there to Continental Europe.[553] Since this thesis analyzes realized investments with a threshold entity value of larger than €150m, the fraction of transactions that were entered into relatively early and in a relatively 'LBO-developed' country is undoubtedly higher.

Following the argumentation in chapter IV.B.3, regional analysis in the remaining part of this thesis differentiates between the UK and Continental Europe (CE), each representing 50% of the total sample.

---

553 See also Braun, C. (1989), pp. 47-68. Further Sapienza, H. J., et al. (1996) find VC markets in the UK to be most like those in the US.

EntryMode

The classification of LBOs by entry mode (chapter II.A.3) differentiates between (i) public-to-private and (ii) private-to-private transactions on a first level and for the latter among divisional, succession and secondary buyouts. The entire sample of 42 realized buyouts comprises four public-to-private and 38 private-to-private entries. The largest fraction of private transactions is the group of 22 divisional buyouts representing 52.4% of the total sample. Further the sample includes ten succession buyouts and six secondary buyouts with respect to the mode of entry. A sub-sample analysis of the remaining empirical analysis alongside the separation in public- and private-to-private entries is not feasible owing to the small number of going private transactions. Therefore and following the argumentation in chapter IV.B.3 the remainder of the analysis differentiates between 16 transactions that were presumably owner-controlled prior to the LBO (ten succession and six secondary buyouts) and 26 transactions that were presumably manager-controlled prior to the LBO, i.e. with dispersed selling ownership (22 divisional buyouts and four going privates).

Timing of Entry and Exit

According to the deal selection criteria, the first LBO of a company under review occurred in Jan-1993. The last considered exit took place in Dec-2004. The earliest exit of the analyzed sample occurred after a 12-month holding period via an IPO in 1994. Given the consideration of completed transactions only, the last entry of an investment under review occurred in Oct-2002. Across the total sample the average (median) holding period equals 30.1 (26.5) months.[554]

It has previously been argued that the extent of *FCF effects* as well as the *variation in the transaction multiple* and therefore the relative importance of components and their contribution to LBO performance varies over time (*H_CV_3*). The median entry date that dichotomizes the sample in *early* and *recent* transactions and is thus applied to test for general time effects of the results is Sep-1998.

---

554 See the upcoming chapter V.D.1 for details regarding the holding period.

Chart 15 Timing of Entry and Exit

Left-hand bars indicate entries, right-hand bars exits; 'Entry' bars split into previously management-controlled (bottom) and previously owner-controlled (top) companies; 'Exit' bars split into IPO (bottom) and secondary buyouts (top); Classification of exit and entry year according to corresponding dates effective

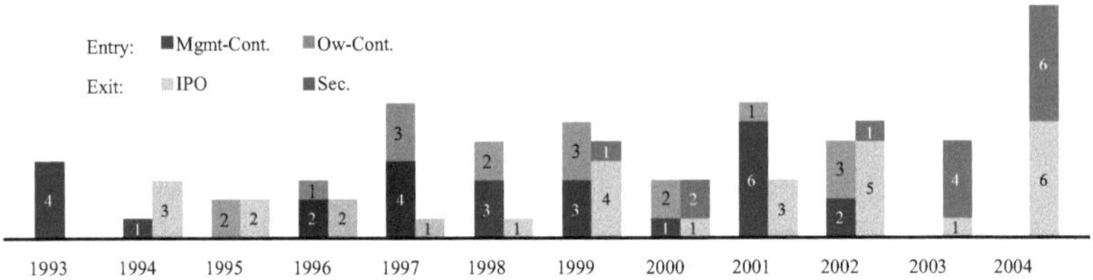

The above Chart 15 displays the distribution of the sample by entry and exit year. Additionally, entry bars separate the mode of entry, as indicated in the previous sample, into previously manager-controlled and previously owner-controlled companies. Exit information separates between the for the analysis relevant modes of IPO and secondary buyout exits. For instance, in 2002 the sample includes five entries, two of which are manager-controlled, and six exits, five of which are IPOs. Accordingly, large secondary buyouts are a phenomenon of recent years, with the first entry into a transaction that was subsequently exited via a secondary taking place in 1997, and the first exit occurring in 1999. In the years 2003 and 2004, secondary exit activity increased notably with ten out of the total of 14 secondary buyout exits taking place in these two years.

2. Purely Internal Perspective Related

2.1 Agency Cost Reduction Related Aspects

2.1.1 Company Size and Profitability at Entry

Various variables can be thought of in order to proxy a firm's size and profitability. Table 8 provides descriptive statistics, first for revenues, EBITDA, EBITDA less capital expenditures, assets, total capitalization and the number of employees as indicator for size, followed by EBITDA-margin, EBITDA less CapEx margin and the EBITA-margin as indicators for the firm's profitability. All variables are characterized by high ranges between the minimum and the maximum value and high standard deviations. This in combination with the skewness of the distributions indicates the relatively high degree of heterogeneity of the sample companies with respect to size and profitability.

Table 8 Company Size and Profitability at Entry

Absolute numbers in €m; foreign currencies converted into € at the respective date effective spot exchange rate; t-1 indicate latest available financial information for twelve months period prior to the entry; IV indicates the corresponding independent variable

	Average	Median	Std. Dev.	Minimum	Maximum	N
Size						
Rev_{t-1} (IV)	707.3	514.3	622.9	86.5	2,616.7	42
$EBITDA_{t-1}$	99.7	75.7	95.7	17.6	513.0	42
$EBITDA\text{-}CapEx_{t-1}$	62.8	48.9	64.5	(24.1)	350.0	38
$Total\ Assets_{t-1}$	727.0	456.2	1,207.3	45.7	6,818.2	35
$Total\ Cap_{t}$	742.8	504.4	712.6	153.9	3,483.0	42
$Employ_{t-1}$	5,103	3,555	3,628	1,020	11,900	31
Profitability						
$EBITDA\text{-}Mrg_{t-1}$ (IV)	17.3%	14.6%	9.0%	5.4%	39.3%	42
$EBITDA\text{-}CapEx\text{-}Mrg_{t-1}$	10.2%	8.9%	7.7%	(10.8%)	35.5%	38
$EBITA\text{-}Mrg_{t-1}$	11.3%	10.8%	5.6%	4.6%	28.6%	37

Variables are presented on a LTM basis. Although operating performance data are adjusted for non-operating one-off items variables might be influenced by operational or macro-economic one-off effects in the one-year period under review. In particular, this might hold to be true for capital expenditures explaining why even negative numbers for $EBITDA\text{-}CapEx_{t-1}$ and $EBITDA\text{-}CapEx\text{-}Mrg_{t-1}$ can be observed.

Owing to previously emphasized restrictions with respect to data availability, some variables can only be computed for a reduced sample of realized LBO transactions as indicated in the far right column. In this respect, the average number of employees prior to the buyout, $Employ_{t-1}$ is only available for 31 out of the 42 companies and hence will limit the analysis of employment effects.

Some brief remarks regarding size and profitability measures with respect to the control variables (i) *Region*, (ii) *EntryMode*, and (iii) *Time*, details of which can be found in Table 52 in the Appendix. The UK sub-sample seems to be more heterogeneous than the CE sub-sample: Whereas UK companies included in the sample were on average 'larger' with respect to all size indicators their median values were generally lower than for CE transactions. Statistically, size and profitability do not differ significantly by region. Furthermore, previously management-controlled companies are not significantly larger in terms of mean and median values than owner-controlled companies. Interestingly though, owner-controlled firms were on average (weak) statistically significantly more profitable than their counterparts, already indicating the support of agency theoretical considerations. The size of analyzed transactions is increasing over time. Average Rev_{t-1} increased (weak significant) from €581.0m for the 21 transactions prior to Sep-1998 to €833.5m for analyzed transactions thereafter.[555] Variations in EBITDA and EBITDA less capital expenditures also indicate highly significant increases in size. The very highly significant rise in total capitalizations implies for the time being that an increase in valuation levels over time amplified the increase in revenues and EBITDA.

2.1.2 *Managerial Ownership*

As theory suggests, management is highly encouraged through equity ownership participation in the course of LBO transactions. On average management owns 11.2% of the company representing on average approximately €23.6m in absolute terms.[556]

Table 9 Managerial Ownership

Relative accrued management ownership stake at exit and the corresponding absolute amount (in €m) based on the initial equity value at entry; IV indicates the corresponding independent variable

	Average	Median	Std. Dev.	Minimum	Maximum	N
λ (IV)	11.1%	10.0%	8.6%	1.2%	40.0%	42
Mgmt Ownership $_{abs}$	23.8	15.9	25.4	1.2	116.2	42

It is important to note that the above numbers do not represent management's cash equity contribution at entry. As repeatedly pointed out elsewhere in this thesis, management incentivation mechanisms are complex including option schemes and leverage effects through sweat equity. Assuming that agreed performance targets are met implies that the management ownership stake generally accrues over time. Owing to the heterogeneity of the sample with respect to size, initial entity and equity value the correlation between managerial ownership in relative and absolute terms is only moderate at 0.48. For the analyzed sample the absolute managerial ownership is, statistically, significantly lower for CE transactions. Significant differences with respect to entry mode and time seem not to exist, either with respect to the relative or the absolute consideration (see Table 53 in the Appendix for details).

2.1.3 *Financing at Entry*

Across the sample of 42 realized transactions the average leverage, according to the debt and equity understanding as defined in chapter II.B, equals 64.3%. In-line with the applied definition for the terminology 'leveraged', the corresponding values range between 50.1% and

---

555 This increase, however, results – other than what one might assume at first – not only from mega-deals included in the recent sub-sample. Also the early sub-sample, with entries prior to Sep-1998, comprises four transactions with Rev_{t-1} in excess of €1bn.

556 In this respect management is defined in a broad sense to comprising further top management positions apart from the Chairman, CEO, CFO and COO. Since the granularity of data regarding the individual positions has not been available, differences might occur across the sample. However, as pointed out earlier, it could be argued that including all equity-incentivized management; facilitates the comparability of the relative managerial ownership stake across transactions of different sizes, assuming that the incentivized management team increases with the size of the company.

82.4% with a relatively low standard deviation of 8.1%. The total mean (median) equity contribution of the analyzed LBOs hence equals 35.7% (34.2%). The average Total Debt to $EBITDA_{LTM}$ ratio is calculated at 4.8x, ranging from 1.8x to 7.1x.[557]

Table 10 Financing at Entry

Leverage, % Equity and % Quasi Equity (as a component of % Equity) expressed as percentage of Total Capitalization; Total Debt and Subordinated Debt expressed in multiples of EBITDA for the LTM period prior to the entry
See Chart 20 on page 194 for the distribution of l_t; IV indicates the corresponding independent variable

	Average	Median	Std. Dev.	Minimum	Maximum	N
l_t (IV)	64.3%	65.8%	8.1%	50.1%	82.4%	42
% Equity $_t$	35.7%	34.2%	8.1%	17.6%	49.9%	42
thereof % Quasi Equity $_t$	23.4%	22.7%	10.9%	5.8%	46.9%	40
Total Debt $_t$	4.8x	4.8x	1.2x	1.8x	7.1x	42
Sub. Debt $_t$	1.5x	1.4x	.7x	.3x	2.9x	29

Sixty-nine percent of the analyzed transactions applied some form of subordinated debt for the financing of the initial investment, which then accounted for approximately one and a half (EBITDA) leverage points on average. Quasi-equity financing is confirmed to be of significant importance in LBO transactions. The financing structure of almost all firms comprises some form of quasi-equity financing instrument as defined in chapter II.B.2.2. In these cases approximately two-thirds of the total equity contributions from the equity investors were on average in the form of preference shares, vendor loans, shareholder loans etc. Falsely considering such quasi-equity financing instruments (in particular shareholder loans) as financial liabilities would significantly distort and disqualify any value creation analysis in LBOs from an equity investor perspective.

Irrespective of *Time*, *EntryMode* and *Region* average gearing ratios are extremely stable, ranging on average ±1% around the total sample average of 64.3%. However, total debt as a multiple of EBITDA for the LTM period prior to the LBO is (weak) statistically significantly higher for recent transactions implying for the time being that entry multiples rose over time in the analyzed sample. Further, quasi-equity financing instruments seem to have increased in popularity over time. The percentage of quasi equity of total capitalization rose with a significance level of below 1% from 19.8% on average for transactions prior to Sep-1988 to an average of 26.3% for the period thereafter (see Table 53 in the Appendix for details).

557 These findings regarding the capital structure of the LBO investments at entry are comparable to the results reported by Weinberger, N. (2005), chapter VI. According to this study of financing determinants of 83 LBOs Total Debt to $EBITDA_{t-1}$ at the time of the entry ranges between 1.6x and 7.6x with an average of 4.6x.

2.2 Management Support Related

2.2.1 Managerial Turnover

22 of the 42 analyzed portfolio companies experienced a change in their top management in the course of the holding period in the form of either a new CEO or CFO.[558] Top-management turnover is exactly evenly split between UK and CE transactions as well as between early and recent transactions. Interestingly, though understandable, according to the descriptive results of the sample, managerial turnover is higher for companies that were presumably management-controlled (15 out of 26 or 57.7%) compared to presumably owner-controlled (seven out of 26 or 42.8%) prior to the LBO. However, owing to the small sample size, this finding is not statistically significant based on the Chi-square test.

2.2.2 Disposals and Acquisitions

During the holding period only six portfolio companies out of the entire sample disposed of significant assets.[559] In light of this low number any sub-sample analysis is obviously by no means feasible and would lack any representativeness; also results do not reveal any major differences regarding the relative split by *Region*, *EntryMode* and *Time*. The 42 sample companies were more acquisitive: Eleven or approximately one quarter of the portfolio companies acquired significant assets during the holding period. Though not being statistically significant owing to the very small sample, previously manager-controlled companies seem to be more acquisitive than previously owner-controlled companies (30.8% compared to 18.8%). According to the 5% threshold level only one sample company acquired as well as divested significantly during the holding period. The descriptive result that on average one out of four portfolio companies undergoes a significant acquisition during the investment period, challenges somewhat the previously presented view that high absolute debt burdens and cash restrictions from debt servicing payments potentially prevent LBO companies from pursuing a growth strategy and undertaking promising add-on acquisitions. In the analyzed sample acquisitive (potentially a buy-and-build) strategies seem to have dominated disposal strategies.

As pointed out earlier, results for FCF components variation analyses will be displayed separately for the *steady* sub-sample of 26 transactions, which neither acquired nor divested in the course of the holding period. In this respect owner-controlled companies seem to be the more 'stable' LBOs with 75% (12 out of 16) having neither significantly divested nor significantly acquired during the holding period compared with the corresponding number of 53.8% for previously management-controlled companies.

---

558 This number is vaguely in line with results presented by Martin, K. J./Mcconnell, J. J. (1989), which report a managerial turnover rate of 41.5% for the 14 months following a takeover.

559 Recall that divestitures and acquisitions are classified as 'significant' and thus considered here if the transaction value exceeds 5% of the firm's total assets in the relevant year.

2.2.3 Experience Index

This thesis operationalizes the experience of the financial sponsor involved in the LBO through the binary variable *ExpInd* taking the value of one for established buyout firms. Based on the Initiative Europe (2004) database that has also been used in part to identify the set of potential transactions, buyout firms will be considered established when they belong to the group of the 20 largest private equity firms according to the cumulated amount invested.

Table 11 Group of Established Buyout Firms

Affiliation based on the cumulated amount invested; no ranking; listing in alphabetical order; considered entity value threshold of €150m in accordance with the criteria for the sample of analyzed transactions; co-investments considered with the fractional equity contribution

3i	Deutsche Bank	PAI
Apax	Doughty Hanson	Permira
BC Partners	Goldman Sachs Capital Partners	Texas Pacific
Candover	Industri Kapital	Charterhouse
Carlyle	KKR	Investcorp
Cinven	Madison Dearborn Partners	Electra
CVC Capital Partners	Nomura	

Source: Initiative Europe (2004)

According to this classification exactly 50% or 21 out of the 42 analyzed realized investments involved an experienced financial sponsor.

3. Purely External Perspective Related

3.1 Conceptual Valuation Framework Related Aspects

Based on theoretical considerations in chapter III.C.1 derived hypotheses regarding the impact of capital market parameters on the variation of the transaction multiple between entry and exit. The risk-free interest rate as well as further parameters to operationalize the capital market environment shall be briefly illustrated / quantified.

3.1.1 Risk-free Interest Rate

The development of the 10-year UK government bond interest rate for the relevant time period is shown in Chart 16. From a level of around 8% the long-term UK government bond rate started to continuously decline in mid 1996. Since late 1998 the rate has oscillated in a relatively narrow range around 5%.

Chart 16 10-year UK Government Bond Rate Jan-1993 to Jan-2005

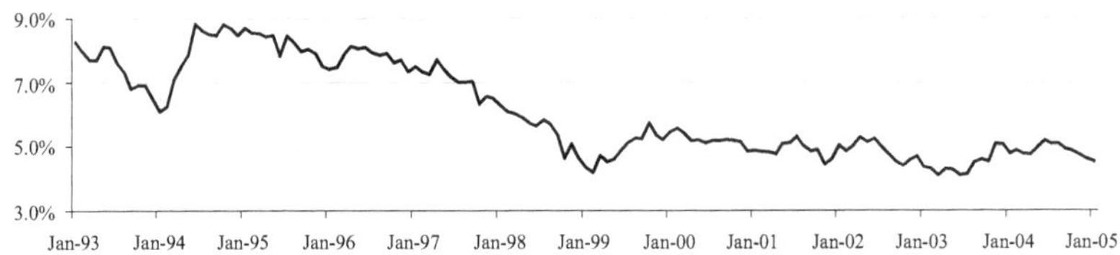

Source: Thomson Financial (2005)

Table 12 Variation in the Risk-free Interest Rate from Entry to Exit

Change in the risk-free interest rate $\Delta\_r_{f,T-t}$ defined as the rate at exit (T) less the corresponding rate at entry (t); IV indicates independent variable

	Average	Median	% Positive Variations	Std. Dev.	Minimum	Maximum	N
$\Delta\_r_{f,T-t}$ *(IV)*	(0.6%)	(0.4%)	21.4%	1.0%	(2.9%)	1.3%	42

In light of this dominant development, it is hardly surprising that for 33 of the 42 analyzed investments the market environment is characterized by a negative interest rate differential from entry to exit; as displayed in Table 12 on average the differential amounts to 0.61%.

3.1.2 Growth

Chapter IV.B.2.1.2 emphasized the general difficulties with operationalizing expected future growth. It has been pointed out that (i) unbiased, objective projections are not available for the entirety of analyzed investments, and that (ii) *Tobin's Q* as a generally applied proxy for growth opportunities is barely feasible in the context of this analysis. In light of these limitations, this thesis applies historically realized growth rates as the corresponding proxies. Following the outlined methodology of analyzing variations in the transaction multiples, variations between the historically realized EBITDA growth rate at exit and at entry are considered.[560] Accordingly:

(85) $$\Delta\_g_{EBITDA} = c\_EBITDA_{t-3,t-1} - c\_EBITDA_{t-1,T-1}$$

560 EBITDA contribution of acquired or divested operations deducted in the nominator or subtracted from the denominator respectively in both EBITDA CAGR ratios in order to derive an adjusted figure. Similar growth as the entire business assumed for acquisitions and divestitures during the holding period; EBITDA-margin of the respective year applied on the hypothetical sales figure. In case no EBITDA figures were available, firm profitability is assumed for the divested or acquired operation.

Table 13 Growth

Δ_gEBITDA defined as the EBITDA CAGR during the holding period less the 2-year period EBITDA CAGR prior to the LBO; EBITDA figures adjusted for acquisition and divestiture activity as detailed in footnote [560]; for 13 investments the EBITDA CAGR for the 2-year period prior to the LBO is not available; in these cases the 1-year period growth rate is applied; Details regarding the EBITDA CAGR during the holding period are discussed in chapter V.D.2.1.1 and Table 23; IV indicates independent variable

	Average	Median	% Positive Variations	Std. Dev.	Minimum	Maximum	N
Δ_g_{EBITDA} (IV)	1.8%	2.8%	64.3%	14.6%	(30.6%)	35.4%	42

As previously detailed the growth variable causes the interdependencies between the internal and the external perspective of the two-tier framework of this thesis. Variations in the firm's growth track during the holding period potentially impact a variation in the transaction multiple. In this respect, the variable anticipates some of the findings regarding variations of operational performance measures during the holding period presented previously and therefore shall only be detailed here to the extent necessary. Of relevance, almost two-thirds of the analyzed investments increase the EBITDA faster during the holding period compared with the 2-year period preceding the buyout. On average annual EBITDA growth under the ownership of the (group of) financial sponsor(s) exceeds annual EBITDA growth prior to the LBO by 1.8%. According to the theoretical considerations in chapter III.C.1 and assuming that this change in growth track is sustained in the future, this increase would merit an increase in the valuation/transaction multiple.

3.2 Capital Market Environment Related Aspects

3.2.1 Equity Market Environment

Chart 17 displays the monthly number of IPOs for the period from Jan-1993 to Jan-2005. As mentioned, the difference between the number at exit and at entry (Δ_#_*IPOs*) will be applied for proxying the relative variation of the equity capital market attractiveness.

Chart 17 Monthly Number of IPOs Jan-1993 to Jan-2005

Combined for UK and Continental Europe

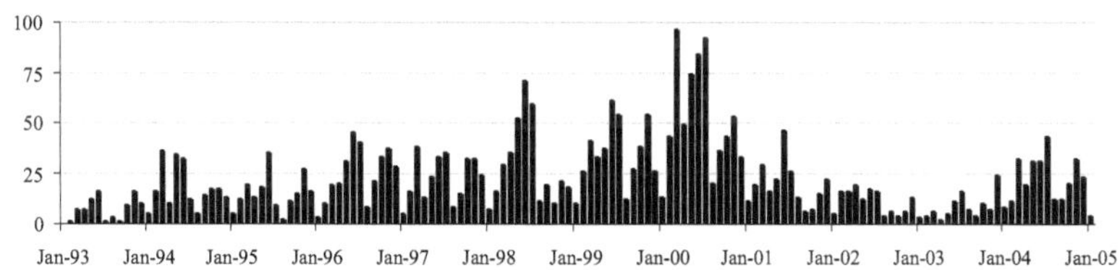

Source: Thomson Financial (2005)

The average monthly number of IPOs for the period under review is 19. IPO activity soared in early 1998 and early 2000 and peaked in the month of Mar-2000 with 96 IPOs.

Table 14 Variation in the Number of IPOs from Entry to Exit

Change in the number of monthly UK and Continental European IPOs $\Delta\_\#\_IPOs_{T-t}$ defined as the number of IPOs at exit (T) less the corresponding number at entry (t)

	Average	Median	% Positive Variations	Std. Dev.	Minimum	Maximum	N
$\Delta\_\#\_IPO_{T-t}$ *(Total Sample)*	6.0	3.0	59.5%	25.4	(45.0)	73.0	42
$\Delta\_\#\_IPO_{T-t}$ *(IPO sample)*	12.3	11.0	67.9%	24.3	(40.0)	73.0	28

A positive variation in this variable might be interpreted as the financial sponsor's timing ability, i.e. the talent to buy in a less attractive equity capital market environment and sell in a relatively more attractive state of the market. Based on Δ_#_*IPOs*, private equity firms seem to possess this ability. Of high statistical significance, with on average 34 IPOs/month, the equity capital market environment is more attractive in the divestment phase than in the acquisition phase with on average 21.5 IPOs/month.[561] 67.9% of the IPO exits occurred in a relatively more attractive environment compared with the entry. By comparison, the corresponding number for the sub-sample of secondary buyout exited LBOs equals 42.9%, confirming the view that secondary buyouts prevail when a relatively unattractive equity capital market environment presumably hampers IPO exits.

3.2.2 Debt Capital Market Environment

In analogy to the number of IPOs, Chart 18 displays the spread for the previously discussed operationalized variable for proxying the debt capital market attractiveness. In the context of value creation analysis in LBOs, a relatively lower spread at exit compared to entry presumably indicates a relatively more attractive debt financing environment. Hence, debt financing multiples are expected to be higher (compared to the entry level of the particular investment), which – following the argumentation of the maximum debt capacity approach – ought to increase the realized transaction multiple at exit.

From levels as low as 2.2% in Mar-2000 the spread peaked at 10.4% in Nov-2002 and continuously decreased thereafter to levels of below 2% in Aug-2004 (see Chart 18). For seven of the eleven relevant transactions with available data Δ_*spread* is negative. At first this indicates a relatively more attractive financing market at exit and hence, following the previously presented argumentation, a presumably higher relative transaction price.

---

561 Based on mean comparison t-test for paired variables.

Chart 18 European High Yield Spread for BB rated Companies Jan-1999 to Jan-2005

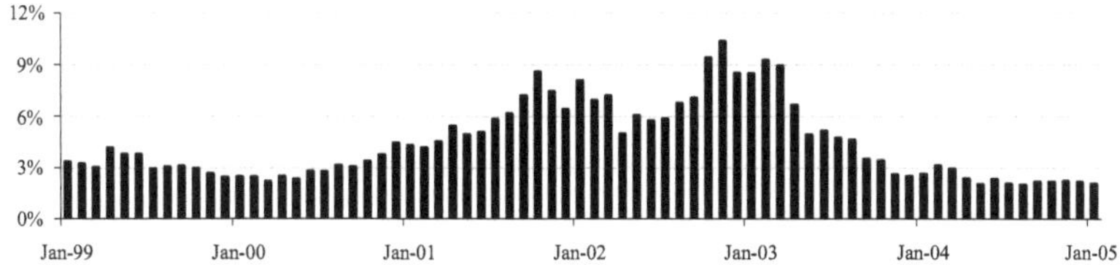

Source: Thomson Financial (2005)

3.3 Information Asymmetries Related Aspects

3.3.1 IPO Exit Characteristics

Table 15 reveals offering details for 28 investments included in the sample that were exited via an IPO. On average the free-float of these companies following the IPO, i.e. the amount of shares sold during the divestment process as percentage of total shares post IPO, equals 55.4% with a standard deviation of 20.2% and a corresponding range of 15.6% to 93.7%.

Table 15 IPO Exit Characteristics

IV indicates α (the remaining LBO equity investor stake including equity and quasi-equity financing instruments) as the independent variable; over-allotment when exercised; PC represents primary component, SC secondary component and EI equity investor

	Average	Median	Std. Dev.	Minimum	Maximum	N
Free-float post IPO	55.4%	56.0%	20.2%	15.6%	93.7%	28
α (IV)	46.0%	44.4%	19.6%	10.1%	84.4%	28
Over-allotment	12.1%	13.0%	2.6%	3.4%	16.2%	20
% PC of Shares Offered	59.7%	63.7%	27.1%	0.9%	100.0%	28
% SC of Initial Shares	37.1%	37.8%	22.7%	0.0%	81.1%	28
% PC to EI	65.5%	66.1%	41.1%	5.9%	175.0%	23
% Proceeds to EI	68.6%	73.1%	28.2%	0.0%	118.3%	28

Based upon signaling consideration in chapter III.C.2.2.1 and the operationalization in chapter IV.B.2.3 the remaining ownership stake α is applied for proxying the exploration of information asymmetries. As pointed out, the remaining stake does not necessarily match one minus the Free Float. The remaining stake also comprises quasi-equity financing instruments that are, post-IPO, still owned by the LBO equity investors. Accordingly, whereas these instruments are considered as an unsold equity component from the point of view of the LBO equity investor they are not accounted for in free float. It can be seen that the company in the sample with the minimum free float has no further outstanding quasi-equity financing instruments following the IPO as the minimum free float equals one minus the maximum remaining stake. Conversely, the investment with the maximum free float of (93.7%)

apparently has further quasi-financing instruments outstanding, implying that the minimum remaining stake of 10.1% exceeds the expected stake of 6.3%.

In 71.4% of these IPO exits the over-allotment option has been exercised, which then amounted to 12.1% of total shares offered. In only two of these cases was the over-allotment exercised in the form of primary shares. Across the 28 transactions the average primary component as percentage of total shares offered amounts to 59.7%. These figures imply that on average the secondary component, i.e. the sale of existing shares by the pre-IPO equity investors, represents 37.1% of the total amount of initial shares pre-IPO, with the remaining ownership stake being diluted to 44.6% on average.

Of particular interest is the information regarding the use of primary proceeds displayed in the penultimate line: ideally it has been argued that proceeds from selling new shares are used to fund growth projects or decrease the firm's third-party financial liabilities. If, however, primary proceeds are used to repay quasi-equity financing instruments, such as shareholder loans provided by the financial sponsors, primary proceeds flow – indirectly – to the LBO equity investors and thus represent a sort of *in disguise secondary component.* Given the excessive use of quasi-equity financing instruments as detailed in chapter V.C.2.1.3, an astonishing 65.5% of primary proceeds were on average used to repay some form of equity investor liabilities.[562]

Even more impressive, all 24 IPO exited portfolio companies that had some form of quasi-equity financing instrument outstanding prior to the IPO used (at least) part of the proceeds to repay equity investor liabilities.[563] A mere three companies had fractions of initial shareholder and vendor loans outstanding following the IPO. Primary proceeds received by the financial sponsor together with the secondary component account on average for 68.6% of proceeds from the IPO.

The typical lock-up period for the remaining stake of the financial sponsor(s) involved in the transaction was 180 trading days (17 out of the 23 for which this data could be collected).

For the analyzed sample of IPO exited LBOs, the raw return on the first trading day compared with the offering price amounts to 1.60%. The excess return equals 1.23%.[564] These numbers are at the lower end of the range when compared with previous studies, which

---

562 Numbers in excess of 100% indicate that new third-party financial liabilities from refinancing in the course of the IPO process were applied to redeem LBO equity investor liabilities.

563 26 IPO exited companies initially applied some form of quasi-equity financing whereof two fully recouped this investment in the course of recapitalizations prior to the IPO.

564 The excess return equals the raw return benchmarked against the return of the DJStoxx index.

generally find IPO exited LBOs to be less underpriced compared with matching non-LBO IPOs.[565]

D. Total Proceeds to Equity Investors

As the discussed prerequisite for any value creation analysis in LBOs, *Total Proceeds* to equity investors are detailed in the following chapters for the analyzed sample of 42 LBO investments. In analogy to the theoretical chapter I, this comprises the decomposition of the LBO transaction model (chapter V.D.1) and the successive detailed discussion of the internal, *FCF effects* (chapter V.D.2) as well as external, *variation in the transaction multiple* (chapter V.D.3) perspective.

1. The LBO Transaction Model

1.1 Financial Leverage and the Variation in the Entity and Equity Value

Before detailing variations in valuations from entry to exit some remarks on the holding period of the LBO investments follow.

Holding Period

The average holding period for the entire sample equals 30.1 months with a median of 26.5 months and a range from seven months to five and a half years.[566]

---

565 For related studies see e.g. Ainina, M. F./Mohan, N. K. (1991), pp. 393ff reporting statistically significant lower excess returns of 2.07% compared with 2.78% for a sample of 92 MBO-IPOs and Saadouni, B. S., et al. (1996) finding mean excess returns of 8.64% and 10.31% for a sample of 39 MBO/non-MBO-IPOs respectively. Hogan, K. M., et al. (2001) report mean excess returns of 7.64% for a sample of 232 IPO exited buyouts. See further Megginson, W. L./Weiss, K. A. (1991), pp. 879-903, Degeorge, F./Zeckhauser, R. (1993), pp. 1323-1348 and , pp. 293-332. The aftermarket performance of the sub-sample of IPO exited LBOs will be given further attention in chapter V.E.2.1.

566 The average number is in line with Holthausen, R. W./Larcker, D. F. (1996) reporting an average holding period for 29.4 months for the analyzed sample of 90 reverse LBOs and broadly in line with the corresponding numbers provided by Kaplan, S. N. (1989a) and Muscarella, C. J./Vetsuypens, M. R. (1990). For a sub-sample of 25 US reverse LBOs entered into in the years 1980 to 1986 Kaplan reports an average holding period of 2.68 years (~32 months); Muscarella and Vetsuypens report 34.7months.

Chart 19 Holding Period Distribution and Descriptive Statistics

In months; holding period defined as difference between entry date effective and exit date effective of the investment

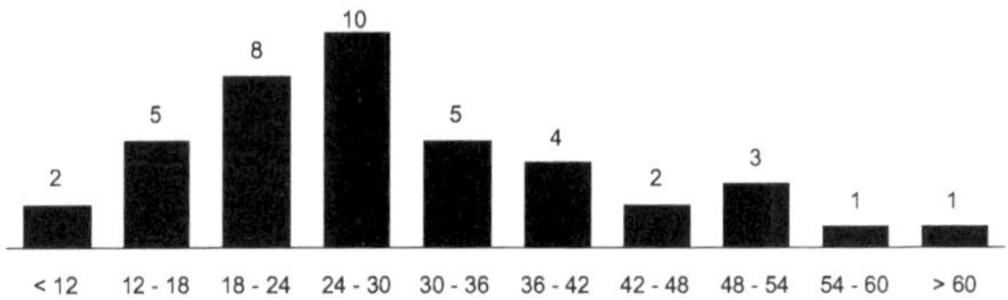

N	42
Average	30.1
Median	26.5
Std. Dev.	13.9
Minimum	7.0
Maximum	66.0

Chart 19 visualizes the slightly left-skewed distribution for the holding period. More than two thirds of the analyzed investments were held less than 36 months; less than 10% of the sample investments were more than 4 years under private ownership by the LBO equity investors. This challenges the frequent argumentation of numerous academics claiming typical investment horizons of three to five or even up to ten years (see discussion in chapter II.A.1).

The average holding period seems to have increased over time. Whereas for the 22 transactions prior to Sep-1998 portfolio companies were held on average 26.9 months by financial sponsor(s) there was a statistically significant increase to 33.3 months for the 22 transactions thereafter. Interestingly, for the analyzed sample the mean/median holding period for previously management-controlled companies is longer (See Table 54 in the Appendix for details). Assuming that the holding period is longer for transactions with higher operational performance improvement potential as related implementations require more time, this finding is well suited to the agency theoretical argumentation that operational performance improvement potentials for management-controlled buyouts exceed those for owner-controlled buyouts.[567]

The finding that investments that are owned by financial sponsors are apparently shorter than generally expected (and presumably alleged by financial sponsors) prompts the questions (i) whether the holding period actually suffices to implement and benefit from positive impacts of the LBO governance structure, and (ii) to what extent value can be created through deleveraging. A relatively short holding period, potentially in combination with high levels of multiple expansion, might point rather to *quick flips* investments and thus challenge the *classical* LBO business model with value being claimed to be generated through restructuring and deleveraging. The forthcoming analysis of the relative composition of *Total Proceeds* as well as relative value creation performance measures will present insights in this respect.

---

567 Forthcoming analyses of the variations in *FCF* components during the holding period will further elaborate on this issue.

Variation in the Entity and Equity Value

The calculation of the appropriate entity and equity value at entry and exit is obviously crucial for any variation analysis though not exactly straightforward. Equation (3) defined that the entity value at entry V_t equals the net capitalization of the transaction, i.e. the sum of all debt- and equity-financing instruments net of any cash, less the transaction costs experienced for entering the transaction. The equity value simply equals the total of all equity-financing instruments. With respect to corresponding exit values a separated consideration of IPO exited and secondary exited transactions is needful.

- For secondary buyout exits, the entity value can be derived similarly to the entry value (and thus equation (3)) based on the funding details of the follow-on LBO. The matching equity value from an LBO equity investor perspective then equals the entity value less any outstanding third-party financial liabilities prior to the secondary buyout funding.
- For IPO exits, the approach is similar though spiked with some peculiarities: the exit entity value is also calculated bottom-up from the post-divestiture capital structure, i.e. as the sum of the firm's market capitalization based on the offering share price plus the amount of net debt post-IPO. However, as mentioned previously an IPO affects the firm's net debt position in various forms. Primary proceeds can either be used for debt repayment and the redemption of LBO equity investor liabilities or kept as cash on a balance sheet. The matching equity value can therefore either be derived (i) as the residual of the entity value less the exact net debt position prior to the IPO (i.e. similar to secondary exits) or (ii) as the sum of secondary proceeds, equity investors liabilities (which are either redeemed with primary proceeds or are still outstanding post-IPO) plus the value of the remaining (though through the primary component diluted) common stock stake. Given the higher accuracy with respect to the exact value at the time of the IPO rather than based on the latest available financial liabilities figure pre-IPO, the second approach is applied. In both cases the implicit assumption is to value the unmonetized, remaining equity stake of the LBO equity investors at the offering price. As pointed out however, pre-LBO equity investors remain exposed to post-IPO performance through the partial exit only. This exposure can have substantial impact on equity investors' return. For the analyzed sample of IPO exited LBOs the mean/median share price 180 trading days after the IPO exceeded the offering price by 20.5% and 0.1% respectively with a range from -47.5% to 369.5%.[568]

[568] The relative performance analysis in chapter V.E will quantify the impact of the aftermarket performance of IPO exited LBOs on equity investor Investment IRRs.

Table 16 displays entity value information at entry and at exit respectively. Given the focus of the analysis with a minimum threshold of €150m, entity values at entry for the companies included in the sample range from €151.2m to €3,317.2m with an average of €695.8m.

Table 16 Entity Value Variation

Absolute numbers in €m; foreign currencies converted into € at the respective date effective spot exchange rates at entry and at exit; entry values are indexed with t; the corresponding exit value with T; g indicates the effective growth rate from entry to exit; c the corresponding CAGR; steady sample comprising investments without any acquisition and divestiture activity during the holding period only

	Average	Median	Std. Dev.	Minimum	Maximum	N
Total Sample						
V_t	695.8	479.5	679.8	151.2	3,317.2	42
V_T	1,039.5	875.1	825.7	222.0	4,566.8	42
g_V_{T-t}	69.9%	61.5%	52.2%	(1.6%)	223.5%	42
c_V_{T-t}	30.5%	20.5%	32.1%	(0.6%)	167.7%	42
Steady Sample						
V_t	631.3	500.7	454.6	151.2	1,772.5	26
V_T	949.4	798.0	606.9	224.7	2,375.0	26
g_V_{T-t}	66.5%	57.1%	49.2%	12.1%	223.5%	26
c_V_{T-t}	34.3%	19.8%	37.0%	3.8%	167.7%	26

The average growth rate in entity value over the average holding period of 30.1 months equals 69.9% with an average CAGR of 30.5%. As for most analyzed variables the g_V_t rate is characterized by a very high variance given the range from (1.6%) to 223.5% and only 42 observations.[569]

Sub-sample Analysis

Table 54 in the Appendix provides the corresponding details for the *Region*, *EntryMode* and *Time* sub-samples. The data confirm the clear trend towards larger LBOs with the average entry entity value being almost double for the equally split sub-samples prior to and after Sep-1998. The corresponding growth rates and CAGRs seem to have slowed down over time potentially indicating reduced value increase contribution through an increase in firm value in recent years, something that will be looked at in more detail in the coming sections. The average entity value CAGR is (weak) significantly higher for previously owner-controlled companies. This is partly due, though, to the on average lower starting value in the form of the entity value at entry.

569 For 41 US reverse LBOs in the years 1976-1987, Muscarella, C. J./Vetsuypens, M. R. (1990) find corresponding annualized mean/median values for the increase in firm size of 97.5% and 34.2% (though with an on average 15% higher average holding period; see footnote[566]), implying an even higher skewness of the results.

Obviously, in the steady sample V_t and V_T as absolute numbers show lower mean and median values in the absence of a few large outliers. Distributions of relative variations (g_V_{T-t}, c_V_{T-t}) are comparable.

Overall patterns for equity value variations as displayed in Table 17 are similar, though obviously reinforced owing to the debt financing leverage effect.[570]

Table 17 Equity Value Variation

Absolute numbers in €m; foreign currencies converted into € at the respective date effective spot exchange rates at entry and at exit; entry values are indexed with t; the corresponding exit value with T; g indicates the effective growth rate from entry to exit; c the corresponding CAGR; steady sample comprising investments without any acquisition and divestiture activity during the holding period only

	Average	Median	Std. Dev.	Minimum	Maximum	N
Total Sample						
E_t	254.3	166.5	232.9	47.5	1,077.8	42
E_T	658.8	503.0	461.8	138.9	2,334.4	42
g_E_{t-T}	215.7%	187.4%	163.1%	16.1%	877.1%	42
c_E_{t-T}	87.4%	47.9%	111.7%	6.0%	578.7%	42
Steady Sample						
Et	240.8	179.3	193.5	47.5	801.3	26
E_T	618.2	480.5	427.8	151.8	1,670.9	26
g_E_{t-T}	203.0%	176.3%	132.4%	59.4%	561.3%	26
c_E_{t-T}	100.6%	57.2%	129.3%	15.9%	578.7%	26

Across the entire sample the equity value increased on average from an initial level of €254.3m during the holding period to an average exit equity value of €658.8m representing a mean growth rate and CAGR of 215.7% and 87.4% respectively.

Effects for the analyzed sub-samples all in all match the ones pointed out in the entity value analysis. Again, the timing sub-sample indicates relatively more attractive transactions for the period prior to Dec-1998. Noteworthy also, the substantial higher average equity value growth rates of CE transactions (See Table 54 in the Appendix for details).

Gearing

Linking variations in the entity value to variations in the equity value Chart 20 provides the distribution of gearing ratios and corresponding descriptive statistics based on (i) the latest financial information prior to the buyout, (ii) the LBO capital structure at entry, and (iii) the capital structure immediately prior to the exit.

570 Important to note though that variations in the equity value can only serve as an indication for value creation since interim equity streams from and to the equityholder are thereby and so far not taken into consideration.

Table 18 Gearing Ratios Pre-LBO, Post-Entry and Pre-Exit

Gearing ratios in 10% intervals; negative number indicates net cash position

	Average	Median	Std. Dev.	Minimum	Maximum	N
Pre-LBO	16.3%	13.2%	18.4%	(12.5%)	67.7%	42
Post-Entry	64.3%	65.8%	8.1%	50.1%	82.4%	42
Pre-Exit	33.4%	32.4%	11.7%	3.6%	63.9%	42
Pre-Exit (Steady Sample)	34.0%	33.1%	9.9%	15.5%	61.2%	26

Chart 20 Gearing Ratios Pre-LBO, Post-Entry and Pre-Exit

Gearing ratios in 10% intervals; negative number indicates net cash position

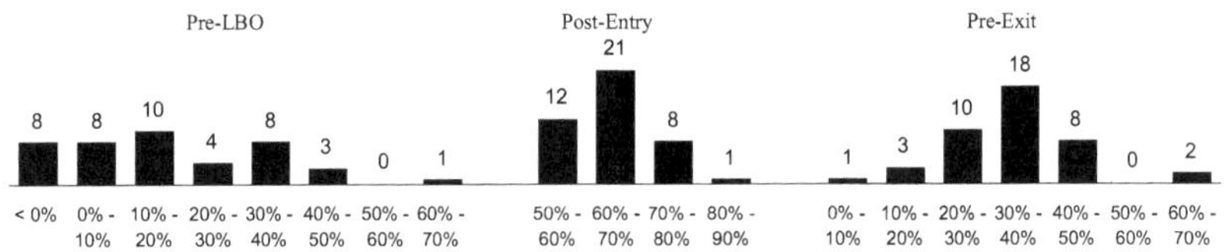

When entering into the investment the average gearing ratio increases from 16.3% to the previously discussed level of 64.3%. From the entry level of 64.3% the average gearing ratio decreases on average for the analyzed sample by 30.9% during the holding period to an exit level of 33.4%. The derived numbers are comparable for the steady sample. Since, however, disposal and acquisition activity affects debt repayment, which (together with the variation in the equity value) drives the decrease in gearing, the variance of the steady sample is obviously lower.

Interestingly, the average pre-exit gearing ratio is statistically significantly higher for recent transactions; obviously in part due to the (significantly) lower mean entity growth rate and CAGR. However, differences could also arise from debt repayment, details of which will be discussed shortly in chapter V.D.2.3.

Based on the conducted variation analysis of the entity and equity valuation as well as the level of net debt for the analyzed LBO investments, Chart 4, which visualized simplistically the LBO analysis, can now illustratively be quantified as shown in Chart 21.

Chart 21 Illustrative LBO Analysis

Based on average numbers for the total sample of 42 analyzed investments as presented in Table 16 and Table 17; accordingly, displayed growth rates are based on individual figures and averaged across the sample (as reported in the tables) and do not correspond to the variation in the absolute average numbers; in €m

For illustrative purposes only, transaction costs are not reported separately and are subsumed with ND_t[571]; no consideration of interim equity streams for the time being; variation in the equity value therefore referred to as Capital Gain

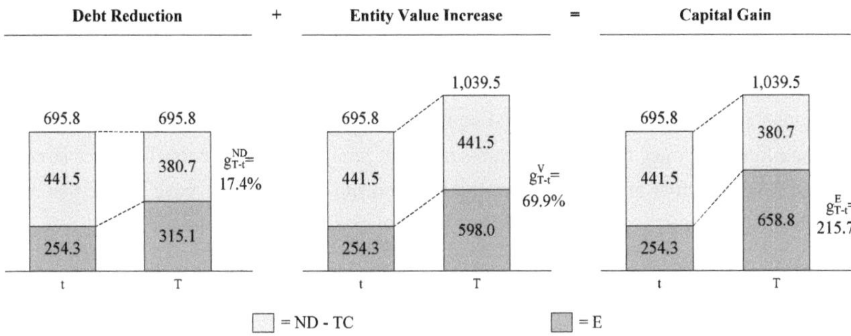

Transaction Costs

Table 19 details for the analyzed sample the distribution characteristics of transaction costs occurred for entering the investment as a percentage of total sources. Transaction costs hereby comprise advisory fees for investment banking, legal, tax and general consultancy advice as well as financing fees for the funding of the transaction. The mean/median percentage of transaction costs amounts to -4.1% with a relatively low standard of 1.7%.

Table 19 Transaction Costs

Transaction costs (TC) as a percentage of Total Sources (TS); TS comprising the entirety of equity and debt financing funds as defined in equation (2)

	Average	Median	Std. Dev.	Minimum	Maximum	N
TC/TS	(4.1%)	(4.1%)	1.7%	(8.3%)	(1.2%)	42

1.2 Components of Total Proceeds to Equity Investors

The following chapter decomposes *Total Proceeds* to equity investors according to the LBO transaction model as detailed in chapter III.A.2. *Total Proceeds* to equity investors differ from

571 ND_T figure of €380.7m displayed here not comparable with ND_T figure reported in Table 31 on page 215 owing to currency translation effects (see also the corresponding footnote [598]).

the difference of the equity values at entry and at exit in the form that interim equity streams and associated transaction costs are considered:

$$(86)\quad TP = E_T - E_t + \sum_{n=t+1}^{T-1} E_n$$ see equation (28), p. 69

For the analyzed sample absolute *Total Proceeds* to equity investors amounted to €439.3m on average, with a median value of €334.2m and a range of between €52.2m and €1,166.5m. Although the previous chapter indicated that investments in the post Sep-1998 sub-sample are significantly larger in terms of entity and equity value, absolute *Total Proceeds* cannot found to be significantly larger for the latter sub-sample of analyzed investments. This fact already indicates less attractive and less performing investments in the recent past; a fact that will further be considered when analyzing relative performance measures in chapter V.E.

Table 20 Total Proceeds to Equity Investors

Absolute numbers in €m; foreign currencies converted into € at the respective date effective spot exchange rates at entry and at exit; entry values are indexed with t; the corresponding exit value with T; steady sample comprising investments without any acquisition and divestiture activity during the holding period only

	Average	Median	Std. Dev.	Minimum	Maximum	N
Total Sample						
ΔE_{abs}	439.3	334.3	297.0	52.2	1,166.5	42
$E_T - E_t$	404.5	313.0	297.4	28.5	1,256.6	42
$E_{t\text{-}T,\ int}$	112.1	80.5	165.5	(101.6)	512.0	13
Steady Sample						
ΔE_{abs}	412.6	343.2	278.4	70.5	1,166.5	26
$E_T - E_t$	377.5	322.4	271.4	70.5	1,166.5	26
$E_{t\text{-}T,\ int}$	182.8	160.0	99.2	99.5	344.9	5

Interim equity streams and transaction costs are not to be neglected. 13 out of the total of 42 transactions, i.e. 31.0% have significant equity streams from and to the equity investors. Ten of these 13 equity streams (23.8% of total investments) have the form of dividend payments to the investors, representing on average for these transactions 33.7% of *Total Proceeds* as defined above.[572] In other words, leaving timing considerations aside (which would amplify the effect further) in ten out of the 42 transactions equity investors realize approximately one third of *Total Proceeds* (representing on average 54.9% of capital invested at entry) prior to the exit of the investment. Only three equity streams have the form of additional equity injections from the equity investor. For these LBOs the additionally contributed equity during the holding period equals 15.5% of the initial equity contribution or –10.1% of *Total Proceeds.*

572 This finding regarding the frequency and also the magnitude of interim equity streams highlights the importance of their consideration and challenges assessments based on neglecting them (see e.g. Cochrane, J. (2005), p. 4).

Not surprisingly equity injections and dividend streams correlate strongly with the company having undertaken a significant acquisition or a recapitalization during the holding period of the investment.[573] Any equity injection is related to a significant add-on acquisition. Only five companies in the steady sample of 26 transactions have interim equity streams; all of which are – in the absence of acquisitions – in the form of dividend payments. Dividend payouts are dependent upon recapitalizations.[574]

Chapter III.A.2 decomposed *Total Proceeds* to equity investors on investment level into (i) *EBITDA Variation*, (ii) *Multiple Variation*, (iii) *Combined EBITDA/Multiple Effect*, (iv) *Cumulated FCF Generation*, and (v) *Transaction Costs*. Expressed relatively:

$$(87)\quad 1=\frac{m_t\Delta C_{T-t}}{TP}+\frac{\Delta m_{T-t}C_T}{TP}+\frac{\Delta m_{T-t}\Delta C_{T-t}}{TP}+\frac{\sum_{n=t}^{T}FCF_n}{TP}-\frac{\sum_{n=t}^{T}TC_n}{TP}$$ see equation (33), p. 70

Table 21 presents the result for decomposing *Total Proceeds* to equity investors on an investment level according to equation (87). The purpose is to provide an indication of the *relative* importance of the five components for *Total Proceeds*. *Relative* implies that the importance of one component here can only be assessed relative to the other components. For the purpose of this analysis *Total Proceeds* are standardized to 100% on investment level.

Table 21 Decomposition of Total Proceeds to Equity Investors according to the LBO Transaction Model

Relative contributions of one of the five components expressed as a percentage of Total Proceeds representing 100% on investment level; steady sample comprising investments without any acquisition and divestiture activity during the holding period only

	Average	Median	% Positive Variations	Std. Dev.	Minimum	Maximum	N
Total Sample							
EBITDA Variation	60.6%	54.9%	97.6%	41.1%	(17.2%)	194.1%	42
Multiple Variation	17.4%	21.1%	73.8%	34.7%	(56.1%)	84.2%	42
Combined Effect	2.7%	7.5%	71.4%	13.8%	(39.0%)	17.6%	42
Cumulated FCF Generation	27.6%	20.9%	85.7%	30.9%	(27.5%)	125.3%	42
Transaction Costs	(8.3%)	(7.1%)	0.0%	5.8%	(24.4%)	(1.4%)	42
Steady Sample							
EBITDA Variation	55.1%	50.0%	100.0%	31.3%	9.4%	121.2%	26
Multiple Variation	21.6%	22.2%	73.1%	33.4%	(40.5%)	84.2%	26
Combined Effect	4.7%	7.8%	73.1%	10.6%	(24.1%)	17.6%	26
Cumulated FCF Generation	26.9%	20.1%	96.2%	22.2%	(1.7%)	81.7%	26
Transaction Costs	(8.3%)	(7.1%)	0.0%	5.9%	(24.4%)	(1.4%)	26

573 See chapter V.C.2.2.2.

574 As discussed in chapter III.B.3 dividend payouts are subject to restrictive debt covenants, which can be circumvented when renegotiating the terms in the course of recapitalizations.

Novel insights regarding the relative importance are attention-grabbing: on average more than 60% of *Total Proceeds* for the analyzed transactions results from variation in the firm's EBITDA level valued with the entry transaction multiple, $m_t\Delta EBITDA_{T-t}$. For 71.4% (30) of the analyzed investments *Multiple Variation* contributed positively to *Total Proceeds*, on average with 17.4% relative to the other components. The combined effect, resulting from the multiplicative conjunction of EBITDA and the corresponding transaction multiple for calculating the entity value, accounts on average for 2.7% of *Total Proceeds*. *Cumulated FCF Generation* adds 27.6% on average and Transaction Costs consummate for the average transaction 8.2% of *Total Proceeds* per transaction. Median values indicate a relatively higher importance of *Multiple Variation* for *Total Proceeds*. For the typical transaction the contribution of EBITDA variation shrinks to 54.9% while the contribution of *Multiple Variation* soars to 21.1%. Owing to outliers and the small sample size standard deviations are relatively high for all components.

With respect to the steady sample the volatility as well as the range of the relative contributions of both *EBITDA Variation* and *Cumulated FCF Generation* decreases considerably. Further, considering *steady* transactions only seems to slightly increase the relative importance of *Multiple Variation* at the expense of *EBITDA Variation*, which seems reasonable given that eleven of the 16 not included investments underwent significant add-on acquisitions.

Sub-sample Analysis

Cumulated FCF Generation gained relative importance as a contributor to *Total Proceeds* over time. Compared with a relative average contribution of 20.5% up to Sep-1998 the corresponding number for recent transactions increased (weak) significantly to 34.7%. Potential reasons can be manifold, but presumably include the longer holding period as well as the lower relative contribution from *Multiple Variation*. The forthcoming regression analyses on the various components of *Total Proceeds* and the overall relative performance will provide further insight in this respect. Interestingly, the relative mean contribution of Transaction Costs is (weak) significantly higher for previously manager-controlled companies (See Table 55 in the Appendix for details).

Based on these first results and despite the heterogeneity of the sample some interesting conclusion can already now be drawn:

- *EBITDA Variation*, i.e. the growth in the cash flow figure for valuation purposes, seems to be by far the most important single driver for TP.[575]
- Cash-generativeness of the business in the form of *Cumulated FCF Generation* seems to be relatively less important than *EBITDA Variation.*
- Variations in the transaction multiple contributed historically on average significantly positively to TP.
- Transaction Costs in LBO investments are substantial, accounting for no less than 8.3% of TP on average.

When interpreting these numbers it's crucial though to be aware that the respective percentages of the components only indicate their *relative* importance for each individual investment. Standardization (to 100%) occurs on investment level.

Given the relative importance of the variation in EBITDA, the following Table 22 decomposes this component in its *Revenue Effect*, its *Margin Effect* and, owing to their multiplicative conjunction, the *Combined Effect.*

Table 22 Components of EBITDA Variation

Relative contributions to Total Proceeds; average values adding up to 60.6% and 55.1% of relative EBITDA Variation contribution to Total Proceeds for the Total and the Steady Sample respectively as indicated in Table 21; steady sample comprising investments without any acquisition and divestiture activity during the holding period only

	Average	Median	% Positive Variations	Std. Dev.	Minimum	Maximum	N
Total Sample							
Revenue Effect	31.4%	23.3%	92.9%	27.7%	(22.5%)	96.4%	42
Margin Effect	25.2%	17.4%	88.1%	28.0%	(15.4%)	96.0%	42
Combined Effect	4.0%	2.3%	78.6%	10.0%	(29.4%)	37.6%	42
Steady Sample							
Revenue Effect	27.8%	19.4%	92.3%	24.3%	(5.3%)	86.3%	26
Margin Effect	23.9%	15.5%	92.3%	25.2%	(15.4%)	90.1%	26
Combined Effect	3.4%	2.6%	84.6%	5.2%	(7.1%)	17.1%	26

Accordingly, an increase in the firm's revenues seems to have historically outweighed the importance of margin improvement for *EBITDA Variation* as contributor to *Total Proceeds.*[576] Obviously, this is something that will be analyzed further in the remaining section in more

575 *Note:* This component refers to the variation in EBITDA for valuation purposes only; improvements in EBITDA however also affect Cumulated FCF Generation as pointed out earlier. The overall effect of an improved operational performance on the performance of LBO transactions will be addressed in the forthcoming chapter V.E. Further as detailed in chapter III.C.1, profitability improvements during the holding period might also affect variations in the transaction multiple. Both aspects further strengthen the relative importance of variations in EBITDA.

576 This finding regarding the relative importance of revenue growth fits well Rogers, P., et al. (2002) calling to "*[f]ocus on growth, not just cost reductions*" (see Rogers, P., et al. (2002), p. 8).

detail, but the result is remarkable: historically, the single most important contributor to *Total Proceeds* to equity investors is revenue growth; i.e. the variation resulting purely from revenue growth of the relevant EBITDA figure for valuation purposes.[577] The table reveals further that 39 and 37 of the considered 42 companies managed to increase revenues and the EBITDA-margin respectively from entry to exit.

The sub-sample analysis (see Table 55 in the Appendix) reveals that the average *Revenue Effect* is (weak) significantly higher for UK transactions. Net of acquisitions and divestitures the relative importance of the revenue effect diminishes for the steady sample.

2. Internal Perspective: FCF Effects

The detailed analysis of *FCF Effects* serves two objectives. First, an analysis of the variation of the constituting components of FCF – separated as discussed in operating cash flow (chapter V.D.2.1) and net-investing cash flow (chapter V.D.2.2) testing previously derived hypotheses with respect to the internal perspective. Second, an analysis of the components of *Cumulated FCF Generation* (chapter V.D.2.3) provides details on deleveraging and its components.

2.1 Operating Cash Flow

2.1.1 Variations of EBITDA, Revenues and EBITDA-Margin

The variation in the EBITDA level from entry to exit represents the starting point for the operating cash flow analysis. Recall that with respect to the identified components of *Total Proceeds* changes in EBITDA affect both the *EBITDA Variation* component as well as the *Cumulated FCF Generation* component.[578]

Three central remarks upfront:

- Across the entire sample an average revenues CAGR of 8.1% in combination with a mean EBITDA-margin CAGR of 7.2% absolute EBITDA increases by as much as 15.8% on average annually.
- Analyses show that including transactions that are disposed off or acquired significant assets during the holding period increases the heterogeneity of the sample. However, especially when considering CAGRs, average and median results are remarkably little affected by the overall disposal and acquisition activity of the sample.

---

577 By contrast, Muscarella, C. J./Vetsuypens, M. R. (1990), p. 1412 conclude for their analyzed sample of 72 LBOs for the years 1976 to 1987 that "*improvements in profitability result mainly from [the] sample firm's ability to reduce costs rather than to generate more revenues or to improve asset turnover.*"

578 As variations in EBITDA and its components for the entire sample are distorted by disposals and acquisitions during the holding period results will again be displayed separately for the *steady sample*.

- Regression results with EBITDA, revenues and EBITDA-margin as independent variables suggest the benefit of further detailing the various FCF constituents.

Table 23 Variations of EBITDA, Revenues and EBITDA-Margin

*Change in EBITDA, revenues and EBITDA-margin between the last LTM period before the entry (t-1) and the last LTM period before the exit (T-1) of the investment; prefix c indicates annualized growth rate (CAGR); steady sample comprising investments without any acquisition and divestiture activity during the holding period only; Z-statistic to test for difference from zero; levels of significance: ***p<0.001, **p<0.01, *p<0.05,(+) p<0.1*

For details regarding absolute variations and growth rates for the holding period of the respective variables see Table 61 in the Appendix

	Average	Median	% Positiv Variations	Std. Dev.	Minimum	Maximum	N
Total Sample							
$c\_EBITDA_{t-1,T-1}$	15.8%***	13.3%	97.6%	10.9%	(11.6%)	47.7%	42
$c\_Rev_{t-1,T-1}$	8.1% ***	6.1%	92.9%	9.3%	(15.4%)	34.4%	42
$c\_EBITDA\text{-}Mrg_{t-1,T-1}$	7.2% ***	6.7%	88.1%	6.5%	(4.3%)	21.8%	42
Steady Sample							
$c\_EBITDA_{t-1,T-1}$	15.9%***	13.3%	100.0%	9.5%	2.5%	47.7%	26
$c\_Rev_{t-1,T-1}$	8.2% ***	5.7%	92.3%	8.8%	(6.4%)	34.4%	26
$c\_EBITDA\text{-}Mrg_{t-1,T-1}$	7.4% ***	8.1%	92.3%	6.3%	(4.0%)	21.8%	26

Variations in EBITDA are remarkable. Across the entire sample LBO companies managed to increase EBITDA by 15.8% annually between the entry and the exit of the investment; with a median EBITDA CAGR of 13.3%. While revenues grew with a CAGR of 8.1% during the holding period, the corresponding EBITDA-margin increased by 7.2% annually. Annualized revenue growth seems to be slightly more volatile than EBITDA CAGRs with a higher standard deviation and a broader range. Since 39 and 37 companies of the total sample succeeded in increasing revenues and EBITDA respectively it is not surprising that the previously formulated expectations are met in the sense that variations in EBITDA, revenues as well as the EBITDA-margin are positive, with a very highly significant difference from zero. In terms of growth from entry to exit, an average revenue increase of 24.5% in combination with a mean EBITDA-margin increase of 16.4% caused EBITDA to grow by 45.3% on average across the entire sample (see Table 61 in the Appendix). These results are best compared to findings reported by Muscarella/Vetsuypens (1990) for a sample of 72 reverse LBOs.[579] Accordingly, the median revenues growth rate and median growth in operating margin amount to 9.40% (N=43) and 23.5% (N=35).[580] These numbers compare with median growth rates for revenues and EBITDA-margin, $g\_Rev_{t-1,T-1}$ and $g\_EBITDA\text{-}Mrg_{t-1,T-1}$, of

579 Comparable to this study Muscarella, C. J./Vetsuypens, M. R. (1990) reports (median) changes of various (relative) accounting measures between the LBO and the exit (IPO). Other *Operational Performance Studies* such as Kaplan, S. N. (1989a), Smith, A. J. (1990a) and Opler, T. C. (1992) report analysis of variances for the years preceding and following the entry LBO transaction.

580 See Muscarella, C. J./Vetsuypens, M. R. (1989), pp. 1399f.

15.6% and 18.1% respectively for the sample analyzed in this thesis.[581] This comparison on the one hand underpins the high relevance of revenue growth for value creation in this analyzed sample. On the other hand given the substantial differences in the considered time period (1976-1987 in Muscarella/Vetsuypens vs. 1993-2004 in this sample) one might hypothesize decreasing operational performance improvement potentials over time.

Steady Sample

The analysis of the steady sample reveals some interesting results in that the corresponding values are surprisingly little affected by disposal and acquisition activity. Average as well as median values for the reduced sample of 26 *steady* investments are almost identical for variations in EBITDA, revenues and EBITDA-margin. For instance, revenues increase with an average CAGR of 8.1% in both samples, which – especially for organic growth – seems remarkably high. This finding seems to contradict the ancient view that LBO candidates are characterized by few growth opportunities and confirms the hypothesis that a shift in the focus of LBO transactions occurred towards operational performance improvement. The regression analysis will provide more insight in this respect. Further, the broad range of all three variables seems to be only to a minor extent attributable to disposals and acquisitions. For the steady sample the heterogeneity of the sample is slightly less pronounced as indicated by lower standard deviations and ranges. However, maximum values are alike for both samples.

Actual Performance Compared with Financing Banks Projections

As detailed in chapter V.A the detailed, novel empirical analysis with comprehensive income statement, cash flow and balance sheet information from prior to the entry throughout the holding period until the exit of the investment builds in part upon confidentially provided information in the form of *financing bank books*. For syndication purpose such documents generally comprise financial projections by the lead financing bank based upon conducted due diligence in the course of the acquisition process.

581 See Table 61 in the Appendix. However, cross-sectional differences with respect to *steady* seem to be much more pronounced in Muscarella/Vetsuypens' sample. Whereas in the analyzed sample, comparable numbers remain broadly unchanged for the *steady sample* (13.6% and 18.1% for changes in revenues and EBITDA-margin respectively), Muscarella/Vetsuypen's figures differ substantially (4.54% and 36.60% for changes in revenues and EBITDA-margin respectively).

Table 24 Actual Performance Compared with Financing Banks Projections

Owing to potential distortions arising for investments with acquisition and divestiture activity during the holding period, and restrictions regarding data availability information is available for a sub-sample of N=14 investments only; T-1 denotes the last full fiscal year (not LTM) prior to the exit, E[T-1] indicates the expectation formed at entry by the financing banks for the corresponding period of time (i.e. the last full fiscal year prior to the exit)

	Average	Median	% Positive Variations	Std. Dev.	Minimum	Maximum	N
$Rev_{T-1} / Rev_{E[T-1]}$	(4.3%)	(5.5%)	28.6%	5.4%	(16.7%)	3.7%	14
$EBITDA_{T-1} / EBITDA_{E[T-1]}$	2.4%	1.9%	57.1%	15.0%	(26.9%)	38.5%	14
$EBITDA\text{-}Mrg_{T-1} / EBITDA\text{-}Mrg_{E[T-1]}$	7.2%	4.1%	64.3%	16.5%	(22.3%)	48.6%	14

Table 24 compares the actually realized performance in the year of the exit with the predicted level for the same year at the time of the entry for *Rev*, *EBITDA* and *EBITDA-Mrg* for a reduced sample with no acquisition and divestiture activity. On average for the analyzed investments financing banks seem to have overestimated growth opportunities but underestimated margin improvements. Ten out of 14 firms in this reduced sample underperform in terms of revenue growth compared with the financing banks projections. More than 70% of the companies don't meet the generally relatively conservative (in particularly compared to management) projections of the financing banks. In terms of EBITDA results are more favorable. On average the portfolio companies exceed the projections formed at entry by 2.4% with a very high standard deviation of 15.0% though resulting from a range of -26.9% to 38.5%. The reason for this outperformance in EBITDA despite missed expectations on *Rev* level is the substantial relative operational performance improvement beyond expectations. The growth rate of $EBITDA\text{-}Mrg_{T-t}$ for nine out of 14 portfolio companies is better than predicted, on average by as much as 7.2%.

Regression Results

Using regression analysis the impact of the previously identified relevant independent variables is quantified with respect to variations in revenue and EBITDA-Margin and therefore on EBITDA; details of which are displayed in Table 33 on page 221 at the end of this chapter.

As predicted, the entry gearing ratio l_t is of high relevance, having a significant negative effect on the annualized revenue growth rate (ß=-0.385; p=0.027) and a positive, though not statistically significant, effect on annualized EBITDA-Margin variations. In line with Hypothesis *H_Int_3* regression results thus imply that excessive gearing seems to impede revenue growth. Phrased differently, faster growing companies seem to be financed with relatively more equity financing instruments. According to the specified regression analysis, a 1% increase in the relative equity contribution coincides with additional annual revenue growth in the magnitude of 0.385%. Arguments for an inverse causality do exist as previously pointed out, as entry capital structure characteristics are potentially based upon financial projections. However, Weinberger (2005) reports such causality for the leverage ratio (i.e. Total Debt to EBITDA) but cannot confirm a significant impact of financial projections on the gearing ratio (i.e. Total Debt as percentage of Total Sources) which is well suited to this analysis and consideration of the gearing ratio.[582] On the aggregated absolute EBITDA level the negative revenue impact (resulting from higher gearing) seems to prevail resulting in a weak significant negative impact of l_t on the EBITDA CAGR. Each 1% increase in gearing sacrifices 0.376% of EBITDA CAGR. Apart from the gearing ratio, size – operationalized through Rev_{t-1} – as well as profitability – operationalized through $EBITDA\text{-}Mrg_{t-1}$ – have a significant negative effect $c\_EBITDA\text{-}Mrg_{t-1,T-1}$ (ß=-4.2 E-5, p=0.076 and ß=-0.271, p=0.49 respectively). While the latter finding confirms hypothesis *H_Int_1b* in that unprofitable firms are relatively more successful in improving overall operational performance expressed in annualized relative variations in the EBITDA-Margin during the holding period the first finding seems to contradict the previously postulated hypotheses based on agency theoretical considerations (*H_Int_1a*) with respect to firm size. Relatively small firms potentially realize high growth rates more easily as growth is a function of the starting value, in this case $EBITDA\text{-}Mrg_{t-1}$. With respect to $c\_Rev_{t-1,T-1}$ tendencies could be found for the profitability at entry and the *EntryMode*, both in accordance with the relevant hypotheses *H_Int_1b* and *H_CV_2*. Accordingly a 1% higher profitability at entry seems to foster higher revenue CAGRs of around 0.229%. Coefficients for the remaining four independent variables on revenue growth are, apart from the Experience Index, negative as hypothesized, though not statistically significant. Five of the remaining eight independent variables for $c\_EBITDA\text{-}Mrg_{t-1,T-1}$ have the predicted, though insignificant, coefficients.

The corresponding determination coefficients R^2 for these regression analyses are 32.3%, 24.8%, and 29.1% respectively.

Stepwise regression results for the *steady sample* are comparable. Additionally, however, the change in management as well as *EntryMode* can be confirmed to have significant impacts. While a changing management seems to positively affect revenue growth, the effect on EBITDA-margin variations is opposite. Portfolio companies with (a) change(s) in top management seem to be characterized by 3.7% higher revenues CAGR though -4.2% less EBITDA-Margin CAGR, obviously offsetting effects on EBITDA level. Interestingly also, for the steady sample LBOs of firms under previously dispersed ownership there was a significant improvement in their EBITDA-Margin during the holding period than for previously owner-controlled LBOs. Supporting hypothesis *H_CV_2* and thus the controlling and monitoring argument of the LBO governance structure, investments with no controlling majority owner prior to the LBO have 4.8% higher EBITDA-Margin CAGR than previously owner-controlled firms.

---

582 See Weinberger, N. (2005), chapter VI.

Sub-sample Analysis

Sub-samples by *Region*, *EntryMode* and *Time* indicate that the annualized EBITDA-Margin growth and as a consequence the EBITDA CAGR are significantly higher for the pre Sep-1998 sub-sample. Compared to an average of 12.8% for recent transactions, EBITDA grows on average as much as 18.7% annually for the 21 pre Sep-1998 investments (See Table 56 in the Appendix for details).

2.1.2 Variations of CoGS-Margin and SG&A-Margin

Table 25 displays the variations of the CoGS-margin and SG&A-margin as the two principal components of the EBITDA-margin. Owing to restrictions of data availability and different accounting standards the components analysis is conducted for a reduced number of transactions as indicated in the far right column.

Table 25 Variations of CoGS-Margin and SG&A-Margin from Entry to Exit

*Change in CoGS-margin and SG&A-margin between the last LTM period before the entry (t-1) and the last LTM period before the exit (T-1) of the investment; prefix c indicates annualized growth rate (CAGR); steady sample comprising investments without any acquisition and divestiture activity during the holding period only; Z-statistic to test for difference from zero; levels of significance: ***$p<0.001$, ** $p<0.01$, * $p<0.05$, $^{(+)}$ $p<0.1$*
For details regarding absolute variations and growth rates for the holding period of the respective variables see Table 62 in the Appendix

	Average	Median	% Negative Variations	Std. Dev.	Minimum	Maximum	N
Total Sample							
c_CoGS-Mrg $_{t-1,T-1}$	(1.1%)*	(1.0%)	68.4%	2.9%	(10.3%)	5.4%	38
c_SG&A-Mrg $_{t-1,T-1}$	(2.2%)*	(2.5%)	64.5%	5.8%	(15.8%)	11.6%	31
SteadySample							
c_CoGS-Mrg $_{t-1,T-1}$	(1.4%)**	(1.0%)	69.6%	2.5%	(10.3%)	1.7%	23
c_SG&A-Mrg $_{t-1,T-1}$	(1.9%)	(2.4%)	65.0%	6.5%	(15.8%)	11.6%	20

68.4% of the considered investments managed to decrease their CoGS-margin during the holding period implying that almost one third of the 39 transactions had to bear increasing CoGS relative to their revenues. The same holds to be true for SG&A costs for a reduced sample of 31 transactions. However, relative annual decreases in CoGS-margin are lower than the comparable number for relative SG&A costs both on average as well as the median. For the median investment, the SG&A-margin decreased by -2.5% annually in relative terms, i.e. to 97.5% of the prior year margin level.[583] The corresponding distribution is more heterogenic as indicated by the higher standard deviation and the broader range between minimum and maximum. This seems intuitive, given that CoGS are predominately driven by material costs, which presumably are less influenceable by post-acquisition operational performance

583 As indicated, numbers need to be interpreted cautiously. For the stated example this implies for instance that the SG&A-margin decreases in the course of one year from (hypothetically) 20% to 19.5% (rather than to 17.5%).

improvement initiatives compared with SG&A and related overhead costs. Since the average CoGS-margin (-55.4% at entry) exceeds the average SG&A-margin (-27.7% at entry) the absolute variation from entry to exit is lower for the latter variable (-1.3% vs. -1.4%. See Table 62 in the Appendix for details).

As expected, variations in CoGS- and SG&A-margin were found to be negative, significantly different from zero for the total sample.

Steady Sample

Conformable to the results presented in Table 23, variations in CoGS-margin and SG&A-margin are relatively stable when considering *steady* transactions only. The median, percentage number of reductions, standard deviations and the range are (almost entirely) identical.

Regression Results

Multivariate regression analyses on $c\_CoGS\text{-}Mrg_{t-1,T-1}$ and $c\_SG\&A\text{-}Mrg_{t-1,T-1}$ (with R^2s of 23.7% and 19.7% respectively) reveal some interesting results. A tendency can be found for Rev_{t-1} in the sense that the larger the firm the less negative is the variation in the CoGS-margin (ß=0.409, p=0.108). This though would contradict hypothesis *H_Int_1a* claiming that larger firms offer more room for (relative) improvement in this respect. *EntryMode* is found to (weak) significantly drive variations in SG&A-margin. Confirming hypothesis *H_CV_2*, variations in SG&A-margin are more favorable (i.e. more negative) presumably for previously management-controlled buyouts. For these investments reductions in SG&A-margin are -0.05% lower (i.e. better). The majority of analyzed independent variables had coefficients with signs as hypothesized; however based on the 10% threshold no further significances can be identified.

Sub-sample Analysis

Univariate analysis confirms the above findings in that the average $c\_CoGS\text{-}Mrg_{t-1,T-1}$ of -1.9% for the CE sub-sample is (weak) significantly lower (i.e. more favorable) than the corresponding -0.1% for the UK sub-sample.

2.1.3 Employment Details and Variation of the R&D-margin

The employment effects of LBOs have always received a great deal of attention. Three quarters of the 21 companies for which relevant employment data are available reduced personnel costs as percentage of sales during the holding period. Moreover, of the four considered EBITDA-margin components, though not mutually exclusive as discussed, the average relative annualized reduction in personnel costs margin is highest. Mean and median CAGRs for the personnel costs margin, $c\_Employ\_Mrg_{t-1,T-1}$, are -2.3% across the holding period for the relevant 21 investments, as expected with a highly significant difference from zero.

Table 26 Employment Details and Variation of R&D-Margin[584]

*Employment details and change in R&D-margin between the last LTM period before the entry (t-1) and the last LTM period before the exit (T-1) of the investment; prefix c indicates annualized growth rate (CAGR); labor productivity defined as revenues per employee; Z-statistic to test for difference from zero; levels of significance: *** p<0.001, ** p<0.01, * p<0.05,(+) p<0.1*

For details regarding absolute variations and growth rates for the holding period of the respective variables see Table 63 in the Appendix

	Average	Median	% Negative Variations	Std. Dev.	Minimum	Maximum	N
$c\_Employ\text{-}Mrg_{t-1,T-1}$	(2.3%)**	(2.3%)	76.2%	3.7%	(11.7%)	6.4%	21
$c\_Employment_{t-1,T-1}$	5.4% *	3.2%	30.0%	11.4%	(12.7%)	37.2%	30
$c\_LaborProd_{t-1,T-1}$	4.5% ***	5.1%	23.3%	6.0%	(7.9%)	19.1%	30
$c\_R\&D\text{-}Mrg_{t-1,T-1}$	(0.4%)	(0.6%)	55.6%	10.4%	(16.3%)	15.3%	9

The question obviously arises whether this reduction in employment costs is due to (i) a decreasing workforce during the holding period, (ii) higher labor productivity, or (iii) a varying composition of the labor force. In this respect more insight is provided through some relevant information for 30 sample investments. Figures as reported in Table 26 invalidate the frequently brought forward argumentation that LBOs go along with negative employment effects. 70% of these 30 investments increased their workforce during the holding period, on average by as much as 5.4% annually or 16.2% throughout the holding period. Though overall employment effects seem to be positive on average, no comment can obviously be made regarding the transfer of jobs to low-wage countries. The structural problem of developed countries that the efficiency focus of LBOs potentially expedites the proceedings of job migration could not be tested for. What can be confirmed however, is that employment increases under-proportionately compared with revenues, indicating a more efficient utilization of human capital as an asset. More than three-quarters of the relevant sub-sample companies manage to increase labor productivity – measured as revenues per employee – during the holding period. The relevant average and median values for $c\_LaborProd_{t-1,T-1}$ is 4.5% and 5.1% respectively.[585]

[584] Given previous findings that results are relatively stable for the *steady sample* with respect to EBITDA and its components (see Table 23 and Table 25) and owing to the reduced number of transactions for the analyzed employment and R&D variables, results are not displayed separately for the steady sample.

[585] Muscarella, C. J./Vetsuypens, M. R. (1990), p. 1401 reports median changes in labor productivity between the LBO and the IPO of 3.14% for a sub-sample of 19 investments. The corresponding number for the analyzed sample here equals 10.2% (see Table 63 in the Appendix) indicating substantially higher productivity improvements.

The effect of LBOs on R&D spending has been subject to controversial discussion.[586] Four of the nine investments for which relevant data are available experienced increasing R&D levels as a percentage of revenues during the holding period. While this challenges the argument of decreasing R&D efforts post-LBO, the result can obviously not be considered representative given the small number of observations.

Regression Results

Regression analyses for the three employment variables show consistent results. Improvements (i.e. positive variations) in $c\_LaborProd_{t-1,T-1}$ are (highly) significantly better for (i) LBOs under previously dispersed ownership, as well as (ii) recent transactions. Such transactions experience, according to the specified regression model, higher annual improvements in labor productivity in the magnitude of 6.3% and 5.1% respectively. Consistently variations in $c\_Employment_{t-1,T-1}$ are significantly lower for previously management-controlled LBOs (ß=-0.109, p=0.037). Hence, results support the previously postulated Hypothesis *CV_2* in that employment effects are less positive for previously manager-controlled LBOs. Findings regarding *Time* imply that – other than initially suggested by Hypothesis *CV_3* – improvements in labor productivity in the course of the LBO were higher in recent transactions.

Further LBOs with changes in top management during the holding period seem to have a tendency to foster relatively more employment than their counterparts with unchanged management (ß=0.079, p=0.105). This fits well the finding that (in particular in the steady sample) a changed management positively affects revenue growth. Results reveal further that LBOs without acquisition and divestiture activity improve labor productivity significantly better (ß=0.049, p=0.040).

Interestingly, a statistically significant negative effect can be found for the gearing ratio. Variations in both personnel costs margin as well as labor productivity are unfavorably related to gearing at entry.[587] Challenging hypothesis *H_Int_2* this implies that the higher the gearing at entry the less favorable (i.e. less negative) are variations in personnel cost margin and the less favorable (i.e. less positive) are variations in labor productivity. Increasing the gearing ratio by 1% (relatively more financial liabilities compared with equity) implies $c\_Employ\text{-}Mrg_{t-1,T-1}$ to be 0.213% higher and $c\_Labor\text{-}Prod_{t-1,T-1}$ to be 0.268% lower. This result could be interpreted as being consistent with the previous finding that leverage seems to restrict revenue

586 See chapter IV.C.1.1.

587 Owing to the reduced sample size of only 21 observations a comprehensive regression including all independent variables can not be conducted. The stepwise approach identified Lev_t as the single significant variable.

growth during the holding period. Given the slackness of employment, increases in labor productivity and thus reductions in personnel cost margins are presumably easier to realize with growing revenues (i.e. increase in labor productivity due to higher revenues with a constant or under-proportionately increasing workforce rather than flat or moderately increasing revenues with a decreasing workforce). Coefficients for the remaining independent variables are non-uniform with no further hypotheses being either validated or invalidated.

The corresponding R^2s for variations in the personnel costs margin, labor productivity and employment are 22.8%, 39.0% and 28.5% respectively for the total sample.

Sub-sample Analysis

As expected the sub-sample analysis with respect to *Region*, *EntryMode* and *Time* coincides with the aforementioned findings. LBOs of previously management-controlled companies increase employment during the holding period by only 2.2% compared to 10.2% for previously owner-controlled firms indicating that revenue increases could be stemmed through productivity improvements rather than recruitment (of weak statistical significance). Though not being statistically significant this higher productivity potential is confirmed by $c\_LaborProd_{t-1,T-1}$, which increased for this group by 5.8% annually from entry to exit compared with 2.5% for pre-LBO owner-controlled companies. Also, labor productivity is significantly higher for the recent transactions sub-sample (7.1% vs. 2.7%). Additionally the sub-sample analysis reveals significances for more favorable annual personnel costs margin reductions for recent transactions (-3.2% vs. -1.2%) and higher labor productivity increases for UK transactions, both findings challenging the respective Hypotheses *CV_3* and *CV_1* (See Table 56 in the Appendix for details).

2.1.4 Variations in Net Working Capital

Variations in NWC and its various components have previously been operationalized as further dependent variables for testing *FCF* effects. Reductions in NWC due to a better NWC management in light of the LBO governance structure are frequently cited as a source of cash in LBO transactions.

Table 27 Variations of Relative Net Working Capital and its Components

*Changes in NWC and its components between the last LTM period before the entry (t-1) and the last LTM period before the exit (T-1) of the investment; 'Narrow' Net Working Capital defined as the sum of inventories and accounts receivable less any accounts payable including prepayments and advances; all variables expressed relative to current year sales; prefix g and c indicate growth rate and annualized growth rate (CAGR) respectively; steady sample comprising investments without any acquisition and divestiture activity during the holding period only; owing to the calculation mode, CAGRs are inappropriate for discussing variations in NWC; Z-statistic to test for difference from zero; Levels of significance: *** p<0.001, ** p<0.01, * p<0.05,(+) p<0.1*

For details regarding absolute variations and growth rates for the holding period of the respective variables see Table 64 in the Appendix

	Average	Median	% Negative Variations	Std. Dev.	Minimum	Maximum	N
Total Sample							
$g\_NWC\text{-}rel_{t-1,T-1}$	(10.8%)	(4.2%)	55.2%	66.4%	(169.5%)	174.9%	29
$c\_Inv_{t-1,T-1}$	(9.2%)***	(7.0%)	75.8%	13.6%	(47.6%)	10.3%	33
$c\_AcRec_{t-1,T-1}$	(4.5%)	(4.7%)	68.8%	12.6%	(50.9%)	15.4%	32
$c\_AcPay_{t-1,T-1}$	(3.3%)	(3.6%)	62.1%	27.5%	(72.9%)	77.8%	29
Steady Sample							
$g\_NWC\text{-}rel_{t-1,T-1}$	(13.2%)	(12.7%)	68.4%	70.9%	(169.5%)	174.9%	19
$c\_Inv_{t-1,T-1}$	(10.3%)**	(7.7%)	76.2%	13.9%	(47.6%)	7.2%	21
$c\_AcRec_{t-1,T-1}$	(4.9%)	(4.8%)	80.0%	9.4%	(32.4%)	14.0%	20
$c\_AcPay_{t-1,T-1}$	1.8%	(4.1%)	61.1%	29.3%	(61.0%)	77.8%	18

Detailed information for a bottom-up calculation of a *narrow* net working capital is available for 29 of the 42 investments. Only slightly more than half of these companies managed to decrease relative NWC in terms of percentage of sales during the holding period. The relative mean and median growth rates are -10.8% and -4.2% respectively.[588] Variations in relative NWC are very highly volatile as indicated by the percentage of positive/negative variations, the very broad range of values and the resulting extremely high standard deviation.[589]

With respect to the three components of NWC, inventories (as % of sales) seem to be most affected by LBO transactions and represent the only variable with the average variation being (very highly) significantly different from zero as expected. Mean and median variations as well as the percentages of negative variations that indicate a favorable impact on NWC (positive variations in the case of accounts payable) are highest for inventories. On average for 33 investments relative inventories decreased with a CAGR of -9.2%. Variations in accounts

588 *Note:* Three companies managed to turn NWC negative, i.e. accounts payable exceeding the sum of inventories and accounts receivable. This illustrates, that given the net calculation of NWC as the sum and difference of its constituent components, calculating CAGRs would be inappropriate as the sign of relative NWC might change in the course of the holding period.

589 Despite the heterogeneity of results this reported mean/median decrease in relative NWC fits well the finding by that LBO-IPOs are characterized by significantly lower NWC compared with a matching sample of non-LBO-IPOs. See Holthausen, R. W./Larcker, D. F. (1996), 315ff.

payable only contributed in 37.9% of the 29 transactions favorably to a reduction in NWC.[590] Like aggregated NWC, all its components are characterized by very high ranges between the minimum and maximum value as well as significant standard deviations indicating the volatility and sensitivity of the variables.[591] Due to this heterogeneity results are relatively less stable for considering steady transactions compared to previous variables. The steady sample confirms the significance of variations in inventories, though.

Regression Results

Reductions in relative aggregated NWC ($g\_NWC_{t-1,T-1}$, R^2=41.2%) are significantly more favorable (i.e. more negative) for larger firms (ß=-3.5 E-4, p=0.044), UK transactions (ß=-0.416, p=0.074) and previously management-controlled transactions (ß=-0.506, p=0.03). Also, as predicted, the lower the profitability prior to the buyout, presumably the higher the need to improve NWC and thus the higher the reductions in relative NWC (ß=2.734, p=0.064). On an aggregated NWC level the findings therefore validate hypotheses *H_Int_1a*, *H_Int_1b*, *H_ CV_1*, and *H_CV_2* (regarding size, leverage, region and entry Mode).

Results for variations in inventories ($c\_Inv_{t-1,T-1}$, R^2=50.3%) are consistent with the above findings in the sense that variations are lower for larger and UK based companies thus giving further support to hypothesis *H_Int_1a* and *H_CV_1*. At first glance seemingly contradictory of aggregated NWC results, inventory reductions are higher for profitable firms. Challenging hypothesis *H_Int_1b*, $c\_Inv_{t-1,T-1}$ is said to be 4.88% lower for each 1% increase in profitability. As will be shown however, these positive effects are overcompensated for by negative effects of profitability on variations in accounts payable.

Relative managerial ownership seems to highly significantly affect variations in accounts receivable in the sense that the higher management's relative equity stake the higher – as postulated in Hypothesis *Int_4* – the reductions in $c\_AccRec_{t-1,T-1}$. The R^2 of the corresponding regression equals 38.1%.

Variations in accounts payable, as the third component of narrow NWC, seem to offset some of the positive effects related to inventories reductions and accounts payable reductions as indicated in Table 27 and confirmed by the regression analysis. Reductions in accounts payable ($c\_AccPay_{t-1,T-1}$, R^2=43.8%), which drive narrow NWC up and thus imply a cash

590 This low number is in line with results reported by Weir, C./Laing, D. (1998), p. 265. According to a sample of 51 MBOs in the years 1987-1993 no more than 45% of the companies manage to increase creditor days, i.e. accounts payable.

591 *Note:* Like with most other variables that consider absolute percentage variations, company and more importantly industry specific factors might distort the comparability of the results, which in particular holds to be true, though, for NWC and its components. E.g. inventory levels at entry range between 0% and 24.4% of revenues owing industry particularities.

outflow for the company are significantly higher (i.e. more negative variations), the larger (ß= -1.8 E-4, p= 0.040) and the more profitable (ß=-2.014, p= 0.001) the firm. Apparently larger and more profitable firms pay faster. On the other hand, variations are favorable (less negative) for UK transactions (ß=0.239, p=0.005) and the higher the gearing ratio of the company (ß=1.028, p=0.020), questioning hypothesis *H_CV_1* and strengthening hypothesis *H_Int_3*. As expected firms with an aggressive capital structure (i.e. high relative debt burden) simply tend to take more time to pay their bills.

Sub-sample Analysis

Coinciding with results of the regression analyses, and thus contrasting hypothesis *H_CV_1*, reductions in relative inventories and increases in accounts payable as a constituting (inverse) component thereof are (weak) statistically more favorable for UK transactions than for CE transactions (-14.1% vs. -4.4% and 4.5% vs. -9.7% respectively) according to unidimensional sub-sample analyses (See Table 56 in the Appendix for details).

2.1.5 Cash Interest Expenses and Cash Taxes

Cash interest and cash taxes paid are the remaining two components of operating cash flow. However, given the peculiarities of these two components pointed out in chapter IV.C.1.1 analyses comparable to the ones conducted yet for the other components of operating cash flow are scarcely meaningful.

Table 28 Variations in Cash Interest

t-1 indicates LTM period prior to the buyout

	Average	Median	Std. Dev.	Minimum	Maximum	N
Int_{Cash} (% of EBITDA) $_{t-1}$	(8.1%)	(3.7%)	12.7%	(43.7%)	5.2%	26
Int_{Cash} (% of EBITDA) $_{t+1}$	(31.9%)	(29.2%)	12.0%	(59.5%)	(12.6%)	27
% Int_{Cash} of Int_{t+1}	73.2%	76.1%	22.4%	28.5%	100.0%	27

With this in mind some interesting observations follow regarding Table 28 for sub-samples of transactions with detailed (cash) interest expense information.[592] The average cash interest expense as percentage of EBITDA of 8.1% for the year prior to the LBO compares with 31.9% for the year following the LBO. In other words almost one third of the firm's (pre-tax and pre depreciation and amortization charge) is pre-committed to debtholder servicing. In cash terms, portfolio companies bear on average 4x the cash interest burden they did prior to the buyout.

592 Cash Interest taken from the company's cash flow statements to quantify effective cash effects of interest payments and expressed as percentage of EBITDA; to avoid one-off distortions arising from the LBO, post-buyout cash interest levels are considered for year t+1.

On average 73.2% of total interest expenses were in the form of effective cash outflows. Most of non-cash effective interest expenses apparently arise from quasi-equity financing instruments. As detailed in chapter II.B.2.2 these hybrid financing instruments are frequently structured with accrued interest payments, implying that interest expenses accrue over time and only become cash effective in combination with the repayment of the notional amount. PIK offers on the one hand the advantage of reducing the cash outflow due to interest payments and thus increasing debt coverage ratios and ultimately leverageability of the company while on the other hand benefiting from the (accounting) interest expense tax shield. This fact in combination with additional arguments subsumed under the tax-savings hypotheses and discussed as a potential source of value in LBO investment in chapter III.B.3.3 should cause effective cash tax rates to decrease following the LBO.

Table 29 Variations in Cash Taxes

t-1 indicates LTM period prior to the buyout; T-1 indicates LTM period prior to the exit

	Average	Median	Std. Dev.	Minimum	Maximum	N
Tax_{Cash} *(% of EBIT)* $_{t-1}$	(22.5%)	(23.4%)	14.5%	(57.9%)	1.5%	26
Ø Tax_{Cash} *(% of EBIT)* $_{t+1,T-1}$	(13.6%)	(9.9%)	14.6%	(58.3%)	2.6%	26

Information on a sub-sample of 26 transactions indicates that the average cash tax rate (relative to EBIT) during the holding period is on average 8.9% lower than the cash tax rate for the year prior to the LBO.[593] Thus testing indirectly for the wealth transfer from the government hypothesis (see chapter III.B.3.3) the presented results give substantial support to this source of value creation in LBOs. However, only 65% of these companies experienced a lower average cash tax rate during the holding period compared with the pre-buyout year.[594]

2.2 *Net Investing Cash Flow*

Apart from the components of operating cash flow, cash outflow for capital expenditures as well as the cash effects of acquisitions and disposals affect FCF available for debt repayment. Variations analysis from entry to exit is conducted for capital expenditures only.

---

593 Cash Taxes taken from the company's cash flow statements to quantify effective cash effects of taxes and limit as far as possible distortions from accounting particularities; to avoid one-off distortions arising from the LBO, entry year t is excluded from the post-buyout average calculation.

594 In this respect it would be beneficial to compare average cash tax rates for the last three years prior to the LBO. Information for the average two year period prior to the LBO was only available for 17 companies and yields comparable results with a mean value of 23.9%. Nine of these 17 companies experienced lower average cash tax rates (as % of EBIT) during the holding period.

Table 30 Variations in Capital Expenditures

*Change in CapEx (expressed as % of Sales) between the last LTM period before the entry (t-1) and the last LTM period before the exit (T-1) of the investment; Prefix c indicates annualized growth rate (CAGR); steady sample comprising investments without any acquisition and divestiture activity during the holding period only; z-statistic to test for difference from zero; Levels of significance: *** $p<0.001$, ** $p<0.01$, * $p<0.05$, $^{(+)}$ $p<0.1$*
For details regarding absolute variations and growth rates for the holding period of the respective variables see Table 65 in the Appendix

	Average	Median	% Negative Variations	Std. Dev.	Minimum	Maximum	N
Total Sample							
$c\_CapEx\text{-}rel_{t-1,T-1}$	(10.1%)***	(7.0%)	68.4%	17.8%	(49.8%)	27.8%	38
Steady Sample							
$c\_CapEx\text{-}rel_{t-1,T-1}$	(10.3%)**	(11.2%)	70.8%	18.8%	(49.8%)	27.8%	24

More than two-third of the 38 relevant companies reduced capital expenditures at exit compared with entry levels. On average capital expenditures (as % of sales) are in absolute terms 1.7% lower at exit than at entry (for details see Table 65 in the Appendix). A relative consideration amplifies this effect: Capital expenditures decreased on average with a CAGR of -10.1%, though again with a high standard deviation of 17.8% and a wide range from -49.8% to 27.8%.[595] Results are only a little different when considering a sub-sample of 24 steady transactions. In particular with respect to capital expenditures it could be argued that results are distorted by focusing on the difference between the LTM period prior to the entry and the particular exit LTM period only. However, the above findings are relatively stable for applying averages of relative capital expenditures during the holding period.

Regression Results and Sub-sample Analysis

For both the total as well as the steady sample neither the regression analyses nor the sub-sample analysis with $c\_CapEx\text{-}rel_{t-1,T-1}$ as the dependent variable reveal significant validating or invalidating results. Signs of the corresponding coefficients are mixed. Annual reductions in relative capital expenditures are higher for profitable, previously manager-controlled early transactions with an experienced sponsor and a change in management during the holding period.

2.3 Cumulated FCF Generation

Having analyzed *FCF effects* through the variation analysis of the various FCF constituents from entry to exit, the objective of the following paragraph is to further detail *Cumulated FCF Generation* as the second component of *Total Proceeds* to equity investors according to the LBO transaction model. By definition, the analysis of differences, be it (i) absolute, (ii) relative,

595 Results are comparable with Holthausen, R. W./Larcker, D. F. (1996), p. 1407 who reports a variation of -11.4% for capital expenditures as % of sales for his sample of 72 reverse LBOs. This number compares with -15.6% for the analyzed sample here (see Table 65 in the Appendix)

or (iii) in CAGR terms, is based on the latest available financial information (*T-1*) prior to the exit only. In doing so the inter-temporal pattern of changes in the variables during the holding period are neglected. Analyzing *Cumulated FCF Generation* and its components produces relief and is done in two respects: first, individual sources and uses of *Cumulated FCF Generation* are discussed. In this respect a 'Net-Debt-Bridge' segues for a 'typical' LBO from the net debt level at entry to the net debt level at exit. Second, an indication for the relative split between *steady* and *improved operational performance* is targeted.

2.3.1 Net-Debt-Bridge

From chapter III.A.2 we recall that *Cumulated FCF Generation* during the holding period is either used for debt repayment purposes (net of additional new borrowings) or distributed to equity investors in the form of dividends (net of equity injections and financing and related transaction costs).

Table 31 Variation in Net Debt from Entry to Exit and Cumulated FCF Generation[596]

Net Debt levels at entry (t) and exit (T), cumulated FCF, debt repayment and interim equity as well as interim transaction costs in €m; foreign currencies converted into € at the respective date effective spot exchange rates at entry; Note that interim equity streams and transaction costs are aggregated across the entire sample

	Average	Median	% Positive Variations	Std. Dev.	Minimum	Maximum	N
ND_t	471.8	347.4	na	483.6	97.7	2,405.2	42
ND_T	395.9	294.8	na	471.6	15.0	2,572.7	42
Cumulated FCF	114.7	72.8	85.7%	166.6	(240.6)	829.0	42
Debt Repayment	75.9	37.0	83.3%	112.8	(169.6)	362.3	42
as % of ND at Entry	17.4%	16.5%	83.3%	22.9%	(37.8%)	92.5%	42
aggregated $E^{Div}/(E^{Inj})$	34.7	0.0	na	103.8	(101.6)	512.0	42
aggregated TC^{Int}	4.0	0.0	na	10.0	0.0	50.0	42

According to Table 31 and in accordance with the valuation at entry[597] when accounting for average transaction costs of €30.3m the mean starting net debt level amounts on average to €471.8m. Mean debt repayment equals €75.9m or 17.4% relative to initial net debt for the entire sample of 42 realized investments resulting in a mean net debt level of €395.9m at exit.[598] From an aggregated, e.g. a Limited Partner perspective, i.e. having invested in each of the analyzed transactions, an interesting observation results with the hypothetical construct of averaging interim equity streams across the entire sample. Accordingly, descriptive results for the analyzed sample imply that only two-third of cumulated FCF is applied for serving the fixed claim, i.e. for repaying third party financial liabilities. The remaining 33% is being used

596 Mean, median results are comparable for the steady sample with substantially lower standard deviations and ranges in the absence of outliers though.

597 Average entry Entity and Equity Value of €695.8m (see Table 16) and €254.3m (see Table 17) respectively.

598 Average exit Entity and Equity Value of €1,039.5m (see Table 16) and €658.8m (see Table 16) respectively. (Difference when subtracting ND owing to currency translation effects)

for serving the contingent, residual claim, i.e. for net distribution to equity investors and payment of related fees.[599] Taking only the actual number of ten transactions with equity dividend streams during the holding period (see chapter V.D.1.1) the relevant number increases from 33% to 76%. The fact that Cumulated FCF and its uses are reported as occurred and not adjusted for different lengths of the investments obviously amplifies the variance of the distributions.

Chart 22 Net-Debt-Bridge from Entry to Exit

Cumulated numbers (no adjustment for the holding period) for each cash flow item standardized with net debt level at entry on investment level and averaged across a reduced sample (N=23) owing to data restrictions in at least one cash flow item; positive values indicate cash inflows, negative values cash outflows; 'Other cash' includes among others one-off restructuring expenses; 'Unexplained' as residual to match independently derived net debt level at exit includes among others accrued interest

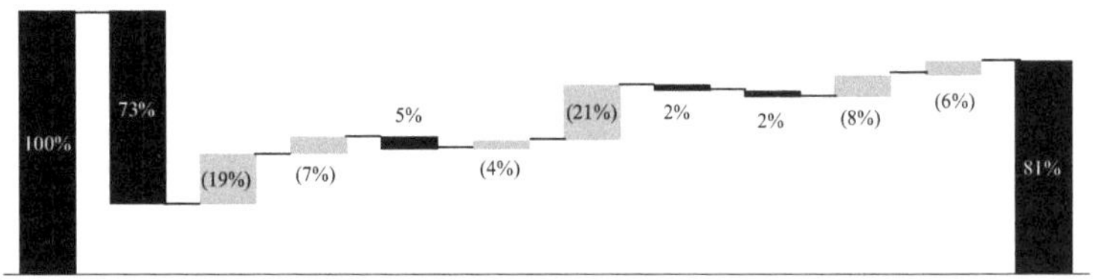

	ND	EBITDA	Cash Interest	Cash Taxes	Delta NWC	Other Cash	CapEx	Dis./ (Acq.)	Add. Debt	E^{Inj}/ (E^{Div})	'Unex-plained'	ND_T
N		23	23	23	23	23	23	23	23	23	23	23
Average		73.4%	-18.9%	-6.9%	5.2%	-3.7%	-21.1%	2.5%	2.4%	-8.3%	-5.4%	80.8%
Median		69%	(17%)	(6%)	4%	(2%)	(16%)	0%	0%	0%	(4%)	85.5%
Std. Dev.		30%	8%	6%	11%	5%	16%	14%	6%	13%	12%	27.1%
Min.		33%	(35%)	(25%)	(21%)	(12%)	(72%)	(23%)	0%	(40%)	(35%)	14.6%
Max.		152%	(6%)	1%	31%	11%	(6%)	52%	27%	0%	21%	157.4%
# Positive		23	0	3	15	1	0	6	4	0	7	23
# Negative		0	23	20	8	16	23	7	0	8	16	0

Chart 22 displays the average contribution of individual operating, investing and financing cash flow items to the variation in net debt relative to the net debt level at entry.[600] These investments with comprehensively available information generate during the holding period on average 73.4% of the initial third party debt burden as cumulated EBITDA. Cumulated capital expenditures account for the largest cash outflow with 21.1% , closely followed by cumulated cash interest expenses (18.9%). Noteworthy, cumulated changes in NWC contribute – on average and for two third of the transactions – positively to net debt reduction. In light of the on average substantial increase in sales during the holding period this implies that NWC is not

599 It has been argued previously that restrictive debt covenants require the renegotiation of third party liabilities and therefore implicitly the repayment of these liabilities for dividends to be distributed to equity investors, implying that all initial debtholder claims have been served.

600 Based on several key indicators the reduced sample is largely representative for the total sample. In both samples revenues increased annually by 8.1%; EBITDA CAGR of 7.2% for the total sample compares to 7.0% for the reduced sample of 23 investments; average ND_T of 80.8% for the reduced sample compares to 82.6% for the total sample.

only reduced in terms of % of sales but also to such an extent that it serves on average as cash contributor. At the time of exit, net debt shrinks on average to 80.8% of the initial amount at entry. The heterogeneity of the sample and the sensitivity of the data are once more highlighted by high standard deviations and ranges for all cash flow items.

2.3.2 Steady vs. Improved Operational Performance

Following the decomposition of *Total Proceeds* into its four components according to equation (33) it has been argued that – other than *EBITDA Variation* and *Multiple Variation* – *Cumulated FCF Generation* is characterized by a *steady* and an *improved operational performance* element. Admittedly, it has already been questioned elsewhere in this thesis to what extent any form of operational performance improvement can be attributed to the LBO transaction as such. It was pointed out in this respect that the theoretically more accurate and valid though in practice relatively arbitrary and questionable approach was to assess how far the LBO improves operations beyond the level to which it would have changed in the absence of the LBO.[601] Regarding the Cumulated FCF component it would nonetheless be of tremendous interest to separate out the steady and improved operating performance element by answering the question what the *Cumulated FCF Generation* would be in the absence of the previously detailed variations of its constituents during the holding period.

To address this question the following analysis builds upon the approach and findings of the preceding net debt variation analysis. The objective is hence to approximate the impact on net debt variation of relevant operational performance components. Absolute EBITDA with the two constituents, revenues and EBITDA-margin, as well as relative capital expenditures are further considered regarding the cumulated impact of variations in these variables: first, Table 31 indicates the relative importance for debt repayment. Second, results in chapter V.D.2.1 and V.D.2.2 indicate variations during the holding period to be highly significantly different from zero. As a matter of course such an approach faces various restrictions and caveats and therefore intends to be purely illustrative. Changes in EBITDA levels affect most remaining operating and investing cash flow components. In order to account for these interdependencies, ratios for cash taxes (as % of EBIT), change in net working capital, other cash items and capital expenditures (all as % of sales) were applied for deriving the corresponding absolute values thereby assuming that the respective ratios are unaffected by changes in the operating performance. Such calculation implicitly builds upon further assumptions: less FCF and accordingly less debt repayment over time increases cumulated cash interest expenses. Given the only minor impact (hypothetical average cash interest rate times the difference in debt repayment due to keeping EBITDA constant) interest expenses were assumed to remain

601 See also methodological considerations in chapter V.B.

constant in absolute terms. No adjustments were made for the cash impact of divestitures and acquisitions, additional borrowings and equity dividends (net of injections).

Regarding absolute EBITDA levels, Chart 22 reveals that of the 73.4% cumulated EBITDA of initial net debt a mere 19.2% remained on average for actual debt repayment owing to operating, investing and also financing cash outflows net of inflows as illustrated. Hypothetically leaving EBITDA at entry levels and thus scarifying the 44.2% mean absolute EBITDA increase for this sample of 23 transactions yields a corresponding number of 57.5% (see Table 32). Meaning, in absence of operational performance improvements cumulated EBITDA on average would have amounted to 57.5% of the initial net debt level. Ceteris paribus the impact on debt repayment is – not surprisingly – substantial: Accounting for interdependencies between EBITDA and the remaining FCF components average debt repayment is calculated to decrease from 19.2% to 9.3%. Whereas at cumulated EBITDA levels of 73.4%, 54.2% thereof is used for anything other than debt repayment; the corresponding number decreases to 48.2% for steady cumulated EBITDA levels of 57.5%.[602] The overall effect of constant EBITDA levels can again be separated into a *constant revenues* and *constant EBITDA-margin* element. In line with the results for the first component of *Total Proceeds*, Variation in EBITDA, the effect of constant revenues outweighs the effect of constant EBITDA margins. Intuitively the effect of variations in relative capital expenditures (as % of sales) on debt repayment is minor compared to constant revenues or constant EBITDA margins; on average cumulated capital expenditures would have been 2.7% higher at 23.8% with a direct impact on debt repayment.

[602] The net cash effect of changes in remaining cash flow items resulting from interdependencies with EBITDA equals approximately 6.0%.

Table 32 Impact of Steady Operational Performance on Debt Repayment

'Constant' means keeping the relevant number (EBITDA, Revenues) or ratio (EBITDA-Margin, CapEx as % of Sales) at the last observable level (i.e. t-1 LTM period) prior to the LBO throughout the holding period of the investment; cumulated EBITDA and debt repayment both expressed in % of net debt at entry compare to the 'as is' values of 73.4% and 19.2% respectively

	Average	Median	Std. Dev.	Minimum	Maximum	N
Constant EBITDA						
Cum EBITDA (% of ND $_t$)	57.5%	53.8%	20.2%	21.8%	92.6%	23
Total DR (% of ND $_t$)	9.3%	8.6%	25.7%	(64.3%)	68.9%	23
Constant Revenues						
Cum EBITDA (% of ND $_t$)	62.2%	61.1%	20.8%	28.2%	99.2%	23
Total DR (% of ND $_t$)	13.2%	9.5%	26.7%	(59.8%)	81.9%	23
Constant EBITDA-Margin						
Cum EBITDA (% of ND $_t$)	68.0%	63.2%	30.1%	26.1%	146.4%	23
Total DR (% of ND $_t$)	13.9%	11.5%	26.3%	(62.3%)	71.5%	23
Constant CapEx (as % of Sales)						
Cum CapEx (% of ND $_t$)	(23.8%)	(19.7%)	17.2%	(68.5%)	(3.3%)	23
Total DR (% of ND $_t$)	15.8%	11.0%	30.3%	(52.3%)	87.5%	23

Summing up, debt repayment in LBO transactions seems to come to a great extent from improved operational performance. Keeping both absolute EBITDA and relative capital expenditures at pre-buyout levels decreases – ceteris paribus – average debt repayment for the reduced sample of 23 transactions from 19.2% to 7.1% implying that performance improvements contribute on average 12.1% of the initial amount of net debt. Theory frequently argues that LBO candidates are characterized by strong and stable operating cash flows with small cash outflows for investing purposes. The presented numbers confirm that based on already existing, steady cash flows LBO companies manage to bear substantial debt burdens with cumulated cash interest payments amounting to on average roughly 30% of cumulated EBITDA. However, above conservative calculations indicate that for debt repayment purposes positive variations in operating and investing cash flow items contribute on average approximately 63%.

Based on this finding the relative importance of improved operational performance for *Cumulated FCF Generation* – as component of *Total Proceeds* – can be approximated. According to Chart 22 the average *Cumulated FCF Generation* before dividend distribution to equity investors and notional debt repayment amounts to 30.5% of net debt at entry. This in combination with the fact that a mean 12.1% of initial net debt arises from improvements; the split between steady and improved operational performance is estimated to average approximately 60.3% vs. 39.7%.

2.4 *Internal Perspective Intermediary Results*

Following the structure of the outlined two-tier framework, the preceding chapters detailed the internal perspective of value creation in LBOs. In a first step the various constituting FCF components (i.e. identified internal perspective *Level I Dependent Variables*) were descriptively and inferringly analyzed as detailed in the research model and copied in extracts in Chart 23. A second step considered aspects of *Cumulated FCF Generation*.

Chart 23 Detailed Research Model – Internal Perspective

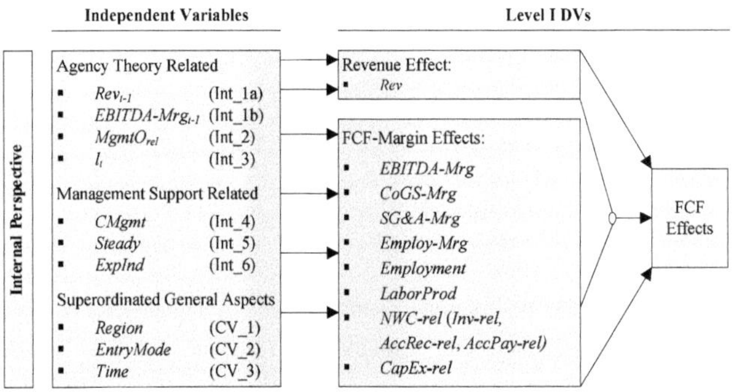

Source: Own Illustration

Table 33 summarizes the regression results for the first step. R square, beta and standardized beta coefficients as well as levels of significance are displayed for the conducted regressions of the identified independent variables on each *Level I Dependent Variable*.

Table 33 Detailed Regression Results – Internal Perspective

ß and standardized ß for all identified Internal Perspective Dependent Variables using comprehensive and stepwise (for c_Employ-Mrg owing to the small sample size of N=20) OLS regression models; findings in accordance with previously postulated hypotheses (including tendencies) in boldface; findings invalidating previously postulated hypotheses (including tendencies) in italic and boldface
*Levels of significance: *** p<0.001, ** p<0.01, * p<0.05,$^{(+)}$ p<0.1*

Dependent Variables	R^2		Independent Variables: Rev_{t-1}	EBITDA-Mrg_{t-1}	Mgmt $Owner_{rel}$	Lev_t	Change Mgmt	Steady	Exp. Index	Region	Entry Mode	Time
EBITDA												
c_EBITDA $_{t-1,T-1}$	24.8%	ß	(.000)	(.037)	(.068)	**(.376)**	.012	.009	(.009)	.018	(.023)	(.050)
		$ß^{stand}$	(.239)	(.030)	(.053)	**(.286)**$^{(+)}$	.056	.042	(.041)	.083	(.101)	(.231)
c_Rev $_{t-1,T-1}$	28.3%	ß	na	**.229**	na	**(.385)**	.029	na	(.013)	na	**(.041)**	na
		$ß^{stand}$	na	**.226**	na	**(.350)** *	.159	na	(.070)	na	**(.219)**	na
c_EBITDA-Mrg $_{t-1,T-1}$	29.1%	ß	***(.000)***	**(.271)**	.028	.047	(.027)	.008	(.003)	.011	.028	(.023)
		$ß^{stand}$	***(.399)***$^{(+)}$	**(.372)***	.211	.059	(.207)	.060	(.026)	.087	.211	(.175)
c_CoGS-Mrg $_{t-1,T-1}$	23.7%	ß	***.000***	.055	.054	(.039)	(.005)	(.004)	(.003)	.009	.002	.004
		$ß^{stand}$	***.409***	.164	.163	(.117)	(.094)	(.072)	(.045)	.160	.032	.067
c_SG&A-Mrg $_{t-1,T-1}$	19.7%	ß	.000	(.196)	.107	.010	.019	(.029)	.027	(.016)	**(.051)**	(.005)
		$ß^{stand}$	.008	(.271)	.159	.016	.160	(.240)	.236	(.133)	**(.418)**$^{(+)}$	(.042)
Employment Details												
c_Employ-Mrg $_{t-1,T-1}$	22.8%	ß	na	na	na	***.213***	na	na	na	na	na	na
		$ß^{stand}$	na	na	na	***.454*** *	na	na	na	na	na	na
c_Employment $_{t-1,T-1}$	39.0%	ß	(.000)	.125	.155	(.147)	**.079**	(.046)	(.037)	(.005)	**(.109)**	(.032)
		$ß^{stand}$	(.050)	.092	.124	(.124)	**.354**	(.201)	(.166)	(.022)	**(.476)***	(.140)
c_LaborProd $_{t-1,T-1}$	28.5%	ß	.000	(.198)	(.046)	***(.268)***	(.028)	**.049**	(.009)	(.014)	**.063**	***.051***
		$ß^{stand}$	.214	(.277)	(.070)	***(.428)****	(.237)	**.407** *	(.080)	(.122)	**.526** **	***.426*** *
NWC												
g_NWC-rel $_{t-1,T-1}$	41.2%	ß	**(.000)**	**2.734**	na	na	na	na	na	**(.416)**	**(.506)**	na
		$ß^{stand}$	**(.347)**$^{(+)}$	**.360**$^{(+)}$	na	na	na	na	na	**(.317)**$^{(+)}$	**(.376)***	na
c_Inv-rel $_{t-1,T-1}$	50.3%	ß	**(.000)**	***(.488)***	.077	.203	(.043)	(.024)	(.039)	**(.088)**	.061	.046
		$ß^{stand}$	**(.586)****	***(.325)***$^{(+)}$	.052	.134	(.160)	(.088)	(.147)	**(.327)**$^{(+)}$	.220	.174
c_AccRec-rel $_{t-1,T-1}$	38.1%	ß	(.000)	(.482)	**(.726)**	.138	(.001)	(.063)	.005	(.020)	.000	.050
		$ß^{stand}$	(.327)	(.336)	**(.529)****	.100	(.005)	(.249)	.019	(.081)	.002	.201
c_AccPay-rel $_{t-1,T-1}$	43.8%	ß	**(.000)**	**(2.014)**	na	**1.028**	na	na	na	**.239**	na	na
		$ß^{stand}$	**(.399)***	**(.638)****	na	**.343** *	na	na	na	**.438** *	na	na
CapEx												
c_CapEx-rel $_{t-1,T-1}$	22.4%	ß	.000	(.339)	.622	.259	(.042)	.005	(.065)	(.065)	(.034)	.042
		$ß^{stand}$	.167	(.164)	.307	.126	(.118)	.014	(.185)	(.185)	(.094)	.120

A meticulous split-up of the various FCF components seems to be highly beneficial:

- First, splitting up absolute EBITDA and further EBITDA-Margin into its constituents reveals significant effects, which seem to partially balance out on an aggregated level and thus would not then have been observable. The same applies to aggregated NWC and its components
- Second, considering various employment details helps to gain a more differentiated understanding of LBO employment effects.

Results regarding the previously postulated hypothesis are mixed:

- *Agency Theory Related.* Overall regression results are slightly supportive for the postulated internal perspective, agency theory related hypotheses
  - Size (hypothesis *H_Int_1b*) seems to be beneficial for NWC reductions but negatively impacting EBITDA improvement. Larger corporations overcompensate for inferior improvements in relative accounts payable through superior improvements in relative inventory levels, which then dominate relative NWC variations. Conversely however, smaller companies have a tendency to outperform with respect to relative CoGS-margin and hence EBITDA-margin variations
  - Hypothesis *H_Int_1b* (profitability) could be validated with respect to revenues growth, EBITDA-margin variations, reductions in NWC and accounts payable as a component thereof in the sense that the lower the profitability prior to the LBO the higher the operational performance improvements and the lower growth in revenues during the holding period
  - Apart from accounts receivable no significance can be found for λ as independent variable. In combination with numerous coefficient signs contrary to those predicted, this questions hypothesis *H_Int_2*
  - The effect of debt financing as a disciplinary tool (hypothesis *H_Int_3*) can be significantly confirmed for NWC components and through coefficients as expected for variations in EBITDA-margin and its components. However, a trade-off seems to exist with respect to revenue growth. Excessive debt financing seems to hamper revenue growth causing the overall impact of the gearing ratio on variations in EBITDA to be negative. This empirically confirms the understanding that faster growing firms are financed through relatively more equity instruments. Interestingly, the effect of the gearing ratio on variations in the personnel costs margin and labor productivity is significantly negative. Improvements in the efficient use of labor seem to suffer from high debt burdens
- *Management Support Related.* Results for operationalization of Management Support, indicate mainly coefficients with signs as predicted though with hardly any significance
  - Variations in the top management (hypothesis *H_Int_4*) seem to coincide with positive employment effects, which is supported through (though not statistically significant) positive effects on revenue growth. Despite numerous coefficient signs as expected, no further significance can be confirmed
  - Similarly, with respect to the divestiture and acquisition activity during the holding period (hypothesis *H_Int_5*), one significant finding can be reported. Acquiring and divesting seems to be a mode of increasing the efficiency through improved labor productivity

— Results for proxying the *experience* level of the private equity investor (hypothesis *H_Int_6*) are non-confirmative. None of the coefficients for any of the analyzed *FCF effects* turned out to be statistically significant. While in the outcome this contrasts findings of previous studies, a major reason for the insignificance might result from the simplistic though appropriate operationalization.[603] As reported in part in chapter IV.B.1.2.3, Kaplan/Schoar (2005) as well as Gottschalg et al. (2004) report significant impacts of the experience level on fund performance.[604] However, other than in this analysis, the experience impact is operationalized and tested for on fund level rather than on the individual investment level. Accordingly, since benefits from experience seem to rather materialize on fund level, it could be hypothesized that experienced funds are characterized by more sophisticated deal selections rather than better-quality management support. In other words experience helps in taking smart individual investment decisions but does not necessarily translate into superior operational performance improvements and hence *FCF effects*. An analysis of the percentage of write-offs by experience (operationalized as stated) could shed further light on this aspect. A further explanation for the insignificance of the fund's experience on operational performance on investment level might be that *PE* firm-specific value addition to LBOs is lower for later stage financing investments.[605]

- *Control Variables*

— With respect to regional considerations (hypothesis *H_CV_1*) UK transactions show as postulated in part significantly more favorable *FCF-effects*. Reductions in NWC (and its components) as well as (though not statistically) EBITDA improvements are larger for UK compared with CE investments

— Testing for the entry mode of the investment reveals for a number of variables statistically significant more favorable variations for previously management-controlled firms thereby confirming hypothesis *H_CV_2*. Apparently, the potential for operational performance improvements seems indeed to be highest in situations where the *change* towards a more shareholder value oriented governance structure is highest, i.e. for investments where previously the separation between ownership and control was comparably large

603 In the absence of feasible alternatives, to avoid multicollinearity of the research model and in particular owing to the small sample size a binary variable has been applied to dummy for being part of the group of highly invested GPs.

604 See Kaplan, S. N./Schoar, A. (2005), pp. 1791-1823 and Gottschalg, O., et al. (2004), pp. 1-53 both of which proxy experience through the sequence number of funds.

605 This view is supported by Sapienza, H. J., et al. (1996) finding that positive impacts from financial sponsors are highest for earlier stage ventures as well as the fact that most positive impacts of experience are reported for VC investments.

— Individual regression results with respect to time considerations (hypothesis *H_CV_3*) are largely unsupportive. Variations in none of the analyzed dependent variables are found to be more favorable for early investments. On the contrary, in fact, labor productivity improvements are significantly better for recent investments

With respect to the analysis of relative operational performance measures in chapter V.E, internal perspective independent variables for which no more than three significant effects could be identified, are excluded from further regression analyses. In detail, this implies that given the constraint with respect to the number of independent variables as well as the two-tier framework of the analysis the internal perspective-specific variables (i) relative managerial ownership stake λ, (ii) change in management *CMgmt*, (iii) divestiture and acquisition activity *Steady*, and (iv) the private equity experience *ExpInd* are not considered in any LBO performance regression analysis.

3. External Perspective: Variation in the Transaction Multiple

The decomposition of *Total Proceeds* according to equation (33) in Table 21 has already indicated that in the past *Multiple Variation* made a significant contribution to equity investors' *Total Proceeds* in this analyzed sample of 42 realized LBO investments. The following chapter further details this external perspective. Apart from descriptive statistics, derived hypotheses are tested for the sub-samples of IPO exited and secondary buyout exited LBOs separately as outlined in the research model.

Table 34 provides descriptive statistics for the $P/EBITDA_{LTM}$ transaction multiples at entry, at exit and their respective variations. Across the entire sample, the portfolio companies experienced an increase in the transaction multiple from 7.2x at entry (ranging from 2.5x to 13.1x) to 8.2x at exit (ranging from 4.6x to 14.0x), representing an average multiple expansion of 1.0x compared to the entry valuation. Given outliers at the upper end of the range, median values are slightly lower with 7.1x at entry and 8.0x at exit. The corresponding multiple expansion equals 1.0x in absolute terms. This is quite remarkable: for the analyzed sample the mean/median transaction multiple increased by as much as 20.2%/13.8% from entry to exit. For 73.8% of the analyzed investments, the $P/EBITDA_{LTM}$ transaction multiple increased from entry to exit. For reasons to be concretized, be it fundamentally, market timing or insider information, financial sponsors benefited historically from investing at comparably low relative price levels and divesting at comparably high relative price levels. In other words LBO performance benefited historically from *buying low and selling high.*

However, the high standard deviation of 1.8x multiple points and the wide range of observations ranging from (2.7x) to 6.0x for the absolute variations not only indicate the heterogeneity of the sample but also point at the tremendous relevance and the impact of variations in the relative valuation as a key value driver in LBO investments. To be considered further, high IPO valuations at exit, especially, cause the corresponding distribution to be left-skewed.

Table 34 Variations in $P/EBITDA_{LTM}$ Transaction Multiples from Entry to Exit

m calculated as entity value at entry and at exit over the corresponding EBITDA for the latest available LTM-period (t-1 and T-1) respectively

	Average	Median	Std. Dev.	Minimum	Maximum	N
Levels						
m_t	7.2x	7.1x	2.1x	2.5x	13.1x	42
m_T	8.2x	8.0x	1.9x	4.6x	14.0x	42

Variations

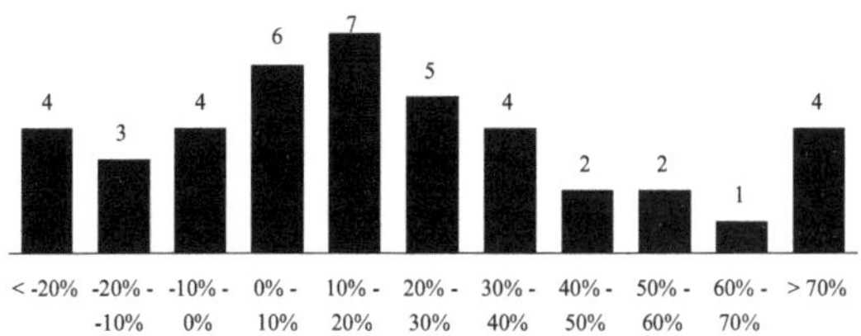

	$g\_m_{t,T}$	$\Delta\_m_{t,T}$
Average	20.2%	1.0x
Median	13.8%	1.0x
Std. Dev.	30.8%	1.8x
Minimum	(25.6%)	(2.7x)
Maximum	101.6%	6.0x

Internal perspective *FCF effects* have been operationalized and analyzed in the form of CAGRs of the various FCF constituents. With respect to the variation in the relative transaction price such CAGR analysis seems little advisable as no continuous variation is expected. The analysis therefore applies the simple variation, i.e. the multiple growth rate $g\_m_{t,T}$. In this light the relationship between the variation in transaction multiples and the corresponding holding period of the investment is of particular interest.

Chart 24 Variation in the Transaction Multiple against Holding Period

Total sample of 42 realized investments; Holding Period in months

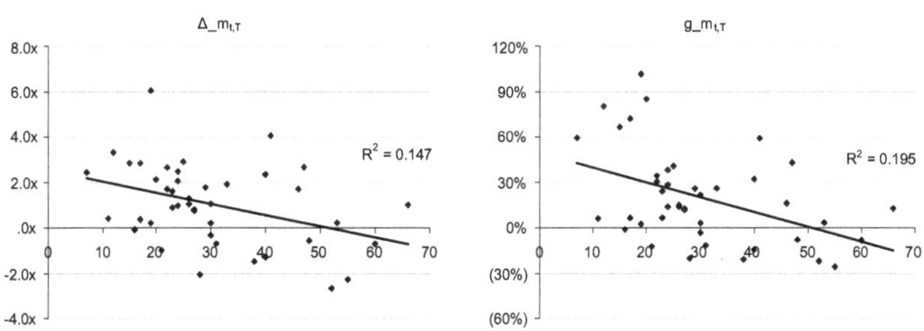

Evidently as displayed in Chart 24, the variation in the transaction multiple and the holding period are negatively related. Few investments with extreme levels of multiple expansion and

comparably short holding periods cause these outliers. These investments have previously been named *quick-flips* elsewhere in this thesis. Decreasing multiple expansion with the holding period is consistent with arguments provided by Ljungqvist/Richardson (2003b). Analyzing the competitive environment in *PE* investing, Ljungqvist/Richardson reason "*that funds that faced though competition when making their investments will* [...] *exit their portfolio holdings later.*"[606] If at the time of the entry competition is severe and *PE* firms potentially overpay, the variation in the transaction multiple will apparently be low or even negative. Conversely, if *PE* firms realized a *lucky buy* at the time of the entry, multiple expansion is expected to be high and *PE* firms might tend to dispose of the investment opportunely. Similarly, the option value to wait with the divestment of the asset also suggests that investments exited after a comparably short holding period are unlikely to be characterized by unfavorable variations in the transaction multiple. If the capital market environment were to be unsatisfactory, the *PE* firm would tend rather to hold on to the investment. As outlined in the research model, the forthcoming regression analysis on the variation in the transaction multiple applies among others, the gearing ratio at entry, l_t, as well as the difference in the number of IPOs, $\Delta\_\#\_IPOs$, to test for the impact of (i) the relative valuation at entry, and (ii) the attractiveness of the capital market environment at exit, respectively.

3.1 Descriptive Differences by Exit Mode

Owing to restrictions with respect to the availability of information, the analysis focuses as pointed out on IPO and secondary buyout exited LBOs only. The entire sample comprises 28 (66.7%) IPO and 14 (33.3%) secondary buyout exits. As detailed in the previously outlined research model, the chosen exit mode shall not be analyzed as dependent variable for the purpose of this thesis. Rather, based on theoretical considerations, the analysis proposes a separate discussion of multiple variation with regard to these two exit modes. Nonetheless, before doing so, some brief though revealing remarks follow, regarding sample characteristics and previously presented results by these considered exit modes; details of which are provided in Table 57 in the Appendix.[607]

With respect to size and profitability prior to the LBO as well as managerial ownership no significant differences between the two sub-samples can be found. For the considered transactions the percentage of common stock is (weak) significantly higher for IPO exited

606 See Ljungqvist, A./Richardson, M. (2003b), p. 5. Among others, Ljungqvist/Richardson argue that investments undertaken in times of intense competition require more and extended hands-on involvement which implies a longer holding period. Related evidence is provided by Bengtsson, O., et al. (2002) (cited in Ljungqvist, A./Richardson, M. (2003b), p. 5) reporting that competition for investments induces VCs to screen less.

607 Non-parametric Mann-Whitney tests are applied to test for mean differences between the samples of IPO exited and secondary buyout exited investments.

transactions. However, this effect is presumably largely attributable to the fact that most of the secondary buyout exited transactions occurred in the sub-sample of a recent transaction for which a significant higher percentage of quasi-equity financing instruments (and hence lower relative common stock contribution) could be found (see chapter C.2.1.3 and Table 53 in the Appendix). Data support the theoretical argument that relatively higher growth rates characterize IPO exited LBO investments. With a mean of 4.0% the variation in the EBITDA growth Δ_g_{EBITDA} is very significantly higher than the corresponding number of -8.6% for secondary buyout exited LBOs.

Further, data seem to confirm the common believe that IPO exits are the preferred exit mode. The operationalization for differences in the prevailing equity capital market attractiveness – the variation in the number of IPOs, *Δ_#_IPOs* – is statistically significantly higher for IPO exited investments, while the operationalization of the debt capital market attractiveness – *Δ_spread* – is not. Similar to *Δ_#_IPOs*, the alternatively considered variables for the operationalization of the variation in the equity capital market attractiveness – the variation in the DJStoxx index as well as the different volume of total equity issuances – are found to be higher for IPO exited investments. Also, the variation in the P/E ratio of the S&P 500 index as a further indicator of the equity capital market attractiveness is found to be very significantly higher for IPO exited LBO investments. This already suggests that the IPO exit mode is chosen in a favorable capital market environment, while the secondary buyout exit is considered as an alternative exit mode, which is potentially supported – but not triggered – by an auspicious debt capital market environment. A beneficial macro-economic environment seems to further foster IPO exits. A tendency can be reported in that the cumulated GDP growth during the holding period is higher for IPO exited investments.

The holding period is longer for secondary exited LBOs; however, the differences apparently vanish when considering the (median) lock-up period for selling down the remaining shares.

3.2 Variation in the Transaction Multiple of IPO Exited LBOs

Table 35 provides descriptive statistics for the absolute entry and exit levels as well as the corresponding absolute and relative variations for $P/EBITDA_{LTM}$ transaction multiples of analyzed IPO exited LBO investments.

Table 35 Variations in $P/EBITDA_{LTM}$ Transaction Multiples from Entry to Exit for IPO Exited LBOs

m calculated as entity value at entry (t) and at exit (T) over the corresponding EBITDA for the latest available LTM-period (t-1 and T-1) respectively; Δ indicates absolute variations, g relative variations

	Average	Median	% Positive Variations	Std. Dev.	Minimum	Maximum	N
Levels							
m_t	7.1x	7.0x	na	2.1x	4.0x	13.1x	28
m_T	8.3x	8.2x	na	1.9x	5.2x	14.0x	28
Variations							
$\Delta\_m_{t,T}$	1.1x	1.0x	78.6%	1.8x	(2.7x)	6.0x	28
$g\_m_{t,T}$	21.6%	13.8%	78.6%	31.2%	(25.6%)	101.6%	28

IPO exited LBOs experience in 78.6% of the cases a multiple expansion; on average by 1.1x $P/EBITDA_{LTM}$ multiple points or 21.6%. The comparison with Table 34 reveals that the distribution of LBOs divested via the public equity market is largely comparable with the distribution of the total sample, already indicating few differences between the distribution for IPO exited and secondary buyout exited LBOs. Notably indeed, IPO exited LBOs seem to be accountable for the lower as well as the upper end outliers of the total sample, though the standard deviations are broadly in line.

Regression Results

The regression analysis with $g\_m_{t,T}$ as the dependent variable and the previously identified independent variables yields remarkable results (see Table 36). Five out of the eight postulated hypotheses can be confirmed.

Table 36 Regression Results – External Perspective IPO Exited LBOs

ß and standardized ß using a stepwise OLS regression model with $g\_m_{t,T}$ as the dependent variable; ; findings in accordance with previously postulated hypotheses (including tendencies) in boldface; findings invalidating previously postulated hypotheses (including tendencies) in italic and boldface
*Levels of significance: *** p<0.001, ** p<0.01, * p<0.05, (+) p<0.1*

	R^2		Δ_r_f	Δ_g_{EBITDA}	$\Delta\_\#\_IPOs$	α	l_t	Region	Entry Mode	Time
			Independent Variables							
$g\_m_{t,T}$	68.3%	ß	***.125***	na	**.004**	**(.292)**	**2.622**	na	**(.226)**	**(.337)**
		$ß^{stand}$	***.465 ****	na	**.313***	**(.263)**	**.763*****	na	**(.353)***	**(.526)****

For the two control variables, *EntryMode* and *Time*, the hypothesized negative relation (see hypothesis *H_CV_2* and *H_CV_3* on page 152) can be validated. Multiple expansion is highly significantly larger for the early sub-sample compared with recent transactions. Also, LBOs of previously owner-controlled companies seem to benefit statistically significantly more from multiple expansion than previously management-controlled companies. Hypothesis *H_CV_1* with respect to *Region* has to be rejected.

Results with respect to the fundamentally derived hypotheses *H_ext_1* and *H_ext_2* are non-significant. Other than the hypothesized negative relation a *positive* relation between the risk-free interest rate differential and the variation in the transaction multiple can be observed. This does not contradict the general finding that the increase in transaction multiples over time coincides as expected with a decreasing risk-free interest rate. However, what cannot be confirmed based upon this sample is that the magnitude of this increase in the transaction multiple relates significantly to the magnitude of the decrease in the risk-free rate. Also, no significant impact can be found for the operationalization of the differential in the expected, risk-neutral growth rate.[608]

Conversely, results regarding the operationalization of the capital market environment and the exploration of potential information asymmetries are very strong. As expected, Δ_#_*IPOs*, the operationalization of the difference in the prevailing equity capital market attractiveness at entry and at exit, is statistically significant (ß=0.313, p=0.033). Apparently, the more attractive the equity capital market at exit compared with the entry, the higher is the variation in the transaction multiple. Regression results indicate that a marginal, positive IPO differential of ten implies ~4% multiple expansion from entry to exit. Further, α, the remaining LBO equity investor interest, is negatively related with multiple expansion. This finding is in accordance with hypothesis *H_ext_4a_IPO* and – when extending the argumentation from underpricing on the variation in the transaction multiple – as analyzed in chapter III.C.2.2.1. Hence, in other words, the less retained by the initial owners, the higher the pricing in the IPO in order to maximize proceeds at the time the majority is sold in a secondary sell-down.

Confirming hypothesis *H_ext_4b*, the variable accounting for the relative entry valuation, l_t, can be found to have a very highly significant impact on the relative variation in the transaction multiples of the analyzed sample of IPO exited LBOs. Seemingly, investments that are financed over-proportionately with debt at the time of entry benefit at exit from multiple expansion. According to the specified regression model a marginal 1% higher gearing ratio at entry implies an approximate 2.6% multiple expansion at exit. Based on equation (64) ($m_t=L_t/l_t$), a relatively low equity contribution at entry might simply imply that relative to the leverage L_t of the transaction the relative purchase price m_t has been low and the investment hence *cheap*. Further, this very significant high impact of l_t might also be the result of signaling aspects. Several models argue that high gearing ratios convey information to the

---

608 As detailed, the operationalization of the *growth* variable is anything but straightforward. The presented regression results do not improve when applying variations of EBITDA during the holding period (i.e. $g\_EBITDA_{t-1,T-1}$ or $c\_EBITDA_{t-1,T-1}$) as indicators.

market.[609] Large pre-IPO gearing ratios are argued to credibly signal firm quality. Debt limits management's discretionary leeway over cash flows and imposes hard budget constraints given the disciplinary role of debt as discussed in chapters III.B.1.2. Accordingly, relatively high levels of debt at entry would not only stand for a lucky buy but also signal firm quality at exit and hence favor a positive variation in the transaction multiple. This alternative explanation would strengthen the initially hypothesized and observed effect and hence might account in part for the high significance.

The *bootstrap approach*[610] has been applied to test the robustness of these regression results given the small sample size of the cross-sectional IPO exit sub-sample. Based on 500 trials the reported significant results can largely be confirmed; only the significance of $\Delta\_\#\_IPOs$ disappears. These results suggest that despite the reduced sample size the reported findings seem to be relatively robust.

Sub-sample Analysis

In accordance with the preceding regression results, the sub-sample analysis confirms some statistically significant differences with respect to *EntryMode* and *Time*. Relative variations in the transaction multiple were found to be (weak) significantly higher for previously owner-controlled LBOs. An average multiple expansion of 14.3% for the 18 previously management-controlled IPO exited LBOs compares with the corresponding number of 34.9% for previously owner-controlled companies. A tendency can be verified for absolute variations. Noteworthy, the ten previous owner-controlled and subsequently IPO exited LBOs under review experienced on average more than two multiple points higher on their exit valuations compared to their entry levels.[611] Further, differences of the absolute and relative variations with respect to the time sub-samples are also (owing to the small sample size only weak) significant. In light of the significantly higher entry transaction multiples but only differing a little from exit transaction multiples for later transactions, variations from entry to exit decreased over time. The average variations of the pre Sep-1998 sub-sample of 1.55x and 30.4% compare with the corresponding numbers of 0.40x and 5.9% respectively for the post Sep-1998 sub-sample. As expected, given the insignificance in the regression analysis, differences for regional sub-samples could not found to be significant (see Table 58 in the Appendix for details).

---

609 See the discussion in chapter III.C.2.2.1 as well as further signaling models such as Ross, S. A. (1977), pp.23-40, Myers, S. C./Majluf, N. S. (1984), pp. 187-221, Narayanan, M. (1988), pp. 39-51 and Heinkel, R./Zechner, J. (1990), pp. 3-24.

610 See e.g. Efron, B./Tibshirani, R. J. (1993) for an introduction to the bootstrap approach.

611 The relatively low average holding period of only 23.5 months for this sub-sample underpins the suspicion that these ten transactions comprise various *quick-flip* LBOs.

3.3 Variation in the Transaction Multiple of Secondary Buyout Exited LBOs

Descriptive statistics comprising absolute entry and exit $P/EBITDA_{LTM}$ transaction multiples as well as the corresponding absolute and relative variations from entry to exit for secondary buyout exited LBOs are displayed in Table 37.

Table 37 Variations in $P/EBITDA_{LTM}$ Transaction Multiples from Entry to Exit for Secondary Buyout Exited LBOs

m calculated as entity value at entry (t) and at exit (T) over the corresponding EBITDA for the latest available LTM-period (t-1 and T-1) respectively; Δ indicates absolute variations, g relative variations

	Average	Median	% Positive Variations	Std. Dev.	Minimum	Maximum	N
Levels							
m_t	7.2x	7.1x	na	2.0x	2.5x	10.4x	14
m_T	8.1x	7.8x	na	2.1x	4.6x	12.1x	14
Variations							
$\Delta\_m_{t,T}$	.8x	.9x	64.3%	1.8x	(2.0x)	4.1x	14
$g\_m_{t,T}$	17.2%	14.6%	64.3%	31.0%	(20.7%)	85.1%	14

Results are broadly comparable to the findings reported for IPO exited LBOs. The average absolute multiple expansion amounts to 0.8x and is hence only slightly lower compared with IPO exits. Considering median variations, differences even vanish entirely. This result is quite astonishing. Even when selling to the credit market, LBO investments seem to have benefited historically, substantially from a flourishing financing market. This exemplarily illustrates that an IPO exit does not necessarily imply the per se preferred exit route.[612] In a favorable financing market environment the *full* exit via a secondary buyout might very well be an attractive alternative. However, the percentage of transactions with multiple expansion is lower. 35.7% of the considered transactions experienced a multiple contraction (compared with 21.4% for IPO exited LBOs).

Correlation Analysis

The reduced sample of only 14 secondary buyout exited LBO investments precludes any inferring analysis. For that reason Table 38 reports basic *Pearson* correlation coefficients for the identified external perspective independent variables only.

612 From a purely financial perspective only and leaving aside further influencing aspects such as the presumably positive public attention of an IPO as well as subjective interests of the management as minority LBO equity investors.

Table 38 Correlation Results – External Perspective Secondary Buyout Exited LBOs

Pearson correlation coefficients for $g\_m_{t,T}$ and identified secondary buyout exit independent variables; findings in accordance with previously postulated hypotheses (including tendencies) in boldface; findings invalidating previously postulated hypotheses (including tendencies) in italic and boldface
*Levels of significance: *** $p<0.001$, ** $p<0.01$, * $p<0.05$, $^{(+)}$ $p<0.1$*

	Independent Variables						
	Δ_r_f	Δ_g_{EBITDA}	Δ_spread	l_t	Region	Entry Mode	Time
$g\_m_{t,T}$	***.423*** $^{(+)}$	(.146)	(.201)	.016	(.306)	.311	***.348***

Analogous to the analyzed sample of IPO exited LBOs, a (weak) significant positive correlation is found between $g\_m_{t,T}$ and Δ_rf challenging the postulated hypothesis *H_ext_1*. Contrary to the findings for the IPO sample and thus contrary to the formulated prediction, a tendency for a positive correlation is also found between $g\_m_{t,T}$ and the *Time* dummy variable. Given the generally more favorable debt financing environment for investments in the recent sub-sample, the variation in the transaction multiple is higher for those secondary buyout exited LBOs. This view is supported by a negative (though unfortunately not significant) correlation between Δ_spread and the variation in *P/EBITDA*.

Sub-sample analysis

For a reduced sample of considered transactions, a tendency for increasing absolute variations in the transaction multiple over time can be reported according to the non-parametric *Mann-Whitney* test for mean differences. The average absolute variation in $P/EBITDA_{LTM}$ between entry and exit increased from 0.44x for the pre Sep-1998 sub-sample to 1.19x for the post Sep-1998 sub-sample. No significant differences are found regarding *Region* and *EntryMode* (see Table 58 in the Appendix for details).

Components of $\Delta\_m_{t,T}$ in Secondary Buyout Exited LBOs

Secondary buyout exited LBOs offer the interesting opportunity to compare the two different funding structures and hence detail components of variations in the transaction multiple. Based upon equation (64), variations in the transaction multiple either result (or better materialize) in a variation in total debt financing (leverage) or equity financing or a combination of both.

$$(88) \quad \Delta\_m_{t,T} = \frac{L_T}{l_T} - \frac{L_t}{l_t}$$

For the analyzed secondary buyout exited transactions Table 39 reports some interesting findings in this respect.

Table 39 Components of Multiple Variation in Secondary Buyout Exited LBOs

Senior Debt and Subordinated Debt financing levels expressed as multiples of the corresponding EBITDA for the latest available LTM-period; total equity contribution expressed as percentage of total sources

	Average	Median	Std. Dev.	Minimum	Maximum	N
At entry *(funding of initial considered LBO)*						
$L_{SD,t}$	3.9x	4.0x	1.0x	1.5x	5.9x	14
$L_{SubD,t}$	1.3x	1.4x	.7x	.3x	2.9x	11
$1\text{-}l_t$ (% $Equity_t$)	33.4%	34.0%	5.3%	23.4%	46.3%	14
At exit *(funding of follow-on LBO)*						
$L_{SD,T}$	4.2x	4.3x	.8x	3.1x	5.7x	13
$L_{SubD,T}$	1.6x	1.6x	.7x	.6x	2.9x	11
$1\text{-}l_T$ (% $Equity_T$)	33.4%	35.2%	7.6%	23.0%	46.5%	13

Accordingly, multiple expansion in secondary buyout exits does not seem to result from increases in the relative equity contribution. Rather, variations seem to be predominately driven by increases in the debt financing ratios. Considering average numbers for the contemplated transactions implies that senior debt as well as subordinated debt financing ratios increased by 0.3x. The resulting combined average variation of approximately 0.6x for *Total Debt* in combination with a flat average, relative equity contribution of 33.4% led to an increase in the mean transaction multiple for secondary buyout exits of 0.9x as reported (see Table 37). These results obviously fit well with findings reported when discussing the financing structure (see Table 10 on page 181 and Table 53 in the Appendix). It has been noted that while gearing ratios (and hence the relative total equity contribution) varied surprisingly little over time, leverage (expressed as multiples of $EBITDA_{LTM}$) increased significantly from 4.5x to 5.1x for the second half of the *Time* sub-sample.

As an interpretation of these results it could be hypothesized that increases in transaction multiples paid are predominantly driven by a favorable and aggressive financing environment rather than necessarily by an increasingly intense competition among financial sponsors.[613] The corresponding line of reasoning is that if competition were to increase and excess funds in the *PE* industry were to be invested desperately than the relative equity contribution ought to increase given the necessity to outbid competing financial sponsors.[614] On the other hand, however, one might argue that increasing financing multiples potentially result from aggressively pushing *PE* firms in order to ensure a competitive edge over competing rivals. Also, even constant gearing ratios might be interpreted as an indication for increasing

613 In particular secondary buyouts are generally characterized by a competitive auction process (see chapter III.C.2.2.2) with the involvement of a variety of *PE* firms.

614 Note, however that constant gearing ratios in combination with increasing leverage obviously imply rising equity contributions expressed as a multiple of *EBITDA*.

competition in the *PE* market for investments. As previously argued, a secondary buyout can be considered as a signal for a less risky investment as the company has already proved its LBO capabilities and demonstrated its ability to cope with the associated heavy debt burden and pressure to improve the operational performance. Such a decreasing investment risk generally justifies not only higher absolute financing ratios (i.e. leverage) but also higher relative debt levels. According to this line of reasoning, gearing ratios were expected to increase; respectively, constant gearing ratios might be interpreted as a result of pressure to bid up and hence bear lower expected rates of return in order to win investments.

3.4 External Perspective Intermediary Results

The previous chapters detailed the external perspective, *variation in the transaction multiple*, separately for IPO exited and secondary buyout exited LBO investments as outlined in the research model in chapter IV.

Chart 25 Detailed Research Model – External Perspective

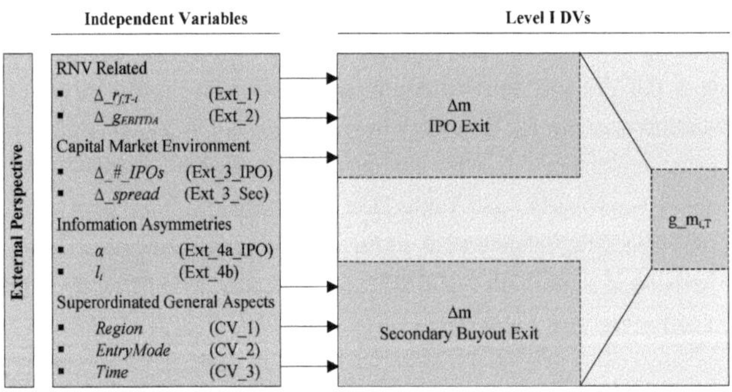

Source: Own Illustration

Key findings are:

- For the entire sample of 42 realized investments $P/EBITDA_{LTM}$ multiples increased from a mean value of 7.2x at entry to a mean value of 8.2x at exit, representing an average multiple expansion of 1.0x or 20.2%. Roughly three quarters of the investments benefited from *buying low and selling high*.

- Somewhat surprisingly, distribution characteristics of multiple expansion for the sub-sample of secondary exited LBO investments are almost identical to those of the IPO exited LBO sample, implying that – in the absence of further aspects – an IPO does not necessarily represent the preferred exit mode.

- Determinants of multiple expansion are largely as predicted.

- The most significant and, for both sub-samples, consistent determinant is the gearing ratio at entry l_t. Accordingly, a high gearing ratio seems to imply a comparably low relative entry transaction price, i.e. a *cheap* investment.
- The effect of the variation in the risk-free interest rate, $\Delta\_r_{f,T\text{-}t}$, is – regardless of the exit mode – positive and thus other than predicted. For the twelve year horizon, decreasing interest rates coincide as expected with multiple expansion. However, this does not hold to be true on investment level. While the variation in the risk-free interest rate increases with the holding period, the variation in the transaction multiple decreases in the holding period. Thus, high multiple expansion – seemingly contradictory – coincides with little variation in the risk-free interest rate and vice versa.
- For the sample of IPO exited investments, the proxy for the equity capital market attractiveness (*Δ_#_IPOs*) is significant as predicted. The correlation coefficient of the corresponding variable for the secondary buyout exited sample, *Δ_spread*, is negative as predicted, though not significant.
- The inclusion of control variables is insightful. Multiple variation is found to be significantly lower for previously management controlled companies. This finding suggests that pre-LBO equity investors share in expected (and empirically confirmed) improvements in operational performance following the LBO entry. Further, whereas multiple expansion decreased over time for IPO exited investments, it increased for secondary buyout exited investments.

- A more detailed consideration of the variation in the transaction multiple for secondary buyout exited investments reveals that increasing leverage ratios are decisive. For one and the same asset financing banks provided historically higher levels of debt financing in secondary buyouts. As hinted, this might reflect a lower degree of uncertainty. However, despite higher leverage, gearing ratios remain constant. In particular for auctioned secondary buyout investments this potentially indicates an increasingly intense competitive environment for *PE* investors.

E. Relative LBO Performance Measures

So far the decomposition of the LBO transaction model (chapter V.D.1) and the underlying effects structured alongside the framework of an internal (chapter V.D.2) as well as an external (chapter V.D.3) perspective of value creation in LBOs have been discussed in detail. The following chapter recombines the two perspectives by assessing in detail LBO investment performance measures and ultimately value creation. Based on considerations in chapter II.C.3 the two primarily analyzed performance measures are *Times Money* (chapter V.E.1) and the

Investment IRR (chapter V.E.2). The brief discussion of (i) *Excess Returns* and (ii) *standardized NPVs* as forms of alternative performance measures concludes (chapter V.E.3).

These analyses provide novel insights in that so far no empirical analysis seems to exist that analyzes and links company- and transaction-specific aspects of LBO performance measures on investment level.

1. Times Money Analysis

1.1 Times Money Descriptive Statistics and Decomposition

Chapter II.C.3.1 discussed the concept of *Times Money* whereby *Total Proceeds* of the investment are considered relative to the amount of capital invested (including equity injections during the holding period) without accounting for the length of the investment.

$$(89)\quad TM = \left(E_T - E_t + \sum_{n=t}^{T} Div_n - \sum_{n=t}^{T} E_{Inj,n}\right) \Big/ \left(E_t + \sum_{n=t}^{T} E_{Inj,n}\right) - 1$$ see equation (13), page 60

The linear calculation of this performance measure, which results from leaving aside the timing aspect, offers the distinctive advantage that similar to equation (33) with respect to *Total Proceeds*, *Times Money* can easily be decomposed into the five components, (i) *EBITDA Variation*, (ii) *Multiple Variation*, (iii) the *Combined EBITDA/Multiple Effect*, (iv) *Cumulated FCF Generation* and (v) *Transaction Costs*. Table 40 provides (i) the corresponding descriptive statistics for the total of 42 analyzed investments, as well as (ii) distribution histograms for the individual components separating out *steady* and *non-steady* investments.

Table 40 Times Money and its Relative Composition

Times Money calculated as Total Proceeds (TP) to equity investors relative to the total amount of Capital Invested (CI)

	Average	Median	% Positive Variations	Std. Dev.	Minimum	Maximum	N
Total Times Money	**2.25x**	**1.94x**	**100.0%**	**1.58x**	**.52x**	**9.10x**	42
EBITDA Variation	1.12x	.98x	97.6%	.85x	(.50x)	4.23x	42
Multiple Variation	.63x	.38x	73.8%	1.09x	(.72x)	4.13x	42
Combined Effect	.14x	.13x	71.4%	.37x	(.93x)	1.29x	42
Cumulated FCF Generation	.49x	.44x	85.7%	.54x	(.41x)	2.55x	42
Transaction Costs	(.14x)	(.13x)	0.0%	.08x	(.42x)	(.03x)	42

Chart 26 Times Money and its Relative Composition

Rationale for clustering the histograms of Times Money and its constituents: respective median values as mid points and ⅓ standard deviation as range; Investments without any acquisition and divestiture activity during the holding period (steady) dark shaded

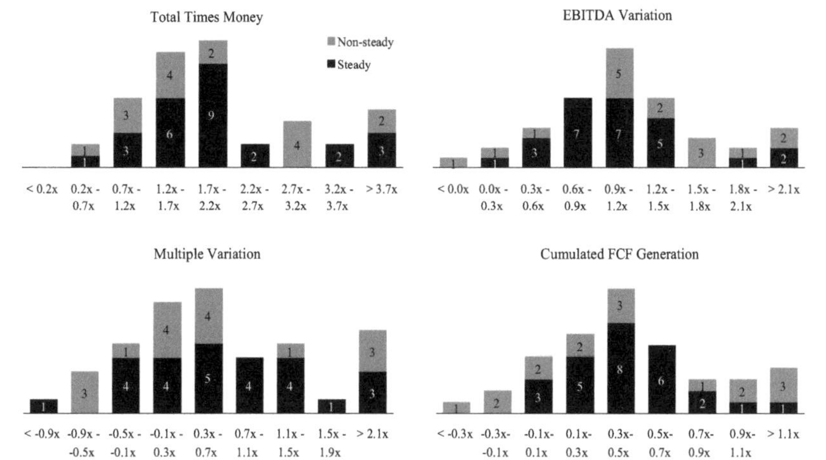

Table 21 previously decomposed *Total Proceeds* to equity investors into the five components whereby absolute *Total Proceeds* were standardized to 100% on the individual investment level. Accordingly, the interpretation of results was how much one of these components contributed relatively to *Total Proceeds* of an investment *compared to the other components*. In this respect, Table 40 has to be interpreted differently: it indicates (averaged across the entire sample) the *absolute contribution of the respective component* to the LBO performance expressed as a multiple of the initial amount invested. *Times Money* as a relative performance measure also enables comparability across various transactions; however, effects are not standardized to 100%.

In light of this understanding Table 40 reveals novel insights regarding the components of LBO investment performance:

Times Money. An equity investor that had invested €1 in each transaction of the analyzed sample of 42 realized LBO investments would have realized an average net capital gain of €2.25. The typical median transaction returned €1.94 of net capital gain. Noteworthy, the *worst* performing transaction of the sample still yielded 0.52x the amount of capital invested at entry. At the upper end of the range the sample is characterized by a few outliers, with five transactions returning in excess of 3.2x the total capital invested. These outliers at the upper end cause the distribution to be left-skewed (see upper-left chart in Table 40). Comparable results on investment level seem not to exist; either in a European context or for LBOs. In the context of direct VC investments Weidig/Mathonet (2004), pp. 1ff report heavily skewed results for a sample of 5,000 US investments. Based on data provided by VentureXperts and Cochrane the authors calculate a mean (median) Times Money multiple of 6.2x (1.5x) with a standard deviation of 53.8%. Further a 30% probability of a total loss was found and the probability to earn in excess of 5x the invested capital surpasses 20%.[615] For a sample of fifty thousand financing rounds Das et al. (2002), pp. 152ff calculate average Times Money multiples of 5.12x and 1.12x for early stage and later stage investments respectively.[616]

EBITDA Variation. The variation in EBITDA from entry to exit for valuation purposes contributed on average the lion's share to the *Times Money* return. A mean EBITDA increase of 45.3% during the holding period of the investment contributed on average 1.12x or 49.8% to *Times Money*.[617] Compared to the remaining components, *EBITDA Variation* is characterized by a relatively low standard deviation. The variance of the distribution decreases further when considering the steady sample only, since transactions that either acquired or divested significantly during the holding period account – as expected – for the majority of outliers at the lower and upper end of the range for this component. As previously pointed out, none of the steady companies experienced decreasing EBITDA levels from entry to exit. Five of the eight transactions with absolute *EBITDA Variation* contributions in excess of 1.5x invested capital are *non-steady*.

Multiple Variation. Table 40 confirms the importance of multiple expansion for historical LBO performance. 28.0% (0.63x) of *Times Money* can ex-post on average be attributed to a variation in the transaction multiple.[617] In other words, leaving the – on average positive – impact of multiple expansion aside, the investor would have earned €1.48 instead of €2.25 for every €1 invested. As illustrated in the corresponding histogram, the distribution is characterized by numerous outliers in the right tail (see lower-left chart in Table 40). The variance of this *Multiple Variation* distribution seems to account to a large extent for the variance of *Times Money* returns.

Cumulated FCF Generation. Debt repayment and interim equity streams contribute on average 0.49x (21.8%) to *Times Money.* The corresponding histogram illustrates that – as expected – *non-steady* transactions account for most of the outliers. Obviously cash in- and outflows from divestitures and acquisitions significantly affect *Cumulated FCF Generation* during the holding period. Therefore, not surprisingly, the standard deviation and maximum observation reduce to 0.34x and 1.46x respectively for the steady sample.

---

615 See Weidig, T./Mathonet, P. Y. (2004), pp. 1ff

616 See Das, S. R., et al. (2002), pp. 152ff.

617 Leaving aside the additional, corresponding fraction from the *Combined Effect*.

Total Transaction Costs in LBO investments are again confirmed to be substantial and amount on average to (0.14x) or (6.2%) of *Times Money*. Interpreting this number has to be done with great caution though. Setting the stage for the LBO transaction model equation (25) derives the equity value at entry as a function of transaction costs associated with the buyout. Therefore any variation and sensitivity analysis with respect to transaction costs automatically affects the equity value at entry and thus double-hits *Total Proceeds* and any related relative performance analysis.

1.2 Separating Steady vs. Improved Operational Performance

The previous decomposition of *Total Proceeds* differentiates among others between *EBITDA Variation* and *Cumulated FCF Generation*. Owing to the fact that these two components are not two mutually exclusive value drivers, the preceding discussion subsumed both components under the internal perspective *FCF effects*. However, the question and critical remark regarding the decomposition of the transaction model as to how much of the LBO performance can be attributed to variations in the firm's operational performance has remained unaddressed so far.

Having separated out *steady* and *improved* operational performance in the context of *Cumulated FCF Generation* (see chapter V.D.2.3.2) this question can now be tackled. Calculations approximated the split between *steady* and *improved* operational performance for *Cumulated FCF Generation*, used for debt repayment and dividend payment purposes, to equal on average 60.3% vs. 39.7%. Meaning, more than 60% of *Cumulated FCF Generation* results on average from improvements in the firm's operations. Applying this split for the average absolute contribution of *Cumulated FCF Generation* to *Times Money* as shown in Table 40, yields corresponding estimations of approximately 0.30x and 0.19x of total capital invested (summing up to the total average contribution of 0.49x).

What does this imply? On average, in the analyzed sample, a mere 0.30x multiple points, representing no better than 13.1% of *Times Money* for these transactions, is estimated to be due to the *steady* operational performance element. The gross of the returns seems to result on average from (i) *improved* operational performance (1.38x or 61.3% of *Times Money* as the sum of EBITDA variation and the relevant *improved element* of *Cumulated FCF Generation*) and (ii) *Multiple Variation* (0.70x or 31.1% of *Times Money*). Therefore, while the firm's cash generativeness at entry together with performance projections drives the leverageability of the buyout, money seems to be earned – and ceteris paribus value created – predominantly through *improvements* in operations rather than deleveraging based on the pre-LBO operating performance.

1.3 *Times Money and the Length of the Investment*

Displaying *Times Money* against the holding period addresses the shortcoming of the *Times Money* performance measure of not accounting for the length of the investment and thus provides some interesting insights in this respect (see Chart 27).

Chart 27 Times Money and its Components against Holding Period

Total sample of 42 realized investments; Holding Period in months; reported R-squares based on basic, univariate OLS regression analyses

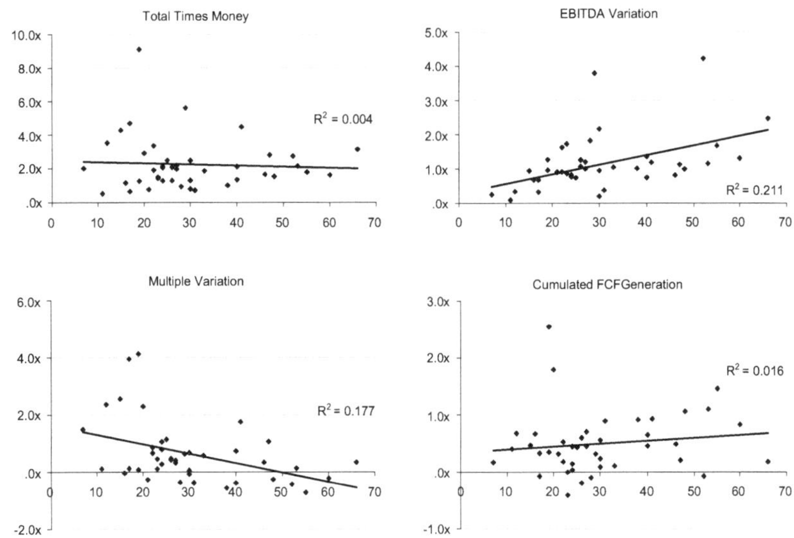

First, other than expected, multiples of the amount of capital invested do not increase with the length of the investment; rather (even) based on the *Times Money* performance indicator an inverse relationship seems to exist between performance and the holding period. This finding seems to support results reported by Phan/Hill (1995) that *"the performance impact of an LBO is far less dramatic over longer time periods."*[618] Given that the amount of *Cumulated FCF Generation* and thus *Total Proceeds* ought to increase over time, this result is astonishing.[619]

Second, as pointed out, the distribution of *Times Money* as such is characterized by some outliers at the upper end and relatively short corresponding holding periods. The lower-left

618 See Phan, P. H./Hill, C. W. L. (1995), p. 732.

619 The effect is clearly expected though for the IRR performance measure given its computation with the exponential impact of the holding period (see chapter V.E.2 for details).

chart – showing the *Multiple Variation* component – confirms findings with respect to the variation in the transaction multiple (see chapter V.D.3 and Chart 24 in particular). Predominately, *quick-flips* cause the relationship between *Multiple Variation* and the holding period to be negative. The *Multiple Variation* component of *Times Money* is (hence) statistically highly significant, negatively dependent on the holding period.

Third, and hardly surprising the *EBITDA Variation* component increases statistically highly significantly in the holding period. Noteworthy in this context, values for the two *EBITDA Variation* component outliers with *Times Money* contributions in excess of 2.5x are not – contrary to what one might assume – negatively distorted by divestitures and acquisitions.

Fourth, contribution from the *Cumulated FCF Generation* component is obviously expected to increase with the length of the investment. However, data can not empirically confirm this relationship, owing to significant distortions from investing (disposals and acquisitions) and financing (new borrowings) cash flow elements during the holding period of the investment.

Sub-sample Analysis

As previously discussed, regression analyses are not conducted for the *Times Money* investment performance measure owing to the deficiency of not accounting for the investment-specific holding period. With respect to the control variables, Mann-Whitney mean comparison tests grouping by *Region*, *EntryMode*, *Time* and *ExitMode* reveal relatively weak significant differences for *Times Money* and its components. A tendency can be found in that CE investments perform better compared to UK investments in terms of *Times Money* (on average 2.73x vs. 1.78x). A tendency also seems to exist for the performance contribution from debt repayment to be higher for investments entered into post Sep-1998. The contribution of *Cumulated FCF Generation* to *Times Money* can be reported to be (weak) significantly higher for secondary buyout exited than IPO exited investments. Whereas *Cumulated FCF Generation* contributes 0.67x *CI* in secondary buyout exited transactions, the corresponding number amounts to only 0.40x *CI* for IPO exited investments (see Table 59 in the Appendix for details).[620]

2. Investment IRR Analysis

2.1 Investment IRR Descriptive Statistics

Descriptive statistics of *Investment IRRs* calculated according to equation (16) are displayed in Table 41. The mean and median *Investment IRRs* of the entire sample amount to 83.0% and

---

[620] This finding apparently results from an on average shorter holding period for IPO exited buyouts (see Table 57 in the Appendix).

57.6% respectively. According to the *Investment IRRs* performance measure, the worst performing transaction in the entire sample still yielded an IRR of as much as 22.4%. The distribution is highly affected by a few outliers as already indicated in the *Times Money* analysis as well as the variation in transaction multiples analysis. The number of 88.8% standard deviation should be kept in mind as it will be referenced shortly when analyzing *Investment IRRs* sensitivities (see chapter V.E.2.2).

Table 41 Investment IRR

Internal Rate of Return with monthly accuracy based on entry and exit date effectives

	Average	Median	Std. Dev.	Minimum	Maximum	N
Investment IRR	**83.0%**	**57.6%**	**88.8%**	**22.4%**	**423.9%**	42

While these numbers might appear high at first glance, they seem not unrealistic. The mean/median *Investment IRR* of the *CEPRES* control sample *CS_2* amounts to 92.0% and 52.0% (see chapter V.A.3). As previously pointed out, a comparison with *Fund/Investor IRRs* reported in recently published *PE Performance Studies* would be misleading for two reasons. First, other than in *Fund/Investor IRRs*, write-offs and underperforming investments are not included in the stated numbers. By comparison, the median *Investment IRR* for the *CEPRES* sample of 436 realized investments including write-offs and underperforming investments equals 15.9%. Second, *Fund/Investor IRRs* are generally reported net of fees and carried interest, which presumably is substantially diluting.

Plotting the IRR against the holding period of the investment and against the capital invested (see Chart 28) reveals that – as expected given the IRR computation – the IRR decreases with the holding period (very highly significant) and with the amount of capital invested (significant).

Chart 28 Investment IRR against Holding Period and Capital Invested

Total sample of 42 realized investments; Holding Period in months; Capital Invested in €m including the initial investment and interim equity injections; Investment IRR and Capital Invested in logarithmic scale

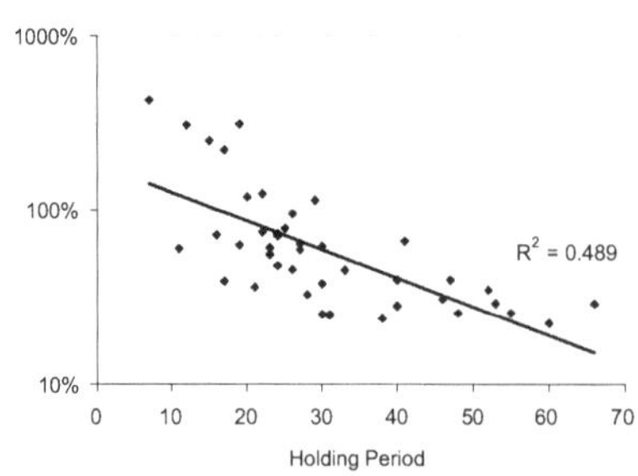

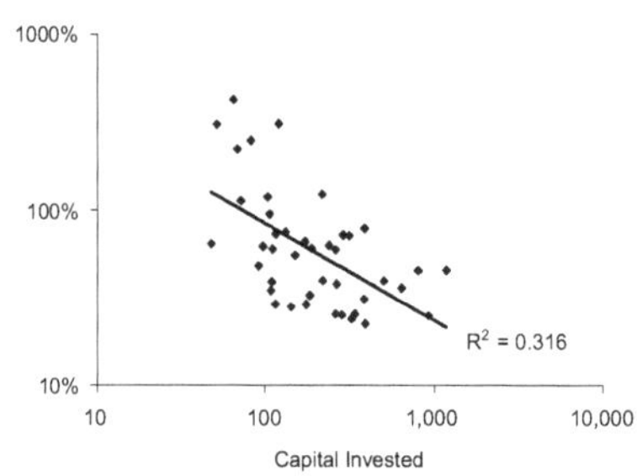

Calculation of a Hypothetical Staged-Exit IRR Accounting for the Equity Capital Market Performance of IPO Exited LBO Investments

So far the performance analysis has implicitly considered – as with secondary buyout exited LBOs – IPO exited investments as full exits. Accordingly, the valuation of divestment proceeds to the LBO equity investors occurred as of the first day of the listing and with the consideration of 100% pre-IPO ownership. However, as briefly pointed out in chapter II.A.4.1, the initial listing of the LBO company as such represents – if at all – only a partial exit for the pre-IPO equityholders. Only if the secondary component comprises a fraction of the equity investors' shares is part of their stake monetized in an IPO. The subsequent further sell-down of these equity holdings – the so-called secondary offering – is subject to/and restricted according to negotiated lock-up agreements between the pre-IPO equity investors and the IPO underwriters.

In this light, the preceding *Investment IRR* calculation applied the IPO offering price for the valuation of 100% of the pre-IPO equity stake. In order to account for this partial exit only and the remaining equity market exposure of the investment from the perspective of the pre-IPO equity investors, a hypothetical *Staged-Exit-IRR* (named IRR_{SE}) can be calculated. Such an IRR considers the share price of the LBO investment at the time when the lock-up period expires for the valuation of the remaining equity stake, which has not been sold at the time of the initial listing.[621]

Table 42 Hypothetical IRR_{SE} Assuming Complete Secondary Sell-down after Lock-up Expiry

Subscription SE indicates staged exit assuming complete sell-down of the remaining ownership stake of pre-IPO equity investors at the day the lock-up period expires; share price performance (until lock-up) represents the actual variation between the offering price (as applied for the preceding IRR calculations) and the closing share price as of the day of the lock-up expiry; for investments with missing information regarding the lock-up period the median value of 180 days has been applied (for 73.9% of the investments the lock-up period equaled 180 days; see chapter V.C.3.3.1); annualization with monthly accuracy

	Average	Median	% Positive Variations	Std. Dev.	Minimum	Maximum	N
Remaining Ownership Stake	43.2%	43.7%	na	19.3%	6.3%	82.1%	25
Share Price Performance	20.5%	0.1%	52.0%	81.6%	(47.3%)	369.5%	25
IRR_{SE}	68.4%	39.2%	na	60.9%	16.6%	220.5%	25

Table 42 provides the corresponding details for IRR_{SE}. For the analyzed sample the initial LBO equity investors remain interested in the investment with a 43.2% post-IPO equity

[621] *Note:* This approach implicitly assumes the complete sell-down of the remaining stake at the expiry of the lock-up. In practice, lock-up agreements are, however, frequently more complex with a staged sell-down of the remaining stake as well as differences of further secondary offerings for the different types of pre-IPO equity investors.

ownership stake.[622] The equity capital market performance of these LBO investments is mixed. Only 52% of the companies outperform their offering price at the time the lock-up period expires. Given some extreme outliers at the upper end of the range the average outperformance is positive with 20.5% while the median value equals 0.1%.

Valuing the remaining LBO equity investor ownership stake with the share price at the time the lock-up period expires and accounting for the associated timing effects of the cash flows (i.e. delayed cash flows from secondary sell-down) results in a comparably lower mean (median) IRR_{SE} of 68.4% (39.2%).[623] Results further indicate that the maximum IRR decreases to 220.5%. It seems that this decrease (similar to the reduced mean/median numbers) results rather from the timing aspect than from lower equity valuations at the expiry. Preceding analyses with respect to the variation in the transaction multiple and the components of *Times Money*, imply that historically numerous IPO exited LBO investments have benefited substantially from multiple expansion between entry and exit. The analysis in chapter V.D.3.2 revealed that such variations result to a great extent from the market environment rather than underlying fundamentals. In this light, it could be supposed that the underperformance following the IPO has a strong negative correlation with the degree of multiple expansion. If this were to be the case, post-IPO equity market performance would correct potentially ill-conceived valuations at the time of the IPO. Surprisingly though, a weak significant *positive* correlation based on the Spearman-Rho test can be found. Accordingly, high levels of multiple expansion at the IPO seem to coincide with a favorable equity capital market performance thereafter and such variations might not be interpreted as potential corrections in the relative valuation.[624] Twelve of the 13 IPO exited investments with an increased share price between the IPO and the end of the lock-up period previously experienced a positive *Multiple Variation*.

Aftermarket Performance of IPO exited LBOs

The preceding calculation of a hypothetical *Staged-Exit-IRR* applied as illustrated the share price performance of the IPO exited LBO until the expiry of the lock-up period. Several papers analyze the post-IPO (accounting and market) performance of IPO exited LBOs in detail

---

622 *Note:* As pointed out when considering the IPO exit statistics in chapter V.C.3.3.1, this number does not (necessarily) imply that pre-IPO equity investors received 56.8% of the post-IPO equity valuation. The ownership stake of pre-IPO equity investors is diluted through the primary component of the listing. *Necessarily* is written in brackets as (part of) the primary proceeds are used as reported for the repayment of quasi-equity financing instruments such as shareholder loans and thus flow to the LBO equity investors.

623 This phenomenon of an on average positive share price performance between the IPO and the expiration of the lock-up period combined with a lower mean/median IRR illustrates the introductorily mentioned reinvestment premise of the *IRR* performance measure. As long as the standard calculated IRR exceeds the annualized stock price performance IRR_{SE} will decrease.

624 An analysis of the variation in the relative (entity) valuation would be subject to even further restrictions and potential distortions such as the specification of the net debt and corresponding $EBITDA_{LTM}$.

yielding mixed results. For the post-offering year Degeorge/Zeckhauser (1993) report significant underperformance in terms of operating income divided by total assets for IPO exited LBOs compared with matching companies.[625] This finding is interpreted to be consistent with informational effects. Accordingly, IPO exited LBOs performing comparably worse than comparison firms is hypothesized to either (i) result from hidden action in the form of manipulation of pre-IPO performance or (ii) arise from hidden information regarding superior private information and the corresponding optimal decision to go public. The corresponding cumulative average excess return of the IPOs benchmarked against a matching firm is negative until the eighth month and increases then (statistically not significant) to 15.2 for the 24 months period. Conversely, Holthausen/Larcker (1996) find significant outperformance in terms of various accounting performance measures for a sample of 89 IPO exited LBOs compared with the corresponding industry for the four consecutive years following the IPO.[626] For the 12-, 24-, 36- and 48-months raw returns of the analyzed sample no significant out-/underperformance compared with the market can be found. Outperformance against the market and a portfolio of matching firms is again found to be significant, with 24.73% and 21.05% respectively, for a sample of 85 IPO exited LBOs analyzed by Mian/Rosenfeld (1993).[627] Based on the finding that abnormal returns were largely driven by takeover activity Mian/Rosenfeld hypothesize that IPOs of LBOs are partially motivated by financial sponsors' desire to exit via a subsequent takeover. Table 43 reports descriptive statistics for an excess return defined as the cumulative return of the IPO exited LBO less the market return.[628]

Table 43 Aftermarket Excess Returns of IPO exited LBOs

*3-, 6- and 9-months aftermarket excess returns for the sample of IPO exited LBOs; excess returns computed by subtracting the market (DJStoxx) return; in order to avoid distortions arising from misspricing and IPO discounts, closing prices for day T+1 were applied; z-statistic to test for difference from zero; levels of significance: *** $p<0.001$, ** $p<0.01$, * $p<0.05$, $^{(+)}$ $p<0.1$*

	Average	Median	% Positive Variations	Std. Dev.	Minimum	Maximum	N
3-months	6.5% *	10.0%	56.0%	13.1%	(13.4%)	26.8%	25
6-months	7.5%	2.9%	56.0%	34.1%	(48.2%)	133.2%	25
-excluding outliers	(0.0%)	0.4%	52.2%	19.8%	(48.2%)	31.0%	23
9-months	12.9%	5.0%	60.0%	55.9%	(64.2%)	205.7%	25
-excluding outliers	(1.5%)	1.6%	56.5%	24.7%	(64.2%)	44.9%	23

Source: DataStream for share price information

For the analyzed sample of IPO exited LBOs a statistically significant outperformance compared with the market portfolio can be found for the 3 months following the IPO. This

625 See Degeorge, F./Zeckhauser, R. (1993), pp. 1338ff.

626 See Holthausen, R. W./Larcker, D. F. (1996), pp. 293ff.

627 See Mian, S./Rosenfeld, J. (1993), pp. 46ff.

628 The performance of the DJStoxx return is applied as market return. The correlation between the considered DJStoxx index and the S&P 500 Composite is – not surprisingly – very highly significant with 96.3%.

significance vanishes thereafter. The distribution parameters for the 6- and 9-months excess return indicate substantial distortion from outliers. Discarding two extreme outperformers (with more than 3x and 4x the standard deviation in excess of the average), the standard deviation decreases substantially and mean/median excess returns are close to zero. LBO stock picking would have been little beneficial, though for the analyzed sample: the percentage of out- and underperformers is almost even.

2.2 *Investment IRR Sensitivity Analyses*

Due to the exponential impact of the holding period and the additive component of *Cumulated FCF Generation*, a decomposition of the IRR comparable to previous analyses with respect to *TP* and *Times Money* is barely feasible. For that reason, the following analysis intends to separate out and approximate the effect of three previously identified key drivers on the calculated *Investment IRRs* of the analyzed sample. Hereby, for each individual investment in the sample, hypothetical IRRs for variations in (i) the transaction multiple, (ii) revenues and (iii) the EBITDA-Margin are calculated. In other words the analysis intends to approximate answers to questions of the type: *What would the IRR have been, if...?*

Transaction Multiple

Assuming no variation in the transaction multiples and calculating hypothetical IRRs with identical entry and exit multiples on investment level, yields an average IRR_{cm}[629] of 46.4% for the entire sample. The *Investment IRR* of a typical transaction in the sample decreases from 57.6% to 40.0%. The second line in Table 44 reports indirectly the relative contribution of multiple variation to the total *Investment IRR* by stating the hypothetical IRR_{cm} as percentage of the *Investment IRR* calculated on investment level and aggregated across the entire sample. Comparable to results presented in Table 21, *Multiple Variation* contributed on average 19.3% to the IRR relative to other components.

Table 44 Hypothetical IRR_{cm} Assuming Constant Transaction Multiples

Annualization with monthly accuracy based on date effectives; subscription cm indicates constant P/EBITDA multiple at entry and exit

	Average	Median	% Negative	Std. Dev.	Minimum	Maximum	N
IRR_{cm}	46.4%	40.0%	0.0%	26.0%	16.4%	159.7%	42
IRR_{cm} / IRR	80.7%	78.8%	0.0%	37.2%	7.4%	159.5%	42

The effect of hypothetically keeping the transaction multiple constant on the distribution of IRRs merits special attention. While standard IRRs are characterized by an immense standard deviation of 88.8% and range of values with some outliers in excess of 200%, the hypothetical

629 Subscription *cm* indicates constant *P/EBITDA* multiple at entry and exit.

IRR_{cm}s are nicely distributed with a standard deviation of no more than 26.0% and a significantly reduced range of 16.4% to 159.7%. This finding emphasizes once again that most of the heterogeneity of *Investment IRRs* results from variations in the transaction multiples. Notably, however, the minimum IRR_{cm} in the analyzed sample still amounts to no less than 16.4%; indicating that sample IRRs benefited from, but were not dependent upon, variations in the transaction multiple.

Chart 29 visualizes the distribution of IRR_{cm} and indicates the sensitivity of the median IRR_{cm} of the entire sample with respect to variations in the transaction multiple.

Chart 29 Distribution of IRR_{cm} and Related Sensitivity

Total sample of 42 realized investments; subscription cm indicates constant P/EBITDA multiple from entry to exit; ceteris paribus sensitivity analysis based on median IRR_{cm} and relative variation in the transaction multiple

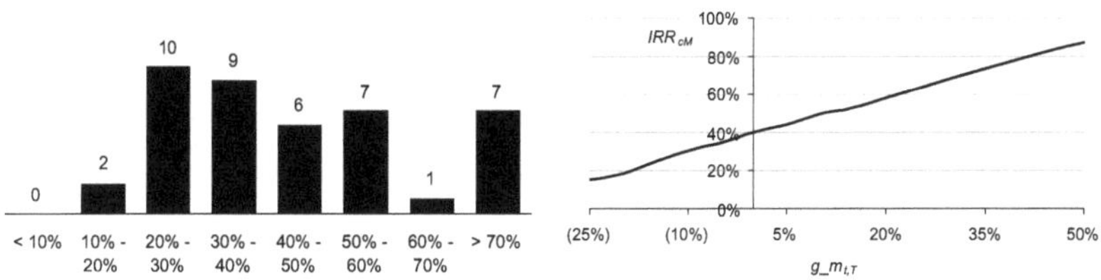

Accordingly, assuming a 20% multiple expansion for each transaction included in the sample, increases the median transaction IRR of the sample from 40.0% to 58.0%.[630]

Revenues

In analogy to the analysis of a constant transaction multiple, Table 45 and Chart 30 display results for the hypothetical case of assuming constant revenues from entry to exit for each of the analyzed investments. In the absence of any growth in revenues and accounting for interim effects on debt repayment the mean and median IRR_{cRev}[631] amounts – ceteris paribus – to 64.2% and 36.3% respectively.[632]

630 This example apparently almost exactly matches the actually observed numbers in the analyzed sample. Including the recorded variation in the transaction multiple of 20.2% as occurred (see Table 34) the median Investment IRR amounts to 57.6%.

631 Subscription *cRev* indicates constant revenues during the holding period.

632 Ceteris paribus (i.e. accounting for interim effects on Cumulated FCF Generation) implies that all other cash flow items were kept as realized in *relative* terms either as % of sales (EBITDA, change in NWC and CapEx) or as % of EBT (Cash Taxes). Circularity with respect to cash interest expense was neglected owing to the minor impact as previously pointed out.

Table 45 Hypothetical IRR_{cRev} Assuming Constant Revenues

Annualization with monthly accuracy based on date effectives; subscription cRev indicates constant revenues at entry and exit; % Negative indicates the percentage of transactions for which hypothetical IRR_{cRev}s would turn negative

	Average	Median	% Negative	Std. Dev.	Minimum	Maximum	N
IRR_{cRev}	64.2%	36.3%	7.1%	89.6%	0.0%	364.5%	42
IRR_{cRev} / IRR	63.6%	71.4%	7.1%	31.9%	0.0%	137.7%	42

Compared to the results for the case of a constant multiple the variance of the distribution remains high due to the discussed outliers arising from *Multiple Variation* whose heterogeneity thus still affects the sample. Expressing IRR_{cRev} as a percentage of the actually realized IRR on investment level and aggregating across the entire sample confirms the tremendous importance of revenue growth for LBO performance. For the median transaction revenue growth contributes 28.6% to the total IRR relative to the other components.

Chart 30 Distribution of IRR_{cRev} and Related Sensitivity

Total sample of 42 realized investments; subscription cRev indicates constant revenues during the holding period; Ceteris paribus sensitivity analysis for the entire sample based on median IRR_{cRev} and annualized revenue growth rates ($c\_Rev_{t-1,T-1}$). Integrated calculation accounts – ceteris paribus – for variations in debt repayment due to revenue variations (see footnote 632).

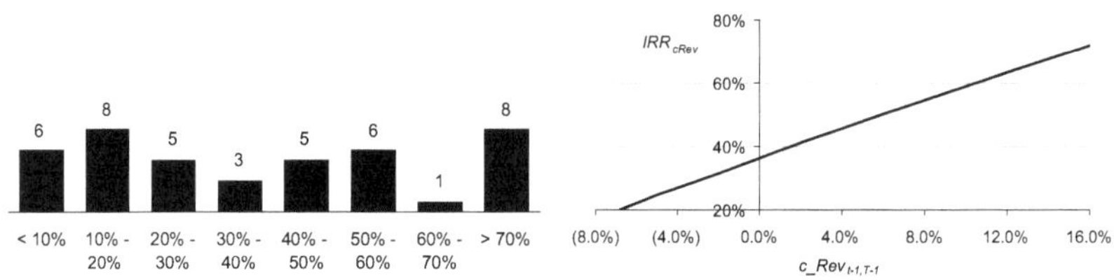

The frequency distribution of IRR_{cRev} in Chart 30 underpins the dependency of IRRs on revenue growth: assuming zero growth 14 transactions (33.3%) in the analyzed sample would yield returns below 20% and three IRRs would hypothetically have turned negative. Accordingly, whereas in the case of transaction multiples investments benefit from but do not depend upon a favorable variation, in the case of revenues, investments clearly rely upon positive revenue growth. The right-hand sensitivity chart indicates that with six percent revenue CAGR from entry to exit for every transaction included in the sample the median IRR would amount to 50.2%.[633]

633 This equals the actual recorded median revenue CAGR of the analyzed sample. See Table 23.

EBITDA-Margin

Third, the impact of a constant EBITDA-margin on sample IRRs is analyzed. All else being equal, keeping the EBITDA-margin for each individual transaction on entry levels decreases the mean and median IRR_{cMrg} [634] to 76.5% and 39.9% respectively.[635]

Table 46 Hypothetical IRR_{cMrg} Assuming Constant EBITDA-Margin

Annualization with monthly accuracy based on date effectives; subscription cMrg indicates constant EBITDA-margin during the holding period; % Negative indicates the percentage of transactions for which hypothetical IRR_{cMrg}s would turn negative

	Average	Median	% Negative	Std. Dev.	Minimum	Maximum	N
IRR_{cMrg}	62.8%	39.4%	2.4%	79.1%	0.0%	389.7%	42
IRR_{cMrg} / IRR	69.4%	73.5%	2.4%	30.3%	0.0%	121.7%	42

The distribution of IRR_{cMrg} resembles the distribution of IRR_{cRev} as being characterized by a few extreme outliers resulting in variations in transaction multiples. The median IRR_{cMrg}/IRR value of 73.5% confirms that EBITDA-margin improvement is of very high importance for value creation; though a slightly less relative contributor to overall IRR than revenue growth (confirming findings in chapter V.D.1.2). The below chart, visualizing the distribution of IRR_{cMrg}, validates this finding in that 21.4% of the analyzed investments would have realized IRR_{cMrg}s below 20% in the absence of EBITDA-margin variations and for one transaction the IRR would hypothetically have turned negative.

Chart 31 Distribution of IRR_{cMrg} and Related Sensitivity

Total sample of 42 realized investments; subscription cMrg indicates constant EBITDA-margin during the holding period; ceteris paribus sensitivity analysis for the entire sample based on median IRR_{cMrg} and annualized EBITDA-margin growth rates ($c\_EBITDA\text{-}Mrg_{t-1,T-1}$); integrated calculation accounts – ceteris paribus – for variations in debt repayment due to EBITDA-margin variations (see footnote [632] for further details)

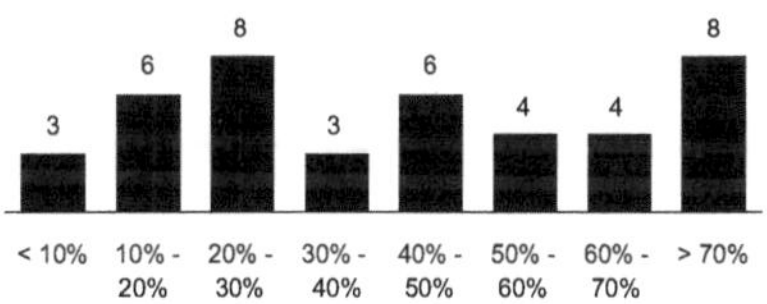

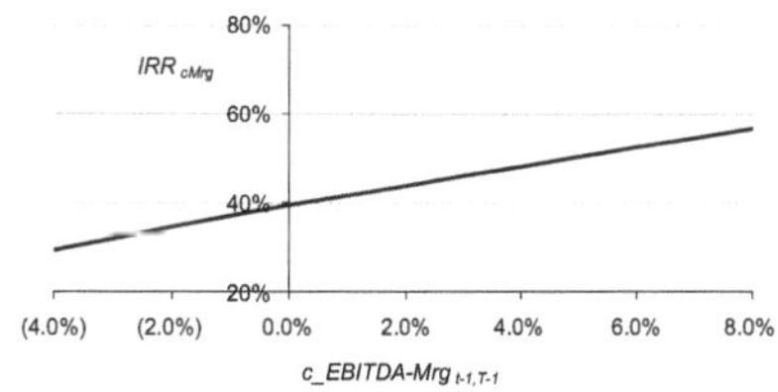

634 Subscription *cMrg* indicates constant EBITDA-Margin during the holding period.

635 See footnote [632] on page 247.

2.3 *Investment IRR Inferring Statistics*

Regression Analysis

The presented research model in chapter IV.A implies that independent variables for which a significant impact on *Level I DVs* could be confirmed (either with respect to the internal or the external perspective) are then applied in a second step as independent variables for analyzing the *Investment IRR* performance measure. As pointed out *Times Money* has not been inferringly analyzed owing to the deficiency of not accounting for the timing aspects of cash flows whereas operationalized *IVs* are in CAGR form.

Concerning the internal perspective, Table 33 revealed that the following independent variables provide (mostly supporting) significant results for at least three operationalized *FCF Effects*: size (Rev_{t-1}), profitability ($EBITDA\text{-}Mrg_{t-1}$), disciplining debt (l_t) as well as the control variable *EntryMode*. With respect to the external perspective Table 36 summarized and indicated the importance of the risk-free interest rate (r_f), the equity market attractiveness (*Δ_#_IPOs*) and the relative entry price (l_t) as well as the two control variables *EntryMode* and *Time*. Significant independent variables for the external perspective were identified separately for the sub-samples of IPO exited and secondary buyout exited investments. *Δ_#_IPOs* correlates negatively and significant at the 1% level with the operationalization of the debt capital market attractiveness *Δ_spread* (-0.657).[636] For that reason, the at first IPO exit-specific operationalization of the equity market attractiveness can also be applied for the entire sample of realized investments when analyzing ex-post value creation through LBO investment performance measures.

Table 47 Regression Results – Investment IRR

ß and standardized ß using a stepwise OLS regression model with logarithm of Investment IRRs (ln_IRR) as the dependent variable; findings in accordance with previously postulated hypotheses (including tendencies) in boldface; findings invalidating previously postulated hypotheses (including tendencies) in italic and boldface
*Levels of significance: *** p<0.001, ** p<0.01, * p<0.05, ^(+)^ p<0.1*

	R^2		Independent Variables: Rev_{t-1}	EBITDA-Mrg_{t-1}	l_t	Δ_r_f	Δ_#_IPOs	Region	Entry Mode	Time
ln_IRR	45.7%	ß	**.000**	(.329)	**4.943**	***.192***	**.009**	(.071)	**(.321)**	**(.473)**
		$ß^{stand}$	**(.221)**	(.039)	**.533*****	***.257***	**.308 ***	(.047)	**(.209)$^{(+)}$**	**(.316)$^{(+)}$**

636 *Note:* the negative correlation coincides with the different predictions of the two corresponding hypotheses (see Table 6). Whereas hypothesis *H_ext_3_IPO* predicts the variation in the transaction multiple (and hence LBO performance) to be higher the higher *Δ_#_IPOs*, hypothesis *H_ext_3_Sec* postulates a negative relationship expecting $g\_m_{t,T}$ to be higher the lower *Δ_spread*.

The gearing ratio (l_t) is obviously highly statistically significant for the *Investment IRR* performance measure. As detailed, a high gearing ratio not only has a disciplining effect with respect to internal *FCF effects* but also can be interpreted as an indicator of an investment with comparably low relative entry valuation and hence potential for multiple expansion. Due to the missing risk adjustment in the *Investment IRR* performance measure the leverage effect apparently implies increasing returns with debt financing. With respect to the remaining two internal perspective (or more precisely agency theory related) *IVs*, *size* and *profitability*, prior to the LBO a tendency can be found for Rev_{t-1} in that smaller companies are comparably better performing in terms of *Investment IRR*.[637] Hardly surprising, given the already offsetting effects with respect to internal perspective, *Level I DVs*, that no significance can be confirmed for $EBITDA\text{-}Mrg_{t-1}$. Concerning the external perspective, capital market related independent variables, the previously identified significances with respect to the variation in the transaction multiple can be confirmed. The capital market environment – operationalized through the difference in the number of IPOs, $\Delta\_\#\_IPOs$ – seems to be crucial in that investments in a favorably developing market are better performing as expected. The seeming controversy regarding the risk-free interest-rate environment also remains. Though weakened compared with the variation in the valuation multiple, a tendency can be found in that investments with a positive differential from entry to exit are better performing.[638]

Regression results with respect to the hypothetically derived *Investment IRRs* for constant transaction multiple IRR_{cm}, constant revenues IRR_{cRev} and constant EBITDA-margin IRR_{cMrg}, during the holding period (see Table 68 in the Appendix) largely confirm previous findings in particular with respect to the sensitivity analysis in chapter V.E.2.2. For the hypothetical constructs of keeping revenues and EBITDA-margin at entry levels the significant impact of the variation in the transaction multiple, and hence of the external perspective remain. Accordingly, as expected, the gearing ratio and the capital market variables remain significant for IRR_{cRev} and IRR_{cMrg}. Additionally, quite an interesting tendency can be found for the hypothetical *Investment IRR* under a constant EBITDA-margin to be relatively higher for previously owner-controlled companies. At closer inspection this seems rational as a constant margin emphasizes the effect of revenue growth on the *Investment IRR* and previous internal perspective *FCF effects* findings indicate higher revenue growth for previously owner-controlled companies. This finding matches regression results with respect to $c\_Rev_{t-1,T-1}$ in

---

637 Given predicted and empirically confirmed offsetting effects with respect to the internal perspective (*FCF-margin effects* vs. *revenue growth*), no corresponding hypothesis for size has been formulated with respect to the LBO investment performance.

638 See the relevant paragraph on the regression results for the variation in the transaction multiple in chapter V.D.3.2 for a related critical discussion.

chapter V.D.2.1.1 as well as internal perspective intermediary findings in chapter V.D.2.4 and Table 33 in particular.

Sub-sample Analysis

Non-parametric mean comparison tests generally confirm the OLS regression results. With a mean (median) figure of 113.4% for the early sub-sample, investments entered into prior to Sep-1998 performed significantly better in terms of *ln_IRR* than investments acquired thereafter (62.2%), i.e. the recent *Time* sub-sample. This outperformance of early transactions is (weak) significantly consistent for all considered hypothetical IRRs. Regardless of stripping out (i) the multiple expansion effect through a hypothetical constant transaction multiple, (ii) the revenue growth effect through hypothetically keeping revenues constant, or (iii) the EBITDA-margin effects through hypothetically keeping the margin constant, empirical results confirm a deteriorating performance (in terms of *Investment IRR*) over time.

Furthermore, for the case of constant revenues, CE transactions show a tendency to perform better than UK transactions. In other words, UK transactions benefited to a greater extent from increasing revenues than CE transactions. This finding is conformable with the results presented in chapter V.D.1.2 and the corresponding Table 55 in the Appendix in that the relative importance of the revenues component of *Total Proceeds* (what has been named *Revenue Effect*) is (weak) significantly higher for UK transactions.

Also consistent with previous findings, a tendency can be found empirically for ln_IRRc_{Mrg} to be higher for previously owner-controlled companies. This implies that – as hypothesized and elsewhere in this thesis empirically indicated – returns of investments in corporations under management control benefit over-proportionately from operational performance improvements expressed through EBITDA-margin expansion.

3. Alternative Performance Measures

This chapter intends to address the shortcoming of the *Investment IRR* in not accounting for the riskiness of the investment. Following introductory considerations, the subsequent paragraphs provide descriptive statistics for *Excess Investment IRRs* and *Standardized NPVs* as two alternative performance measures for ex-post value creation analysis. Illustratively, the impact of considering the rate of return of an alternative investment opportunity as the appropriate discount rate can be shown. These alternative performance measures will not be analyzed inferringly regarding the impact of the identified IVs given that the consideration of an alternative investment opportunity presumably already controls for some of the considered external perspective aspects.

3.1 Excess Investment IRRs

Excess Investment IRRs express the abnormal return of a *PE* investment compared with the public market portfolio.

(90) $ER_i = IRR_i - IRR_k$ see equation (17), page 64

Table 48 displays the corresponding details for the sample of analyzed investments. Next to the *Investment IRR* of an individual *PE* investment, the hypothetical IRRs for (i) a constant transaction multiple (*cm*), (ii) constant revenues (*cRev*), and (iii) constant EBITDA-margin (*cMrg*) throughout the holding period are considered in analogy to the *Investment IRR* sensitivity analysis in chapter V.E.2.2. The IRR of the PM investment is based upon the performance of the DJStoxx index for the comparable investment period from the entry (*t*) to the exit (*T*) of the investment.

Table 48 Excess Investment IRRs

Excess IRRs calculated on investment level as Investment IRR less corresponding IRR of the DJStoxx Index for the comparable holding period (i.e. investment at time t and divestment at time T); subscription cm indicates constant multiples at entry and exit (see Chart 29 for details); subscription cRev indicates constant revenues throughout the holding period (see Chart 30 for details), cMrg constant EBITDA-margin (see Chart 31for details)

	Average	Median	% Positive Variations	Std. Dev.	Minimum	Maximum	N
$IRR - IRR_{DJStoxx,t\text{-}T}$	80.2%	49.7%	100.0%	85.1%	10.9%	411.7%	42
$IRR_{cM} - IRR_{DJStoxx,t\text{-}T}$	43.6%	41.2%	97.6%	24.3%	(4.6%)	138.3%	42
$IRR_{cRev} - IRR_{DJStoxx,t\text{-}T}$	61.4%	31.5%	90.5%	86.8%	(30.4%)	352.2%	42
$IRR_{cMrg} - IRR_{DJStoxx,t\text{-}T}$	59.9%	32.6%	95.2%	76.4%	(25.6%)	377.5%	42

Most importantly, none of the considered investments underperformed compared to the DJStoxx index. The minimum *ER* amounts to 10.9%; the median *ER* amounts to as much as 49.7%. *ERs* for the hypothetical IRRs confirm findings of the IRR sensitivity analysis adjusted for the impact of abnormal returns *ER*. Accordingly, considering constant transaction multiples reduces the standard deviation of the distribution significantly. However, the interpretation of ER_{cM} seems questionable. *Investment IRRs* with constant multiples put the emphasis on the impact of the internal perspective for value creation. When detailing the external perspective it has been shown that external, capital market environment related aspects, such as the IPO attractiveness as well as the risk-free discount rate, have a significant impact on the variation in the transaction multiple. Apart from this, the relatively higher importance of revenue growth compared with EBITDA-margin improvement is confirmed. In the hypothetical case of constant revenues throughout the holding period, 9.5% of the investments yield negative *ERs* whereas for the case of constant margins the corresponding number equals 4.8%.

3.2 Standardized NPVs

As pointed out in chapter II.C.3.3 three different, illustrative rates of return of alternative investment opportunities will be applied for deriving NPVs on investment level.

- A *representative Fund IRR*, calculated based on results reported by two recent *PE Performance Studies*:[639] $r_K = r_{PE\ Studies} = 18.9\%$.
- The *median Investment IRR* of the *CEPRES* control sample CS_2:[640] $r_K = r_{CS\_2} = 52.0\%$.
- The *median* IRR_{cm} as calculated in chapter V.E.2.2: $r_K = r_{IRRcm} = 40.0\%$.

In order to ensure comparability across the various investments NPVs are standardized by indexing the initial equity contribution E_t to one. Table 49 reports the corresponding details.

Table 49 Standardized NPVs

Entire sample of 42 realized LBO investments; NPVs standardized on investment level by indexing E_t to 1

	Average	Median	% Positive Variations	Std. Dev.	Minimum	Maximum	N
$NPV\ (r_k = r_{PE\ Studies})$	1.15	0.74	100.0%	1.23	0.13	6.60	42
$NPV\ (r_k = r_{CS\_2})$	0.26	0.05	52.4%	0.92	(0.64)	4.08	42
$NPV\ (r_k = r_{IRRcM})$	0.49	0.18	59.5%	1.02	(0.47)	4.81	42

Considering the *representative Fund IRR* as the appropriate discount rate yields an average, standardized NPV of 1.15, implying that for an investor with 18.9% opportunity cost of capital the average investment in the sample would have created €1.15 of value for each €1 invested. In accordance with previous results, each investment would have created value from this perspective. However as previously pointed out, *Fund IRR*s comprise not only successfully realized LBO investments but also write-offs and underperforming investments. This view apparently questions the applicability of $r_{PE\ Studies}$ as the appropriate discount rate.

The NPV calculation based on r_{CS_2} overcomes this deficiency by applying the median IRR of successfully realized investments only. As expected – given the median IRR of the control sample (52.0%) being close to the reported median IRR for the analyzed sample (57.6% see Table 41) – the median NPV is close to zero. Almost half of the investments would hereby *not* have created value when applying r_{CS_2} as r_k.

The rationale for considering r_{IRRcm} is the fact that in practice ex-ante IRR calculations are – in the absence of further insights – generally based on the assumption of a constant transaction multiple. Accordingly, $r_{IRRcm} = 40.0\%$ could be regarded as the opportunity costs of capital based on the investments' operating performance. Due to the on average significantly positive impact of the external market environment and hence positive variations in the transaction

---

639 The reported figure represents the average fund IRR of two recent PE Performance Studies (see chapter I.A.2.3). Kaplan, S. N./Schoar, A. (2005) report a mean fund IRR of 18% for buyout funds for an analyzed sample of 166 buyout funds; Ljungqvist, A./Richardson, M. (2003a) report a mean fund IRR of 19.81% for 73 mature funds.

640 For details regarding the *CEPRES* control sample see chapter V.A.3.

multiple, the NPV for r_{IRRcm} amounts on average to 0.49 and is positive for 59.5% of the analyzed investments.

The high sensitivity of the NPV to the applied discount rate is obvious. To further illustrate this dependency, Chart 32 plots the NPV against continuous discount rates in the range of 0% to 100% for all investments of the analyzed sample. Again the impact of the variation in (i) the transaction multiple, (ii) revenues, and (iii) EBITDA-margin from entry to exit shall be demonstrated by displaying the corresponding NPV separately.[641] The implications are revealing:

- First, the upper-left chart reveals that assuming a zero discount rate the average standardized NPV amounts to 2.25. As a zero discount rate implies no time value of money, this number matches the average *Times Money* as reported in Table 40. Considering the other extreme and following the definition that the IRR is the discount rate that implies a zero NPV, the median standardized NPV line crosses the y-coordinate at the median *Investment IRR* of 57.6%. The concave shape obviously results from the exponential impact of time and mean/median values for the holding period of greater than one.

- Second, the vertical distance between the average and the median line in the upper-left chart illustrates once more the heterogeneity of the sample with respect to the impact of a few outliers at the upper end. In accordance with previous findings this distances reduces to almost zero when considering NPV_{cm} with constant transaction multiples. The preceding implication with respect to *Times Money* and *Investment IRR* hold true. According to Table 40, the combined contribution of the *Multiple Variation* and the *Combined Earnings/Multiple Variation* component amounts to 0.77x. This implies *Times Money* with constant transaction multiple to be 1.48x, which exactly equals the mean NPV_{cm} for r_k = zero (see upper right chart). Similarly, the median NPV_{cm} line crosses the y-coordinate at the median IRR_{cm} of 40.0% (see Table 44).

- Third, previously argued implications with respect to constant revenues and constant EBITDA-margins are confirmed. In both cases the impact on value creation is substantial, with revenue growth being the larger contributor to NPVs (see lower left-hand and right-hand charts respectively).

---

641 The corresponding adjustments to the NPV on investment level are made – in analogy to the IRR sensitivity analysis in chapter V.E.2.2 – in the equity valuation at exit E_T. Interdependencies of constant revenues and constant EBITDA-margins with Cumulated FCF Generation are considered..

Chart 32 Standardized Mean/Median NPVs against the Alternative Rate of Return

Entire sample of 42 realized LBO investments; NPV values standardized to one; subscription cm indicates constant multiples at entry and exit (see Chart 29 for details); subscription cRev indicates constant revenues throughout the holding period (see Chart 30 for details), cMrg constant EBITDA-Margin (see Chart 31 for details)
The upper line in each chart represents the average, the lower line the median

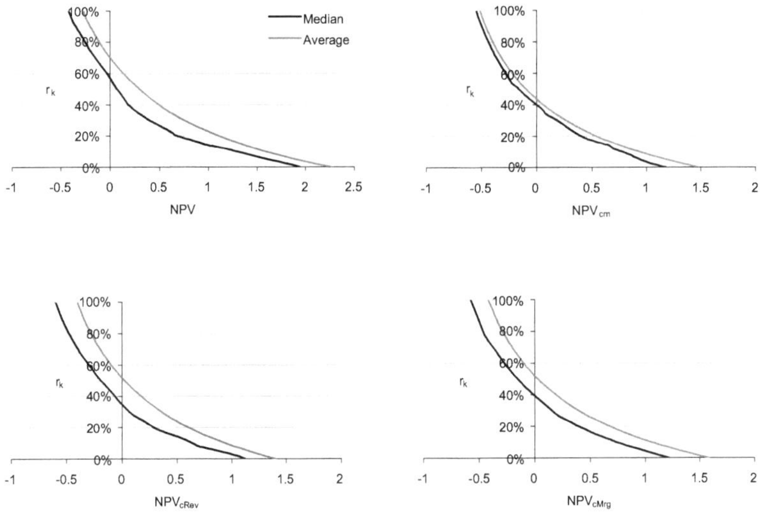

3.3 LBO Performance Measure Correlation Analysis

This thesis introductorily discussed and empirically analyzed various different ex-post value creation and LBO investment performance measures. Although each measure is imperfect in some respect, it contributes to the understanding of value creation in LBOs on investment level. A brief discussion of the corresponding correlations shall conclude here.

Table 50 LBO Performance Measure Correlation Analysis

Entire sample of 42 realized LBO investments; subscription cm indicates constant multiples at entry and exit; subscription cRev indicates constant revenues throughout the holding period, cMrg constant EBITDA-Margin; NPVs standardized on investment level by indexing E_t to one; subscriptions of NPVs specify the applied discount rate with PE Studies representing a representative fund IRR and, CS_2 being the median Investment IRR of the CEPRES control sample

	Times Money				Investment IRR				Alternative Measures			
	Total TM	Δ EB ITDA	Δ m	Σ FCF	IRR	IRR_{cm}	IRR_{cRev}	IRR_{cMrg}	ER	$NPV_{PE\ Studies}$	NPV_{CS_2}	NPV_{IRRcM}
Total TM	1.00	**0.28**	**0.78** [2]	0.44	**0.58** [3]	0.65	0.55	0.57	0.55	**0.94**	**0.82**	**0.86** [3]
Δ EB ITDA		1.00	**(0.26)** [1]	(0.22)	(0.19)	0.18	(0.31)	(0.22)	(0.25)	0.09	(0.08)	(0.04)
Δ m			1.00	0.28	0.76	0.43	0.77	0.76	0.76	0.87	0.88	0.88
Σ FCF				1.00	0.19	0.44	0.30	0.20	0.22	0.39	0.34	0.36
IRR					1.00	**0.60**	**0.97**	**0.98** [2]	0.99	**0.75**	**0.85**	**0.82** [3]
IRR_{cm}						1.00	0.58	0.51	0.56	0.76	0.77	0.78
IRR_{cRev}							1.00	0.93	0.97	0.72	0.83	0.80
IRR_{cMrg}								1.00	0.97	0.72	0.81	0.78
ER									1.00	0.72	0.82	0.80
$NPV_{PE\ Studies}$										1.00	0.96	0.98
NPV_{CS_2}											1.00	0.80
NPV_{IRRcM}												1.00

Table 50 displays the correlations between the various analyzed LBO investment performance measures, clustered alongside *TM*, *Investment IRR* and *Alternative Measures*. Particularly noteworthy findings are circled and in boldface.

- First, *EBITDA Variation* correlates negatively with *Multiple Variation*. Seemingly, the understanding that companies that managed to improve their operations during the holding period merit a positive variation in the transaction multiple seems to be flawed. Rather, the previous derived implications that (i) investments that offer huge potential for operational performance improvement demand a purchase price premium at entry, and (ii) variations in the transaction multiple are, by a long way, mostly driven by external, capital market environment aspects, seem to be confirmed.

- Second, due to the heterogeneity of the $g\_m_{t-1,T-1}$ distribution, TM and *Investment IRR* correlate much more positively with (proxies for) *Multiple Variation* (IRR_{cRev} and IRR_{cMrg}) than with proxies for *EBITDA Variation* (IRR_{cm}). As a consequence the *Investment IRR* actually correlates negatively with *EBITDA Variation*.

- Third, *TM* and *Investment IRR* have a high (and very significant) correlation with 0.58. However, regarding their respective correlations with the various NPV measures, *TM* apparently seems to be the better proxy for *value creation* than the *Investment IRR*. Obviously, the lower the considered rate of return for the alternative investment opportunity, the more this holds true. Only for very high levels of r_k does the *Investment IRR* correlate higher than *Times Money* with the standardized NPV in the analyzed sample.

VI. Conclusion

This thesis aims to shed light on value creation in LBOs from an equity investor perspective on investment level. Introductorily (and in more detail in the research model), two sets of questions have been laid out that are identified as research gaps in LBO literature and therefore are intended to be addressed herewith. First, the question regarding the individual components of/and their relative contribution to *TP* and subsequently value creation in LBO investments. Second, the question regarding internal as well as external aspects and determinants affecting the variation of these components and hence driving value creation in LBO investments.

A. Components of/and their Relative Contribution to Value Creation Measures

Based upon the calculation of *Total Proceeds* this thesis analyzed (i) *Times Money*, (i) *Investment IRRs*, and (iii) *Excess Returns* as well as *Standardized NPVs*.

- *Times Money (TM)* has the repeatedly stated shortcoming of neither accounting for the timing of the cash flows nor the associated risk. However, given its practical relevance and ease of decomposition into the identified five components of value creation, *TM* has been descriptively analyzed in chapter V.E.1. Accordingly, an investor who invested €1 in the portfolio of analyzed LBO investments would have earned €2.25 in return. The median *TM* in the sample amounts to 1.94x.
- *Investment IRR* overcomes the deficiency of *TM* with respect to the timing of cash flows. The missing risk consideration remains, though. Chapter II.C.3.2 argued that given *PE* fund dynamics the *Investment IRR* nonetheless might represent an appropriate performance measure for ex-post value creation. Furthermore, the fact that the *Investment IRR* accounts for neither the systematic nor the unsystematic risk of the particular investment provides the benefit that the inferring analysis in chapter V.E.2 can comprise, along with variables for company- and transaction-specific aspects, variables for market and macroeconomic aspects. For the analyzed sample of 42 realized investments, the mean (median) *Investment IRR* amounts to 83.0% (57.6%).
- *Alternative Performance Measures* intend to address the shortcoming of the *Investment IRR* with respect to the consideration of risk. The difficulty of specifying the appropriate discount rate has been discussed in chapter II.C.2. Apart from the fact that standard capital market models fail to assess an appropriate equity beta for a portfolio investment, there seems to be a common understanding in that systematic as well as unsystematic risk is priced in *PE* investing. *Excess Returns* compared with the *PM* still amount to 49.7% for the median investment (mean 80.2%). In light of the high *Investment IRRs*, Standardized NPVs

are on average positive, i.e. value has been created for the three considered alternative rates of return $r_{PE\ Studies}$, r_{CS_2} and r_{IRRcm}.

The starting point for the theoretical as well as empirical analysis was the decomposition of TP to equity investors according to the LBO transaction model into the non-mutually exclusive components (i) *EBITDA Variation*, (ii) *Multiple Variation*, (iii) *combined EBITDA/Multiple effect*, (iv) *Cumulated FCF Generation*, and (v) *Transaction Costs.*

EBITDA Variation and Cumulated FCF Generation

EBITDA Variation for valuation purposes represents according to this decomposition by far the most important single component and accounts on average for 60.6% of *TP* relative to the other components and for 45.3% of *Times Money*. The corresponding figures for *Cumulated FCF Generation* used for debt repayment or dividend distribution purposes are 27.6% and 21.8% respectively. This has various implications.

First, the relatively small contribution of debt repayment is remarkable. The understanding of LBOs as means to mostly create value (i.e. increasing the equity rate of return) through benefiting from returns on invested capital in excess of (after-tax) debt financing costs, i.e. through deleveraging, seems obsolete. The importance of operational performance improvement outweighs by far the pure deleveraging effect. This implication is further enforced when taking into account that part of the stated figures for deleveraging obviously result from operational improvements during the holding period. Accounting for these interdependencies, the pure contribution of the firm's steady performance for debt repayment and potentially distribution of interim dividends to equity investors has been approximated at 13.1% of *Times Money* only.

Second, these figures apparently imply that the ancient understanding of the ideal LBO candidate as being characterized by large and stable cash flows needs to be revised. Rather, based on the outlined findings, an ideal LBO candidate seems to be characterized by substantial restructuring and hence operational performance improvement *potential* at entry. Such potential is intended to materialize during the holding period until the exit in *EBITDA Variation*. In simple words, most value is created by selling the LBO company with a higher EBITDA level than when it was initially bought. The business' prevailing ability to generate cash at entry can of course not be underestimated as (in combination with projections) it sets the basis for the LBO financing structure, which clearly affects the value creation in LBOs substantially. However, whereas in early-stage *VC* investments this understanding is well-established it is remarkable that even in large-scale LBO investments, from an equity investor perspective money is earned mostly through operational performance improvement.

Third, the differences in the aforementioned figures regarding the average, relative importance of the component (vis-à-vis) the other components, compared with the average absolute importance for *Times Money*, implies already that the third primary component, *Multiple Variation*, accounts for most of the heterogeneity and extreme tails of the *Times Money* distribution. In other words, the average relative importance of *EBITDA Variation* and *Cumulated FCF Generation* decreases in the average, absolute *Times Money* consideration at the expense of the *Multiple Variation* component.

Variation in FCF Components

Splitting up EBITDA in a first step in its two primary components, revenue and EBITDA-margin reveals the importance of both of these components. An average revenue CAGR of 8.1% in combination with an average EBITDA-margin CAGR of 7.2% during the holding period imply EBITDA to increase on average 15.8% annually. These results, in particular with respect to revenue growth, are comparable for the *steady sample*, implying that historically LBO investments benefited substantially from organic growth. To put this in numbers, even leaving aside for the moment the impact on *Cumulated FCF Generation* as well as the Combined EBITDA/Multiple effect, revenue growth contributed on average more than 31% to TP (i.e. relative to the other components). Still, the average EBITDA-margin improvement is remarkable: for an imaginary, average investment with say 10% EBITDA-margin at entry and 3 years holding period the results imply an increase in the EBITDA-margin to 12.3% at exit. For a reduced sub-sample it appears that this increase in EBITDA-margin exceeds the previous formulated expectations at entry, whereas forecasts with respect to revenue growth are generally not met. As expected, improvements in SG&A-margin (in relative terms) contribute most to these EBITDA-margin improvements.

Whereas the personnel cost margin is found to decrease and hence contribute to EBITDA-margin improvements, employment levels are found to increase by as much as 5.4% on average annually during the holding period of an average LBO investment. Hence, promoting LBO investments as socially beneficial, this thesis actually reports a mean/median increase in employment levels of as much as 16.2% and 7.0% respectively during the holding period with 70% of the analyzed investments experiencing positive variations. A main aspect of the nonetheless decreasing personnel cost margin might be the fact that a sizeable fraction of not only management but also other employees is incentivized through variable equity-linked compensation components.

Reductions in relative NWC levels are significant, with the decrease in relative inventory levels accounting for most of this positive effect. For more than three-quarters of the considered investments inventories decrease in relative terms; on average by as much as -17.1%. Similarly the generally predicted decrease in relative capital expenditures can be confirmed; with variations being negative as predicted for about two-thirds of the investments and the mean/median annual decrease amounting to -10.3%/-11.2%.

Despite these improvements, however, capital investment spending still accounts for most of the cash outflow during the holding period. Using a net debt-bridge from entry to exit, total cumulated EBITDA generation during the holding period is found to be eaten up mostly by CapEx (28.7%) and cash interest expenses (25.7%). Including further cash flow components, net debt is found to decrease on average (median) by 19.2% (14.5%) only.

Multiple Variation

Pure *Multiple Variation* accounts on average for 17.4% in relative terms compared to the other components of *TP* and for 28.0% in absolute terms of *Times Money*. This increase is due to the heterogeneity of the distribution of the variations in the transaction multiple. For a few investments, multiple variation accounts for most of *Times Money* and hence obviously affects the average contribution to this performance measure across the entire sample to a larger extent as when standardized to 100% on investment level first.

The reason for this substantial contribution of *Multiple Variation* is that historically almost three-quarters of the analyzed transactions experienced a $P/EBITDA_{LTM}$ multiple expansion between the entry and the exit of the investment; on average by as much as 20.2% or 1.0x multiple points. A few transactions in the sample, named *quick flips*, are characterized by high levels of multiple expansion in combination with a comparably short holding period. Interestingly, in light of the financing as well as debt and equity capital market environment of the analyzed time period 1993–2004, IPO exited investments are on average not characterized by significantly higher levels of multiple expansion compared with secondary buyout exited LBO investments. This might imply that – apart from further influencing considerations and purely based upon the realizable price decision criterion – secondary buyout exits do not necessarily need to be considered as the exit of second choice. Comparing the funding structure of secondary buyout transactions reveals that on average a combination of increasing leverage (both in terms of senior as well as subordinated debt) and constant gearing ratios causes the positive multiple expansion. Apart from attributing the increasing leverage entirely to a more favourable financing environment, it might be interesting to consider a second fact. Secondary buyouts are presumably less risky/volatile (i.e. with more predictable cash equity streams) investments and hence merit higher levels of debt financing.

Transaction costs are quite substantial in LBO investments. Entry transaction costs account for no less than 4.1% of Total Sources to fund the transaction. In combination with any interim transaction costs the total contribution amounts to -8.3% relative to the other components and to -6.2% of *Times Money* in absolute terms. Provocatively, transaction costs represent roughly one-third of *Cumulated FCF Generation* and hence about half of total debt repayment from an aggregated perspective.

B. Determinants of Value Creation in LBO Investments

In order to account for the duality in the LBO value creation process of (i) company- and transaction-specific factors on the one hand, as well as (ii) external factors on the other hand this thesis has applied a two-tier framework. Such conceptual framework helps to structure the analysis of determinants of value creation in a first step. Based thereupon the corresponding hypotheses were derived and empirically tested in a second step. Apart from the higher level of granularity, the separate consideration of internal and external aspects and, therefore, of the aggregated perspective, provides the opportunity to reveal potentially offsetting effects. The following summarizes findings for the identified and tested determinants and discusses some implications.

- *Size*. Although some evidence could be found for larger firms offering (as expected) more operational performance improvement potential, smaller firms do perform better on an aggregated perspective. Apparently, the negative effect of size on revenue growth in combination with the growth rate arithmetic seems to dominate. Considering smaller investment as the superior investment choice might be injudicious though. As introductorily pointed out when considering the *Investment IRR* in more detail, this performance measure abstracts from accounting for the absolute amount invested. From a fund perspective with a limited amount of realizable investment opportunities given restrictions regarding resources and time, it might very well be preferable to invest more money in a relatively less performing investment. In other words, given the opportunity costs of uninvested capital the aggregated fund return might actually be higher when choosing the larger though comparably lower IRR investment. Nonetheless, in terms of *Investment IRR*, smaller firms outperform larger firms as reported.

- *Profitability*. As predicted less profitable firms seem to offer more operational performance improvement potential and are hence better performing investments in terms of *Investment IRR*. Although the significance vanishes on the aggregated performance level results are consistent and as predicted for internal *FCF effects*. Potential interdependencies of profitability with financing parameters cannot be found. Accordingly, searching for companies with comparably low/depressed levels of profitability seems to be a viable investment selection criterion given that the potential to overly increase profitability levels is simply higher.

- *Managerial Incentivation*. Owing to the irrelevancy with respect to the variation in internal perspective *FCF effects*, managerial ownership has not been considered further regarding the impact on LBO value creation and performance measures. In other words, while managerial incentivation as such represents a crucial and undoubted aspect of *PE* investing, the relative managerial ownership stake does not seem to serve as an indicator for LBO performance as no linear relationship with positive *FCF effects* can be found.

- *Disciplining Debt*. A high gearing ratio at entry is – as consistently predicted – a highly relevant determinant for LBO investment performance. Not only does it serve high levels of debt financing as a disciplinary tool with respect to positive internal perspective *FCF effects*, but also it seems that the gearing ratio represents a positive indicator for *Multiple Variation*. Most importantly, apart from the basic leverage effect on the equity rate of return, a high entry gearing ratio stands for an attractive entry purchase price for reasons discussed. The implication for *PE* investing is that relatively high gearing ratios at entry not only formally decrease the ex-ante expected equity rate of return but also limit the potential for beneficial multiple expansion. In other words, relatively high purchase prices that potentially coincide with high gearing ratios should not have the delusive effect of overrating exit opportunities and overestimating exit multiples.
- *Management Support*. The analysis of internal perspective *FCF effects* found hardly any support for *Management Support*. Presumably, other than with respect to early stage *VC* investing, large scale buyouts potentially offer fewer opportunities for *PE* firms to establish hands-on operational involvement as a differentiating criterion. Implications are far-reaching. At first, *PE* firm experience seems not to be a direct determinant of LBO investment performance. However, as hinted in the intermediary results regarding the internal perspective, *PE* firm experience might materialize as a differentiating value-adding criterion on fund level regarding superior investment selection capabilities. In other words, experienced funds just do smarter deals. The discussion regarding the impact on LBO investment performance is controversial though. Superior selection capabilities might indeed affect LBO investment performance indirectly. Experienced *PE* firms potentially identify investment opportunities in which their operational and strategic involvement facilitates realize an *Investment IRR* that justifies the capital commitment. Broadly speaking, adding value through experience does not necessarily imply a (linear) relation with the LBO performance measure.
- *Fundamental Value Drivers*: Disappointingly, no statistical significance can be confirmed regarding the impact of fundamental value drivers identified in the context of the RNV theorem. The differential in the realized EBITDA growth rate prior to the LBO and during the LBO holding period as proxy for differences in growth expectations seems to have only a little relevance for the variation in the relative valuation and hence on LBO investment performance. Similarly, the differential in the prevailing risk-free interest rate seems not to be a determinant of LBO investment performance as predicted. Given the outlined

interdependencies with the holding period this differential may even have a controversial impact.

- *Capital Market Attractiveness*: Proxies for differentials in the debt and equity capital market attractiveness were found to be significant with respect to both the external as well as the LBO investment performance perspective. Accordingly, LBO investment timing capabilities seem to be a crucial determinant for the corresponding performance. The profane *buy low and sell high* view can be transformed to the equity capital market attractiveness in that buying in a minimally attractive but selling in a highly attractive market environment turns out to be a significant determinant for multiple variation and hence LBO investment performance. The impact of potential information asymmetries in the divestment process could only be tested for with respect to the external perspective of IPO exited LBO investments. Hereby multiple expansion coincides with the fraction of equity ownership sold. As pointed out, the causality can be discussed critically though. LBO equity investors might take advantage from comparably high valuation levels by selling a high fraction of their stake. However, the theoretical line of reasoning assumes that the IPO price range is – together with the primary and secondary component – endogenously set by the LBO equity investors. IPO equity investors hereby have a limited possibility to react by impacting the price (for successful IPOs) within this set price range only.

Testing for the three control variables *Region*, *EntryMode* and *Time* turned out to be insightful.

- *Region*: The distinction between more and less shareholder value oriented countries is not conclusively unequivocal. On the one hand few variations in NWC and its components support the prediction of the working hypothesis in that more shareholder value oriented countries are characterized by more favorable variations. On the other hand, however, no significant variations can be found either regarding further internal perspective *FCF effects*, or with respect to the external perspective variations in the transaction multiple. Also, the effect with respect to value creation/the performance of the LBO investment is not significant. On the other hand no significance could be found for the contrary effect in that LBO investments in relatively less shareholder value oriented countries offer more potential to improve the operational performance given potentially depressed profitability levels. However, since the formulation of the hypothesis is already apparently controversial as discussed, no final conclusion and implication shall be drawn with respect to regional considerations here.

- *Time*: Interestingly, internal perspective *FCF effects* are not found to be significantly better for the sub-sample of early investments: in other words, good news for *PE* firms in that potentials for operational performance improvements seem not to vanish over time. Recent transactions alike still offer substantial improvement opportunities. The concern that the potential to benefit from the (as learned) key contributor to *TP* and LBO investment performance decreases over time cannot be confirmed. However, despite (i) favorable developments regarding the debt financing markets and thus the opportunities to exit via a secondary buyout (and substantial multiple expansions for these exit modes comparable with prior IPO exits), as well as (ii) the 1999/2000 IPO boom phase in the recent sub-sample, the variation in the transaction multiple decreases significantly over time for the analyzed sample. This negative effect prevails when considering LBO investment value creation/performance. Early investments outperform recent investments. Sub-sample results indicate that the decrease in multiple expansion over time results from significantly increased relative transaction prices at entry. A potential implication apart from the well-established argument that increasingly intense competition in the *PE* market drives up relative prices might be that given more intense competition, timing capabilities of *PE* firms are less pronounced.

- *EntryMode*: The thesis distinguishes previously owner-controlled and previously management-controlled companies. As theoretically argued and subsequently predicted, empirical support could be found that *FCF effects* during the holding period of the investment are higher for previously management-controlled companies. In other words, benefits of the LBO governance structure such as the alignment of interests and the monitoring and control effects seem to be limited and already partially implemented prior to the LBO for previously owner-controlled companies. Interestingly though, these improvements and the corresponding higher growth rates of *FCF* seem to be anticipated by the market, in particular the seller: the variation in the transaction multiple is significantly lower for previously management-controlled companies, implying that entry prices (and hence the corresponding transaction multiple) seem to reflect the superior improvement potential. It might be argued that this presumably relatively higher entry transaction multiple comprises a control premium reflecting the anticipated opportunities for value creation in previously management-controlled companies. This finding of comparably lower variations in transaction multiples for going privates and divisional buyouts matches nicely the findings of substantial acquisition premia paid in going private transactions. In light of this argumentation the observed degree of multiple expansion in the analyzed sample of 20.2% on average and positive for almost three-quarters of the investments, is even more remarkable. Abstracting from further impacting factors (such as the capital market environment), the above argumentation implies that previously management-controlled investments that require the payment of a control premium at entry, should rather experience a multiple contraction at exit since then much of the benefits arising from operational performance improvements have already been realized. In other words, the relative valuation of *all* investments at exit (regardless of their mode of entry) should not comprise such a control premium. Accordingly, it could be hypothesized that the multiple expansion of previously owner-controlled investments represents a purer indicator for externally induced variations in the multiple since doing so compares the valuations on a like-for-like basis regarding the ownership structure and hence disregards potential control premia. The fact that the percentage of investments under previous management control that experienced a multiple expansion (81.3%) exceeds the corresponding percentage for pre-LBO owner-controlled companies (69.2%) supports this line of reasoning. For this sub-sample the multiple increased on average by as much as 24.2% up to the time of the exit.

The analysis reveals that the investment performance decreases with the holding period of the investment. The decomposition analysis provides further insight in that the outperformance of these investments with, by comparison, short holding periods results from the negative correlation between holding period and the variation in the transaction multiple. These investments, combining short holding periods in combination with high levels of multiple expansion were named *quick flips*. As most of these investments are succession buyouts it might be hypothesized that these investments predominantly created value at the expense of uninformed, private pre-buyout shareholders by arbitraging between private and public/institutional private markets.

C. Discussion and Outlook

The purpose of this thesis is the analysis of value creation in LBO investments from an equity investor perspective. The empirical results with respect to the components and determinants of value creation in LBO investment as summarized in the preceding chapter are to a large extent novel and insightful. Throughout the conceptual and empirical analysis associated challenges have been emphasized and critically discussed, key aspects of which shall briefly be highlighted.

The holistic view, i.e. the conjoint consideration of (i) internal, company- and transaction-specific aspects, as well as (ii) external, capital market environment related aspects, resulting from the objective function *value creation in successful LBO investments from an equity investor perspective*, bears three major, related challenges.

- The decomposition of *Total Proceeds* as the pre-requisite for value creation analysis according to the LBO transaction model might be considered commonly exhaustive but falls short in being mutually exclusive. As pointed out *EBITDA Variation* and *Multiple Variation* interfere in that, theoretically, changes in (i) the firm's profitability, as well as its (ii) long-term expected, future growth rate impact the transaction multiple.
- The discussion of individual sources of value creation structured alongside the conceptual two-tier framework of an internal and external perspective addresses various determinants.

However, despite this holistic view, there are likely to be further non-considered aspects that affect value creation in LBO investments.

- In light of the quantitative nature of the empirical analysis, the operationalization of various rather qualitative aspects is troublesome. This concerns in particular the involvement of the financial sponsor, referred to as *Management Support*.

Empirical results for the analysis of 42 realized LBO investments seem to partially alleviate these concerns. First, the theoretically predicted interference between variations in the operational performance and variations in the transaction multiple cannot – as discussed – be empirically confirmed. Rather, improvement potentials seem to be anticipated by selling shareholders at entry inducing them to demand a premium. Such premium apparently negatively affects *Multiple Variation*. Second, the R^2 of the *Investment IRR* regression analyses (see chapter 2.3) are remarkably high, implying that the identified determinants explain a relatively large fraction of total value creation in LBO investments.

However, the empirical analysis itself is without any doubt characterized by limitations.

- First, and most importantly, owing to restrictive, though necessary, deal selection criteria and constraints regarding data availability, the analyzed sample comprises no more than 42 realized LBO investments. While the novelty of the analyses justifies the relatively small sample size, comparable tests on selected findings with larger sample sizes are desirable in order to confirm the generality of the derived implications.
- Second, the analysis focuses on successfully realized LBO investments only. As repeatedly pointed out, write-offs and underperforming investments, which as learned substantially affect *PE* fund performance, are not considered. Given this survivor bias the implications are constrained to successful LBOs only.
- Third, given the focus of the thesis, comparisons with a matching sample of companies that did not experience a LBO, were not conducted.
- Fourth, as with any empirical analysis of quantitative nature, data availability and data consistency impose restrictions. As briefly pointed out previously this concerns among other things accounting data in general and the calculation of LTM figures and comprehensive cash flow information during the holding period in particular.

As a consequence, conducted sub-sample analyses and regression-based findings regarding the determinants of value creation have to be interpreted with great caution and strictly within the scope of this thesis.

Nonetheless, several aspects give confidence with respect to the validity and generality of reported key findings.

- First, several main implications drawn from the empirical analysis are based upon, and confirmed by various different analyses and tests. Separately derived findings with respect to the internal as well as external perspective coincide with respect to the effect on LBO performance measures. Also, in particular with respect to these LBO performance measures, the relative importance of components for value creation in LBO investments and the respective determinants are consistent for the different analyzed measures. Inconsistencies of the numerous analyses and tests were not found.

- Second, the magnitude of mean/median and standard deviations of the derived *Investment IRR* are broadly validated. With respect to a control sample of aggregated cash flow based *Investment IRRs*, distribution characteristics for *Investment IRRs* of the analyzed sample are highly comparable. Further, differences to recently reported *Fund IRRs* are explicable. As outlined the focus on realized investments as well as the consideration net of fees and carried interest substantially dilutes comparable *Fund IRRs*. Also in this context, cross-sectional analyses of these *Fund IRR*s justify relatively higher *Investment IRRs* for a sample of larger, predominantly IPO exited LBO investments of experienced funds.[642] The relative validity of *Investment IRR* distribution characteristics is of particular relevance as it provides confidence regarding the highly sensitive bottom-up calculation of *Investment IRRs* based on transaction prices, entry and exit capital structures and interim equity streams.

To conclude, the empirical analysis seems to address and meet the introductorily formulated questions and expectations. Based upon a conceptual, holistic framework, components of value creation in LBOs on investment are quantified and descriptively analyzed. The impact of various theoretically derived determinants of value creation can be quantified. Apart from this, additional insights arising from the novel database contribute to a more objective debate regarding *PE* investing in general. A comparison of various LBO performance measures completes the analysis. Clearly, further comparable studies with an alternative or extended set of investments are desirable to challenge and preferably confirm the derived findings and implications. Also in this respect, further detailed empirical studies regarding the impact of individual aspects of value creation on the actual LBO performance on investment level would be valuable.

---

642 See Kaplan, S. N./Schoar, A. (2005), pp. 1791-1823. Experienced funds are, among others, more likely to successfully realize LBO investments.

Appendix

Appendix A Details regarding the derivation of equation (81) in chapter III.C.2.2.1

Starting point is the expected end of period 1 utility according to equation (79).

$$(91)\quad E\left(U(\widetilde{W}_1)\right)=\alpha\left[p\mu+(1-p)\mu(\alpha,Dis)\right]+M\widetilde{r}_M+\left[W_0+(1-\alpha)(\mu(\alpha,Dis)-Dis)-I\right]$$

$$-\frac{b}{2}\left[\alpha^2\sigma^2+M^2\sigma_M^2+\alpha^2p(1-p)(\mu-\mu(\alpha,Dis))^2\right]$$

Substituting for $\mu(\alpha,Dis)$, equation (77) and for δ equation (73) yields

$$(92)\quad E\left(U(\widetilde{W}_1)\right)=\alpha p\mu+(1-p\alpha)\mu^L(\alpha)+\frac{\bar{r}_M^2}{2b\sigma_M^2}+W_0-I$$

$$-\frac{b}{2}\left[\alpha^2\sigma^2+\alpha^2p(1-p)(\mu-\mu(\alpha,Dis))^2\right]$$

Setting $\mu=\mu(\alpha,Dis)$ for the optimal *Dis* equation (92) reduces to

$$(93)\quad E\left(U(\widetilde{W}_1)\right)=\alpha p\mu+(1-p\alpha)\mu^L(\alpha)+\frac{\bar{r}_M^2}{2b\sigma_M^2}+W_0-I$$

With $\mu_\alpha^L(\alpha)=\frac{\alpha}{1-\alpha p}b\sigma_L^2$ the first order condition of equation (93), $\frac{\partial E\left(U(\widetilde{W}_1)\right)}{\partial\alpha}=0$

$$(94)\quad p\mu+\alpha b\left(\sigma_L^2-\sigma^2\right)-p\mu^L(\alpha)=0$$

which is satisfied for

$$(95)\quad \sigma^2=\sigma_L^2+\frac{p}{\alpha b}\left(\mu-\mu^L(\alpha)\right)$$

In combination with equation (77), the signaling schedule for the firm's variance according to equation (81) results.

$$(96)\quad \sigma^2(\alpha,Dis)=\sigma_L^2+\frac{(1-\alpha)p}{(1-\alpha p)\alpha b}Dis$$

Appendix B Predicted Signs of Coefficients for Internal Perspective Regression Results

Table 51 Predicted Signs of Coefficients for Internal Perspective Regression Results

Based upon (i) postulated hypotheses in chapter IV.B and (ii) expected variations of internal perspective dependent variables according to chapter IV.C; prefix c indicates CAGR during the holding period, prefix g indicates growth rate from the entry (t) to the exit (T)

	Independent Variables									
Dependent Variables	**Rev_{t-1}**	**EBITDA-Mrg_{t-1}**	**λ**	**I_t**	**CMgmt**	**Steady**	**ExpInd**	**Region**	**Entry Mode**	**Time**
EBITDA										
$c\_EBITDA_{t-1,T-1}$	+	-	+	+	+	-	+	-	+	-
$c\_Rev_{t-1,T-1}$	0	+	0	-	+	0	+	0	-	0
$c\_EBITDA\text{-}Mrg_{t-1,T-1}$	+	-	+	+	+	-	+	-	+	-
$c\_CoGS\text{-}Mrg_{t-1,T-1}$	-	+	-	-	-	+	-	+	-	+
$c\_SG\&A\text{-}Mrg_{t-1,T-1}$	-	+	-	-	-	+	-	+	-	+
Employment Details										
$c\_Employ\text{-}Mrg_{t-1,T-1}$	-	+	-	-	-	+	-	+	-	+
$c\_Employment_{t-1,T-1}$	+	-	+	+	+	-	+	-	-	-
$c\_LaborProd_{t-1,T-1}$	+	-	+	+	+	-	+	-	+	-
NWC										
$g\_NWC\text{-}rel_{t-1,T-1}$	-	+	-	-	-	+	-	+	-	+
$c\_Inv_{t-1,T-1}$	-	+	-	-	-	+	-	+	-	+
$c\_AccRec_{t-1,T-1}$	-	+	-	-	-	+	-	+	-	+
$c\_AccPay_{t-1,T-1}$	+	-	+	+	+	-	+	-	+	-
CapEx										
$\Delta CapEx\text{-}rel_{t-1,T-1}$	-	+	-	-	-	+	-	+	-	+

Appendix C Details by Sub-samples

Table 52 Details for Size and Profitability Variables by Sub-samples

Mean and median values of size and profitability variables by Region, EntryMode and Time sub-samples; absolute numbers in €m (converted at the respective date effective spot exchange rate) except for employment; relevant number of transactions displayed separately when reduced compared with total sample; IV indicates applied independent variables
*Mann-Whitney test applied for mean difference tests; levels of significance: *** $p<0.001$, ** $p<0.01$, * $p<0.05$, $^{(+)}$ $p<0.1$*

			By Region		By EntryMode		By Time	
		Total Sample	UK	CE	Mgmt-Controlled	Owner-Controlled	Pre Sep-1998	Post Sep-1998
	N	42	21	21	26	16	21	21
Size								
Rev $_{t-1}$ *(IV)*	Average	707.3	804.9	609.6	788.2	575.7	581.0	833.5$^{(+)}$
	Median	514.3	496.9	531.8	591.8	365.1	401.1	718.9
EBITDA $_{t-1}$	Average	99.7	117.1	82.3	113.6	77.1	70.3	129.1**
	Median	75.7	58.9	81.8	75.7	64.5	42.1	109.0
	N	38	20	18	23	15	20	18
EBITDA-CapEx $_{t-1}$	Average	62.8	68.5	56.5	67.9	55.1	43.8	83.9 **
	Median	48.9	40.2	56.9	50.9	40.9	24.7	69.1
	N	35	18	17	23	12	20	15
Assets $_{t-1}$	Average	727.0	953.6	487.1	888.0	418.4	730.8	722.0
	Median	456.2	457.9	400.0	456.2	362.2	328.5	459.7
Total Cap $_t$	Average	742.8	887.4	598.2	847.2	573.0	513.4	972.2***
	Median	504.4	489.5	536.0	573.4	386.7	366.1	777.2
	N	31	16	15	19	12	18	13
Employ $_{t-1}$	Average	5,103	5,672	4,497	5,880	3,874	4,492	5,950
	Median	3,555	4,338	3,049	4,747	2,829	3,225	4,997
Profitability								**
EBITDA-Mrg $_{t-1}$ *(IV)*	Average	17.3%	18.0%	16.6%	17.2%	17.5%	16.1%	18.5%**
	Median	14.6%	14.9%	14.4%	14.0%	16.6%	14.7%	14.4%
	N	38	20	18	23	15	20	18
EBITDA-CapEx-Mrg $_{t-1}$	Average	10.2%	9.4%	11.0%	9.3%	11.4%	8.3%	12.2%
	Median	8.9%	8.8%	9.1%	8.8%	11.2%	8.6%	9.1%
	N	37	17	20	23	14	20	17
EBITA-Mrg $_{t-1}$	Average	11.3%	11.8%	11.0%	10.5%	12.7%$^{(+)}$	11.1%	11.7%
	Median	10.8%	9.9%	11.0%	9.1%	12.6%	10.4%	10.8%

Table 53 Details for Managerial Ownership and Financing at Entry Variables by Sub-samples

Mean and median values of managerial ownership and financing at entry by Region, EntryMode and Time sub-samples; absolute numbers in €m (converted at the respective date effective spot exchange rate); relevant number of transactions displayed separately when reduced compared with total sample; IV indicates applied independent variables
*Mann-Whitney test applied for mean difference tests; levels of significance: *** $p<0.001$, ** $p<0.01$, * $p<0.05$, (+) $p<0.1$*

		Total Sample	By Region		By EntryMode		By Time	
			UK	CE	Mgmt-Controlled	Owner-Controlled	Pre Sep-1998	Post Sep-1998
	N	42	21	21	26	16	21	21
Managerial Ownership								
λ (IV)	Average	11.1%	12.4%	9.8%	11.1%	11.0%	12.4%	9.8%
	Median	10.0%	10.0%	10.0%	8.7%	10.4%	12.0%	7.2%
$Mgmt\_Owner_{abs}$	Average	23.8	29.6 *	18.0	27.1	18.4	22.2	25.4
	Median	15.9	27.0	11.5	15.9	15.0	15.2	16.0
Financing at Entry								
l_t *(IV)*	Average	64.3%	63.2%	65.4%	64.5%	63.9%	64.0%	64.6%
	Median	65.8%	65.2%	66.0%	66.1%	65.4%	64.8%	66.0%
L_t	Average	4.8x	4.8x	4.7x	4.8x	4.7x	4.5x	5.1x (+)
	Median	4.8x	4.9x	4.7x	4.9x	4.6x	4.5x	4.9x
	N	29	15	14	17	12	11	18
$Sub.Debt_t$	Average	1.5x	1.5x	1.4x	1.6x	1.2x	1.5x	1.4x
	Median	1.4x	1.5x	1.3x	1.7x	1.3x	1.6x	1.4x
	N	40	21	19	24	16	19	21
% Quasi Equity $_t$	Average	23.4%	27.1% (+)	19.4%	22.0%	25.7%	20.3%	26.3%**
	Median	22.7%	27.0%	19.2%	22.4%	25.2%	19.1%	24.3%

Table 54 Details for Entity and Equity Value and Leverage Variations by Sub-samples

Mean and median values of holding period (HP), entity and equity value variations by Region, EntryMode and Time sub-samples; absolute numbers in €m (converted at the respective date effective spot exchange rate)
*Mann-Whitney test applied for mean difference tests; levels of significance: *** $p<0.001$, ** $p<0.01$, * $p<0.05$, (+) $p<0.1$*

		Total Sample	By Region: UK	By Region: CE	By EntryMode: Mgmt-Controlled	By EntryMode: Owner-Controlled	By Time: Pre Sep-1998	By Time: Post Sep-1998
	N	42	21	21	26	16	21	21
HP	Average	30.1	29.3	30.9	31.3	28.1	26.9	33.3 *
	Median	26.5	26.0	27.0	28.5	25.5	23.0	30.0
Entity Value Variation								
V_t	Average	695.8	833.4	558.1	791.1	540.8	471.8	919.7 **
	Median	479.5	457.6	511.8	526.8	380.5	312.8	736.3
V_T	Average	1,039.5	1,188.4	890.5	1,118.1	911.7	796.2	1,282.8 (+)
	Median	875.1	750.7	876.7	898.4	736.5	611.3	1,070.0
g_V_{t-T}	Average	69.9%	62.7%	77.1%	64.7%	78.4%	89.0%	50.8% *
	Median	61.5%	53.3%	63.8%	44.1%	69.7%	80.8%	45.5%
c_V_{t-T}	Average	30.5%	25.3%	35.7%	24.3%	40.5% (+)	42.7%	18.3% *
	Median	20.5%	19.2%	22.1%	16.5%	27.3%	26.6%	15.9%
Equity Value Variation								
E_t	Average	254.3	300.2	208.3	287.4	200.4	176.0	332.6 **
	Median	166.5	160.2	172.8	195.8	136.9	119.7	265.0
E_T	Average	658.8	722.1	595.5	674.1	633.9	550.6	767.0
	Median	503.0	515.7	490.3	528.2	468.4	421.0	607.2
g_E_{t-T}	Average	215.7%	172.9%	258.5%	195.9%	247.9%	271.3%	160.1% *
	Median	187.4%	153.4%	206.6%	141.3%	210.0%	213.3%	129.1%
c_E_{t-T}	Average	87.4%	64.1%	110.8%	69.2%	117.0%	127.5%	47.4% *
	Median	47.9%	43.2%	60.3%	41.4%	71.3%	66.1%	39.3%
Gearing Ratio								
l_T	Average	33.4%	35.1%	31.6%	34.3%	31.9%	29.7%	37.0% *
	Median	32.4%	32.3%	32.4%	34.3%	31.8%	31.2%	35.2%

Table 55 Details for Total Proceeds and its Components by Sub-samples

Mean and median values for Components of Total Proceeds (TP) by Region, EntryMode and Time sub-samples
*Mann-Whitney test applied for mean difference tests; levels of significance: *** p<0.001, ** p<0.01, * p<0.05,* (+) *p<0.1*

			By Region		By EntryMode		By Time	
		Total Sample	UK	CE	Mgmt-Controlled	Owner-Controlled	Pre Sep-1998	Post Sep-1998
	N	42	21	21	26	16	21	21
Relative Composition of Total Proceeds								
EBITDA Variation	Average	60.6%	64.7%	56.4%	62.9%	56.7%	58.7%	62.4%
	Median	54.9%	58.5%	47.7%	54.9%	54.0%	55.8%	54.0%
Multiple Variation	Average	17.4%	12.5%	22.4%	14.9%	21.6%	23.7%	11.2%
	Median	21.1%	21.8%	20.4%	19.8%	22.2%	19.3%	21.8%
Combined Effect	Average	2.7%	3.5%	1.8%	1.2%	5.1%	4.2%	1.1%
	Median	7.5%	7.8%	7.1%	3.3%	8.1%	7.4%	7.8%
$\sum$ *FCF*	Average	27.6%	28.7%	26.5%	30.3%	23.2%	20.5%	34.7%(+)
	Median	20.9%	17.4%	22.7%	19.9%	21.3%	9.3%	28.7%
TC	Average	(8.3%)	(9.5%)	(7.1%)	(9.3%) (+)	(6.6%)	(7.1%)	(9.4%)
	Median	(7.1%)	(7.5%)	(7.0%)	(8.0%)	(6.6%)	(6.7%)	(8.4%)
Components of EBITDA Variation								
Revenue Effect	Average	31.4%	39.0% (+)	23.9%	30.2%	33.4%	28.4%	34.5%
	Median	23.3%	33.3%	22.8%	23.3%	24.2%	19.4%	32.0%
Margin Effect	Average	25.2%	23.6%	26.9%	27.8%	21.0%	24.9%	25.6%
	Median	17.4%	19.2%	15.3%	17.4%	17.5%	25.5%	14.0%

Table 56 Details for Dependent Variables by Sub-samples – Internal Perspective

Mean and median values of dependent variables by Region, EntryMode and Time sub-samples; relevant number of transactions displayed separately when reduced compared with the total sample
*Mann-Whitney test applied for mean difference tests; levels of significance: *** p<0.001, ** p<0.01, * p<0.05, (+) p<0.1*

		Total Sample	By Region		By EntryMode		By Time	
			UK	CE	Mgmt-Controlled	Owner-Controlled	Pre Sep-1998	Post Sep-1998
	N	42	21	21	26	16	21	21
EBITDA								
c_Rev $_{t-1,T-1}$	Average	8.1%	9.2%	7.0%	6.5%	10.7%	9.1%	7.1%
	Median	6.1%	6.0%	6.1%	5.7%	7.1%	6.5%	5.7%
c_EBITDA $_{t-1,T-1}$	Average	15.8%	16.5%	15.1%	14.8%	17.4%	18.7%	12.8% *
	Median	13.3%	13.5%	13.0%	13.0%	14.4%	17.7%	11.8%
c_EBITDA-Mrg $_{t-1,T-1}$	Average	7.2%	6.9%	7.5%	7.8%	6.1%	9.0%	5.3% *
	Median	6.7%	5.4%	8.0%	8.2%	5.2%	9.0%	4.2%
	N	38	17	21	24	14	20	18
c_CoGS-Mrg $_{t-1,T-1}$	Average	(1.1%)	(0.1%)	(1.9%) (+)	(0.8%)	(1.6%)	(1.5%)	(0.7%)
	Median	(1.0%)	(0.3%)	(1.4%)	(0.4%)	(1.6%)	(1.4%)	(0.4%)
	N	31	14	17	20	11	17	14
c_SG&A-Mrg $_{t-1,T-1}$	Average	(2.2%)	(3.3%)	(1.2%)	(3.3%)	(0.1%) (+)	(1.9%)	(2.5%)
	Median	(2.5%)	(3.5%)	(0.7%)	(3.8%)	0.9%	(2.7%)	(1.6%)
Employment Details								
	N	21	13	8	12	9	10	11
c_Employ-Mrg $_{t-1,T-1}$	Average	(2.3%)	(2.7%)	(1.6%)	(1.2%)	(3.7%)	(1.2%)	(3.2%) (+)
	Median	(2.3%)	(3.0%)	(1.0%)	(1.6%)	(3.2%)	(1.0%)	(3.8%)
	N	30	16	14	18	12	18	12
c_Employment $_{t-1,T-1}$	Average	5.4%	4.2%	6.8%	2.2%	10.2% (+)	6.7%	3.4%
	Median	3.2%	2.6%	4.4%	1.9%	7.0%	3.6%	1.6%
	N	30	16	14	18	12	18	12
c_LaborProd $_{t-1,T-1}$	Average	4.5%	5.9%	2.9% (+)	5.8%	2.5%	2.7%	7.1% *
	Median	5.1%	6.1%	3.5%	5.4%	3.5%	4.6%	7.3%
NWC								
	N	29	13	16	18	11	15	14
g_NWC-rel $_{t-1,T-1}$	Average	(10.8%)	(27.4%)	2.7%	(4.9%)	(20.6%)	(25.0%)	4.4%
	Median	(4.2%)	(12.7%)	(0.1%)	(2.2%)	(4.2%)	(8.5%)	2.3%
	N	34	16	18	22	12	18	16
c_Inv-rel $_{t-1,T-1}$	Average	(9.0%)	(14.1%)	(4.4%) (+)	(8.4%)	(9.9%)	(8.0%)	(10.1%)
	Median	(6.4%)	(10.0%)	(3.7%)	(6.4%)	(6.4%)	(7.1%)	(5.2%)
	N	32	14	18	21	11	17	15
c_AccRec-rel $_{t-1,T-1}$	Average	(4.5%)	(7.2%)	(2.5%)	(4.3%)	(4.9%)	(5.7%)	(3.2%)
	Median	(4.7%)	(6.7%)	(3.6%)	(4.7%)	(3.6%)	(4.7%)	(4.7%)
	N	29	13	16	18	11	15	14
c_AccPay-rel $_{t-1,T-1}$	Average	(3.3%)	4.5%	(9.7%) (+)	(1.6%)	(6.1%)	(0.2%)	(6.6%)
	Median	(3.6%)	4.6%	(5.6%)	(0.8%)	(5.0%)	(0.4%)	(5.6%)
CapEx								
	N	38	20	18	23	15	20	18
c_CapEx-rel $_{t-1,T-1}$	Average	(10.1%)	(11.5%)	(8.6%)	(11.9%)	(7.5%)	(11.5%)	(8.7%)
	Median	(7.0%)	(10.5%)	(6.4%)	(9.7%)	(6.0%)	(8.5%)	(6.4%)

Appendix D Details by Exit Mode

Table 57 Details for Independent Variables and Internal Perspective Dependent Variables by Exit Modes

Mean and median values of independent variables and internal perspective dependent variables by IPO exited and secondary buyout exited sub-samples; Rev_{t-1} in €m, Holding Period in months, L_t expressed as multiple of $EBITDA_{LTM}$; l_t, % Common Stock and % Quasi Equity as % of TS
*Mann-Whitney test applied for mean difference tests; levels of significance: *** $p<0.001$, ** $p<0.01$, * $p<0.05$, (+) $p<0.1$*

		Rev_{t-1}	EBITDA-Mrg_{t-1}	λ	L_t	l_t	% Common Stock (+)	% Quasi Equity
IPO Exits	Average	701.5	17.5%	11.2%	4.7x	63.1%	15.8%	22.6%
	Median	454.9	14.6%	10.6%	4.6x	64.5%	12.8%	21.6%
Secondary Buyout Exits	Average	718.8	16.9%	10.9%	5.0x	66.6%	8.5%	24.9%
	Median	574.9	14.7%	9.1%	5.0x	66.0%	7.6%	23.7%

		Δ_rf	$Δ\_g_{EBITDA}$ **	$Cum\_GDP_{t,T}$	Δ_P/E **	Δ_#_IPO *	Δ_Spread	HP
IPO Exits	Average	(0.63%)	3.9%	7.8%	4.0%	277.4%	(1.85%)	28.3
	Median	(0.59%)	5.3%	6.8%	(5.5%)	60.3%	(2.09%)	25.0
Secondary Buyout Exits	Average	(0.56%)	(8.1%)	6.0%	(12.4%)	19.8%	(0.41%)	33.7
	Median	(0.33%)	(4.9%)	4.9%	(17.3%)	(19.6%)	(1.00%)	29.0

		$c\_Rev_{t-1,T-1}$	$c\_EBITDA_{t-1,T-1}$ *	c_EBITDA-$Mrg_{t-1,T-1}$	c_CoGS-$Mrg_{t-1,T-1}$	c_SG&A-$Mrg_{t-1,T-1}$	c_Employ-$ment_{t-1,T-1}$
IPO Exits	Average	9.7%	18.4%	8.1%	(1.1%)	(2.3%)	5.9%
	Median	6.3%	16.8%	8.9%	(1.0%)	(2.6%)	3.3%
Secondary Buyout Exits	Average	4.8%	10.6%	5.3%	(1.3%)	(2.0%)	2.9%
	Median	5.8%	11.3%	4.3%	(0.9%)	(2.1%)	0.8%

		c_Labor $Prod_{t-1,T-1}$	g_NWC-$rel_{t-1,T-1}$	$c\_Inv\text{-}rel_{t-1,T-1}$	c_AccRec-rel	c_AccPay-rel	c_CapEx-$rel_{t-1,T-1}$
IPO Exits	Average	4.6%	(15.9%)	(8.8%)	(4.6%)	(2.5%)	(10.9%)
	Median	5.1%	(6.4%)	(7.2%)	(4.7%)	(3.5%)	(8.5%)
Secondary Buyout Exits	Average	3.9%	5.2%	(9.5%)	(4.2%)	(5.9%)	(7.9%)
	Median	4.4%	4.8%	(4.1%)	(4.7%)	(5.0%)	(5.0%)

Table 58 Details for Transaction Multiples and their Absolute as well as Relative Variations by Sub-samples – External Perspective

Mean and median values for absolute and relative variations in the transaction multiple by Region, EntryMode and Time sub-samples; DV indicates applied dependent variable
*Mann-Whitney test applied for mean difference tests; levels of significance: *** $p<0.001$, ** $p<0.01$, * $p<0.05$, $^{(+)}$ $p<0.1$*

			By Region		By EntryMode		By Time	
		Total Sample	UK	CE	Mgmt-Controlled	Owner-Controlled	Pre Sep-1998	Post Sep-1998
Total Sample								
	N	42	21	21	26	16	21	21
m_t	Average	7.2x	7.3x	7.1x	7.1x	7.2x	6.8x (+)	7.6x
	Median	7.1x	7.1x	6.9x	6.8x	7.1x	6.5x	7.3x
m_T	Average	8.2x	8.1x	8.3x	8.0x	8.6x	8.0x	8.4x
	Median	8.0x	8.1x	7.9x	7.9x	8.0x	7.7x	8.1x
$\Delta\_m_{t,T}$	Average	1.04x	.85x	1.23x	.82x	1.41x	1.26x	.82x
	Median	1.04x	.98x	1.70x	1.04x	1.02x	1.02x	1.05x
$g\_m_{t,T}$	Average	20.2%	13.9%	26.4%	17.7%	24.2%	25.6%	14.7%
	Median	13.8%	12.7%	21.7%	13.8%	13.8%	12.9%	13.9%
IPO Exited								
	N	28	15	13	18	10	18	10
m_t_IPO	Average	7.1x	7.1x	7.1x	7.2x	7.0x	6.6x *	8.2x
	Median	7.0x	7.1x	6.8x	7.0x	6.8x	6.5x	7.8x
m_T_IPO	Average	8.3x	8.2x	8.4x	7.9x	9.0x	8.1x	8.6x
	Median	8.2x	8.1x	8.6x	7.8x	8.4x	7.8x	8.4x
$\Delta\_m_{t,T}\_IPO$	Average	1.14x	1.06x	1.23x	.65x	2.02x	1.55x (+)	.40x
	Median	1.04x	1.02x	1.77x	.71x	1.70x	1.69x	.93x
$g\_m_{t,T}\_IPO$	Average	21.6%	16.8%	27.2%	14.3% (+)	34.9%	30.4% (+)	5.9%
	Median	13.8%	13.8%	26.0%	9.6%	23.0%	25.0%	10.3%
Secondary Buyout Exited								
	N	14	6	8	8	6	3	11
m_t_Sec	Average	7.2x	7.6x	7.0x	7.0x	7.6x	8.0x	7.0x
	Median	7.1x	7.1x	7.1x	6.8x	7.2x	7.8x	7.1x
m_T_Sec	Average	8.1x	7.9x	8.2x	8.2x	7.9x	7.6x	8.2x
	Median	7.8x	7.9x	7.8x	7.9x	7.8x	7.7x	7.9x
$\Delta\_m_{t,T}\_Sec$	Average	.84x	.34x	1.22x	1.19x	.38x	(.44x)	1.19x
	Median	.93x	.08x	1.38x	1.38x	.04x	(.08x)	1.70x
$g\_m_{t,T}\_Sec$	Average	17.2%	6.7%	25.1%	25.3%	6.4%	(2.7%)	22.7%
	Median	14.6%	1.2%	19.0%	19.0%	2.4%	(1.0%)	21.7%

Table 59 Details for Times Money and its Components by Sub-samples

Mean and median values of Times Money (TM) and its Components by Region, EntryMode, Time and ExitMode sub-samples
*Mann-Whitney test applied for mean difference tests; levels of significance: *** $p<0.001$, ** $p<0.01$, * $p<0.05$, $^{(+)}$ $p<0.1$*

		Total Sample	By Region UK	By Region CE	By Entry Mode Mgmt-Control	By Entry Mode Owner-Control	By Time Pre Sep-1998	By Time Post Sep-1998	By Exit Mode IPO	By Exit Mode Sec
	N	42	21	21	26	16	21	21	28	14
TM	Average	2.25x	1.78x	2.73x	2.11x	2.49x	2.66x	1.85x	2.40x	1.96x
	Median	1.94x	1.54x	2.01x	1.72x	2.04x	2.01x	1.65x	1.94x	1.86x
EBITDA Variation	Average	1.12x	1.05x	1.19x	1.15x	1.08x	1.29x	.95x	1.24x	.88x
	Median	.98x	.99x	.96x	.96x	1.01x	.99x	.95x	.98x	.91x
Multiple Variation	Average	.14x	.11x	.17x	.10x	.20x	.21x	.07x	.19x	.04x
	Median	.13x	.12x	.13x	.04x	.14x	.15x	.11x	.15x	.04x
Combined Effect	Average	.63x	.36x	.90x	.51x	.83x	.87x	.40x	.70x	.50x
	Median	.38x	.28x	.63x	.34x	.44x	.41x	.34x	.38x	.37x
$\sum$FCF	Average	.49x	.38x	.61x	.48x	.52x	.42x	.57x	.40x$^{(+)}$	.67x
	Median	.44x	.40x	.45x	.37x	.45x	.31x	.53x	.31x	.66x
TC	Average	(.14x)	(.13x)	(.14x)	(.14x)	(.13x)	(.13x)	(.15x)	(.14x)	(.14x)
	Median	(.13x)	(.13x)	(.13x)	(.14x)	(.13x)	(.13x)	(.14x)	(.13x)	(.13x)

Table 60 Details for Realized Investment IRR and Hypothetical Investment IRRs by Sub-samples

Mean and median values of Times Money and its Components by Region, EntryMode, Time and ExitMode sub-samples
Hypothetical IRRs indexed with (i) cm indicating constant multiple from entry to exit, (ii) cRev indicating constant revenues during the holding period and (cMrg) indicating constant EBITDA Margin during the holding period
*Mann-Whitney test applied for mean difference tests; levels of significance: *** $p<0.001$, ** $p<0.01$, * $p<0.05$, $^{(+)}$ $p<0.1$*

		Total Sample	By Region UK	By Region CE	By Entry Mode Mgmt-Control	By Entry Mode Owner-Control	By Time Pre Sep-1998	By Time Post Sep-1998	By Exit Mode IPO	By Exit Mode Sec
	N	42	21	21	26	16	21	21	28	14
IRR	Average	83.0%	65.2%	100.8%	69.3%	105.2%	113.4%*	52.6%	97.7%	53.6%
	Median	57.6%	48.0%	63.1%	42.4%	63.3%	62.2%	39.7%	57.6%	51.2%
IRR_{cM}	Average	46.4%	44.3%	48.5%	44.0%	50.4%	53.7%$^{(+)}$	39.1%	50.0%	39.3%
	Median	40.0%	36.3%	41.7%	35.8%	41.6%	48.5%	36.3%	43.1%	38.2%
IRR_{cRev}	Average	64.2%	45.9%	82.5%	55.2%	78.8%	91.7%$^{(+)}$	36.7%	75.2%	42.2%
	Median	36.3%	21.4%	43.6%	32.6%	45.6%	43.6%	21.4%	35.9%	40.2%
IRR_{cMrg}	Average	62.8%	47.0%	78.5%	48.4%	86.0%	86.8%$^{(+)}$	38.7%	74.0%	40.3%
	Median	39.4%	39.9%	36.0%	30.1%	47.4%	40.4%	38.9%	39.4%	38.2%

Appendix E Additional FCF Details

Table 61 Detailed Variations of EBITDA, Revenues and EBITDA-Margin

Change in EBITDA, revenues and EBITDA-margin between the LTM period (t-1) before the entry and the LTM period (T-1) before the exit of the investment; prefix Δ and g indicate absolute variation and growth rate from entry to exit respectively; Δ_EBITDA and Δ_Rev in €m (converted at the entry date effective spot exchange rate); steady sample with 26 investments without any acquisition and divestiture activity during the holding period
*Z-statistic to test for difference from zero; Levels of significance: *** $p<0.001$, ** $p<0.01$, * $p<0.05$, (+) $p<0.1$*

	Average	Median	% Positive Variations	Std. Dev.	Minimum	Maximum	N
Total Sample							
Δ_EBITDA $_{t-1,T-1}$	33.9 ***	29.2	97.6%	29.5	(20.8)	147.2	42
g_EBITDA $_{t-1,T-1}$	45.3%***	37.6%	97.6%	41.5%	(18.6%)	215.0%	42
Δ_Rev $_{t-1,T-1}$	139.5 **	80.5	92.9%	240.2	(206.2)	1,358.4	42
g_Rev $_{t-1,T-1}$	24.5%***	15.6%	92.9%	29.7%	(24.3%)	118.2%	42
Δ_EBITDA-Mrg $_{t-1,T-1}$	2.6% ***	2.3%	88.1%	2.4%	(1.4%)	8.7%	42
g_EBITDA-Mrg $_{t-1,T-1}$	16.4%***	18.1%	88.1%	14.6%	(12.8%)	49.3%	42
Steady Sample							
Δ_EBITDA $_{t-1,T-1}$	31.9 ***	26.6	100.0%	25.7	3.9	114.2	26
g_EBITDA $_{t-1,T-1}$	0.4 ***	34.8%	100.0%	31.7%	6.4%	156.8%	26
Δ_Rev $_{t-1,T-1}$	161.2 **	86.4	92.3%	280.9	(13.0)	1,358.4	26
g_Rev $_{t-1,T-1}$	22.8%***	13.6%	92.3%	27.9%	(6.4%)	109.4%	26
Δ_EBITDA-Mrg $_{t-1,T-1}$	2.6% ***	2.3%	92.3%	2.4%	(0.8%)	8.7%	26
g_EBITDA-Mrg $_{t-1,T-1}$	15.3%***	17.7%	92.3%	13.6%	(12.8%)	43.5%	26

Table 62 Detailed Variations of CoGS-Margin and SG&A-Margin

Change in CoGS- and SG&A-margin between the LTM period (t-1) before the entry and the LTM period (T-1) before the exit of the investment; prefix Δ and g indicate absolute variation and growth rate from entry to exit respectively; steady sample with 26 investments without any acquisition and divestiture activity during the holding period
*Z-statistic to test for difference from zero; levels of significance: *** $p<0.001$, ** $p<0.01$, * $p<0.05$, (+) $p<0.1$*

	Average	Median	% Negative Variations	Std. Dev.	Minimum	Maximum	N
Total Sample							
Δ_CoGS-Mrg $_{t-1,T-1}$	1.4% **	1.1%	31.6%	2.5%	(5.0%)	7.7%	38
g_CoGS-Mrg $_{t-1,T-1}$	(2.8%)*	(1.7%)	68.4%	6.5%	(23.8%)	12.9%	38
Δ_SG&A-Mrg $_{t-1,T-1}$	1.3% *	0.7%	35.5%	3.6%	(4.7%)	12.8%	31
g_SG&A-Mrg $_{t-1,T-1}$	(3.0%)	(6.0%)	64.5%	13.7%	(31.1%)	35.8%	31
SteadySample							
Δ_CoGS-Mrg $_{t-1,T-1}$	1.6% **	1.0%	30.4%	2.4%	(1.7%)	7.7%	23
g_CoGS-Mrg $_{t-1,T-1}$	(3.4%)*	(1.9%)	69.6%	5.8%	(23.8%)	3.9%	23
Δ_SG&A-Mrg $_{t-1,T-1}$	0.8%	0.6%	35.0%	3.7%	(4.7%)	12.8%	20
g_SG&A-Mrg $_{t-1,T-1}$	(1.7%)	(4.6%)	65.0%	15.6%	(31.1%)	35.8%	20

Table 63 Additional Employment Details and Detailed Variation of R&D-Margin[643]

Employment details and change in R&D-margin between the LTM period (t-1) before the entry and the LTM period (T-1) before the exit of the investment; prefix Δ and g indicate absolute variation and growth rate from entry to exit respectively
*Z-statistic to test for difference from zero; levels of significance: *** p<0.001, ** p<0.01, * p<0.05,(+) p<0.1*

	Average	Median	% Negative Variations	Std. Dev.	Minimum	Maximum	N
Δ_Employ-Mrg $_{t-1,T-1}$	1.0% *	0.9%	23.8%	1.8%	(2.6%)	5.0%	21
g_Employ-Mrg $_{t-1,T-1}$	(3.9%)(+)	(4.3%)	76.2%	10.3%	(26.7%)	28.3%	21
Δ_Employment $_{t-1,T-1}$	495 (+)	266	30.0%	1,500	(3,206)	4,828	30
g_Employment $_{t-1,T-1}$	16.2%**	7.0%	30.0%	31.5%	(27.7%)	120.4%	30
g_LaborProd $_{t-1,T-1}$	11.5%***	10.2%	23.3%	15.2%	(16.2%)	47.9%	30
Δ_R&D-Mrg $_{t-1,T-1}$	0.3%	0.2%	33.3%	0.9%	(1.4%)	1.5%	9
g_R&D-Mrg $_{t-1,T-1}$	1.6%	(1.3%)	55.6%	20.9%	(26.8%)	43.2%	9

Table 64 Detailed Variations of Relative Net Working Capital and its Components

Changes in NWC and its components between the LTM period (t-1) before the entry and the LTM period (T-1) before the exit of the investment; 'narrow' NWC defined as the sum of inventories and accounts receivable less any accounts payable including prepayments and advances; all variables expressed relative to current year revenues; prefix Δ and g indicate absolute variation and growth rate from entry to exit respectively
*Z-statistic to test for difference from zero; levels of significance: *** p<0.001, ** p<0.01, * p<0.05,(+) p<0.1*

	Average	Median	% Negative Variations	Std. Dev.	Minimum	Maximum	N
Total Sample							
Δ_NWC-rel $_{t-1,T-1}$	(0.8%)	(0.2%)	55.2%	5.5%	(14.1%)	11.6%	29
Δ_Inv-rel $_{t-1,T-1}$	(1.1%)**	(0.7%)	75.8%	1.9%	(4.6%)	3.4%	33
g_Inv-rel $_{t-1,T-1}$	(17.1%)***	(13.0%)	75.8%	24.8%	(81.0%)	17.3%	33
Δ_AccRec-rel $_{t-1,T-1}$	(1.1%)	(0.7%)	68.8%	4.0%	(14.4%)	7.7%	32
g_AccRec-rel $_{t-1,T-1}$	(6.3%)	(8.0%)	68.8%	24.6%	(47.9%)	86.1%	32
Δ_AccPay-rel $_{t-1,T-1}$	(1.3%)	(0.9%)	62.1%	5.1%	(17.8%)	7.4%	29
g_AccPay-rel $_{t-1,T-1}$	(0.5%)	(9.3%)	62.1%	44.4%	(90.5%)	107.0%	29
Steady Sample							
Δ_NWC-rel $_{t-1,T-1}$	(1.7%)	(1.5%)	72.2%	4.7%	(12.1%)	9.2%	18
Δ_Inv-rel $_{t-1,T-1}$	(1.4%)**	(1.1%)	76.2%	1.8%	(4.6%)	1.5%	21
g_Inv-rel $_{t-1,T-1}$	(17.8%)**	(13.5%)	76.2%	23.1%	(81.0%)	17.3%	21
Δ_AccRec-rel $_{t-1,T-1}$	(1.0%)	(0.7%)	80.0%	2.5%	(9.5%)	3.1%	20
g_AccRec-rel $_{t-1,T-1}$	(10.6%)*	(10.0%)	80.0%	16.2%	(42.5%)	21.4%	20
Δ_AccPay-rel $_{t-1,T-1}$	(0.9%)	(1.1%)	61.1%	4.0%	(9.8%)	7.4%	18
g_AccPay-rel $_{t-1,T-1}$	5.7%	(9.8%)	61.1%	47.9%	(90.5%)	107.0%	18

643 Due to the findings in Table 23 and Table 25 that results are relatively stable for the steady sample and owing to the reduced number of transactions for the analyzed employment and R&D variables, results are not displayed separately for the steady sample.

Table 65 Detailed Variations of Capital Expenditures

*Change in CapEx (expressed as % of revenues) between the LTM period (t-1) before the entry and the LTM period (T-1) before the exit of the investment; prefix Δ and g indicate absolute variation and growth rate from entry to exit respectively Z-statistic to test for difference from zero; levels of significance: *** p<0.001, ** p<0.01, * p<0.05,(+) p<0.1*

	Average	Median	% Negative Variations	Std. Dev.	Minimum	Maximum	N
Total Sample							
$\Delta\_CapEx\text{-}rel_{t-1,T-1}$	1.7% *	0.7%	31.6%	4.5%	(2.9%)	20.8%	38
$g\_CapEx\text{-}rel_{t-1,T-1}$	(15.6%)**	(18.8%)	68.4%	34.6%	(71.9%)	70.2%	38
Steady Sample							
$\Delta\_CapEx\text{-}rel_{t-1,T-1}$	0.8% **	0.9%	29.2%	1.6%	(2.3%)	3.6%	24
$g\_CapEx\text{-}rel_{t-1,T-1}$	(16.1%)**	(20.4%)	70.8%	34.4%	(71.9%)	70.2%	24

Appendix F Additional Regression Details

Table 66 Independent Variables Correlation Matrix

	Internal Perspective							External Perspective				Control Variables		
	Rev_{t-1}	$EBITDA\text{-}Mrg_{t-1}$	l_t	λ	*CMgmt*	*Steady*	*ExpInd*	Δ_r_f	*Δ_gEBITDA*	*Δ_#_IPOs*	α	*Region*	*Entry Mode*	*Time*
Rev_{t-1}	1.00	(0.42)	0.22	(0.24)	0.10	0.11	0.23	0.10	(0.16)	(0.35)	(0.20)	0.16	0.21	0.17
$EBITDA\text{-}Mrg_{t-1}$		1.00	0.05	0.05	(0.12)	(0.09)	(0.11)	0.04	0.10	0.15	0.05	0.08	0.14	(0.02)
l_t			1.00	(0.12)	(0.18)	(0.00)	(0.07)	(0.30)	(0.15)	(0.28)	0.21	(0.14)	0.04	0.04
λ				1.00	(0.21)	(0.29)	(0.03)	(0.04)	0.01	0.03	(0.19)	0.15	(0.15)	0.01
CMgmt					1.00	0.04	0.04	(0.06)	(0.17)	(0.17)	0.10	0.00	0.00	0.14
Steady						1.00	0.11	0.17	(0.32)	0.13	0.16	(0.10)	0.10	(0.21)
ExpInd							1.00	(0.01)	(0.18)	(0.13)	(0.25)	(0.19)	0.10	(0.08)
Δ_r_f								1.00	(0.09)	(0.15)	0.19	0.22	0.45	0.08
Δ_gEBITDA									1.00	0.33	(0.05)	0.01	(0.19)	0.08
Δ_#_IPOs										1.00	(0.09)	(0.08)	(0.45)	(0.10)
α											1.00	(0.19)	0.10	(0.08)
Region												1.00	0.05	0.10
EntryMode													1.00	(0.10)
Time														1.00

Table 67 OLS Regression Premises Tests

	$c\_EBITDA_{t-1,T-1}$	$c\_Rev_{t-1,T-1}$	$c\_EBITDA\text{-}Mrg_{t-1,T-1}$	$c\_CoGS\text{-}Mrg_{t-1,T-1}$	$c\_SG\&A\text{-}Mrg_{t-1,T-1}$	$c\_Employ\text{-}Mrg_{t-1,T-1}$	$c\_Employment_{t-1,T-1}$	$c\_Labor\text{-}Prod_{t-1,T-1}$	$g\_NWC\text{-}rel_{t-1,T-1}$
VIF (max)	2.067	1.261	2.067	2.133	2.376	1.000	1.879	1.879	1.330
Durbin-Watson	1.435	1.457	1.911	1.867	2.320	1.977	1.653	2.209	1.963
KS Z-Statistics	1.113	1.061	.846	1.211	.439	.641	.993	.681	1.125

	$c\_Inv\text{-}rel_{t-1,T-1}$	$c\_AccRec\text{-}rel_{t-1,T-1}$	$c\_AccPay\text{-}rel_{t-1,T-1}$	$c\_CapEx\text{-}rel_{t-1,T-1}$	g_m_{t,T_IPO}	ln_IRR	ln_IRR_{cM}	ln_IRR_{cRev}	ln_IRR_{cMrg}
VIF	1.976	1.960	1.609	1.983	1.750	1.609	1.785	1.744	1.742
Durbin-Watson	2.035	1.679	2.285	2.569	1.880	2.084	2.183	2.253	2.346
KS Z-Statistics	1.023	1.038	.847	.555	.821	.900	.421	.743	1.053

Table 68 Regression Results – Hypothetical Investment IRRs

ß and standardized ß using stepwise OLS regression models with logarithm of Investment IRRs as the dependent variable; hypothetical IRRs indexed with (i) cm indicating constant multiple from entry to exit, (ii) cRev indicating constant revenues during the holding period and (cMrg) indicating constant EBITDA Margin during the holding period; findings in accordance with previously postulated hypotheses (including tendencies) in boldface; findings invalidating previously postulated hypotheses (including tendencies) in italic and boldface

*Levels of significance: *** $p<0.001$, ** $p<0.01$, * $p<0.05$, $^{(+)}$ $p<0.1$*

	R^2		Independent Variables: **Rev_{t-1}**	**EBITDA-Mrg_{t-1}**	**I_t**	**Δ_r_f**	**Δ_#_IPOs**	**Entry Mode**	**Time**
ln_IRR$_{cM}$	21.9%	ß	(.000)	(.906)	**1.422**	.049	.007	(.075)	(.096)
		$ß^{stand}$	(.124)	(.173)	**.245**	.105	.093	(.078)	(.103)
ln_IRR$_{cRev}$	32.5%	ß	.000	(.988)	**8.756**	***.393***	.011	(.218)	(.504)
		$ß^{stand}$	(.184)	(.074)	**.582 ****	***.346*** (+)	.253	(.091)	(.215)
ln_IRR$_{cMrg}$	22.2%	ß	.000	1.530	**5.279**	.275	**.005**	**(.684)**	(.596)
		$ß^{stand}$	(.179)	.100	**.312** (+)	.201	**.299** (+)	**(.242)**	(.216)

Bibliography

Achleitner, Ann-Kristin; Schiereck, Dirk; Wahrenburg, Mark (2003): Meinungsspiegel zum Thema: Going Private, in: Betriebswirtschaftliche Forschung und Praxis, vol. 55, pp. 199-207.

Achleitner, Ann-Kristin; Wahl, Simon (2003): Corporate Restructuring in Deutschland – Eine Analyse der Möglichkeiten und Grenzen der Übertragbarkeit US-amerikanischer Konzepte wertsteigernder Unternehmensrestrukturierungen auf Deutschland, Sternenfels

Ainina, M. Fall ; Mohan, Nancy K. (1991): When LBOs go IPO, in: Journal of Business Finance & Accounting, vol. 18 (no. 3), pp. 393-403.

Akerlof, George A. (1970): The market for 'lemons': quality and the market mechanism, in: Quarterly Journal of Economics, vol. 84 (no. 3), pp. 488-500.

Alchian, Armen A.; Demsetz, Harold (1973): The property right paradigm, in: Journal of Economic History, vol. 33, pp. 16-27.

Allen, Franklin; Faulhaber, Gerald (1989): Signaling by underpricing in the IPO market, in: Journal of Financial Economics, vol. 23, pp. 303-323.

Allen, Franklin; Santomero, Anthony M. (1997): The theory of financial intermediation, in: Journal of Banking & Finance, vol. 21 (no. 11/12), pp. 1461-1485.

Allen, Jay (1996): LBOs - the evolution of financial structures and strategies, in: Journal of Applied Corporate Finance, vol. 8 (no. 4), pp. 18-29.

Amihud, Yakov (1989): Leveraged management buyouts and shareholders' wealth, in: Amihud, Yakov: Leveraged Management Buyouts, Homewood, Illinois, pp. 3-34.

Amihud, Yakov; Mendelson, Haim (1986): Asset pricing and the bid-ask spread, in: Journal of Financial Economics, vol. 17 (no. 2), pp. 223-250.

Anders, George (1992): The barbarians in the boardroom, in: Harvard Business Review, vol. 70 (no. 4), pp. 79-87.

Andres, Christian; Betzer, André; Hoffmann, Mark (2004): Going private via LBO - shareholder gains in the European market, Working Paper, University of Bonn, pp. 1-39.

Angbazo, Lazarus A.; Mei, Jianping; Saunders, Anthony (1998): Credit spreads in the market for highly leveraged transaction loans, in: Journal of Banking & Finance, vol. 22 (no. 10), pp. 1249-1282.

Arbeitskreis Finanzierung (1990): Arbeitskreis Finanzierung der Schmalenbach-Gesellschaft/ Deutsche Gesellschaft für Betriebswirtschaft e.V.: Analyse für die Entwicklung eines Buy-out Marktes notwendigen Bedingungen in der Bundesrepublik Deutschland unter besonderer Berücksichtigung von MBOs, Schmalenbachs Zeitschrift für betriebswirtschaftliche Forschung, vol. 42, pp. 830-850.

Aron, Debra (1988): Ability, moral hazard, firm size, and diversification, in: The Rand Journal of Economics, vol. 19 (no. 1), pp. 72-87.

Asquith, Paul (1983): Merger bids, uncertainty, and stockholder returns, in: Journal of Financial Economics, vol. 11 (no. 1), pp. 51-84.

Asquith, Paul; Wizman, Thierry A. (1990): Event risk, covenants, and bondholder returns in leveraged buyouts, in: Journal of Financial Economics, vol. 27 (no. 1), pp. 195-213.

Backhaus, Klaus; Erichson, Bernd; Plinke, Wulff; Weiber, Rolf (2003): Multivariate Analysemethoden - Eine anwendugsorientierte Einführung, 10. Auflage, Heidelberg, Springer.

Bader, Hanspeter (1996): Private Equity als Anlagekategorie: Theorie, Praxis und Portfoliomanagement für institutionelle Investoren, Bern, Switzerland, Haupt.

Baker, George P (1992): Beatrice: A Study in the Creation and Destruction of Value, in: Journal of Finance, vol. 47 (no. 3), pp.1081-1119.

Baker, George P; Jensen, Michael C.; Murphy, Kevin (1988): Compensation and incentives - practice vs. theory, in: Journal of Finance, vol. 43 (no. 3), pp. 593-616.

Baker, George P.; Montgomery, Cynthia A. (1994): Conglomerates and LBO associations: a comparison of organizational forms, Harvard Business School working paper, Harvard, MA, pp. 1-34.

Baker, George P.; Smith, George D. (1998): The new financial capitalists: Kohlberg Kravis Roberts and the creation of corporate value, Cambridge, U.K., Cambridge University Press.

Baker, George P.; Wruck, Karen H. (1989): Organizational changes and value creation in leveraged buy-outs: the case of O.M. Scott & Sons Company, in: Journal of Financial Economics, vol. 25 (no. 2), pp. 163-190.

Ballwieser, Wolfgang (1993): Methoden der Unternehmensbewertung, in: Gebhardt, Günther; Gerke, Wolfgang; Steiner, Manfred: Handbuch des Finanzmanagements, Instrumente und Märkte der Unternehmensfinanzierung, München, Beck, pp. 151-176.

Ballwieser, Wolfgang; Schmid, Helmut (1990): Charakteristika und Problembereiche von Management Buyouts (I), in: WiSu - Das Wirtschaftsstudium, vol. 5, pp. 299-305.

Barney, Jay B.; Busenitz, Lowell; Fiet, James O.; Moesel, Doug (1996): New venture team's assessment of learning assistance from venture capital firms, in: Journal of Business Venturing, vol. 11 (no. 4), pp. 257-272.

Barney, Jay B.; Wright, Patrick M. (1988): On becoming a strategic partner: The role of human resources in gaining competitive advantage, in: Human Resource Management, vol. 37 (no. 1), pp. 31-46.

Baron, David P. (1982): A model of the demand for investment banking advertising the distribution services of new issues, in: Journal of Finance, vol. 37 (no. 5), pp. 955-976.

Barry, Christopher B. (1994): New directions in research on venture capital finance, in: Financial Management, vol. 23 (no. 3), pp. 3-15.

Barry, Christopher B.; Muscarella, Chris J.; Peavy, John W. III; Vetsuypens, Michael R. (1990): The role of venture capitalists in the creation of public companies: evidence from the going public process, in: Journal of Financial Economics, vol. 27 (no. 2), pp. 447-471.

Baysinger, Barry; Hoskinsson, Robert E. (1989): Diversification strategy and R&D intensity in multiproduct firms, in: Academy of Management Journal, vol. 32 (no. 2), pp. 310-332.

Becker, Reimund (2000): Buy-outs in Deutschland: Handbuch für Manager, Consultants und Investoren, Cologne, Germany, Deutscher Wirtschaftsdienst.

Bengtsson, Ola; Kaplan, Steven N.; Martel, Frederic; Strömberg, Per (2002): Investment screening and market conditions: evidence from venture capital, Unpublished working paper, University of Chicago

Benston, Georg J.; Smith, Clifford W. (1976): The transaction cost approach to the theory of financial intermediation, in: Journal of Finance, vol. 31 (no. 2), pp. 215-231.

Berg, Achim (2005): What is strategy for buyout associations?, Berlin, VWF.

Berg, Achim; Gottschalg, Oliver (2003): Understanding value generation in buyouts, INSEAD Working Paper Series, Fontainebleau, France. http://ssrn.com/abstract=500942, pp. 1-47.

Berger, Matthias (1993): Management buy-out und Mitarbeiterbeteiligung - Finanzwirtschaftliche Analyse von Konzepten zur Übernahme von Unternehmen durch Management und Belegschaft, Köln, Botermann.

Berglöf, Erik (1994): A control theory of venture capital finance, in: Journal of Law, Economics and Organization, vol. 10, pp. 247-267.

Berle, Adolph A.; Means, Gardiner C. (1932): The modern corporation and private property, New York, Commerce Clearing House.

Bhagat, Sanjai; Shleifer, Andrei; Vishny, Robert (1990): Hostile takeovers in the 1980s: the return to corporate specialization, in: Baily, M. N.; Winston, C: Brookings Papers on Economic Activity: Microeconomics, Washington, Brookings Institution, pp. 1-84.

Bhide, Amar V. (1990): Reversing corporate diversification, in: Journal of Applied Corporate Finance, vol. 3 (no. 2), pp. 70-81.

Bhide, Amar V. (1993): The hidden costs of stock market liquidity, in: Journal of Financial Economics, vol. 34, pp. 31-51.

Bieler, Stefan (1996): Die Unternehmernachfolge als finanzwirtschaftliches Problem, Wiesbaden, Gabler.

Bilo, Stéphanie (2002): Alternative asset class - publicly traded private equity - performance, liquidity, diversification potential, and pricing characteristics, Bamberg, Germany

Black, Fisher; Jensen, M.; Scholes, Myron (1972): The capital asset pricing model: some empirical tests, in: Jensen, Michael C.: Studies in the theory of capital markets, New York, Praeger, pp. 79-121.

Bodie, Zvi; Kane, Alex; Marcus, Alan J. (1999): Investments, Fourth Edition, McGraw-Hill International Editions.

Booth, James R.; Smith, Richard L. (1986): Capital raising, underwriting and the certification hypothesis, in: Journal of Financial Economics, vol. 15 (no. 1/2), pp.261-281.

Borden, Arthur M. (1974): Going private - old tort, new tort or no tort?, in: NYU Law Review, vol. 49, pp. 987-1042.

Bortz, Jürgen (2005): Statistik für Human- und Sozialwissenschaftler, 6. Auflage, Heidelberg, Springer.

Bradley, Michael; Desai, Arnand; Kim, E. Han (1988): Synergistic gains from corporate acquisitions and their division between the stockholders of target and acquiring firm, in: Journal of Financial Economics, vol. 21 (no. 1), pp. 3-40.

Braun, Christoph (1989): Leveraged Buyouts: Theoretische Grundlagen und empirischer 3-Länder-Vergleich, München-Unterföhring, Germany, GBI.

Brealey, Richard A.; Myers, Stewart C. (2003): Principles of corporate finance, 7th edition, Boston, MA, Irwin/McGraw-Hill.

Brettel, Malte (2002): Entscheidungskriterien von Venture Capitalists: Eine empirische Analyse im internationalen Vergleich, in: Die Betriebswirtschaft, vol. 62 (no. 3), pp. 305-325.

Brettel, Malte; Meier, Degenhard; Reißig-Thust, Solveig (2004): Vertragsgestaltung von Venture Capitalists und Business Angels im Vergleich, in: Die Betriebswirtschaft, vol. 64 (no. 4), pp. 431-447.

Brinkrolf, Andreas (2002): Managementunterstützung durch Venture-Capital-Gesellschaften, Wiesbaden, DUV.

Broda, Björn M. (2003): Mezzanine Finance - Finanzierungslücken flexibel schließen, in: Der Schweizer Treuhänder, 2003 (no. 11), pp. 977-980.

Brophy, David J.; Guthner, Mark W. (1988): Publicly traded venture capital funds: implications for institutional 'Fund-of-Funds' manager, in: Journal of Business Venturing, vol. 3 (no. 1), pp. 187-206.

Brück, Marco (1998): Beteiligung an Unternehmen: Desinvestition und Lösung von Engagements - ein Entscheidungsmodell, Bamberg, Difo-Druck.

Bruton, Gary D.; Scifres, Elton (1992): Leveraged buyouts: their impact on R&D spending, in: Management International Review, vol. 32 (no. 1), pp. 7-21.

Bull, Ivan (1989): Financial performance of leveraged buyouts: an empirical analysis, in: Journal of Business Venturing, vol. 4 (no. 4), pp. 263-279.

Burch, Timothy R.; Nanda, Vikram (2003): Divisional diversity and the conglomerate discount: evidence from spinoffs, in: Journal of Financial Economics, vol. 70 (no. 1), pp. 69-98.

Burgel, Oliver; Murray, Gordon C. (2000): The impact of fund size and investment preferences on venture capitalist's returns, in: Proceedings of the Twenty-Second Annual Entrepreneurship Conference, Wellesley/MA/US.

Butler, Paul A. (2001): The alchemy of LBOs, in: The McKinsey Quarterly, (no. 2), pp. 140-151.

Bygrave, William D.; Fast, Norman; Khoylian, Roubina; Vincent, Linda; Yue, William (1989): Early rates of return of 131 venture capital funds started 1978-1984, in: Journal of Business Venturing, vol. 4 (no. 1), pp. 93-105.

Bygrave, William D.; Timmons, Jeffry A. (1992): Venture Capital at the Crossroads, Boston, MA, Harvard Business School Press.

Campbell, Tim S.; Kracaw, William A. (1980): Information production, market signaling, and the theory of financial intermediation, in: Journal of Finance, vol. 35 (no. 4), pp. 863-882.

Cannella, Alberta A., Jr.; Hambrick, Donald C. (1993): Effects of executive departures on the performance of acquired firms, in: Strategic Management Journal, vol. 14 (Special Issue), pp. 137-152.

Capen, E. C. ; Clapp, R. V.; Campbell, W. M. (1971): Competitive bidding in high risk situations, in: Journal of Petroleum Technology, June 1971, pp. 641-653.

Carow, Kenneth A.; Roden, Dianne M. (1997): Determinants of the stock price reaction to leveraged buyouts, in: Journal of Economics and Finance, vol. 21 (no. 3), pp. 49-59.

Cassing, John; Douglas, Robert W. (1980): Implications of the auction mechanism in Baseball's free agent draft, in: Southern Journal of Economics, vol. 47 (no. 1), pp. 110-121.

CEPRES (2005): Financial information provider for leveraged buyouts, www.cepres.com

Chase, William C.; Simon, Herbert (1973): Perception in chess, in: Cognitive psychology, vol. 4, pp. 55-81.

Chatterjee, Sayan (1986): Types of synergy and economic value: the impact of acquisitions on merging and rival firms, in: Strategic Management Journal, vol. 7 (no. 2), pp. 119-139.

Cheung, Steven N. (1970): The structure of a contract and the theory of a non-exclusive theory, in: Journal of Law and Economics, vol. 13 (no. 1), pp. 49-70.

Child, John (1984): Organizations: a guide to problems and practice, London, Harper & Row.

Choo, Freddie; Trotman, Ken T. (1991): The relationship between knowledge structure and judgment for experienced and inexperienced auditors, in: Accounting Review, vol. 66 (no. 3), pp. 464-485.

Clarkson, Peter M.; Dontoh, Alex; Richardson, Gordon; Sefcik, Stephan E. (1991): Retained ownership and the valuation of initial public offerings: Canadian evidence, in: Contemporary Accounting Research, vol. 8, pp. 115-131.

Coase, Ronald H. (1960): The problem of social cost, in: Journal of Law and Economics, vol. 3 (no. 1), pp. 1-44.

Cochrane, John (2005): The risk and return of venture capital, in: Journal of Financial Economics, vol. 75 (no. 1), pp. 3-52.

Coffee, John C. Jr.; Lowenstein, Louis; Rose-Ackerman, Susan (1988): Knights, raiders, and targets - the impact of the hostile takeover, Oxford, Oxford University Press.

Cohen, Jacob; Cohen, Patricia; West, Stephen G.; Aiken, Leona A. (2003): Applied multiple regression/correlation analysis for the behavior sciences, Mahwah, Erlbaum.

Colman, Robert D. (1981): Overview of leveraged buyouts, in: Lee, Steven J.; Colman, Robert D.: Handbook of Mergers, Acquisitions and Buyouts, Englewood Cliffs, NJ, Prentice Hall.

Cook, Douglas O.; Easterwood, John C.; Martin, John D. (1992): Bondholder wealth effects of management buyouts, in: Financial Management, vol. 21 (no. 1), pp. 102-113.

Cornett, Marcia M; Travlos, Nickolas G. (1993): Going private buyouts and determinants of shareholders' returns, in: Journal of Accounting, Auditing & Finance, pp. 1-30.

Cotter, James F.; Peck, Sarah W. (2001): The structure of debt and active equity investors: the case of the buyout specialist, in: Journal of Financial Economics, vol. 59 (no. 1), pp. 101-147.

Courteau, Lucie (1995): Under-diversification and retention commitments in IPOs, in: Journal of Financial and Quantitative Analysis, vol. 30 (no. 4), pp. 487-517.

Cox, James C.; Isaac, Mark R. (1984): In search of the winner's curse, in: Economic Inquiry, vol. 22, pp. 579-592.

Cox, John C.; Ross, Stephan A.; Rubinstein, Mark (1979): Option pricing - a simplified approach, in: Journal of Financial Economics, vol. 7 (no. 3), pp. 229-263.

Cullinan, Geoffrey; Le Roux, Jean-Marc; Weddigen, Rolf-Magnus (2004): When to walk away from a deal, in: Harvard Business Review, vol. 82 (no. 4), pp. 96-104.

Cumming, Douglas J.; MacIntosh, Jeffrey G. (2003): A cross-country comparison of full and partial venture capital exits, in: Journal of Banking & Finance, vol. 27, pp. 511-548.

Cutler, David M. ; Summers, Lawrence (1988): The costs of conflict and financial distress: evidence from the Texaco-Pennzoil litigation, in: RAND Journal of Economics, vol. 19 (no. 2), pp. 157-172.

Das, Sanjiv R.; Jagannathan, Murali; Sarin, Atulya (2002): The private equity discount, in: Journal of Investment Management, vol. 1 (no. 1), pp. 152-177.

Datar, Srikant M.; Feltham, Gerald A.; Hughes, John S. (1991): The role of audits and audit quality in valuing new issues, in: Journal of Accounting and Economics, vol. 14 (no. 1), pp. 3-49.

De Clerq, Dirk; Sapienza, Harry J. (2002): Knowledge-based antecedents of venture capital firm value added, in: Proceedings of the Twenty-Second Annual Entrepreneurship Conference, Wellesley/MA/US.

DeAngelo, Harry; DeAngelo, Linda E. (1987): Management buyouts of publicly traded corporations, in: Financial Analyst Journal, vol. 43 (no. 3), pp. 38-49.

DeAngelo, Harry; DeAngelo, Linda E.; Rice, Edward M. (1984): Going private: minority freezeouts and shareholder wealth, in: Journal of Law and Economics, vol. 27, pp. 367-401.

DeAngelo, Harry; DeAngelo, Linda E.; Rice, Edward M. (1994): Going private: the effects of a change in the ownership structure, in: Stern, Joel M.; Chew, Donald: The revolution in corporate finance, 2nd edition, Cambridge, MA, Blackwell Publishing, pp. 602-610.

DeAngelo, Harry; Masulis, Ronald W. (1980): Optimal capital structure under corporate and personal taxation, in: Journal of Financial Economics, vol. 8 (no. 1), pp. 3-29.

DeAngelo, Linda E. (1986): Accounting numbers as market valuation substitutes: a study of management buyouts of public shareholders, in: Accounting Review, vol. 61 (no. 3), p. 400-420.

DeGeorge, Francois; Zeckhauser, Richard (1993): The reverse LBO decision and firm performance: theory and evidence, in: Journal of Finance, vol. 48 (no. 4), pp. 1323-1348.

Demougin, Dominique; Jost, Peter-J. (2001): Theoretische Grundlagen der Prinzipal-Agenten-Theorie, in: Jost, P. J.: Die Prinzipal-Agenten-Theorie in der Betriebswirtschaftslehre, Stuttgart, Schaeffer-Poeschel, pp. 45-81.

Demsetz, Harold (1964): The exchange and enforcement of property rights, in: Journal of Law and Economics, vol. 7 (no. 1), pp. 11-26.

Demsetz, Harold (1967): Towards a theory of property rights, in: American Economic Review, vol. 57 (no. 2), pp. 347-359.

Denis, David J. (1994): Organizational form and the consequences of highly leveraged transactions: Kroger's recapitalization and Safeway's LBO, in: Journal of Financial Economics, vol. 36 (no. 2), pp. 193-224.

Denis, David J.; Serrano, Jan M. (1996): Active investors and management turnover following unsuccessful control contests, in: Journal of Financial Economics, vol. 40 (no. 2), pp. 239-266.

Desbrières, Philippe; Schatt, Alain (2002): The impact of LBOs on the performance of acquired firms: the french case, in: Journal of Business Finance and Accounting, vol. 29 (no. 5), pp. 695-729.

Diamond, Douglas W.; Dybvig, Philip H. (1983): Bank runs, deposit insurance and liquidity, in: Journal of Political Economy, vol. 91 (no. 3), pp. 401-419.

Diller, Christian; Kaserer, Christoph (2005): What drives cash flow based European private equity returns? Fund inflows, skilled GPs and/or risk?, RICAFE working paper no. 15

Downes, David H.; Heinkel, Robert (1982): Signaling and the valuation of unseasoned new issues, in: Journal of Finance, vol. 37 (no. 1), pp. 1-10.

Drukarczyk, Jochen (1999): Finanzierung - Eine Einführung, Stuttgart, Germany, Lucius & Lucius.

Duffie, Darrel (1988): Security markets: stochastic models, Boston, Academic Press.

Duffner, Stefan (2005): Agency Problems in Venture Capital Financing - The Issues, Trust and the Real World, Bamberg, Difo-Druck.

Easterwood, John C. (1998): Divestments and financial distress in leveraged buyouts, in: Journal of Banking & Finance, vol. 22, pp. 129-159.

Easterwood, John C.; Seth, Anju; Singer, Ronald F. (1989): The impact of leveraged buyouts on strategic direction, in: California Management Review, vol. 32 (no. 1), pp. 30-43.

Eddey, Peter H.; Lee, Kin Wai; Taylor, Stephen L. (1996): What motivates going private: an analysis of australian firms, in: Accounting and Finance, Vol. 36 (May), pp. 31-50.

Edwards, Robert D.; Magee, John (1976): Technische Analyse von Aktientrends, Darmstadt, Hoppenstedt.

Efron, Bradley; Tibshirani, Robert J. (1993): An introduction to bootstrap, New York, Chapman and Hall.

Eisenhardt, Kathleen M. (1989): Agency theory: an assessment and review, in: Academy of Management Review, vol. 14 (no. 1), pp. 57-74.

Evans, Frank C.; Bishop, David M. (2001): Valuation for M&A - building value in private companies, NY, John Wiley and Sons.

EVCA (2003): EVCA guidelines, Zaventem, Belgium, European Private Equity and Venture Capital Association (EVCA).

EVCA (2004): Pan-European survey of performance - from inception to 31 December 2003, www.evca.com, European Private Equity and Venture Capital Association (EVCA).

Fabozzi, Frank; Francis, Jack C. (1979): Mutual funds systematic risk for bull and bear markets: an empirical examination, in: Journal of Finance, vol. 34 (no. 5), pp. 1243-1250.

Fama, Eugene F. (1970): Efficient capital markets: a review of theory and empirical work, in: Journal of Finance, vol. 25 (no. 2), pp. 383-417.

Fama, Eugene F. (1980): Agency problems and the theory of the firm, in: Journal of Political Economy, vol. 88 (no. 2), pp. 288-307.

Fama, Eugene F. (1991): Efficient capital markets II, in: Journal of Finance, vol. 46 (no. 5), pp. 1575-1614.

Fama, Eugene F.; French, Kenneth R. (1997): Industry costs of equity, in: Journal of Financial Economics, vol. 43 (no. 1), pp. 133-156.

Fama, Eugene F.; Jensen, Michael C. (1983): Separation of ownership and control, in: Journal of Law and Economics, vol. 26 (no. 2), pp. 301-325.

Fama, Eugene F.; Jensen, Michael C. (1985): Organization forms and investment decisions, in: Journal of Financial Economics, vol. 14 (no. 2), pp. 101-119.

Färber, Heijo (2005): Determinanten der Entscheidung für eine Börseneinführung, Hamburg, Germany, Kovac.

Fenn, George W.; Liang, Nellie; Prowse, Stephen (1997): The private equity market: an overview, in: Financial Markets, Institutions and Instruments, vol. 6 (no. 4), pp. 1-105.

Forst, Martin (1993): Struktur und Stabilität eines Leveraged Management Buy-out, Dissertation University of Cologne.

Frankfurter, George M.; Gunay, Erdal (1992): Management buy-outs: the sources and sharing of wealth between insiders and outsiders, in: Quarterly Review of Economics and Finance, vol. 32 (no. 3), pp. 82-95.

Fried, Vance H.; Bruton, Gary D.; Hisrich, Robert D. (1998): Strategy and the board of directors in venture capital-backed firms, in: Journal of Business Venturing, vol. 13 (no. 6), pp. 493-503.

Fried, Vance H.; Hisrich, Robert D. (1988): Venture capital research: past, present, and future, in: Entrepreneurship Theory and Practice, vol. 1 (no. 1), pp. 15-28.

Fried, Vance H.; Hisrich, Robert D. (1992): Venture capital and the investor, in: Management Research News, vol. 15 (no. 4), pp. 28-39.

Frommann, Holger (1992): Die Finanzierung von Management Buy-Outs, in: Luetjen, Gerd: Firmenübernahme durch Management und Belegschaft, Wiebaden, Gabler, pp. 105-134.

Furubotn, Eirik G.; Pejovitch, Svetozar (1972): Property rights and economic theory: a survey of recent literature, in: Journal of Economic Literature, vol. 10 (no. 4), pp. 1137-1162.

Furubotn, Eirik G.; Pejovitch, Svetozar (1974): The economics of property rights, Cambridge, Ballinger publishing company.

Gale, Ian; Stiglitz, Joseph E. (1989): The informational content of initial public offerings, in: Journal of Finance, vol. 44 (no. 2), pp. 469-477.

Garfinkel, Michelle R. (1989): The causes and consequences of leveraged buyouts, in: Federal Reserve Bank of St. Louis, September, pp. 23-34.

Garvey, Gerald T. (1992): Leveraging the underinvestment problem: how high debt and management shareholdings solve the agency costs of free cash flow, in: The Journal of Financial Research, vol. 15 (no. 2), pp. 149-166.

Gifford Jr., Dun (2001): Why debt can hurt corporate growth, in: MIT Sloan Management Review, no. 42 (no. 3), p. 18.

Gilson, Stuart C. (1989): Management turnover and financial distress, in: Journal of Financial Economics, vol. 25 (no. 2), pp. 241-262.

Gleisberg, Ralf (2003): Börsengang und Unternehmensentwicklung: der Einfluss veränderter Eigentums- und Kontrollstrukturen, Wolfratshausen, Germany, Going-Public-Media.

Gompers, Paul A. (1994): The rise and fall of venture capital, in: Business and Economic History, vol. 23, pp. 1-24.

Gompers, Paul A. (1996): Grandstanding in the venture capital industry, in: Journal of Financial Economics, vol. 42 (no. 1), pp. 133-156.

Gompers, Paul A. (1998): Venture capital growing pains: should the market diet?, in: Journal of Banking & Finance, vol. 22, pp. 1089-1104.

Gompers, Paul A. (2002): Corporations and the financing of innovation: the corporate venturing experience, in: Economic Review, vol. 87 (no. 4), pp. 1-18.

Gompers, Paul A. ; Lerner, Joshua (1997): Venture capital fundraising, firm performance, and the capital gains tax

Gompers, Paul A.; Lerner, Joshua (1999a): An analysis of compensation in the U.S. venture capital partnership, in: Journal of Financial Economics, vol. 51 (no. 1), pp. 3-44.

Gompers, Paul A.; Lerner, Joshua (1999b): How are venture capitalists compensated?, in: Gompers, Paul A.; Lerner, Joshua: The Venture Capital Cycle, Cambridge, MA, MIT Press, pp. 57-94.

Gompers, Paul A.; Lerner, Joshua (1999c): The venture capital cycle, Cambridge, MA, MIT Press.

Gompers, Paul A.; Lerner, Joshua (2000a): The challenge of performance assessment, in: Lake, Rick; Lake, Ronald: Private Equity and Venture Capital: A Guide for Investors and Practitioners, London U.K., Euromoney Books, pp. 249-259.

Gompers, Paul A.; Lerner, Joshua (2000b): Money chasing deals? The impact of fund inflows on private equity valuations, in: Journal of Financial Economics, vol. 55 (no. 2), pp. 281-325.

Gordon, M.J. (1962): The investment, financing and valuation of the corporation, Illinois

Gorman, Michael J.; Sahlman, William A. (1989): What do venture capitalist do?, in: Journal of Business Venturing, vol. 4 (no. 4), pp. 231-248.

Gottschalg, Oliver; Phalippou, Ludovic; Zollo, Maurizio (2004): Performance of private equity funds: another puzzle?, INSEAD Working Paper Series, Fontainebleau, France, pp. 1-53.

Graebner, Ulrich A. (1991): Die Auseinandersetzung um Leveraged Buyouts, Frankfurt a. M., Germany, Fritz Knapp.

Grammatikos, Theoharry; Makhija, Anil K.; Thompson, Howard E. (1988): Financing corporate takeovers by individuals seeking control, in: Managerial and Decision Economics, vol. 9, pp. 227-235.

Gräper, Matthias (1993): Management-Buy-Out: eine empirische Analyse zur deutschen Entwicklung bis 1990, Kiel, Wissenschaftsverlag Vauk.

Grinblatt, Mark; Hwang, Chuan Y. (1989): Signalling and the pricing of new issues, in: Journal of Finance, vol. 44 (no. 2), pp. 383-420.

Groh, Alexander P. (2004): Risikoadjustierte Performance von Private Equity-Investitionen, Darmstadt, Germany, Technische Universität Darmstadt, 327.

Grossman, Sanford J.; Hart, Oliver (1982): Corporate financial structure and managerial incentives, in: McCall, J. J.: The Economics of Information and Uncertainty, Chicago, IL, University of Chicago Press, pp. 107-140.

Grossman, Sanford J.; Hart, Oliver (1983): An analysis of the principal-agent problem, in: Econometrica, vol. 51, pp. 7-45.

Gull, Jason (1999): Methodologies of marketing private equity returns, in: Venture Capital Journal, vol. 39 (no. 6), pp. 46-48.

Hagenmüller, Moritz (2004): Investor Relations von Private Equity Partnerships, Sternenfels, Verlag Wissenschaft und Praxis.

Hamada, Robert S. (1969): Portfolio analysis, market equilibrium and corporation finance, in: Journal of Finance, vol. 24 (no. 1), pp. 13-31.

Harris, Milton; Raviv, Artur (1991): The theory of capital structure, in: Journal of Finance, vol. 46 (no. 1), pp. 297-355.

Hart, Oliver (1983): The market mechanism as an incentive scheme, in: Bell Journal of Economics, vol. 14 (no. 2), pp. 366-382.

Hartmann-Wendels, Thomas; Pfingsten, Andreas; Weber, Martin (1998): Bankbetriebslehre, Berlin, Springer.

Hatzig, Christoph (1995): Unternehmensbewertung und Kaufpreisfindung beim Management Buy-Out (MBO) - Eine ökonomische Analyse unter besonderer Berücksichtigung von Informationsvorteilen des Managements, Hamburg, Germany, S + W Steuer- und Wirtschaftsverlag.

Heinkel, Robert; Zechner, Josef (1990): The role of debt and preferred stock as a solution to adverse investment incentives, in: Journal of Financial and Quantitative Analysis, vol. 25 (March), pp. 3-24.

Hellmann, Thomas F. (1994): Financial structure and control in venture capital, Working Paper, Standford University, Standford, US

Hellmann, Thomas F. (1998): The allocation of control rights in venture capital contracts, in: RAND Journal of Economics, vol. 29 (no. 1), pp. 57-76.

Hellmann, Thomas F.; Puri, Manju (2002): Venture capital and the professionalization of start-up firms: empirical evidence, in: Journal of Finance, vol. 57 (no. 1), pp. 169-197.

Hellwig, Martin (1991): Banking, financial intermediation and corporate finance, in: Giovannini, Alberto; Mayer, Colin: European financial integration, Cambridge, Cambridge University Press, pp. 35-63.

Henriksson, Roy D. (1984): Market timing and mutual fund performance: an empirical investigation, in: Journal of Business, vol. 57, pp. 73-96.

Henriksson, Roy D.; Merton, Robert C. (1981): On market timing and investment perfromance. II. Statistical procedures for evaluating forecasting skills, in: Journal of Business, vol. 54, pp. 513-533.

Herrmann, Volker (2002): Marktpreisschätzung mit kontrollierten Multiplikatoren, Lohmar/Köln, Eul.

Hershman, Arlene (1969): The spin-off - one minus one equals three?, in: Dun's Review, vol. 93 (no. 3), pp. 31-33.

Hielscher, Udo; Zelger, Hansjörg; Beyer, Sven (2003): Performancemessung und Reporting von Venture Capital-/Private Equity Gesellschaften, in: Finanzbetrieb, 7-8/2003, pp. 498-505.

Himmelberg, Charles P.; Hubbard, R. Glenn; Palia, Darius (1999): Understanding the determinants of managerial ownership and the link between ownership and performance, in: Journal of Financial Economics, vol. 53 (no. 3), pp. 353-384.

Hinz, Holger; Dörscher, Martin (2003): Mezzanine Capital - Ein flexibles Finanzierungsinstrument für KMU, in: Discussion Paper der Universität Flensburg - Internationales Institut für Management, no. 5/2003,

Hite, Gailen L.; Owers, James E.; Rogers, Ronald C. (1987): The market for interfirm asset sales: partial sell-offs and total liquidations, in: Journal of Financial Economics, vol. 18, pp. 229-252.

Hite, Gailen L.; Vetsuypens, Michael R. (1989): Management buy-outs of divisions and shareholder wealth, in: Journal of Finance, vol. 44 (no. 4), pp. 953-970.

Hoffmann, Peter; Ramke, Ralf (1992): Management buy out in der Bundesrepublik Deutschland - Anspruch, Realität und Perspektiven, 2nd edition, Berlin, Germany, Erich Schmidt Verlag.

Hogan, Karen M.; Olson, Gerald T.; Kish, Richard J. (2001): A conmparison of reverse leveraged buyouts and original initial public offers: factors impacting their issuance in the IPO market, in: The Financial Review, vol. 38, pp. 1-18.

Holmstrom, Bengt; Tirole, Jean (1993): Market liquidity and performance monitoring, in: Journal of Political Economy, vol. 101, pp. 678-709.

Holthausen, Robert W.; Larcker, David F. (1996): The financial performance of reverse leveraged buyouts, in: Journal of Financial Economics, vol. 42 (no. 3), pp. 293-332.

Hoskisson, Robert E.; Turk, Thomas A. (1990): Corporate restructuring: governance and control limits of the internal capital market, in: Academy of Management Journal, vol. 15 (no. 3 (March)), pp. 459-477.

Houlden, Brian (1990): Buyouts and beyond: motivations, strategies and ownership changes, in: Long Range Planning, vol. 23 (August), pp. 73-77.

Hull, John C. (2003): Options, futures and other derivative securities, 5th edition, New Jersey, Prentice Hall.

Huydts, Henrik J. M. A. (1992): Management Buyout als strategische Option zur Regelung der Nachfolge in mittelgrossen Familienunternehmen : Erfolgsfaktoren und Gestaltungsvarianten, Dissertation, Hochschule St. Gallen.

Ibbotson, Roger G.; Jaffe, Jeffrey F. (1975): 'Hot' issues markets, in: Journal of Finance, vol. 30 (no. 4), pp. 1027-1042.

Ick, Matthias (2005): Performance measurement and appraisal of private equity investments relative to public equity markets, Working Paper, University of Lugano, pp. 1-53.

Inderbitzin, Michael (1993): Going Private und dem Going Private ähnliche Sachverhalte, Zürich, Switzerland, Schulthess.

Inderst, Roman; Müller, Holger M. (2004): The effect of capital market characteristics on the value of start-up firms, in: Journal of Financial Economics, vol. 72, pp. 319-356.

Initiative Europe (2004): Information provider for leveraged buyouts, www.initiative-europe.com.

Ippolito, Richard A.; James, William M. (1992): LBOs, reversions and implicit contracts, in: Journal of Finance, vol. 47 (no. 1), pp. 139-168.

Ivanova, Ana; Tzvetkova, Rossitza (2001): Exit-Strategien bei Private Equity Investments, in: Grünbichler, Andreas; Graf, Steffen; Gruber, Alfred: Private Equity und Hedge-Funds: Alternative Anlagekategorien im Überblick, Frankfurt a. M., Frankfurter Allgemeine Buch, pp. 165-193.

Jakoby, Stephan (2000): Erfolgsfaktoren von Management Buyouts in Deutschland, Cologne, Germany, Josef Eul.

Jansen, Stephan A.; Picot, Gerhard; Schiereck, Dirk (2001): Internationales Fusionsmanagement - Erfolgsfaktoren grenzüberschreitender Unternehmenszusammenschlüsse, Stuttgart, Schäffer-Poeschel.

Jeng, Leslie A.; Wells, Philippe C. (2000): The determinants of venture capital funding: evidence across countries, in: Journal of Corporate Finance, vol. 6, pp. 241-289.

Jensen, Michael C. (1968): The performance of mutual funds in the period 1945-1964, in: Journal of Finance, vol. 23 (no. 2), pp. 389-416.

Jensen, Michael C. (1972): Optimal utilization of market forecasts and the evaluation of investment performance, in: Szego, G. P.; Shell, Karl: Mathematical methods of investment and finance, Amsterdam, North-Holland Publishing Company,

Jensen, Michael C. (1986): Agency costs of free cash flow, corporate finance, and takeovers, in: American Economic Review, vol. 76 (no. 2), pp. 323-329.

Jensen, Michael C. (1989a): Active investors, LBOs and the privatization of bankcruptcy, in: Journal of Applied Corporate Finance, vol. 2 (no. 1), pp. 35-44.

Jensen, Michael C. (1989b): Eclipse of the public corporation, in: Harvard Business Review, vol. 67 (no. 5), pp. 61-74.

Jensen, Michael C. (1993): The modern industrial revolution, exit, and the failure of internal control systems, in: Journal of Finance, vol. 48 (no. 3), pp. 831-880.

Jensen, Michael C.; Kaplan, Steven N.; Stiglin, Laura (1989): Effects of LBO's on tax revenues of the U.S. treasury, in: Tax Notes, vol. 42 (February), pp. 727-733.

Jensen, Michael C.; Meckling, William (1976): Theory of the firm: managerial behavior, agency costs, and ownership structure, in: Journal of Financial Economics, vol. 3 (no. 4), pp. 305-360.

Jensen, Michael C.; Murphy, Kevin (1990a): CEO incentives: it's not how much you pay, but how, in: Harvard Business Review, vol. 68 (May-June), pp. 138-147.

Jensen, Michael C.; Murphy, Kevin (1990b): Performance pay and top-management incentives, in: Journal of Political Economy, vol. 98, pp. 225-264.

Jensen, Michael C.; Ruback, Richard S. (1983): The market for corporate control, in: Journal of Financial Economics, vol. 11 (no. 1-4), pp. 5-50.

Jones, Charles M.; Rhodes-Kropf, Matthew (2003): The price of diversifiable risk in venture capital and private equity, Working Paper, Columbia University Graduate School o Business, pp. 0-40.

Jost, Peter J. (1998): Strategisches Konfliktmanagement in Organisationen: eine spieltheoretische Einführung, Wiesbaden, Gabler.

Kagel, John H; Levin, Dan (1986): The Winner's Curse and public information in common value auctions, in: American Economic Review, vol. 76 (no. 5), pp. 894-920.

Kagel, John H; Levin, Dan; Battlio, R.; Meyer, D. J. (1989): First-price common value auctions: bider behavior and the Winner's Curse, in: Economic Inquiry, vol. 27 (no. 2), pp. 241-258.

Kagel, John H.; Levin, Dan (1999): Common Value Auctions with Insider Information, in: Econometrica, vol. 67 (no. 5), pp. 1219-1238.

Kagel, John H.; Richard, Jean-Francois (2001): Super-experienced bidders in first-price common-value auctions: rules of thumb, nash equilibrium bidding, and the winner's curse, in: Review of Economics and Statistics, vol. 83 (no. 3), pp. 408-419.

Kahan, Marcel; Klausner, Mike (1993): Antitakeover provisions in bonds: bondholder protection or management entrenchment?, in: UCLA Law Review, vol. 40 (April), pp. 931-982.

Kaplan, Steven N. (1989a): The effects of management buy-outs on operating performance and value, in: Journal of Financial Economics, vol. 24 (no. 2), pp. 217-254.

Kaplan, Steven N. (1989b): Management buyouts: evidence on taxes as a source of value, in: Journal of Finance, vol. 44 (no. 3), pp. 611-632.

Kaplan, Steven N.; Ruback, Richard S. (1995): The valuation of cash flow forecasts: an empirical analysis, in: Journal of Finance, vol. 50 (no. 4), pp. 1059-1093.

Kaplan, Steven N.; Schoar, Antoinette (2005): Private equity performance: returns, persistence and capital flows, in: Journal of Finance, vol. 60 (no. 4), pp. 1791-1823.

Kaplan, Steven N.; Stein, Jeremy (1993): The evolution of buyout pricing and financial structure in the 1980s, in: Quarterly Journal of Economics, vol. 108 (no. 2), pp. 313-358.

Kaplan, Steven N.; Stein, Jeremy C. (1990): How risky is the debt in highly leveraged transactions?, in: Journal of Financial Economics, vol. 27 (no. 1), pp. 215-245.

Kaplan, Steven N.; Stromberg, Per (2003): Financial contracting theory meets the real world: evidence from venture capital contracts, in: Review of Economic Studies, vol. 20 (no. 2), pp. 281-315.

Karsunky, Robert (1992): Entwicklung eines funktionenorientierten "Leveraged-Management-Buy-Out"-Modells und Beurteilung seiner Strukturierungs- und Finanzierungsalternativen in der Bundesrepublik Deutschland, Grossbritannien und Frankreich, Frankfurt a. M., Peter Lang.

Kaserer, Christoph; Diller, Christian (2004): European private equity funds - a cash flow based performance analysis, Working Paper, University of Munich, pp. 1-47.

Keese, Christoph (2005): Warum Franz Müntefering mit seinen Thesen irrt, in: Die Welt, Berlin, 17. April 2005.

Kelleners, André (2004): Risikoneutrale Unternehmensbewertung und Multiplikatoren, Wiesbaden, DUV.

Kessel, Annette (1995): Der Leveraged Buyout in den USA und der Bundesrepublik Deutschland, Frankfurt a. M., Peter Lang.

Kessel, Bernd (1991): Management Buy-out - Grundlagen und Probleme, Frankfurt a. M., Peter Lang.

Kessel, Bernd (1998): Leveraged Buy-Out der Aktiengesellschaft: Ein interdisziplinärer Ansatz, Wirtschaftsrecht und Wirtschaftsverfassung, Frankfurt a. M., Peter Lang.

Kieschnick, Robert L. (1998): Free cash flow and stockholder gains in going private transactions revisited, in: Journal of Business Finance & Accounting, vol. 25, pp. 187-202.

Kim, E. Han; Schatzberg, John D. (1987): Voluntary corporate liquidations, in: Journal of Financial Economics, vol. 19 (no. 2), pp. 311-328.

Kim, Wi Saeng; Lyn, Esmeralda O. (1991): Going private: corporate restructuring under information asymmetry and agency problems, in: Journal of Business Finance & Accounting, Vol. 18 (5), pp. 637-648.

Kitching, John (1989): Early retuns on LBOs: a transatlantic study sheds new light on how and why they work, in: Harvard Business Review, vol. 67 (Nov-Dec), pp. 74-81.

Kitzmann, Jana (2005): Private equity in Deutschland: zur Performance von Management-Buy-outs, Wiesbaden, DUV.

Klein, Benjamin; Leffler, Keith (1981): The role of market orces in assuring contractual performance, in: Journal of Political Economy, vol. 89, pp. 615-641.

Knoblauch, Björn (2002): Value creation strategies for companies in private equity portfolios, unpublished document, Hicks, Muse, Tate & Furst Center for Private Equity Finance, McCombs School of Business, University of Texas at Austin, Austin

Koehnemann, Marc (2005): Weshalb gehen Venture Capitalists nicht an die Börse? Untersuchung der Eignung des Geschäftsmodells "Venture Capital" für eine Börsennotierung am Beispiel der deutschen VC-Industrie, Marburg, Germany, Tectum.

Kon, Stanley; Jen, Frank C. (1979): The investment performance of mutual funds: an empirical investigation of timing, selectivity, and market efficiency, in: Journal of Business, vol. 52, pp. 263-289.

Korsukéwitz, Karl (1976): Die Prüfung der Beteiligungswürdigkeit nicht emmissionsfähiger Unternehmungen durch Beteiligungsgesellschaften, Berlin.

Kraft, Volker (2001a): Empirische Ergebnisse zu Private Equity - Investitionen in Turnaround-Unternehmen, in: Grünbichler, Andreas; Graf, Steffen; Gruber, Alfred: Private Equity und Hedge-Funds: Alternative Anlagekategorien im Überblick, Frankfurt a. M., Frankfurter Allgemeine Buch, pp. 125-164.

Kraft, Volker (2001b): Private Equity für Turnaround-Investitionen: Erfolgsfaktoren in der Managementpraxis, Frankfurt a. M., Campus.

Kropp, Matthias (1992): Management Buy-outs und die Theorie der Unternehmung, Wiesbaden, Germany, Gabler.

Kulinski, Jan; Schiereck, Dirk (2003): Unternehmensnachfolge mit Börsenrückzug und Private Equity: Friedrich Grohe, in: Lange, Werner; Schiereck, Dirk: Nachfolgefragen bei Familienunternehmen: Unternehmenskauf und Private Equity als Alternative zur Börse, Heidelberg, Finanz Colloquium, pp. 179-208.

Kürsten, Wolfgang (1994): Finanzkontrakte und Risikoanreizproblem - Mißverständnisse im imformationsökonomischen Ansatz der Finanztheorie, Wiesbaden, Gabler.

Kürsten, Wolfgang (1995): Unternehmenswachstum, Kapitalstruktur und informationsökonomische Komplikationen, in: Bühner, Rolf; Haase, Klaus-Dietmar; Wilhelm, Jochen: Die Dimensionierung des Unternehmens, Stuttgart, Schäffer-Poeschel, pp. 227-258.

Lakonishok, Josef; Shleifer, Andrei; Vishny, Robert (1994): Contrarian investment, extraploration, and risk, in: Journal of Finance, vol. 49 (no. 5), pp. 1541-1578.

Laux, Helmut (1998): Entscheidungstheorie, 4. Auflage, Berlin/Heidelberg, Springer.

Lee, Chiun I.; Rosenstein, Stuart; Rangan, Nanda; Davidson, Wallace N. III (1992): Board composition and shareholder wealth: the case of management buyouts, in: Financial Management, vol. 21 (no.1), pp. 58-72.

Lee, D. Scott (1992): Management buyout proposals and inside information, in: Journal of Finance, vol. 47 (no. 3), pp. 1061-1079.

Lehn, Kenneth; Poulsen, Annette (1989): Free cash flow and stockholder gains in going private transactions, in: Journal of Finance, vol. 44 (no. 3), pp. 771-788.

Lehn, Kenneth; Poulsen, Annette (1990): The economics of event risk: the case of bondholders in leveraged buyouts, in: Journal of Corporation Law, vol. 15 (no. 2), pp. 199-217.

Lei, David; Hitt, Michael A. (1995): Strategic restructuring and outsourcing: the effect of mergers and acquisitions and LBOs on building firm skills and capabilities, in: Journal of Management, vol. 21 (no. 5), pp. 835-859.

Leland, Hayne E.; Pyle, David H. (1977): Informational asymmetries, financial structure, and financial intermediation, in: Journal of Finance, vol. 32 (no. 2), pp. 371-387.

Leopold, Günter; Frommann, Holger; Kühr, Thomas (2003): Private Equity - Venture Capital: Eigenkapital für innovative Unternehmer, 2nd edition, München, Germany

Lerner, Joshua (1994a): Venture capitalists and the decision to go public, in: Journal of Financial Economics, vol. 35 (no. 3), pp. 293-316.

Lerner, Joshua (1994b): Venture capitalists and the oversight of private firms, Harvard University unpublished manuscript

Lerner, Joshua (2001): A note on private equity fundraising process, Harvard Business School note, Cambridge, MA, pp. 1-6.

Lerner, Joshua; Schoar, Antoinette (2004): The illiquidity puzzle: theory and evidence from private equity, in: Journal of Financial Economics, vol. 72 (no. 1), pp. 3-40.

LeRoy, Stephen F. (1989): Present value, in: Eatwell, J.; Milgate, M.; Newman, P.: Finance, London, pp. 237-242.

Levitt, Barbara; March, James G. (1988): Organizational learning, in: Annual Review of Sociology, vol. 14, pp. 319-340.

Lichtenberg, Frank; Siegel, Donald S. (1990): The effects of leveraged buyouts on productivity and related aspects of firm behavior, in: Journal of Financial Economics, vol. 27 (no. 1), pp.165-194.

Liebeskind, Julia P.; Wiersema, Margarethe; Hansen, Gary (1992): LBOs, corporate restructuring, and the incentive-intensity hypothesis, in: Financial Management, vol. 21 (no. 1), pp. 73-88.

Lintner, John (1965): The valuation of risk assets and the selection of risky investments in stock portfolios and capital budgets, in: Review of Economics and Statistics, vol. 47 (no. 1), pp. 13-37.

Ljungqvist, Alexander; Richardson, Matthew (2003a): The cash flow, return and risk characteristics of private equity, Stern School of Business working paper, New York, NY, pp. 1-41.

Ljungqvist, Alexander; Richardson, Matthew (2003b): The investment behavior of private equity fund managers, Stern School of Business working paper, New York, NY, pp. 1-35.

Long, William F.; Ravenscraft, David J. (1993a): Decade of debt: lessons from the LBOs in the 1980s, in: Blair, Margaret M.: The deal decade: what takeovers and leveraged buyouts mean for corporate governance, Washington, D.C., Brookings Institution, pp. 205-237.

Long, William F.; Ravenscraft, David J. (1993b): The financial performance of whole company LBOs, Center of Economic Studies discussion paper, no.#CES 93 16, Washington, DC, pp. 0-36.

Long, William F.; Ravenscraft, David J. (1993c): LBOs, debate and R&D intensity, in: Strategic Management Journal, vol. 14 (no. 4 (Summer Special Issue)), pp. 119-135.

Loughhran, Tim; Ritter, Jay (1993): The timing and subsequent performance of IPOs: the U.S. and interantional evidence, Unpublished working paper, University of Illinois, Urbana-Champaign, IL

Lowenstein, Louis (1985): Management buyouts, in: Columbia Law Review, vol. 85 (no. 4), pp. 730-784.

Lubatkin, Michael H. (1987): Merger strategy and stockholder value, in: Strategic Management Journal, vol. 8 (no. 1), pp. 39-54.

Luippold, Thomas L. (1992): Management Buy-Outs - Evaluation ihrer Einsatzmöglichkeiten in Deutschland, 2nd edition, Stuttgart, Germany, Paul Haupt.

MacMillan, Ian C.; Kulow, David M.; Khoylian, Roubina (1989): Venture capitalists' involvement in their investments: extent and performance, in: Journal of Business Venturing, vol. 4 (no. 1), pp. 27-47.

Maddala, George S. (1991): A perspective on the use of limited-dependent and qualitative variables models in accounting reserach, in: The Accounting Review, vol. 66 (no. 4), pp. 788-807.

Magowan, Peter A. (1989): The case for LBOs: the Safeway experience, in: California Management Review, vol. 32 (no. 1), pp. 9-19.

Mahajan, Jayashree (1992): The overconfidence effect in marketing management predictions, in: Journal of Marketing Research, vol. 29 (no. 3), pp. 329-342.

Maloney, Michael T.; McCormick, Robert E.; L., Mitchell Mark (1993): Managerial decision making and capital structure, in: Journal of Business, vol. 66 (no. 2), pp. 189-217.

Manigart, Sophie; De Waele, Koen; Wright, Mike; Robbie, Ken; Desbrières, Philippe; Sapienza, Harry J. ; Beekman, Amy (2002): Determinants of required return in venture capital investments: a five country study, in: Journal of Business Venturing, vol. 17 (no. 4), pp. 291-312.

Manne, Henry G. (1965): Mergers and the market for corporate control, in: Journal of Political Economy, vol. 73 (no. 2), pp. 110-120.

Marais, Laurentius; Schipper, Katherine; Smith, Abbie (1989): Wealth effects of going private for senior securities, in: Journal of Financial Economics, vol. 23 (no.1), pp. 155-169.

Mares, Vlad; Harstad, Ronald M. (2003): Private information revelation in common-value auctions, in: Journal of Economic Theory, vol. 109 (no. 2), pp. 264-282.

Markides, Constantinos C. (1997): Strategic innovation, in: MIT Sloan Management Review, vol. 38 (no. 3), pp. 9-23.

Markowitz, Henry (1952): Portfolio selection, in: Journal of Finance, vol. 7 (no. 1), pp. 77-91.

Marris, Robin (1963): A model of the managerial enterprise, in: Quarterly Journal of Economics, vol. 77 (May), pp. 185-209.

Marten, Kai-Uwe (1995): Empirische Analyse des Prüferwechsels im Kontext der Agency- und Signalling-Theorie, in: Zeitschrift für Betriebswirtschaft, vol. 65 (no. 7), pp. 703-727.

Marten, Kai-Uwe; Köhler, Annette G. (1999): Due Diligence in Deutschland, in: Finanzbetrieb, 11/1999, pp. 337-348.

Martin, John D.; Petty, William J. (1983): An analysis of the performance of publicly traded venture capital comapnies, in: Journal of Financial and Quantitative Analysis, vol. 18 (no. 3), pp. 401-410.

Martin, Kenneth J. ; McConnell, John J. (1989): Corporate performance, corporate takeovers and management turnovers, in: Journal of Finance, vol. 46 (no. 2), pp. 671-688.

Masulis, Ronald W. (1980): The effects of capital structure changes on security prices: a study of exchange offers, in: Journal of Financial Economics, vol. 8 (no. 2), pp. 139-178.

Megginson, William L.; Weiss, Kathleen A. (1991): Venture capitalist certification in initial public offerings, in: Journal of Finance, vol. 46 (no. 3), pp. 879-903.

Meier, Degenhard (2005): Post-investment value addition to buyouts - a study on European private equity firms' post-investment value addition to buyouts, Wiesbaden, DUV.

Merton, Robert C. (1981): On market timing and investment performance. I. An equilibrium theory of value for market forecasts, in: Journal of Business, vol. 54, pp. 363-406.

Mian, Shehzad ; Rosenfeld, James (1993): Takeover activity and the long-run performance of reverse leveraged buyouts, in: Financial Management, vol. 22 (no. 4), pp. 46-57.

Miller, Edward M. (1977): Risk, uncertainty, and divergence of opinion, in: Journal of Finance, vol. 32 (no. 4), pp. 1151-1168.

Miller, Merton H. (1977): Debt and taxes, in: Journal of Finance, vol. 32 (no. 2), pp. 261-278.

Mills, Karen G. (2000): LBO returns in the United States: what will it take to succeed in the new era of LBOs?, in: Lake, Rick; Lake, Ronald: Private Equity and Venture Capital: A Guide for Investors and Practitioners, London U.K., Euromoney Books, pp. 261-273.

Mittendorfer, Roland (2001): Finanzierungsmodelle von Leveraged Buyouts, in: Stadler, Wilfried: Venture Capital und Private Equity: Erfolgreich wachsen mit Beteiligungskapital, Köln, Deutscher Wirtschaftsdienst, pp. 141-184.

Modigliani, Franco; Miller, Merton H. (1958): The cost of capital, corporation finance and the theory of investment, in: American Economic Review, vol. 48 (no. 3), pp. 261-297.

Modigliani, Franco; Miller, Merton H. (1963): Corporate income taxes and the cost of capital: a correction, in: American Economic Review, vol. 53 (no. 3), pp. 433-443.

Moeller, Hans P. (1985): Die Informationseffizienz des Deutschen Aktienmarktes - Eine Zusammenfassung und Analyse Empirischer Untersuchungen, in: Zeitschrift für betriebswirtschaftliche Forschung, vol. 37, pp. 500-518.

Mols, Niels P. (2000): Dual channels of distribution: a transaction cost analysis and propositions, in: International Review of Retail, Distribution and Consumer Research, vol. 10 (no. 3), pp. 227-246.

Morck, Randall; Shleifer, Andrei; Vishny, Robert (1988): Management ownership and market valuation: an empirical analysis, in: Journal of Financial Economics, vol. 20 (no. 1/2), pp. 293-315.

Moreland, Robert; Reyes, Jesse E. (1992): The debate over performance, in: Venture Capital Journal, vol. 32 (no. 10), pp. 44-48.

Morris, Peter (2005): Private equity - which exit?, Morgan Stanley Fixed Income Research, 18-Feb-2005, pp. 1-12.

Moskowitz, Tobias J.; Vissing-Jörgensen, Annette (2002): The returns to entrepreneurial investment: a private equity premium puzzle?, in: American Economic Review, vol. 92 (no. 4), pp. 745-778.

Mossin, Jan (1966): Equilibrium in capital asset market, in: Econometrica, vol. 34 (no. 4), pp. 768-783.

Müller, Oliver (2003): Mezzanine Finance - Neue Perspektiven in der Unternehmensfinanzierung, Swiss Private Equity and Corporate Finance Association, Bern-Stuttgart-Wien, Haupt.

Müller-Trimbusch, Jobst (1999): High-Yield-Anleihen: Perspektiven für die Risikofinanzierung deutscher Unternehmen, Wiesbaden, DUV.

Murray, Gordon C. (1995): Evolution and change: an analysis of the first decade of the UK venture capital industry, in: Journal of Business Finance and Accounting, vol. 22 (no. 8), pp. 1077-1106.

Murray, Gordon C. (1999): Early-stage venture capital funds, scale economics and public support, in: Venture Capital, vol. 1, pp. 351-384.

Muscarella, Chris J.; Vetsuypens, Michael R. (1989): A simple test of Baron's model of IPO underpricing, in: Journal of Financial Economics, vol. 24 (no. 1), pp. 125-135.

Muscarella, Chris J.; Vetsuypens, Michael R. (1990): Efficiency and organizational structure: a study of reverse LBOs, in: Journal of Finance, vol. 45 (no. 5), pp. 1389-1413.

Myers, Raymond H. (1986): Classical and Modern Regression With Applications, Boston, Duxbury Press.

Myers, Stewart C. (1977): Determinants of corporate borrowing, in: Journal of Financial Economics, vol. 5 (no. 2), pp. 147-175.

Myers, Stewart C.; Majluf, Nicolas S. (1984): Stock issues and investment policy when firms have information investors do not have, in: Journal of Financial Economics, vol. 13 (no. 2), pp. 187-221.

Narayanan, MP (1988): Debt versus equity under asymmetric information, in: Journal of Financial and Quantitative Analysis, vol. 23 (no. 1), pp. 39-51.

Newbould, Gerald D.; Chatfield, Robert E.; Anderson, Ronald F. (1992): Leveraged buyouts and tax incentives, in: Financial Management, vol. 21 (no. 1), pp. 50-57.

Ofek, Eli (1994): Efficiency gains in unsuccessful management buyouts, in: Journal of Finance, vol. 49 (no. 2), pp. 637-654.

Opler, Tim C. (1992): Operating performance in leveraged buyouts: evidence from 1985-1989, in: Financial Management, vol. 21 (no. 1), pp. 27-34.

Osborne, MFM (1959): Brownian motion in the stock market, in: Operations Research, vol. 7 (March/April), pp. 145-173.

Oskamp, Stuart (1982): Overconfidence in case-study judgements, in: Kahneman, Daniel; Slovic, Paul; Tversky, Amos: Judgement under uncertainty: heuristics and biases, Cambridge, UK, pp. 287-293,

Otto, Hans J. (1990): Management Buy-Out und Belegschafts Buy-Out, in: Assmann, Heinz D.; Schütze, Rolf A.: Handbuch des Kapitalanlagerechts, München, Beck, pp. 834-872.

Paisner, Guy (2005): FN Profile: CVC rules the European roost, in: Financial News Online, www.efinancialnews.com, 12-Sep-2005, pp. 1-3.

Palepu, Krishna G. (1990): Consequences of leveraged buyouts, in: Journal of Financial Economics, vol. 27 (no. 1), pp. 247-262.

Phan, Phillip H.; Hill, Charles W. L. (1995): Organizational restructuring and economic performance in leveraged buyouts: an ex post study, in: Academy of Management Journal, vol. 38 (no. 3), pp. 704-739.

Picot, Arnold; Bortenlänger, Christine; Röhrl, Heiner (1997a): Organization of electronic markets: contributions of new institutional economics, in: Information Society, vol. 13 (no. 1), pp. 107-123.

Picot, Arnold; Dietl, Helmut; Franck, Egon (1997b): Organisation - eine ökonomische Perspektive, Stuttgart, Schäffer-Poeschel.

Picot, Arnold; Reichwald, Ralf; Wigand, Rolf (2001): Die grenzenlose Unternehmung: Information, Organisation und Management, 4. Auflage, Wiesbaden, Gabler.

Pliska, Stanley R. (1997): Introduction to mathematical finance - discrete time models, Massachusetts, Blackwell Publishers.

Prahalad, CK; Hamel, Gary (1990): The core competence of the corporation, in: Harvard Business Review, vol. 68 (no. 3), pp. 79-91.

Pratt, Shannon P. (1990): Discounts and premia, in: Valuation of closely held companies and inactively traded securities, Charlottesville, VA, The Institute of Chartered Financial Analysts, pp. 38-50.

Pratt, Shannon P.; Reilly, Robert F.; Schweihs, Robert P. (2000): Valuing a business: the analysis and appraisal of closely held companies, Chicago, Dow Jones-Irwin.

Prester, Melanie (2002): Exit-Strategien deutscher Venture Capital Gesellschaften, Münster, Germany, LIT.

Rajan, Raghuram; Servaes, Henri; Zingales, Luigi (2000): The cost of diversity: the diversification discount and inefficient investment, in: Journal of Finance, vol. 55 (no. 1), pp. 35-80.

Ramu, Shiva S. (1999): Restructuring and break-ups – corporate growth through divestitures, spin-offs, split-ups and swaps, New Dehli, Response Books.

Richard, Jörg; Weinheimer, Stefan (2002): Handbuch Going Private, Recht und Wirtschaft, Heidelberg

Richter, Frank (2001): Simplified discounting rules in binomial models, in: Schmalenbach Business Review, vol. 53 (no. 3), pp. 175-196.

Richter, Frank (2002a): Logische Wertgrenzen und subjektive Punktschätzungen - Zur Anwendung der risikoneutralen (Unternehmens-) Bewertung, unter Mitwirkung von Christian Timmreck, in: Heintzen, M; Kruschwitz, L: Unternehmen bewerten, Berlin, 59-73.

Richter, Frank (2002b): Simplified discounting rules, variable growth, and leverage, in: Schmalenbach Business Review, vol. 54 (no. 2), pp. 136-147.

Richter, Frank (2004a): Relativer Unternehmenswert, in: Richter, Frank; Timmreck, Christian: Unternehmensbewertung - Moderne Instruments und Lösungsansätze, Stuttgart, Schaeffer-Poeschel, pp. 367-380.

Richter, Frank (2004b): Valuation with or without personal income taxes, in: Schmalenbach Business Review, vol. 56 (no. 1), pp. 20-45.

Richter, Frank (2005): Mergers & Acquisitions : Investmentanalyse, Finanzierung und Prozessmanagement, München, Vahlen.

Richter, Frank; Herrmann, Volker (2003): Pricing with performance-controlled multiples, in: Schmalenbach Business Review, vol. 55 (no. 3), pp. 194-219.

Richter, Frank; Timmreck, Christian (2003): M&A Optionen sind Real(e) Optionen - Wirtschaftlichkeitsanalyse von M&A Transaktionen dargestellt von Vendor Loans, in: Hommel, Ulrich; Scholich, Martin; Baecker, Philipp: Real Optionen - Konzepte, Praxis und

Perspektiven strategischer Unternehmensfinanzierung, Oestrich-Winkel/Frankfurt a.Main, Germany, pp. 243-256.

Ritter, Jay (1984): The 'hot issue' market of 1980, in: Journal of Business, vol. 57, pp. 215-240.

Ritter, Jay (1991): The long-run performance of initial public offerings, in: Journal of Finance, vol. 46 (no. 1), pp. 3-27.

Ritter, Jay (1999): Initial public offerings, in: Logue, Dennis; Seward, James: Handbook of modern finance, Boston, US, Warren, Groham & Lamont RIA Group, Chapter D11.

Rock, Kevin (1986): Why new issues are underpriced, in: Journal of Financial Economics, vol. 15 (no. 1/2), pp. 187-212.

Rogers, Paul; Holland, Tom; Haas, Dan (2002): Value acceleration: lessons from private-equity masters, in: Harvard Business Review, vol. 80 (no. 6), pp. 5-11.

Rosenstein, Joseph; Bruno, Albert V.; Bygrave, William D.; Taylor, Natalie T. (1993): The CEO, venture capitalists, and the board, in: Journal of Business Venturing, vol. 8 (no. 2), pp. 99-113.

Ross, Stephen A. (1973): The economic theory of agency: the principal's problem, in: American Economic Review, vol. 63 (no. 2), pp. 134-139.

Ross, Stephen A. (1976): The arbitrage theory of capital asset pricing, in: Journal of Economic Theory, vol. 13, pp. 341-360.

Ross, Stephen A. (1977): The determination of financial structure: the incentive-signalling approach, in: Bell Journal of Economics, vol. 8 (no. 1), pp. 23-40.

Ross, Stephen A. (1987): Arbitrage and martingales with taxation, in: Journal of Political Economy, vol. 95 (no. 2), pp. 371-393.

Ross, Stephen A.; Westerfield, R. W.; Jaffe, J. (2002): Corporate finance, New York, USA, McGraw-Hill.

Ross, Stephen A.; Westerfield, Randolph W.; Jordan, Bradford D. (2000): Fundamentals of corporate finance, New York, USA, McGraw-Hill.

Rotemberg, Julio ; Saloner, Garth (1994): Benefits of narrow business strategies, in: American Economic Review, vol. 84 (no. 5), pp. 1330-1349.

Ruback, Richard S. (2002): Capital cash flows: a simple approach to valuing risky cash flows, in: Financial Management, vol. 31 (no. 2), pp. 85-103.

Rudolph, Bernd (2004): Analyse hybrider Finanzierungsinstrumente: Mezzanine-Kapital, in: Zeitschrift für das gesamte Kreditwesen, 2004 (no. 1), pp. 12-16.

Ruhnka, John C.; Young, John E. (1991): Some hypotheses about risk in venture capital investing, in: Journal of Business Venturing, vol. 6 (no. 2), pp. 115-133.

Saadouni, Brahim S.; Briston, RJ; Mallin, CA (1996): Unseasoned equity offerings MBO-IPOs vs. non-MBO-IPOs, in: Journal of Business Finance & Accounting, vol. 23 (no. 1), pp. 47-60.

Sahlman, William A. (1990): The structure and governance of venture capital organizations, in: Journal of Financial Economics, vol. 27 (no. 2), pp. 473-521.

Samdani, Sam G. ; Butler, Paul; McNish, Rob (2001): The alchemy of leveraged buyouts, in: Budde, Florian; Farha, Gary A.; Frankemölle, Heineret al: Value creation: strategies for the chemical industry, Weinheim, Wiley-VCH, pp. 93-107.

Sapienza, Harry J. (1992): When do venture capitalists add value?, in: Journal of Business Venturing, vol. 7 (no. 1), pp. 9-27.

Sapienza, Harry J.; Manigart, Sophie; Vermeir, Wim (1996): Venture capitalist governance and value added in four countries, in: Journal of Business Venturing, vol. 11 (no. 6), pp. 439-469.

Schafstein, David (1988): The disciplinary role of takeovers, in: Review of Economic Studies, vol. 55 (no. 182), pp. 185-200.

Schefczyk, Michael (2004): Erfolgsstrategien deutscher Venture Capital Gesellschaften, 3rd edition, Stuttgart, Schäffer-Poeschel.

Schipper, Katherine; Smith, Abbie (1991): Effects of management buyouts on corporate interest and depreciation tax deductions, in: Journal of Law and Economics, vol. 34 (no. 2), pp. 295-341.

Schmid, Helmut (1994): Leveraged Management Buy-Out: Begriff, Gestaltungen, optimale Kapitalstruktur und ökonomische Bewertung, Frankfurt. a. M., Peter Lang.

Schmidt, Daniel (2003): Private equity, stocks- and mixed asset portfolios: a bootstrap approach to determining performance characteristics, diversification benefits and optimal portfolio allocation, Working Paper, University of Frankfurt, pp. 0-54.

Schmidt, Daniel; Nowak, Eric; Knigge, Alexander (2004): On the performance of private equity investments: does market timing matter?, Working Paper, Goethe-University of Frankfurt and University of Lugano, pp. 1-33.

Schmidt, Daniel; Wahrenburg, Mark (2004): Contractual relations between European VC-funds and investors: the impact of reputation and bargaining power on contractual design, RICAFE working paper no. 008

Schmidt, Reinhard H. (1988): Neuere Property Rights-Analysen in der Finanzierungstheorie, in: Budäus, Dietrich; Braun, Wolfram: Betriebswirtschaftslehre und Theorie der Verfügungsrechte, Wiesbaden, Gabler, pp. 239-267.

Schmidt, Reinhard H.; Terberger, Eva (1997): Grundzüge der Investitions- und Finanzierungstheorie, Wiesbaden, Germany, Gabler.

Schmidtke, Axel (1985): Die Praxis des Venture-Capital-Geschäfts, Landsberg am Lech, Moderne Industrie.

Schober, Andreas (1996): Die EVCA-Richtlinien zur Performancemessung, BVK Dokumentation Nr. 1, Berlin 1996

Scholes, Myron; Williams, Joseph (1971): Estimating betas from nonsynchronous data, in: Journal of Financial Economics, vol. 5 (no. 3), pp. 309-328.

Schröder, Christoph (1992): Strategien und Management von Beteiligungsgesellschaften: ein Einblick in Organisationsstrukturen und Entscheidungsprozesse von institutionellen Eigenkapitalinvestoren, Baden-Baden

Schulz, Eckehard (2000): Die Finanzierung von Existenzgründungen: eine informationsökonomische Analyse, Frankfurt a. M., Peter Lang.

Schwenkedel, Stefan (1991): Management Buyout: Ein neues Geschäftsfeld für Banken, Wiesbaden, Germany, Gabler.

SEC (2001): Excerpts from speeches by the staff of the office of the Chief Accountant through December 6, 2001, http://www.sec.gov/info/accountants/speechoutline.htm

Seth, Anju; Easterwood, John C. (1993): Strategic redirection in large management buyouts: the evidence from post-buyout restructuring activity, in: Strategic Management Journal, vol. 14 (no. 4), pp. 251-273.

Sharpe, William F. (1964): Capital asset pricing: a theory of market equilibrium under conditions of risk, in: Journal of Finance, vol. 19 (no. 3), pp. 425-442.

Sharpe, William F. (1994): The sharpe ratio, in: Journal of Portfolio Management, vol. 21 (no. 1), pp. 49-58.

Shepherd, Dean A.; Zacharakis, Andrew; Baron, Robert A. (2003): VC's decision processes: evidence suggesting more experience may not always be better, in: Journal of Business Venturing, vol. 18 (no. 3), pp. 381-401.

Shleifer, Andrei (1986): Do demand curves for stocks slope down?, in: Journal of Finance, vol. 41 (no. 3), pp. 579-590.

Shleifer, Andrei; Summers, Lawrence (1988): Breach of trust in hostile takeovers, in: Auerbach, Alan: Corporate takeovers: causes and consequences, Chicago, University of Chicago Press, pp. 33-69.

Shleifer, Andrei; Vishny, Robert (1986): Large shareholders and corporate control, in: Journal of Political Economy, vol. 94 (no. 3), pp. 461-488.

Shleifer, Andrei; Vishny, Robert (1989): Management entrenchment, in: Journal of Financial Economics, vol. 25 (no. 1), pp. 123-139.

Shleifer, Andrei; Vishny, Robert (1997a): The limits of arbitrage, in: Journal of Finance, vol. 52 (no. 1), pp. 35-55.

Shleifer, Andrei; Vishny, Robert (1997b): A survey of corporate governance, in: Journal of Finance, vol. 52 (no. 2), pp. 737-783.

Singh, Harbir (1993): Challenges in researching corporate restructuring, in: Journal of Management Studies, vol. 30 (no. 1), pp. 147-172.

Skryzcki, Cindy (1988): Impact on R&D is newest worry about LBOs, in: The Washington Post, pp. H1, H5.

Smith, Abbie J. (1990a): Corporate ownership structure and performance: the case of management buyouts, in: Journal of Financial Economics, vol. 27 (no. 1), pp. 143-164.

Smith, Abbie J. (1990b): The effects of leveraged buyouts, in: Business Economics, vol. 25 (no. 2), pp. 19-25.

Spielmann, Urs (1994): Der Generationenwechsel in mittelständischen Unternehmungen bei Gründern und Nachfolgern, Dissertation, Hochschule St. Gallen

Spremann, Klaus (1989): Agent and principal, in: Bamberg, G.; Spremann, Klaus: Agency theory, information and incentives, Berlin, Springer, pp. 3-37.

Spremann, Klaus (1990): Asymmetrische Information, in: Zeitschrift für Betriebswirtschaft, vol. 60, pp. 561-586.

Spremann, Klaus (1991): Investition und Finanzierung, 4. verbesserte Auflage, Munich, Oldenbourg.

Stewart, Bennett G. III; Glassman, David M (1988): The motives and methods of corporate restructuring - part II, in: Journal of Applied Corporate Finance, vol. 1, pp. 79-88.

Stiglitz, Joseph E. (1974): On the irrelevance of corporate financial policy, in: American Economic Review, vol. 64 (no. 6), pp. 851-866.

Stiglitz, Joseph E.; Weiss, Andrew (1981): Credit rationing in markets with imperfect information, in: American Economic Review, vol. 71 (no. 3), pp. 393-410.

Stulz, René M. (1990): Managerial discretion and optimal financing policies, in: Journal of Financial Economics, vol. 26 (no. 1), pp. 3-27.

Süchting, Joachim (1995): Finanzmanagement - Theorie und Politik der Unternehmensfinanzierung, 6th edition, Wiesbaden, Germany, Gabler.

Summers, Lawrence H. (1989): Taxation and corporate debt, hearing before the Committee on Finance - U.S. Senate, first session, January 25, 1989

Suni, Juha (2002): Mezzanine finance in leveraged buyouts, Working Paper, Helsinki University of Technology.

Then Bergh, Friedrich (1998): Leveraged Management Buyout: Konzept und agency-theoretische Analyse, Wiesbaden, Germany, Deutscher Universitätsverlag.

Thompson, Steve; Wright, Mike; Robbie, Ken (1992a): Buy-Outs, divestment, and leverage: restructuring transactions and corporate governance, in: Oxford Review of Economic Policy, vol. 8 (no. 3), pp. 58-69.

Thompson, Steve; Wright, Mike; Robbie, Ken (1992b): Management equity ownership, debt and performance: some evidence from the U.K. management buyouts, in: Scottish Journal of Political Economy, vol. 39 (no. 4), pp. 413-430.

Thomson Financial (2005): Financial information provider, www.thomson.com.

Thum, Oliver (2004): Besonderheiten bei der Bewertung von Private Equity-Targets, in: Richter, Frank; Timmreck, Christian: Unternehmensbewertung : moderne Instrumente und neue Ansätze, Stuttgart, Schäffer-Poeschel, pp. 217-231.

Tietzel, Manfred (1981): Die Ökonomie der Property-Rights: Ein Überblick, in: Zeitschrift für Wirtschaftspolitik, vol. 30 (no. 3), pp. 207-243.

Torabzadeh, Khalil M.; Berlin, William J. (1987): Leveraged buyouts and shareholder returns, in: The Journal of Financial Research, vol. 10 (no. 4), pp. 313-319.

Travlos, Nickolas G.; Cornett, Marcia M. (1993): Going private buyouts and determinants of shareholders' returns, in: Journal of Accounting, Auditing & Finance, pp. 1-3.

Trester, Jeffrey J. (1998): Venture capital contracting under asymmetric information, in: Journal of Banking & Finance, vol. 22 (no. 6-8), pp. 675-699.

Treynor, Jack L. (1965): How to rate management of investment funds, in: Harvard Business Review, vol. 43 (no. 1), pp. 63-75.

Treynor, Jack L.; Mazuy, Kay (1966): Can mutual funds outguess the market, in: Harvard Business Review, vol. 44 (July), pp. 131-136.

Tripp Howe, J (1988): Junk bonds. Analysis & portfolio strategies, Chicago, Probus Publishing.

Tyebjee, Tyzoon T.; Bruno, Albert V. (1984): A model of venture capital investment activity, in: Management Science, vol. 30 (no. 9), pp. 1051-1066.

Vermaelen, Theo (1981): Common stock repurchases and market signaling - an empirical study, in: Journal of Financial Economics, vol. 9 (no. 2), pp. 139-183.

Volkart, Rudolf (1999): High Yield Debt als Finanzierungsinstrument - Kapitalkosten, Risiko-Rendite-Struktur und Agency-Aspekte, in: Der Schweizer Treuhänder, 1999 (no. 12), pp. 1233-1246.

von Daniels, Holger (2004): Private Equity Secondary Transactions - Chancen und Grenzen des Aufbaus eines institutionalisierten Secondary Market, Wiesbaden, DUV.

Wallace, Anise (1988): A bruising battle over bonds, in: New York Times, NYC, November 27, 1988, D1.

Wallner, Nicholas (1980): Leveraged buyouts: a review of the state of the art, in: Mergers & Acquisitions, Winter 1980, pp. 16-26.

Warga, Arthur; Welch, Ivo (1993): Bondholder losses in leveraged buyouts, in: Review of Financial Studies, vol. 6 (no. 4), pp. 959-982.

Warner, Jerold B. (1977): Bankruptcy costs: some evidence, in: Journal of Finance, vol. 32 (no. 2), pp. 337-347.

Weidig, Tom; Mathonet, Pierre Yves (2004): The risk profiles of private equity, SSRN Working Paper Series, http://ssrn.com/abstract=495482, pp. 1-33.

Weinberger, Nick (2005): Determinanten der Finanzierung von Leveraged Buyouts - Eine empirische Analyse anhand von Leveraged Buyouts in Europa zwischen 2000 und 2003, Working Paper.

Weir, Charlie; Laing, David (1998): Management buy-outs: the impact of ownership changes on performance, in: Journal of Small Business and Enterprise Development, vol. 5 (no. 3), pp. 261-269.

Welch, Ivo (1989): Seasoned offerings, imitation costs, and the underpricing of initial public offerings, in: Journal of Finance, vol. 44 (no. 2), pp. 421-449.

Westerwelle, Guido (2005): Äußerungen der SPD-Spitze zu Wirtschaftsinvestitionen in Deutschland, Rede im Deutschen Bundestag am 21. April 2005, Germany

Wiersema, Margarethe F.; Liebeskind, Julia P. (1995): The effects of leveraged buyouts on corporate growth and diversification in large firms, in: Strategic Management Journal, vol. 16 (no. 6), pp. 447-460.

Wilhelm, Jochen E. M. (1985): Arbitrage theory: introductory lectures on arbitrage based financial asset pricing, Berlin, Springer.

Williamson, Oliver E. (1975): Markets and hierarchies: analysis and anti-trust implications, New York, Free Press.

Williamson, Oliver E. (1985): The economic institutions of capitalism: firms, markets, relational contracting, New York, Free Press.

Witt, Peter (2003): Corporate Governance - Systeme im Wettbewerb, Wiesbaden, DUV.

Wöginger, Helmut (2004): Bewertung von Synergien bei Mergers&Acquisitions - Das Synergy-Value-Concept, in: Richter, Frank; Timmreck, Christian: Unternehmensbewertung - Moderne Instruments und Lösungsansätze, Stuttgart, Schaeffer-Poeschel, pp. 235-262.

Wright, Mike; Coyne, John; Mills, Adam (1987): Management buy-outs, Cambridge/London

Wright, Mike; Hoskisson, Robert E.; Busenitz, Lowell W. (2001): Firm rebirth: buyouts as facilitators of strategic growth and entrepreneurship, in: Academy of Management Executive, vol. 15 (no. 1), pp. 111-125.

Wright, Mike; Robbie, Ken (1996): The investor-led buy-out: a new strategic option, in: Long Range Planning, vol. 29 (no. 5), pp. 691-702.

Wright, Mike; Robbie, Ken (1997): Venture capitalists and serial entrepreneurs, in: Journal of Business Venturing, vol. 12 (no. 3), pp. 227-249.

Wright, Mike; Robbie, Ken (1998): Venture capital and private equity: a review and synthesis, in: Journal of Business Finance & Accounting, vol. 25 (no. 5/6), pp. 521-570.

Wright, Mike; Robbie, Ken (1999): Management buy-outs and venture capital: into the next millenium, Cheltenham, UK, Edward Elgar.

Wright, Mike; Wilson, Nick; Robbie, Ken; Ennew, Christine T. (1994): Restructuring and failure in buy-outs and buy-ins, in: Business Strategy Review, vol. 5 (no. 2), pp. 21-40.

Wruck, Karen H. (1989): Equity ownership concentration and firm value: evidence from private equity financings, in: Journal of Financial Economics, vol. 23 (no. 1), pp. 3-28.

Wunsch, Gerhard; Schreiber, Helmut (1984): Stochastische Systeme, Berlin, Technik.

Zahra, Shaker A.; Fescina, Michael (1991): Will leveraged buyouts kill U.S. corporate research and development?, in: Academy of Management Executive, vol. 5 (no. 4), pp. 7-21.

Zarowin, Paul (1990): What determines earnings-price ratios: revisited, in: Journal of Accounting, Auditing & Finance, vol. 5, pp. 439-454.

Zimmermann, Heinz; Bilo, Stéphanie; Christophers, Hans; Degosciu, Michèl (2004): The risk and return of publicly traded private equity, WWZ/Department of Finance, Working Paper No. 1/05, pp. 1-24.

Zollo, Maurizio; Gottschalg, Oliver (2004): When experience hurts - experimental learning, perceived task homogeneity and the confidence trap, Working Paper of the INSEAD-Wharton Alliance